VER

INLET

NORTH VANCOUVER

ARK

STREET

STREET

STREET

STREET

STREET

THE AMBITIOUS CITY
A HISTORY OF THE CITY OF NORTH VANCOUVER

THE AMBITIOUS CITY
A History of the City of North Vancouver

Warren Sommer

Harbour Publishing

CONTENTS

INTRODUCTION

F rom the time of its inception North Vancouver had a strong sense of its own identity and an indestructible confidence in its own future. Writing in March 1907, just days before the city's incorporation became official, George Bartley, editor of the community's first newspaper, summarized his impressions of the city:

> North Vancouver is unique among Canadian towns. Its population is an incarnation of indomitable activity, unintermittently obsessed with development schemes, not frenzied, yet possessed and inflamed by the spirit of advancement. The town seems to grow daily under the eye of observation. It is not a miracle, but it is a prodigy of progress.

It was Bartley who coined the term "the Ambitious City" in his inaugural edition of the *Express* in 1905. The city was not yet a city, but its aspirations were boundless. The community was still young and in the eyes of Bartley and his coterie, a new City of North Vancouver had every prospect of supplanting Vancouver as the province's principal urban centre.

As they were quick to point out, North Vancouver enjoyed a long shoreline with a deep harbour. There was potential for a bridge across the Second Narrows, thus connecting the city with the Great Northern Railway to the south and the proposed Vancouver, Westminster and Yukon Railway to the north. Much of the untold mineral, agricultural and forest wealth of the province's interior would flow through the city to markets overseas. Wharves and factories would line the North Shore's waterfront. A city of well-built houses set among spacious parks would rise on the slopes above. With most of the future city's land mass owned by the North Vancouver Land and Improvement Company, the Lonsdale Estate and Alfred St. George Hamersley, the new city would be easy both to plan and to create. People dared to think of a population numbering in the tens of thousands if not the hundreds of thousands.

It was a bold and courageous dream. At first, everything seemed to go well. Lots were sold, businesses were opened and houses were built. Much of the civic infrastructure was put in place: electric lights, a telephone service, sidewalks, street lights and most importantly, a streetcar system. Schools were built to serve a growing population. Societies and clubs began to function. Whether gathering for a community work bee, attending a meeting, going to church, participating in team sports, or joining in the city's impressive Dominion Day celebrations, North Vancouver residents demonstrated their commitment to their town and to each other. In the early 1900s a city was developing, but so was a community.

The city began with great expectations but was soon beset by hard times. After a period of rampant speculation and construction, a severe economic depression hit the community in 1913. Hundreds of property owners lost their investments and the city's debt began to grow. The much-vaunted northern railway proved a hollow delusion. The bridge was built, but not until 1925. Due to its poor design, it was repeatedly hit by passing vessels and was often out of service. Although the Harbour Commissioners' railway reached the city in 1929, the short section of railway (the Pacific Great Eastern Railway's North Shore Division) with which it connected was closed just months before. If that was not enough, the Great Depression hit in 1929. People lost their jobs and went hungry. Unable to pay taxes, many lost their properties as well. The city became land-rich, but its tax revenues plummeted as its debt load increased. In 1933, the province took action, abolishing the elected council and appointing its own commissioner to oversee the city's return to solvency.

A less determined population might well have given up. Certainly, many people did leave the community, but others came to replace them, if only to secure affordable housing. People tightened their belts and worked together as never before, neighbour helping neighbour, forging friendships in the process. The *North Shore Press* retained confidence in the community's future, in 1931 issuing a special supplement lauding the progress of the previous quarter-century. Writing in the *Vancouver Sun*, Herb Morden was equally positive, noting that "despite many ups and downs, destiny has dealt many kindnesses to the North Shore." Morden recalled the words spoken by the community's first mayor Arnold Kealy when the city's street lights were first turned on in 1906. For Morden, Kealy's words were as relevant in 1936 as they were thirty years before: "These lights that glitter tonight for the first time in the community are a prophecy of greater things that will make us more than a second to the city across the inlet."

Optimism aside, it took a war to put the city back on the path to recovery. During the 1940s, Burrard Dry Dock and North Van Ship Repairs, the city's two largest industries, thrived as thousands of workers flocked to work in ship construction.

Labour issues were dealt with expeditiously. The ferries were crowded to the point of overflowing and houses were built by the hundreds. The city boomed once again. Government by commissioner reversed the city's fortunes and the province authorized a return to elected government in 1944. With the war over, returning servicemen and women came to North Vancouver to find homes and begin families. Writer after writer noted a spirit of renewed confidence in the air. As Alan Jessup noted in the *Vancouver Daily Province Magazine* in October 1947:

> *Word began to get out that North Vancouver was the place to live. There were practically no holdups or robberies; your curtains stayed clean longer because there were fewer industrial chimneys; land was cheap and Vancouver was so far away your husband stayed home nights . . . Old-timers have always known that North Vancouver was the best place to live but they had a hard time getting anyone to listen . . .*

The city has never looked back. The growth that began after the war has continued through the turn of the millennium. The city built reserves to fund its infrastructure and facilities rather than rely on borrowing. Over time its "heritage fund" became the envy of other municipalities, including the District of North Vancouver whose politicians made repeated overtures for amalgamation. The city's port facilities continued to develop in the 1960s and 1970s, featuring large bulk freight terminals on a scale unimaginable at the time of the city's founding. With so much industry at its doorstep, the city developed an environmental consciousness years before the movement became widespread.

Although its footprint and layout originates in decisions made a century ago, today's city owes much of its character to only a few years' worth of productive planning. The Official Community Plan of 1980, the GVRD's Official Regional Plan of 1980 and the institution of Seabus in 1977 have led to the revitalization of Lower Lonsdale and the redevelopment of much of Central Lonsdale. Older single-family houses and modest apartment blocks have given way to higher-quality and higher-density development, much of it connected by attractive walkways and plazas to a waterfront park and pedestrian piers. For the majority of residents the quality of life is high.

Throughout the city's first century, residents endured a series of misfortunes of comic if not epic proportions. Yet they never lost their strong sense of self. North Vancouver, it is clear, is no mere suburb. Although residents traditionally commuted to jobs in Vancouver, the industrial and commercial development of the last half-century has substantially changed the situation. By 2001, almost half the city's workforce laboured on the North Shore. As the city enters its second century as an incorporated municipality, it is impressively clear that much of its early ambition has been achieved.

The North Vancouver shoreline c. 1898, with St. Paul's Roman Catholic Church and the Mission Reserve on the left, the Moodyville Sawmill on the right, and the partially cleared townsite in the centre.
City of Vancouver Archives, CVA MiP51.1-3

1 MILLTOWN AND MISSION 1792–1875

O ne day in the summer of 1896, anthropologist Charles Hill-Tout boarded the ferry *Senator* at its berth in Vancouver and crossed the inner harbour. As he peered over the water, Hill-Tout sighted the village of Moodyville, home to one of the largest sawmills in the province. Square-rigged sailing ships lined its docks. Steam and smoke billowed high above them, and angry sounds erupted from the mill. An assortment of wood-frame buildings climbed the hill and punctuated the shore, and remnants of an ancient forest darkened the slopes beyond.

When the ferry docked at the foot of the trail that was later to become Lonsdale Avenue, Hill-Tout walked ashore. The tower of the Roman Catholic mission church soon came into view, with dozens of cottages clustered around it like chicks around a mother hen. This was the Mission Reserve, the site of a permanent Squamish village since the early 1860s. Hill-Tout entered the village, and found the elders of the community assembled to meet him.

Hill-Tout had come to speak to the oldest member of the band, a man he described as a "decrepit creature, stone-blind from old age." Hill-Tout learned that Mulks, the man whose stories he hoped to record, was close to a century old, his mother having been in her teens when George Vancouver had visited Howe Sound a hundred years before. The elders had prepared a table for the meeting, placing tally sticks at intervals along its length. Each stick represented a chapter in the story Mulks had agreed to tell. The old man spoke at length, beginning his recitation "in a loud, high-pitched key, as if he were addressing a large audience in the open air":

> *In the beginning there was water everywhere and no land at all. When this state of things had lasted for a long while, the Great Spirit determined to make land appear. Soon the tops of the mountains showed above the water and they grew and grew until their heads reached the clouds. Then he made the lakes and rivers, after that the trees and animals. Soon after this had been done, Kalana, the first man, was made.*

Hill-Tout recorded the old man's story as fully as he could, given his limited understanding of the archaic Squamish Mulks spoke. He published his findings the following year in an account that described not only the creation of the Squamish people, but also a series of plagues—floods, snow storms, and illness—sent by the Great Spirit to punish the Squamish for their transgressions.

Hill-Tout and his contemporaries had developed theories about how aboriginal people had travelled from Asia to North America, but Squamish oral traditions placed little emphasis on where their ancestors had come from. Instead, they focussed on how the Squamish people had been created, and how they were connected to other human beings and other living creatures. The Squamish who lived along the shores of Burrard Inlet and neighbouring Howe Sound saw themselves as an integral part of the natural world rather than as its masters.

When first explored by Europeans, the area around Burrard Inlet was dotted with Halkomelem- and Squamish-speaking villages. These were home to the Squamish, the Musqueam and the Tsleil-Waututh people. Some of these villages were permanent winter villages; others were seasonal encampments. Just how long each of these First Nations had inhabited the inlet is clouded by a confusion perhaps brought about by the major population upheavals that occurred in the late eighteenth and early nineteenth centuries. Villages were decimated by smallpox and then transformed by the influence of the Europeans.

Interest in the region had been spurred by Captain James Cook's voyage to the northwest coast of North America in 1778. The first Europeans known to have sighted and entered English Bay were a group of Spanish sailors under the command of José Maria Narváez, aboard the schooner *Santa Saturnina* in 1791. Cook's expedition had sparked a lucrative trade in sea otter fur, which gave rise to friction with the Spanish, who claimed control over the territory. In 1792, diplomacy prevailed as Britain sent Captain George Vancouver to the Northwest Coast to negotiate the details of a treaty with the Spanish.

Archibald Menzies, the Vancouver expedition's botanist, reported deserted villages in Birch Bay, Howe Sound, and Jervis and Burrard Inlets. Peter Puget, who served with Vancouver, also recorded his impressions, noting of the Natives he encountered near Whidbey Island: "the small pox most have had, and most terribly pitted they are; indeed many have lost their Eyes and no Doubt it has raged with uncommon inveteracy among them."

A century later, the smallpox epidemic that had so devastated the Natives of the area had become part and parcel of their oral histories. The venerable Mulks, who had told Charles Hill-Tout the story of Squamish people's creation, also told him about their near demise: "A dreadful skin disease, loathsome to look upon, broke out upon all alike. None were spared. Men, women, and children sickened, took the disease and died in agony by the hundreds, so that when the spring arrived and fresh food was procurable, there was scarcely a person left of all their numbers to get it. Camp after camp, village after village, was left desolate . . ." Contemporary scholarship suggests that a great smallpox epidemic hit the people living around the Strait of Georgia in 1782–83. Some accounts place the population loss at over 90 percent of the Native population of the day: tens, if not hundreds, of thousands of people. During the course of his research, Hill-Tout compiled a list of Squamish place names around the inlet. Some of these may have been the sites of former villages or camps, and most were abandoned at the time of his investigations.

Unlike Narváez, Vancouver did find the First Narrows, and ventured into the inner harbour. On June 13, 1792, within sight of the future city of North Vancouver, he was "met by about fifty Indians, in their canoes, who conducted themselves with the greatest decorum and civility, presenting us with several fish, cooked, and undressed, of the sort already mentioned as resembling the smelt. These good people, finding we were inclined to make some return for their hospitality, shewed much understanding in preferring iron to copper." The Natives were probably from the Squamish village of Homulchesan located along the Capilano River near its mouth. The party was also visited by a group of Natives who approached from the south shore, possibly from the village of Whoi-Whoi, later to become the site of Lumberman's Arch in Stanley Park. Second Lieutenant Peter Puget recorded the encounter in his log, noting that his visitors had been astonished by the firing of muskets. Puget's entry in his log also suggested that although the Squamish possessed copper ornaments, Vancouver's party was likely the first group of Europeans to reach the inner harbour.

Only nine days after first entering the inlet, Vancouver rowed south to rejoin his ships at Birch Bay. As he approached Spanish Banks he was astounded to see two Spanish vessels lying at anchor near Point Grey. These were the schooners *Sutil* and *Mexicana*, commanded by Dionisio Alcalá Galiano and Cayetano Valdés y Flores. Despite his initial shock, Vancouver and the Spaniards got on well, exchanged details of their explorations, and agreed to meet within the coming days. Eager to learn more about the inlet, a party of Spaniards embarked in a longboat, making their way through the First Narrows, past the site of what was to become North Vancouver, and on to the head of Indian Arm. During their exploration of the inlet, the British and the Spanish were impressed by the grandeur of the scenery they passed. On June 14, 1792 Vancouver entered the first written description of the North Shore:

> The shores of this channel, which after Sir Harry Burrard of the navy, I have
> distinguished by the name of "Burrard's Channel," may be considered, on the
> southern side of a moderate height, and though rocky, well covered with trees of a
> large growth, principally of the pine tribe. On the northern side, the rugged snowy

barrier, whose base we had now nearly approached, rose very abruptly, and was only protected from the wash of the sea by a very narrow border of low land.

The Spaniards also consigned their thoughts to paper. Alcalá Galiano mused on the magnificent wilderness:

The shores are steep and rocky, with mountains of considerable height, with a mantle of tall close spaced conifers, and impenetrable underbrush. Many streams of fresh water, and some cascades, flowed from the melted snow of these mountains, which joined the range to the west that could be seen through the ravines. The mild temperature, the beauty and lushness of the various greens, the multitude of wild roses, and several meadows with small fruits, blackberries and gooseberries, made it a delightful visit . . .

Neither the British nor the Spanish expeditions commented on the potential wealth that the forests and the adjacent deep-sea harbour might afford enterprising settlers. Although Captain Cook had found magnificent timber with which to repair his ships while visiting Nootka Sound, the Northwest Coast was simply too far away from markets to make logging and milling operations financially viable. Decades were to pass before Europeans returned to the inlet. In the interim, the lives of those who had lived there since time immemorial returned to normal as the local First Nations resumed harvesting the wealth of the rivers, forests and sea, and celebrated their cultural traditions through dance, storytelling and song.

By the early 1820s Mulks was a young man. As a child he had undoubtedly heard stories about white-skinned men who had visited his people in large sea-going vessels. He may also have learned how the Musqueam people, whose principal village was just south of English Bay, had received a visit in 1808 from another group of Europeans led by Simon Fraser. Fraser had come overland from eastern Canada, exploring the west on behalf of the Montreal-based North West Company. Two decades later, Fraser's company had been absorbed by the Hudson's Bay Company, which started a fur trading post at Fort Langley. Britain had established its dominance over the local fur trade, and soon began work on colonizing and populating the area as part of the British Empire.

In February 1859, one year after the establishment of British Columbia as a British colony, Governor James Douglas issued his first proclamation regarding the disposal of Crown lands. The first point in the proclamation was unequivocal: "All the lands of British Columbia, and all the mines and minerals therein, belong to the Crown in fee." Douglas's proclamation ignored potential land claims by the Squamish, Musqueam, Tsleil-Waututh or any other First Nations. The price at which Crown lands would be made available was kept low to encourage settlement.

The colony's land disposal policies evolved over time, but were always essentially based on the "pre-emption" concept of permitting qualified persons to acquire provisional title to publicly owned land. Adult, male British subjects (or adult males seeking naturalization) who were over the age of eighteen were authorized to pre-empt up to 160 acres of previously unclaimed land, provided it was not reserved for a townsite, military reserve, other reserves or use by the aboriginal population. Pre-emptors were required in theory to live continuously on their land and to make improvements such as erecting buildings and fences, removing the forest cover, and establishing cultivated fields. With these improvements made, a certificate of improvement could be issued, and upon payment of a fee to a land registry office, a Crown grant would be issued, giving the pre-emptor clear title to his property.

Those who purchased land in the colonial capital of New Westminster had high hopes for its economic future. Not only was the developing city the capital of a vast, new colony, it was the gateway to the rich agricultural lands of the Fraser Valley and the mineral wealth of the interior. The Royal Engineers had prepared a detailed plan for the city complete with formal avenues, parks and squares. Wharf facilities and business blocks soon appeared with houses, churches and government buildings on the slopes above.

Such considerations played a major role when New Westminster architect and contractor T.W. Graham and his partner, carpenter George Scrimgeour, filed a claim for 150 acres of heavily forested land on the northern side of Burrard Inlet about four miles above the First Narrows in November 1862. Graham and Scrimgeour's claim, described as Lot 272, lay at the foot of a slope covered with firs and cedars of incredible proportions, some of them exceeding twelve feet in diameter. As

Ships berthed at the Moody, Dietz, and Nelson Sawmill, with wharf and houses, 1872.

North Vancouver Museum and Archives, 3779

the slope neared the inlet, it levelled out, and then fell once again as it plunged into the harbour. A nearby creek (later known as Lynn Creek) flowed year-round, providing a source of water and power. Graham and Scrimgeour increased their timber reserves in January 1863, when their associate Philip Hicks filed a claim for Lot 273, a 194-acre property lying just west of Lot 272. This land was to become the site of one of the largest sawmills of its day, and a key component of the future City of North Vancouver.

With well over three hundred acres of heavily timbered land in hand, Graham and Scrimgeour's Pioneer Mills opened for business in June 1863, offering fir, cedar and spruce lumber as well as tongue-and-groove flooring, "at prices lower than Puget Sound lumber." The mill's owners were perhaps encouraged by the words of John Robson, editor of New Westminster's *British Columbian*, who extolled the virtues of Burrard Inlet's forest resources. Robson was so impressed by what he had seen that he encouraged the lumbermen of eastern British North America to consider expanding their operations to the inlet. The two centre-discharge waterwheels of Pioneer Mills drove two massive circular saws, one located above the other as the radius of one alone was insufficient to cut the massive logs felled on the slopes. The mill also boasted a twenty-two-inch planing machine and various other items of equipment. Operations in the forest were less mechanized, with teams of oxen dragging the logs to tidewater or directly to the mill. The mill's capacity of forty thousand feet in twenty-four hours may have been modest but was apparently more than sufficient to meet demand.

The mill dispatched its first shipment of lumber in August 1863, two months after beginning operations. Twenty-five thousand feet of three-inch planks were stowed aboard the steamer *Flying Dutchman* and sent to New Westminster. These planks had been ordered as reinforcements for the levee along the New Westminster waterfront. The mill subsequently sent lumber to markets on Vancouver Island as well as in New Westminster, but orders fell short of what had been anticipated. Both the editor Robson and the owners of the Pioneer Mills had failed to consider not only the limited extent of the local market, but also competition from mills in New Westminster and the need for representation in markets abroad. In December 1863, just six months after opening the mill, Graham and his colleagues decided to cut their losses and offer their entire operation for sale by public auction. The sale was conducted at Valentine's Hall in New Westminster on December 16. Only two men placed bids, with grocer and riverboat man John Oscar Smith narrowly winning over local entrepreneur Sewell Prescott Moody.

An expenditure of just $8,000 had given James Oscar Smith not only a sawmill, but one million feet of logs cut and ready for milling, rights to 480 acres of forest, and two and a half yokes of oxen. In March 1864 the renamed Burrard Inlet Mills was operating once again. Smith placed advertisements in the New Westminster and Victoria newspapers offering fir, cedar and spruce lumber. Smith enjoyed significant success, sending order after order to Victoria, Nanaimo and several other destinations. More remarkably, he also secured a number of foreign orders, sending a shipment of lumber to Valparaiso, Chile, aboard the *Brewster* in August 1864. Three months later the barque *Ellen Lewis* stopped at the mill and was filled with 277,500 feet of lumber and 16,000 pickets. When the ship set sail for

Adelaide, it appeared that Smith was beginning to succeed where Graham had failed. However, because the mill lacked the capacity to handle large orders in a timely manner, it had taken seven months to load the *Ellen Lewis*.

To make matters worse, Smith had borrowed heavily to purchase the mill and his creditors were impatient for repayment. The operation may have been succeeding, but not quickly enough. Smith, on the edge of financial ruin, was forced to offer up for sale not just the mill and its 480 acres but also a number of personal items including his shotgun and a mahogany table. The auction was held in the very chambers where he had purchased the mill just twelve months earlier, and the successful bidder was none other than Sewell Prescott Moody.

Born into a staunch Methodist family in Maine, "Sue" Moody arrived in the Northwest at the height of the Fraser River gold rush. His first known business venture was in New Westminster, where he bid on a number of contracts for road construction. In late 1862 Moody joined forces with Moses C. Ireland, one of the more colourful characters of the colonial period. Like Moody, Ireland was a native of Maine and had a good eye for a promising business venture. The two formed a partnership in New Westminster to buy a herd of cattle in Oregon and drive it north for sale to the beef-starved residents of British Columbia. The venture turned their investment of $2,600 into a sum several times larger, which they invested in the construction of a sawmill in New Westminster the next year. Competition from other mills and the hazards of navigation on the lower Fraser, however, rendered the venture unsuccessful.

Moody's foray into the lumber business had roughly coincided with the ventures of T.W. Graham and John Oscar Smith, and neither Moody's New Westminster operation nor Burrard Inlet Mills had achieved short-term success. Those who were present in Valentine's Hall when the auctioneer's gavel came down for the last time and the mill on Burrard Inlet was acquired by yet another New Westminster businessman must have wondered how Moody could succeed where others had failed. Moody, after all, was still a relatively young man and his record in business was mixed.

Moody had acquired Burrard Inlet Mills at the end of January 1865 in partnership with Moses C. Ireland and James van Bramer. Moody himself oversaw the mill's operations, returning it to production within a month of the purchase. By May 1865 Moody had shipped his first load of lumber overseas, on the barque *Glimpse* bound for Sydney, Australia. Other exports followed in rapid succession, carried on ships destined for Adelaide and Mexico. By 1866, the quality of Moody's product began to be better known and ships bound for Australia, Peru and China berthed at his docks. Improvements to the mill's capacity had accelerated production and ships also began to be loaded with increasing speed. Where four ships had been loaded in 1864, five were loaded in 1866. By 1867 the number increased to seven ships bound for Hawaii, New Zealand, Chile and other destinations.

If Moody and his partners allowed themselves to experience any degree of euphoria, it must have been tempered by the fear of competition. The firm was well aware of the mills in Puget Sound that offered similar products at prices comparable to its own. Moody and Company's enterprise on Burrard Inlet was only under way when a far greater threat appeared in the person of Captain Edward

Sawmill owner Sewell Prescott Moody and his associates George Washington Haynes (left) and Josias Charles Hughes (right), c. 1870.

City of Vancouver Archives, CVA Port P861 N383

Stamp. Stamp had first visited British Columbia in 1857 when, as the commander of a merchant vessel carrying timber from Puget Sound to Australia, he took some time to examine the timber resources on the west coast of Vancouver Island. He moved to Victoria in 1858 and after several false starts entered the lumber business in 1860 as commission agent for the Anderson Company of London. With considerable bombast, he successfully lobbied the colonial government for rights to timber along the Alberni Canal and built a steam-powered mill where the city of Port Alberni stands today. The Anderson Mill exported eight million board-feet of lumber in 1862 but Stamp's relationship with the Anderson Company soured and he left its employ the same year. In the fall of 1863 he returned to England where he formed the British Columbia and Vancouver Island Spar, Lumber and Saw Mill Company with several investors.

On returning to British Columbia, Stamp threatened to locate a new mill in the United States unless the colonial government gave in to a number of demands. These included a twenty-one-year lease of fifteen thousand acres of timbered land at the remarkably low rate of one cent per acre, the right to cut timber on government reserves (such as the military reserves on Burrard Inlet), the right to purchase twelve hundred acres of pasturage (to provide food for the oxen he expected to acquire as draft animals) and the right to import leather and iron for use in the mill free of duty. In a colony with few opportunities to promote industry, settlement and trade, the government had little alternative but to acquiesce to the majority of Stamp's requests.

In the summer of 1865, Stamp's mill rose in a clearing along the south shore of Burrard Inlet, directly opposite Moody's mill. A combination of British capital and government concessions had placed Stamp in an advantageous position. As his rival's mill began to take shape, Moody crafted a carefully worded letter to

Logging with oxen, Burrard Inlet, c. 1889. As they moved inland, early loggers on the inlet used teams of oxen, and later, horses, to move felled logs to tidewater. By the early 1900s, animal power was superseded by steam-powered donkey engines.

City of Vancouver Archives, CVA Log P3

the mainland colony's governor, Edward Seymour. Moody noted that he and his partners were operating on the same 480 acres they had originally acquired from John Oscar Smith and that their timber reserves were in imminent danger of being exhausted. Their firm had developed a successful foreign trade in lumber and spars and had brought jobs and prosperity to the colony. It was only right, Moody implied, that his company's mill be placed on the same footing as Stamp's by being awarded the rights to an additional five thousand acres of timber.

Moody's request fell on fertile ground, and his company was awarded the rights to four thousand acres of timber in the Lynn Creek watershed, well within reach of his mill. Recognizing the limited demand for lumber in the mainland colony, Moody began to look for more foreign markets. The nearest were on the west coast of the United States, and these were largely controlled by timber brokers in San Francisco. In the mid-1860s, Californians acquired much of their lumber from mills in Puget Sound. Lumber shipped from Burrard Inlet had a reputation for being of inferior quality and difficult to load in the area's treacherous currents. Moody confronted these allegations head-on, travelling to San Francisco in June 1867 and departing with orders totalling 1.4 million feet of lumber. Stamp, in San Francisco at the same time as Moody, relied on contacts overseas to secure his export orders.

Recognizing that land fronting on tidewater in Burrard Inlet was potentially valuable if only for its timber, a number of other New Westminster residents had also begun to pre-empt parcels in the area. Mention of an "Indian Lodge" in one of the pre-emption records is perhaps the first written evidence of Squamish occupation of the site that was later to become the Mission Reserve. Known to the Natives as Ustlawn, its site allowed for easy beaching of canoes and its clear waters of Mosquito Creek offered a ready supply of drinking water. In 1864 the settlement had been home to only four families, including those of Chief Skwatatxwamkin and his nephew Chief Snatt. The establishment of the first mill on the north side of Burrard Inlet would have elicited curiosity among the local First Nations people. When a second mill appeared, the roar of machinery and the loud thump of logs echoed from both shores. Sites long used for gathering food and other resources were destroyed as loggers moved farther along the shore and farther up the slopes. Some Natives, however, learned that the European presence afforded opportunities not only for trade but also for employment. Ustlawn began to grow as additional Squamish families settled alongside the village's four founding families.

But it was not only First Nations who saw the advantages that the two mills offered. The earliest pre-emptions on the north shore of the inlet by Graham and Scrimgeour, Philip Hicks and Frederick Howson had been followed by 160-acre claims by Ira Sacket and Colley Lewis on January 12, 1864. In the absence of maps and survey posts, early pre-emptors described their claims with reference to pre-existing landmarks. Sacket described his land as follows: "On the west it is joined by the claim of Colley Lewis. The Indian Lodge is distant from my house about one mile. On the east it is joined by the land of the sawmill but not immediately, as there is no corner post set by them. On the claim is at present one dwelling house and a large barn."

Chief Snatt from the "Indian Lodge," or Ustlawn, felt that Lewis's claim was a threat to the pre-existing land claims of his own people and paid a visit to New Westminster to appeal to Chartres Brew, chief magistrate of the mainland colony. Brew appears to have sided with the Squamish and authorized Snatt to "take away the post and at the same to notify Lewis that [Brew] had ordered him to do so." Lewis's claim subsequently lapsed, but despite Brew's ruling, the property was taken up by Alexander Merryfield three and a half years later. Claims for parcels nearby continued to be filed until 1872, by which time the entire shoreline of what was to become the City and District of North Vancouver had become the subject of pre-emptions. Throughout the 1860s, Chief Snatt and his people had managed to retain de facto title to the thirty-acre property they had settled on beginning in the early 1860s. The Squamish people had also tightened their grip on the village of Homulchesan at the mouth of the Capilano River, and had successfully foiled Sapper John Linn when he attempted to acquire land at the mouth of Seymour River. Despite these minor victories, the question of aboriginal title was one that would continue to vex the Squamish for many generations.

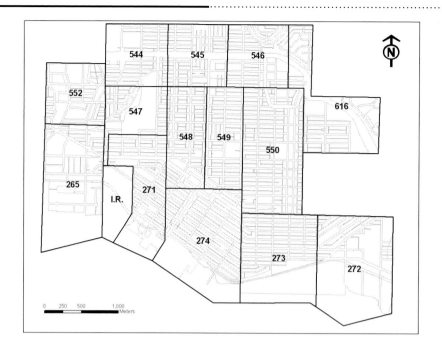

These district lots were to comprise the City of North Vancouver.

Map by Perry Beck, City of North Vancouver

In theory, land policy throughout British North America had long been subject to the provisions of the Royal Proclamation of 1763. This document established the Crown as the ultimate custodian of colonial lands. It forbade colonial governors from disposing of land within their jurisdictions unless title to that land had been acquired from its original inhabitants through treaty or sale. But in the eyes of James Douglas's successors, the First Nations people who lived in British Columbia had no rights of property. The views of colonial secretary William A.G. Young were typical of the time: "The Indians have no right to any land beyond . . . their actual requirements, for they really have never actually possessed it."

In the face of such sentiments, it is remarkable that the Squamish people managed to secure the lands they did along the shores of the inlet. By 1869, several Squamish families were living at Chief Snatt's settlement of Ustlawn. What may once have been a seasonal campground was now a permanent and growing settlement, and it was apparent that Snatt and his people would soon require additional land. One man who ought to have been aware of this was Captain John Deighton, a Yorkshire-bred mariner who had exchanged life at sea for a position behind a bar. Deighton, more popularly known as "Gassy Jack," had settled with his Squamish wife on the south side of the inlet in 1867, building a saloon just to the west of Captain Stamp's mill. His attempt in May 1869 to pre-empt ten acres of waterfront land just east of the Squamish settlement was actively resisted by Snatt and his people, who had already seen their original reserve reduced in size following the retirement of Governor Douglas. Snatt was not alone in his protest, having solicited significant support from the Roman Catholic Church.

Members of the Missionary Order of the Oblates of Mary Immaculate (OMI), a Roman Catholic order founded in France in 1816, had visited Ustlawn as early as May 1863, when Father Gendre made his first trip to the North Shore. Snatt and his wife had already been converted to Roman Catholicism and had been baptized by Father Leon Fouquet, OMI, in New Westminster in 1863. By late 1868 Snatt and his people had erected a church in their village, with lay brothers associated with the Oblates assisting in its completion. The church—later named St. Paul's—served both sacred and secular purposes, proclaiming Squamish conversion to the Roman Catholic faith as well as Squamish ownership of the land on which it stood.

Snatt and the Oblates soon found that the colonial bureaucracy had little patience with their protest. After consulting with an Oblate priest, Snatt went to visit the authorities with a letter outlining his objections to Deighton's claim. The letter was received by Chartres Brew, who according to an Oblate chronicler, "seemed annoyed on reading the letter, and tore part of it in small pieces. [Nor] did he speak nicely to Snatt [telling] him that the place there was not at all their land." A subsequent letter to Joseph Trutch, the chief commissioner of lands and works, referred to the Squamish as a "troublesome tribe . . . likely to give the scattered white population of the inlet a great deal of trouble." Writing to his bishop shortly before the affair was concluded, Father Paul Durieu, OMI, lamented:

> *Everything possible is being done to deprive the natives of their land, for whom they haven't yet deigned to mark off the reserves. Snatt has had to strive to prevent losing the land on which we have built the church. I was obliged to run around for ten days, finding the judge, the policeman, and finally drafting a petition in form. Did you know that Judge Ball registered the white claim taking all Snatt's land at Burrard Inlet, leaving the natives naught but the land on which the church stands and a large native lodge?*

Moodyville shoreline from the west, 1860s, showing the debris left by early hand-logging on the slopes in the foreground.

North Vancouver Museum and Archives, 9233

The petition Durieu drafted on behalf of Snatt and sixty-five other members of his community noted the Squamish people's long-standing occupation of the site and their previous complaints about European intrusions, and it respectfully demanded "that there be left for us two hundred acres of land having sixty chains [400 metres] of frontage along the sea." In the end, the Squamish were allotted a thirty-five-acre reserve, a third of which was subject to tidal inundation.

While Snatt and his people were fighting for their piece of the inlet's north shore, Moody and company were developing a community of their own. During the 1860s and 1870s the mill was expanded and production increased. The settlement around the mill began to assume the shape of a small town. The mill and its environs were owned by the company but community connections were developing nonetheless, often at the initiative of the mill owners themselves.

Moody and his partners may have possessed both vision and ambition, but none were particularly wealthy. This was corrected in 1866, when James van Bramer and Moses C. Ireland's roles in the partnership were taken up by Hugh Nelson and George Dietz. Nelson and Dietz had become prominent figures in the mainland colony, having operated several businesses including the British Columbia and Victoria Express Company, a firm that carried goods between Victoria and Yale. Nelson's other business interests included the Yale Steam Navigation Company and Dietz's included a number of mining concerns. The new partners brought capital to the mill, enabling Moody to undertake a number of productive initiatives including the construction of a new sawmill, the acquisition of a sailing barque and

Steam and smoke emanate from the Moodyville Sawmill, c. 1890. The ship Valparaiso *is anchored on the right.*
City of Vancouver Archives, CVA Mi p22

the building of a number of support facilities. The new steam-powered mill was the most significant undertaking, leading to greatly increased lumber production and hence, increased profit that made the other ventures possible.

Moody, Dietz and Nelson's faith in the potential of the inlet was shared by several outside observers. The captain of the *Jeddo*, whose ship had visited the inlet sometime before mid-1866, wrote to his company's agents:

This is, without exception, one of the finest harbours I ever saw. It is locked in all round with high lands, covered with trees three hundred feet high, so that no wind or sea can hurt ships, and very easy for access for the largest ships afloat, and good anchorage. It is, likewise, a good place for loading. The ships can moor head and stern about half a cable's length from the mills, in six fathoms of water. There are about eighty or one hundred inhabitants employed at the saw mills. I should think in a short time this will become a very extensive place of business in the lumber and spar trade, as I understand it is the best lumber on the coast, or perhaps in the world; and according to my judgement, I should think it could not be surpassed.

When John Robson ventured into Burrard Inlet in mid-1868, some months after his previous visit, he found a palpable difference in Moody's mill and the settlement that had grown up around it: "The beautiful sunny side of the slope is now dotted with the neat cabins of hardy woodmen . . . while the wharf accommodation has been gradually creeping into the sea until a dozen of ships might now find ample room with depth of water sufficient to float the *Great Eastern* . . . and so facile of access that the largest ships can come right alongside under sail where they may be undisturbed by wind and wave."

With the new steam-powered and original water-powered facilities combining to manufacture a variety of products, the North Shore mill truly began to prosper. Most of its output was now being shipped to the southern hemisphere. A series of gold rushes in Australia in the 1850s had led to increased prosperity and to the growth of towns and cities, all of which required vast supplies of construction materials. The growth of the sugar industry in Hawaii in the 1860s also fuelled the demand for North American lumber, and a series of events in Chile—ranging from economic booms to war to earthquakes—created a further demand for lumber well into the 1870s. The opening up of China to trade with the West had led to the growth of Shanghai, with a corresponding demand for building materials that continued for decades to come.

Moody's actions indicate that he was an enlightened businessman who realized contented employees made good workers. He supported initiatives to promote sobriety, learning, religion and harmony in his community. He had permitted the holding of religious services on the mill property as early as June 1865, when John Robson's brother Ebenezer Robson, a Methodist minister then based in New Westminster, rode to Burrard Inlet and then travelled by canoe to the mill. Robson reported preaching to a congregation of fifteen, noting that his audience had been most attentive and that he had been invited to return. This was likely the first time a Protestant clergyman had conducted services on the inlet.

In January 1869 the Mount Hermon Masonic Lodge was established in the small

Moodyville's Mount Hermon Masonic Lodge, painted by John de Forest, c. 1901. The lodge was the first fraternal organization established on the inlet.

City of Vancouver Archives, CVA Out P.1179 N 733

community with Moody as a charter member. Another major development came a few days later with the establishment of the New London Mechanics Institute in the Masonic Hall. Mechanics' Institutes were a remarkable creation of the Victorian age. Designed to provide the working classes, skilled artisans in particular, with opportunities for education and personal "improvement," they served as a positive alternative to the gin halls and pubs that "degraded" the working classes. The mill community never had a church of its own, but the New London Mechanics Institute made its premises available to any visiting clergyman. The Bible headed the list of the Institute's initial set of library books, many selected by Moody while visiting San Francisco. Texts on philosophy, geology, chemistry and natural history followed, supplemented by volumes on American statesmen and politics.

During Moody's regime, mill society was predominantly young and male but racially diverse. Managers were mostly American or British while tradesmen were predominantly from the Maritime provinces. Labourers and longshoremen were for the most part First Nations from the Squamish community to the west, which grew as Natives relocated from Howe Sound. There was also a contingent of Chinese workers, many of them former gold miners. As time passed the ethnic mix was enriched by the arrival of Hawaiians, Chileans and others.

Unskilled workers could earn twenty to thirty dollars per month, plus board, based on a twelve-hour day and six-day workweek. Benefits as we know them today were non-existent, though employees were entitled to "a hurried one half-hour break for lunch." The workforce tended to be itinerant, with many labourers working for only a few weeks before moving on. Although most aboriginal employees lived in homes on the Mission Reserve, the mill provided accommodation for the others.

By the 1880s, the Moodyville Sawmill employed a multi-racial workforce, including whites, Squamish, Chinese, and Kanakas (Hawaiians). William Nahanee, son of a Kanaka father and Squamish mother, stands at the centre of the group.
City of Vancouver Archives, CVA Mi N26 p.2

Housing was racially and socially segregated, the unmarried mill workers living in bunkhouses behind the mill with separate buildings for Caucasians, Chinese and a growing number of Hawaiians. Some of these latter employees, known locally as "Kanakas," had arrived after leaving the employ of Hudson's Bay Company posts at Fort Langley and elsewhere. Others were crewmen who jumped ship when their vessels were in port.

Moody's New England Calvinist morality and sound business sense forbade the establishment of either hotels or saloons in the small community. Mill employees seeking a drink and female society were obliged to travel across the inlet to the hamlet of Granville, a.k.a. Gastown, where retired riverboat captain Gassy Jack Deighton and his Squamish wife operated their rollicking Globe Hotel and bar. The difference in the two settlements was clearly evident to those who visited the inlet. James McCulley, a young sailor who deserted his ship for Moody's mill in 1875, subsequently wrote to his parents in England: "There is a library and papers with reading room which is a great boon and places Moodyville far ahead of the neighbouring mills and villages which nearly all boast of a rum mill or two . . . Nothing of the kind is allowed on Moody's land." Captain W.J. Lees of the British barque *Chelsea* also complimented the mill's managers on their policy of prohibition: "The crew here are free from the temptations of the grog shop, and no idlers are allowed about the place."

The consumption of alcohol, of course, was one of few pleasures available to the non-Native men of the inlet who worked long hours, lived generally without female companionship and whose close quarters offered few outlets for social or physical recreation. For the aboriginal population, the effects of liquor could be severe. With no tradition of social drinking or moderation, the consumption of alcoholic beverages by Native employees was particularly worrisome for the mill owners, as widespread intoxication could halt production for a day or more. The Indian Liquor Ordinance of 1867 had forbidden the sale or supply of liquor to Native people (save for medicinal purposes) but it proved difficult to enforce. First Nations could be particularly vulnerable to the allures of the liquor pedalled illegally by men such as Maximilien Michaud, who operated the New Brighton Hotel, a fashionable resort at the Burrard Inlet terminus of the road from New Westminster.

Isolation generally mitigated the negative effects of alcohol among the workers at the mill. A ferry service provided by Welshman John "Navvy Jack" Thomas in his rowboat was the sole formal connection between the two sides of the inlet until Captain James van Bramer's steam-powered ferry *Seafoam* entered service in 1868. Gassy Jack Deighton's attempt in 1869 to secure land—potentially as a site for a saloon—near what later became the Mission Reserve had been quashed with the help of the Oblate missionaries. In early 1874, however, William Bridges succeeded in acquiring a licence to sell liquor from premises about a mile west of the mill, near the foot of what was later to become Lonsdale Avenue. Although his attempt to construct a trail to the mill was thwarted by Josias C. Hughes, a friend and employee of Moody, Bridges' waterfront hostelry and bar were nonetheless built, temptingly close to both the mill and the Mission Reserve.

Although many who worked at Moody's mill may have been tempted by liquor, non-Native workers were challenged in other ways as well. During its earliest years, there were very few women at the settlement. The absence of a significant population of white women in early British Columbia was a matter of concern to the colonial government and even attracted the eye of *The Times* (of London), which wrote in 1863: "There is probably no country where the paucity of women in comparison with men is so injuriously felt . . . Oh! If fifty or one hundred should arrive from England every month until the supply equalled the demand, what a blessing it would be to us and the colony at large!" Of sixty women who arrived in the colony in 1862 via a "bride ship" sponsored by the Anglican Church, at least one found her way to Burrard Inlet: Miss Emma E. Tammage married R.H. Alexander, who later became manager of the Hastings Mill (as Stamp's mill became known as after his death in 1872).

Many men followed the example of the fur trade and formed liaisons with Native and mixed-race women. Such relationships—dubbed "country marriages"—generally lacked the sanction of either the state or the church but many endured nonetheless. There were also relationships that ended in misfortune. Moodyville pioneer Alice Springer Crakanthorp recalled James van Bramer having a country marriage that ended when he returned to the United States, taking the couple's two daughters—but not his wife—with him. Crakanthorp also identified Alexander Merryfield as having an aboriginal partner, but the relationship ended when he refused to bow to pressure from the Oblates to formally marry.

A few men were reported to have practised polygamy. Alice Crakanthorp's daughter Muriel noted that some of the men who lived on Brigham Terrace had two or three wives:

> First, they would have an Indian wife, and then, perhaps, later, the white wife would come along from somewhere, perhaps come out on a sailing ship, and the Indian wife would have to go, she being only a common law wife. And, then again, other men may have had two or three Indian women living with them; two or three wives, but the Roman Catholic priests put a stop to that; made them marry; there were getting to be so many little ones.

Moody himself took a First Nations wife, without the benefit of clergy. Little is known about the relationship except that it produced two children, George and Anita, and may have ended by July 1869 when Moody married nineteen-year-old Janet Watson in an Anglican ceremony in Victoria. The new Mrs. Moody continued to live in Victoria, preferring its amenities to those of the village on the inlet. In later years, Moody's Victoria-born children attempted to hide the fact of their father's earlier marriage and offspring. As Moody's granddaughter Jean Greenwood recalled, "My parents didn't tell us these Indian children were my grandfather's children. They said that when the Indians admired someone, they took his name. They didn't want to tell us they were considered bastard children . . . It was very sad that those things happened. It was hard for them to get employment, an education."

By 1870, the settlement around the mill was becoming a sizeable community with a workforce of perhaps a hundred supplemented by a growing number of wives and children. The appearance of school-age children in the settlement necessitated the establishment of the Burrard Inlet School District in mid-1870. The new school

General Store on the wharf at Moodyville, undated. An elevated plank walk leads to the shanties on the hillside behind.

British Columbia Archives, 9314

district encompassed both sides of the inlet, but its first schoolhouse was located at Moody's Mill (as the community was then called), since that settlement had the greater number of school-age children. Moody, Dietz and Nelson arranged for the construction of a one-room school, and mill superintendent George Washington Haynes persuaded his sister Laura to travel from Maine to take up the post of schoolteacher at a salary of forty dollars per month. Laura Haynes later recalled the considerable challenges her new position demanded:

> *When we reached our destination even my enthusiasm was dampened a little. The whole settlement seemed built on a sawdust pile and the noise from the mill itself was with us from dawn till dusk. Our house was a shack of green lumber, but we soon made it more or less attractive. The school itself was a one-room building, also on the sawdust pile. In fact, it was around the school that they used to burn the refuse from the mill so that many a time the children had to be dismissed after a half day session, and sent home with streaming eyes and noses.*

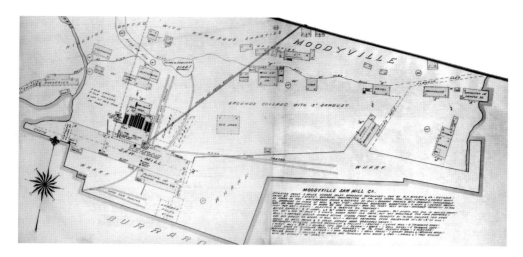

Dakin's Fire Insurance Map of the Moodyville Sawmill, 1889, shows the wharf, mill buildings, general store, and hotel in the foreground, the Chinese "Rookeries" on the left, and the single men's tenements and shanties on the hillside behind.

University of British Columbia Library, Special Collections, 63514 V3D3 1889

Miss Haynes began her career at Moody's Mill with thirteen students, a number that grew to forty within two years. This growth resulted in the creation of the Granville School District to serve the inhabitants of the inlet's southern shore.

By then, the newly created province of British Columbia had passed its first Public Schools Act, requiring that anyone teaching in the province be a British subject. As an American Miss Haynes was compelled to relinquish her post to New Brunswick native Margaret Thain, the wife of one of the mill's longshoremen. Thain served as the community's schoolteacher until 1876, by which time a new school building, described by the provincial inspector of schools as being "out of the way of the smoke and din of the mills," had been built. During these first years the inspector provided positive reports on the management of the school and the progress of its students, noting in 1872 that the school was "orderly and quiet." With its new community facilities, the settlement at Moody's Mill attracted favourable comments from visitors to the inlet who described both the physical attractiveness and high moral tone of what Mrs. Thain had by then dubbed "Moodyville."

Booming economies in the southern hemisphere and sound local management led to the mill's continued prosperity through the late 1860s and into the 1870s. In 1869, lumber from Moody's Mill filled the holds of about two dozen ships, their cargoes bound for ports in Australia, Hawaii, South America, California and Britain. Moody's own barque, the *Delaware*, sailed to California on no less than three occasions. Under Moody's direction, the number of cargoes shipped from his docks had increased from just six in 1865 to forty-five in 1869.

With the mill's future seemingly secured, Moody and his partners continued to improve its facilities. Communication with the outside world was addressed in 1869 when the partners installed a telegraph line between the mill and New Westminster. The line followed the road between the Royal City and the hotel at Brighton before crossing the inlet in an underwater cable. In 1872, the firm completed a dock in New Westminster and began to diversify its activities by acquiring a silver mine at Hope. A few months later, in the spring of 1873, Moody announced his intent to increase his mill's power and capacity by constructing five new boilers. Nothing, it appeared, could stop the dreams of the enterprising Mr. Moody.

But Moody and his partners suffered a major setback two days before Christmas 1873, when a fire in the lamp room spread quickly through the steam-powered

Margaret Thain, second schoolteacher at Moodyville, was married to stevedore Captain Murray Thain, Burrard Inlet's first harbour master.

City of Vancouver Archives, CVA Port P449.1 & .2

section of the mill. Flames leapt high into the sky, creating an eerie sight for those who watched the destruction from the rival mill across the inlet. In the light of day the devastation proved immense. Undeterred, Moody set about rebuilding, using the old water-powered mill to cut the required materials and engaging John Hendry, a millwright born in New Brunswick, as project supervisor. Remarkably, the mill was rebuilt and ready for production by March 1874, its capacity having been increased significantly during the reconstruction.

The threat of fires was but one to the dangers faced by the sawmill owner. Coastal travel was another. Moody had a narrow escape in January 1875, when travelling north from California aboard the steamer the *Los Angeles*. The ship's propeller shaft snapped eighty-eight hours out of San Francisco, leaving the vessel powerless and adrift. Though no one had been injured and the ship had been towed safely into Astoria, Oregon, the event was but one of a series of incidents involving poorly maintained and sometimes irresponsibly captained vessels along the coast. Moody's next maritime adventure had a less fortunate ending. He and scores of other passengers bound for San Francisco boarded the aging steamer the *Pacific* in Victoria in November 1875. Sailing in the dark, the *Pacific* collided with the *Orpheus* off Cape Flattery and sank within an hour. Four weeks later bits and pieces of the *Pacific* began to appear on the beach below Victoria's Beacon Hill. Amid the flotsam and jetsam, the most remarkable find was a painted fragment of board bearing a hurriedly pencilled inscription: "S. P. Moody—all lost."

DREAMERS AND SCHEMERS 1876–1886

Moody's untimely death, coming as it did shortly after British Columbia had entered Confederation, coincided with the dawn of a new age for those who lived and worked in the westernmost province. A railway linking the Pacific province with the Canadian heartland had been promised, and those who lived in British Columbia began to dream of access to wealthy eastern markets. The peopling of the Canadian West would require the very building materials that British Columbia possessed in such abundance, and the timber trade could not help but benefit. The province's ports would also prosper, as ships from "the Orient" transferred their cargoes onto trains departing for the east. The anticipation spread that British Columbia would cease to be a frontier society and great cities would emerge where railways met the sea. Burrard Inlet might well become the Liverpool of the Pacific and a key component of what was in time referred to as the "all-red route" from Britain to China, Japan and India.

During the colonial period, commercial activity along Burrard Inlet's northern shore had largely been limited to that of a single enterprise. Ironically, many of the men who had controlled that enterprise were American. Moody had been born in Maine and maintained his American status throughout his life in British Columbia, going so far as to have British subjects in his employ pre-empt land on his behalf. He had even held July Fourth celebrations at the mill. Those overtly loyal to the Crown had to travel across the inlet for observances of the Queen's birthday.

Several of Moody's partners had also been Americans. Moses C. Ireland was a native of Maine, and James van Bramer was from New York. George Dietz's origins are unknown. In 1875, his name was inexplicably deleted from references to the firm, probably because he was beginning to exhibit the outward symptoms of insanity. George Washington Haynes, who served as one of Moody's logging camp superintendents and later as superintendent of the mill, was like Moody a native of Maine. Andrew Welch, who had quietly been taken into the partnership in the late 1860s, was a San Francisco businessman. Of Moody's other major associates, only Hugh Nelson from Ireland and Josias Hughes of Upper Canada could claim to have been born under the British flag. As the century wore on, however, those

Moodyville as seen from Burrard Inlet, late 1800s. The ferry Senator, named in honour of Hugh Nelson, and the tug Etta White are berthed on the left.
North Vancouver Museum and Archives, 8139

in command of the mill and those who developed the community around it were increasingly British.

With Moody dead, Dietz descending into madness and Andrew Welch residing in California, Hugh Nelson assumed management of the firm. One of Nelson's first acts was to reorganize the firm under the name of the Moodyville Sawmill Company. Moody might be dead, but his name lived on in the name of both his community, officially christened in 1875, and the mill. Nelson's desire to bring new capital into the company resulted in the recruitment of several additional partners, including a number of distinguished British-born businessmen and professionals from New Westminster and Victoria: bank manager James Burns, barrister Montague William Tyrwhitt Drake, ship's chandler Peter McQuade and riverboat captain John Irving.

Having assumed leadership of the mill, Nelson set about putting his own stamp on the business, ensuring that it remained one of the top three export enterprises in the province. Nelson recognized the benefits that the Canadian Pacific Railway would bring and lobbied for Moodyville to be made its western terminus. He was quick to embrace technological change, overseeing the installation of electric lights in the settlement early in 1882, just two years after Edison had patented the invention. Moodyville's were the first electric lights in the province, and news of their installation so intrigued the mayor and council of the City of Victoria that they decided to visit the mill en masse. Their party arrived at Moodyville late one night shortly after midnight, hauling Nelson and machinist J.S. Randall from their beds to show them the lights. Those with a technical bent were surely impressed by Randall's description of how the electric lamps worked: there were ten lights in total, each providing two thousand candles' worth of illumination.

Nelson also implemented a number of improvements to the inlet's infant transportation system. Having arrived in British Columbia in 1858, Nelson had seen the construction of a series of trails linking Burrard Inlet with New Westminster, at that time the largest urban centre on the BC mainland. For Moodyville, the most important of these trails was the route that connected the resort hamlet of New Brighton with the "Royal City" of New Westminster. New Brighton stood near the site of what was later to become Hastings Park and the Pacific National Exhibition fairgrounds but was then best known as the site of Maximilien Michaud's hotel and picnic grounds. By 1868, the state of the trail was such that horse-drawn stages were able to travel between the two centres, with Captain James van Bramer's vessel *Seafoam* completing the connection to the north side of the inlet. By 1873, van Bramer had augmented the *Seafoam* with the *Chinaman*, another small steam-powered vessel. Van Bramer's vessels are said to have served the inlet via a triangular route, wherein the ferries met the stage at New Brighton, crossed the inlet to Moodyville, recrossed the inlet to the Hastings Mill, then returned to New Brighton.

In the mid-1870s the *Lily* and the *Union* were brought into service on the inlet. The *Lily* was a forty-three-foot vessel built for van Bramer in Victoria and fitted with engines pulled from the *Seafoam*. The product of frontier ingenuity, the *Union* consisted of little more than a threshing machine engine mounted on a roughly built scow. A pair of wooden cogs propelled two side-mounted paddlewheels. The vessel lost power whenever its whistle was sounded and, in the absence of

Hugh Nelson, partner with Sewell Moody and George Dietz in what ultimately became known as the Moodyville Sawmill. After leaving the mill, Nelson became active in public life, becoming a MLA, MP, senator, and lieutenant-governor of the province.
City of Vancouver Archives, CVA Port P457 N1066

Ferry Senator, *with passengers near the bow, berthed in Vancouver. In the 1890s,* Senator *made regular trips between Vancouver and Moodyville, and later, to the foot of Lonsdale Avenue in North Vancouver.*

City of Vancouver Archives, CVA BO P62

a reverse gear, could only go straight ahead. Those who travelled on the *Union* could be knocked off their feet and hurled overboard as it abruptly stopped or got under way, resulting in the affectionate nicknames *Sudden Jerk* and *Hell-a-Roaring*. Passengers wishing to preserve their dignity doubtless preferred to journey aboard the *Lily* or the *Chinaman* and were surely relieved when the less eccentric steamer *Leonora* (named in honour of van Bramer's daughter) appeared on the inlet in 1876. In 1880, the recently incorporated Moodyville Ferry Company built a new steamer at Moodyville and put it into service under the command of Captain Hugh Stalker. Named the *Senator* in honour of newly appointed senator Hugh Nelson, the vessel served the residents of Moodyville into the early 1900s.

This collection of steamers was indicative of the inlet's highly successful economy in the 1870s, despite a general slowdown in the colony's interior. The Moodyville and Hastings mills hummed with activity, fed by loggers who moved from place to place as they harvested what appeared to be a never-ending supply of timber. On the inlet's southern shore, the hamlet of Granville continued to grow, its several saloons enjoying the spirited support of loggers, mill workers and sailors from the schooners, barques and brigantines that called to pick up lumber. On the northern shore, a handful of farmers, including the Hugh Burr family at the mouth of Seymour Creek and the John Linn family at the mouth of Lynn Creek, eked out a living selling dairy products to the Moodyville and Hastings mill communities. The Squamish villages at the mouths of Mosquito Creek and the Capilano River also

Moodyville Hotel, initially operated by Captain William Power, and later, by Charles Mee. The hotel, with its well-stocked bar, did not open until after the death of Sewell Moody, whose puritanical bent forbade the presence of alcohol in his small community.

North Vancouver Museum and Archives, 884

grew, but as in the previous decade, it was the sawmill that elicited the attention of visitors from distant lands. Visiting the mill in 1882, surveyor Newton H. Chittenden noted the technological supremacy and scale of its operations:

> *Their great mill, furnished with ten electric lights for night work, completely equipped with double circular and gang saws, edgers, scantling, planing, and lathe machines, and employing a hundred men, [was] cutting up huge logs at the rate of from 75 to 100 thousand feet daily or from 20 to 25 million feet a year. Quite a fleet of ships lay waiting for their cargoes for China, Japan, Australia, and the West Coast of South America. The town with its mill, machine shop, store, hotel, boarding house, and numerous dwellings, and the shipping in front, presented the most interesting scene of activity on the Inlet.*

Chittenden's reference to a hotel suggests that Moody's position on hotels in Moodyville may have been reversed by Nelson. It is certain that there was a hotel in Moodyville by the early 1880s: operated by Captain William Power, who had previously operated hostelries in Yale and New Westminster, much of its success was due to his personal popularity. Writing in 1904, newspaperman D.W. Higgins remembered, "Nearly every early resident of Yale, Vancouver, and Victoria will readily recall the personality of Captain William Power . . . The Captain, who was an Irishman, was a splendid specimen of manhood and an accomplished athlete." Power's commanding presence also made an impression on Vancouver pioneer businessman Frank W. Hart: "At the Moodyville Hotel the caterer was a great big man, great big 'corporation' in front, big Englishman, everybody liked him, and he shook hands with us, and when he laughed he would shake, too, all over. He had been a millionaire, or something, friend of [David] Oppenheimer's; well up in society; earls or something . . ." Captain Power extended gracious hospitality to those who practised moderation and dealt discreetly but firmly with those who did not.

Captain William Power, the gregarious manager of the Moodyville Hotel and prominent speculator in North Shore properties.
British Columbia Archives, ZZ-95310

At the time of the 1881 Canadian census, the first to include BC, Moodyville remained a multiracial society dominated by unmarried males. More than two thirds of its population of 196 residents was male, and of these 80 percent were over the working age of fourteen. Almost three-quarters of working-age residents came from English-speaking countries, while slightly over one-quarter traced their origins to places as diverse as mainland Europe, China, the West Indies, Latin America and the Sandwich Islands (as Hawaii was then known). None of these figures account for the dozens of First Nations who lived on nearby reserves but who came to the mill to work, trade or make purchases at its store. Nor do the figures account for the crews of visiting ships, which in 1881 included men from Malaya and the Philippines as well as Europe and North America.

Over time, clear patterns of physical separation became evident in the small community. Early residents interviewed by Vancouver city archivist Major James Skitt Matthews recalled the community's social and racial divisions in detail:

Around the mill was "The Spit," reclaimed from the sea by the dumping of slabs and sawdust. Firmed by traffic, it became the rendezvous for all sports and games. Eastward from it extended Kanaka Row with houses on both sides. At the end of Kanaka Row a skid road turned due north, from which the bears often ate the dog fish oil with which the skids were greased. West of the mill were the "Rookeries," the Chinese shanties. Leading up the hill were Canary Lane or Walk, and Maiden Lane, so named because there were no maidens there.

The settlement also possessed a "Frenchman's Row," Brigham Terrace and the hilltop area of "Nob Hill," echoing San Francisco's prestigious neighbourhood. Axel Nyman, who was born in Moodyville in 1886, recalled the cluster of dwellings from which the mill's senior staff could survey the activity below them: "The big shots lived up the hill, Nob Hill we used to call it. That's where the manager's house was, and others like the chief engineer, the foreman, and all like that. The school teacher lived there too and a few others like office guys, paymaster, and so on."

Nob Hill's "Big House," officially known as Invermere, became the focal point for high society on the north side of the inlet. People who were invited there enjoyed high social status and eagerly participated in entertainments arranged by Nelson and his successors. Guests included people occupying similar positions on the south side of the inlet such as Hastings Mill manager R.H. Alexander and his wife; itinerant clergymen; well-heeled visitors from New Westminster, Victoria and San Francisco; and the captains of visiting ships. The latter would sometimes bring their wives and children, who often joined ships' commanders while their ships were at sea. Entertainments included piano recitals, singing, croquet and in later years tennis.

When not at work, mill employees undertook a range of recreational activities. For some, a trip to William Bridges' saloon—located near what was to become the foot of Lonsdale Avenue—provided an opportunity to drink and carouse out of sight of disapproving matrons in the village. Others continued the long-established tradition of travelling over to Granville to drink or play cards. Some such games spanned several days, in at least one instance forcing the Hastings Mill to cease operations for lack of staff. Those of a literary bent could visit the Mechanics Institute's library, which at its peak housed over six hundred volumes and subscribed to about two dozen periodicals. One such publication was the short-lived but spirited *Moodyville Tickler,* the first newspaper on the inlet. Edited and published by William Colbeck, the paper printed just three or four issues, mixing gentle satire with stern analysis of the major political issues of the day. Its inaugural issue offered tongue-in-cheek advice to potential advertisers:

> *Notices of deaths, unless accompanied by a special fee, will be restricted to two lines and a half, but an enclosed five dollar bill (silver taken at a discount), will ensure a double-leaded, double black-edged column, devoted to praises of the deceased, and enumerating his peculiar vices (if he had any). His pedigree will be traced back to the Conquest, and his whole career will be "done up," so brown that his dearest relative, not even his mother-in-law, would be able to recognize the picture.*

The "Big House" on Moodyville's "Nob Hill," home of a succession of mill managers and site of numerous social events— including tennis parties—for the inlet's social elite in the 1880s and 1890s.
City of Vancouver Archives, CVA Out P232**

the picture.

Benjamin Springer, manager of the Moodyville Sawmill after Hugh Nelson's retirement in 1882. Springer was also a local lay magistrate and land speculator.

City of Vancouver Archives, CVA Port 542 (cropped)

Frances (Richards) Springer, wife of Moodyville Mill manager Ben Springer and doyenne of North Shore society in the 1880s.

City of Vancouver Archives, CVA Port P118.2

Employees could also attend the family dances and religious services held in the Institute's hall. The mill's management arranged occasional outings for its employees, events presaging the outdoor recreational activities that later became part and parcel of North Vancouver life. While hiking in the forest does not seem to have been pursued by many, picnicking was a popular pastime. Former resident Matthew Sergius Logan remembered one such event, organized by Moody just months before his death: "There was nowhere to picnic, much, to go for a picnic in 1875; everything was forest, but there was a bit of grass and a bit of pasture up Seymour Creek flats, so one day we all got on a scow, at the invitation of Moody, and took all the people of Moodyville for a picnic up Seymour Creek."

Alice Crakanthorp, daughter of mill manager Benjamin Springer, recalled similar excursions when much of the population of Moodyville travelled by steamer to Granite Falls in Indian Arm, sometimes accompanied by the captains of visiting ships and their wives. For those who lived within the settlement, sandwiched as it was between the forest and the sea, such expeditions must have been memorable indeed. After the picnic the party would return to Moodyville, where all were "invited to the cookhouse for dinner or supper, and after that [to a] dance in the Mechanics Institute." As a child, Mrs. Crakanthorp had considered attending a dance in the Mechanics Institute the pinnacle of social achievement: "I used to think if I could only get to the Masonic Hall, I should attain something—the style and ceremony of it!"

Benjamin Springer became full-time mill manager in 1882 after Hugh Nelson had retired to focus on his position in the Senate. Ownership of the mill passed to Welch, Rithet and Company, with the Californian Welch being the principal owner. Springer's appointment as mill manager assured continuity, since he had previously served as mill foreman and was well aware of the traditions of the operation. Springer continued to operate the enterprise in much the same way as his predecessors, and his wife Frances Springer soon established herself as the leader of high society on the north shore of the inlet just as Mrs. Alexander had on the south. Benjamin and Frances Springer soon made their mark in local history as the parents of the first white child born on Burrard Inlet: Mabel Ellen Springer was born in Moodyville on April 29, 1875.

Benjamin Springer also represented the law in Moodyville. During the 1870s and 1880s, it was practice for the managers of Burrard Inlet's two sawmills to serve as lay magistrates. Such men were not trained in the law, lawyers being rather scarce in British Columbia at the time. Instead, they were perceived as educated men whose characters and backgrounds suggested intelligence, fairness and good judgment. Hugh Nelson had also served as a magistrate in Moodyville. James Raymur and R.H. Alexander filled similar positions on the south side of the inlet. In 1891 Moodyville also gained its own police force, when the British Columbia Police assigned George Calbick to the position of constable. Illicit activity appears to have been a concern in Moodyville in the 1880s, with most of the infractions related to alcohol abuse. Having acquired the services of a policeman, the citizens of Moodyville determined to build a jail, conveniently located behind the hotel.

Concern about the deleterious effects of alcohol was an ongoing and central theme in the small community's life. Moodyville women regularly attended meetings of the Women's Christian Temperance Union on the inlet's south shore. The liquor trade among Native people was especially worrisome and remained a major concern throughout the 1880s. Limiting liquor abuse by Natives was one of many projects taken up by the Oblate priests.

The Oblates' influence was beginning to grow throughout the Lower Mainland, with Father Paul Durieu the most influential among them. Durieu had been born in France in 1830, entered the Oblate order in 1848, and was ordained six years later. After several years' service in Washington, he moved north to take up duties first in Esquimalt, then in Sechelt, Kamloops and New Westminster. Durieu assumed responsibility for the operation of St. Mary's Mission, at Mission in the Fraser Valley, in 1867. He probably first encountered members of the Squamish First Nation while posted in Sechelt and New Westminster, and he initiated efforts to convert them in the mid-1860s.

Influenced by Jesuit activities in South America, Durieu devised a controversial method of organizing Native communities under strict church control that became known as the "Durieu system." A central characteristic of the system, according to anthropologist Wilson Duff, was that "the people were moved to a new location where they built a village of modern-style houses and a dominating church." For the Squamish, whose main settlements were at the head of Howe Sound, this new location was the site in North Vancouver the Oblates at first renamed Sacred Heart, then St. Paul's, but which was commonly known as "The Mission." To be admitted to this model Christian village, residents had to forswear non-Christian beliefs and live like Europeans. Durieu and his fellow priests established a hierarchy of officials at each consolidated village, appointing "watchmen" to act as the priests' eyes and ears and "policemen" to enforce Oblate rules. They even appointed "chiefs" who sometimes vied for influence with hereditary and government-appointed leaders.

Louis Miranda, who grew up on the Mission Reserve, recorded his mother's memories of the inner workings of the Durieu system:

> [A watchman] would walk all through the mission during the day, and after dark he would sneak up close to the house and listen to what was going on in the home. If he heard anyone singing an Indian song or heard the older people talking of the Indian culture, he would report it to the Bishop, and the next Sunday that party . . . would be asked to come forward and kneel before the Bishop and the Chief. Then the Bishop would ask the watchman to come forward and make his report . . . speak to the accused party, and he would be fined five to twenty-five dollars.

Public humiliations such as these were central to Durieu's system, and under some Oblate priests, punishments extended to flogging and other extreme measures. Strict discipline, and punishment followed by forgiveness, instilled dependency in the Natives and ensured continuing Oblate control at the Mission Reserve and other First Nations settlements throughout the province. In return Natives were offered rapid indoctrination into the mysteries of the European culture that was gaining the upper hand in their changing world, a promise that continued to draw

Father Paul Durieu, OMI, 1890s. Durieu was largely responsible for the establishment of the Mission Reserve and for the conversion of many of its Squamish inhabitants to Roman Catholicism. He served as Bishop of New Westminster from 1890 to 1899

Archives of the Archdiocese of Vancouver

In the white community, the cultural makeover of the Squamish brought about by the Durieu system was viewed as a miracle. The view of the area's Indian agent P. McTiernan was typical of outside observers:

> *I am happy to be able to report that there is a very marked increase in the Indian population of Burrard Inlet Mission . . . At the Mission they have fifty-two nice and well-built cottages, in regular rows, with good, wide streets. They have a splendid new church, which was dedicated on the 20th June last. It cost them—exclusive of their own labour—$3,500. It is considered the best finished church in the province. On the day of the dedication there were about 1,000 Indians present, men, women, and children, all cleanly and well dressed. They were very much admired and praised by the large number of white people who attended the dedication on that day.*

The Mission Reserve, c. 1886, with St. Paul's Roman Catholic Church in the centre.
North Vancouver Museum and Archives, 1452

Oblate visitors to the village were perhaps even more enamoured with what they encountered. If approaching from the inlet, visiting priests were greeted by a flagpole flying pennants inscribed "Religion," "Temperance" and "Civilization." As these visitors walked up the beach, the church and the village's houses rose in front of them. As Father J.M. LeJacq reported to his family in 1887:

front of them. As Father J.M. LeJacq reported to his family in 1887:

> *Seen from the bay, the Indian village offers an appealing sight . . . All the houses, well aligned and painted white, have an air of light heartedness and propriety . . . But what is most striking is the church, crowned with a magnificent belltower. It occupies the centre of the village at a respectful distance from the homes, and is surrounded by verdant pasture . . . At the extremity of the village is the cemetery, which is well kept. In the middle there is a huge wooden cross.*

The pervasive influence of the Oblates eventually extended into education, though Squamish children would not have a school until many years later. Although much of what the Oblates ultimately achieved would later be called into question, their concern for the physical and economic well-being of their converts was not. The Oblate priests joined government officials to arrest a recurrence of smallpox in the inlet in 1862. Furthermore, it was the Oblates who consistently supported the Native population in its struggles for land, sometimes incurring the anger of the provincial government.

During the 1880s First Nations people continued to make up much of the Moodyville sawmill's workforce, and according to the Department of Indian Affairs

received wages as high as those paid to "the best white labourers." Most Squamish worked as longshoremen while others served in logging camps on the lower coast, felling timber and transporting it to tidewater to be boomed. Native employees at the mill could amass considerable savings but used them in a manner their non-Native neighbours viewed with chagrin. Feasting and gift-giving, or "potlatching," was a central component of traditional Native life and one that non-Natives struggled to understand. Reverend George Grant recalled one potlatch, noting how a man known as "Big George" had worked at the Moodyville sawmill until he had saved about $2,000:

> *Instead of putting this in a Savings Bank, he had spent it all on "stores" for a grand "Potlatch," summoning Siwashes from far and near to come, eat, drink, dance, be merry and receive gifts. Nearly a thousand assembled; the festivities lasted a week; and everybody got something, either a blanket, musket, bag of flour, box of apples, or tea and sugar. When the fun was over, "Big George" now penniless, returned to the mill to carry slabs at $20 a month.*

Potlatches and feasts were held most often during the winter, as they had been for countless centuries. For Native people, winter had traditionally been a time when little work was done, the harvesting and processing of salmon, berries, roots and other foodstuffs having been conducted in the spring, summer and fall. However, in the new wage economy, a week-long absence of the Native workforce could result in major disruptions in the sawmills. When demand for lumber was high, the Moodyville sawmill operated night and day, and stability in its workforce was crucial. Further disruptions occurred when Natives began to travel at harvest time to work at farms in the upper Fraser Valley. Native priorities became increasingly

incompatible with those of the mill, and inevitably management began to look for other sources of labour.

The long-awaited link with central Canada had begun to approach the Pacific in 1885–86, and the location of the railway's terminus dominated public debate. Although North Shore landowners advocated a site near the Moodyville sawmill, the provincial government's promise of six thousand acres of mostly flat land west of the Hastings Mill resulted in the first steam engine rolling into "Vancouver" on May 23, 1887. Granville had acquired what one observer dubbed a "bombastic swaggering" new name, under which the newly incorporated city embarked on an era of tremendous growth.

If any gloom persisted in Moodyville, it was confined to a few and was likely short-lived. Vancouver, after all, was but a short ferry ride away. The Second Narrows invited bridge construction, and once-forested land was now cleared and ready for development. Furthermore, North Shore lumber was readily available for the construction of the emerging metropolis and demand for export timber remained healthy. Moodyville residents thus continued to live much as they had before, males working at the mill and shipyard, females keeping house and children going to school.

By the end of the 1880s, however, subtle changes began to take place. Japanese workers began to appear at the mill, where they joined aboriginal and Chinese labourers carting slabs and other waste. The number of Chinese workers also grew,

The Star Gang of longshoremen at Moodyville. Prior to the adoption of the principle of equalization of hours, Burrard Inlet's longshoremen were organized into a series of gangs, entry into which was highly restricted. The Star Gang included men of British, Kanaka, Native and Chilean origin.

North Vancouver Museum and Archives, 4846

while the Native workforce began to dwindle. According to Axel Nyman, many Native people preferred to work elsewhere: "The Native Indians preferred to go fishing and hop-picking in the summer time. They would leave the mill with the result that more Chinese and Japanese got the jobs. So eventually they lost those jobs. The better workers among them would work on the longshore end of it." Some Chinese were employed as domestic servants and laundrymen, assuming work formerly done by Natives. Alice Crakanthorp remembered how her mother Mary Richards Springer at first hired Squamish women to do her laundry but turned to the Chinese at the Rookeries to do the work instead. Despite their important contribution, the Moodyville Chinese experienced the same kind of discrimination that was prevalent throughout the province. Rodger Burnes recalled watching Chinese workers being bullied by boom men at the mill:

The Chinese had a bunk house also at the foot of the hill on the edge of deep water. By walking on the logs when the boom men were not at work these Chinese would fish off the logs. But woe and behold if the boom men caught them doing that. They would be chased off at once and if caught on a log before they could reach the shore they were in trouble. The boom men would get at each end of the log and roll it while those on the shore would throw stones and sticks at the men.

During the same period, Chilean sailors also settled in the area and sought work at the sawmill. The sailors usually followed a routine of jumping or deserting ship, hiding out in the woods at the base of Grouse Mountain until their ship left, and then seeking accommodation and work with friends in town. Impoverished by the economic depression that befell the province in the early 1890s, some of these mariners initially squatted on property owned by the Moodyville Mill and later on the federally owned foreshore, where they established a small community. As the *Vancouver Daily World* advised its readers a few years later:

Two years ago when the depression was at its worst and the Moodyville mills were practically shut down, the directors of the Moodyville Lands Timber and Trading Company decided to tax all who had dwelling houses on their lands $5 a month. This created quite an exodus of Chileans from Moodyville and they applied to their consul for advice and assistance. Mr. Morris, after a lengthy correspondence with the Ottawa authorities, advised them to settle on the foreshore of North Vancouver on Dominion lands, where, in all likelihood, they would remain undisturbed. They followed his advice. Pedro Flores, the veteran Chilean who came here over 20 years ago, was the first to erect his cabin and now there is quite a little settlement consisting of Chileans and their families, exclusively on the foreshore of the Inlet. They have named it New Valparaiso.

Some of these mariners were of mixed Spanish and South American Indian blood and found themselves in a society that considered them more Native than European. A few married into non-Native families, and others married Native women and settled on the Mission Reserve. Surnames such as Cordocedo, Miranda, Gonzales and Flores thereby joined the British and other European surnames used by the Squamish.

years but racial barriers hampered their assimilation into European society. Owing to their dark skin, meagre formal educations and a record of working in unskilled jobs, they found their upward social mobility as restricted as that of their Chilean, Asian and First Nations neighbours. Over time some Kanakas made their way to the "Kanaka Ranch" situated on Vancouver's Coal Harbour, squatting in shacks built on the beach. Others such as the Nahus and the Nahanees remained on the North Shore, marrying Squamish women and adding to the ethnic diversity of the Squamish community.

An account by Alice Crakanthorp is revealing of the type of racial friction encountered in early Moodyville:

> We had a teacher at the school named McMillan, and he whipped the Indian boys unmercifully; he would go out in the bush and cut a switch, and whip them with it . . . The Indian boys resented this, and showed their resentment by draping an apple tree in his garden with dead snakes . . . When the tree was shaken the dead snakes began to wriggle and drop to the ground; it was horrible.

Speaking to Major Matthews in 1938, Lena Randall Blaney, who grew up in Moodyville in the 1890s, related her memories of the clash of cultures at the time and spoke of her family's relations with the Squamish people: "I liked most of them, but Mother was terrified." Mrs. Blaney remembered an occasion where she had walked to the Mission Reserve with her mother. "On the way back, the Indians were singing and dancing and fighting, some of them in the nude; Mother was in a terrible state, but we walked through and they did not bother us."

Such accounts suggest that Bishop Durieu and his priests may have exaggerated their impact on the daily lives of the Squamish. An anecdote by Ruby Springer Bauer, about her family's washerwoman Louisa, adds to this notion:

The Nahanee family of Moodyville. The family's patriarch, Hawaiian-born "Joe" Nahanee, retired from the fur trade to work at the Hastings Sawmill and lived at Coal Harbour's Kanaka Ranch. His son, William, married a Squamish woman, Mary See-em-ia, and moved to Moodyville prior to settling on the Mission Reserve. Members of other Kanaka families—the Eihus and the Nahus—are also in the photograph.
North Vancouver Museum and Archives, 4847

Bauer, about her family's washerwoman Louisa, adds to this notion:

> [Louisa] had children, and sent them to the Protestant school. Louisa was proud of her children, and looked after them, and did her best for them . . . It seems the Roman Catholic priest did not like Louisa sending her children to the Protestant school, and shook his head; told her it was "bad" business, and gently admonished her. And, as a final argument added, "You know where you'll go, Louisa? You'll go to hell, surely." So Louisa replied, "Ah, lots of nice people go to hell nowadays."

Reports from the local Indian agents in this period indicate their general satisfaction with relations between Natives and non-Natives in the area. In the 1880s, agents also reported a steady increase in Native population numbers, despite annual spikes in the death rate occasioned by influenza, measles and tuberculosis. Much of this population increase was attributed to the eradication of smallpox, to good hygiene and to improved "morality." The report of the Indian agent for 1888 suggested that conditions on the Mission Reserve were due in great measure to the ministrations of Paul Durieu:

> The Mission Indians at Burrard Inlet are an excellent band. Their nice white clean houses with their fine church is a credit to them; their streets are laid out in regular order; they have street lamps and sanitary regulations which they observe strictly; the men, women and children dress as cleanly and well as any white people. Although living quite close to the City of Vancouver, their women—young or old—or their boys are never found loitering on the streets either by day or night. There are a number of able bodied men in the village who work almost continually at the saw mills and receive as high wages as is paid to the best white laborers. Their morality is evidenced by the steady increase in their number, notwithstanding the number of their children who died last winter. These Indians are under the strict religious care of his Lordship Bishop Durian [sic] who devotes a great deal of time and attention to them.

Annual tallies of the inlet's First Nations population confirm the agent's claim that the population on the Mission Reserve was "steadily increasing in number." In 1880, the population at the Mission stood at 123. By 1885, the number had grown to 206. In 1888, 296 Native people lived at the reserve, while another 62 lived in Moodyville. In the early 1890s, however, population levels declined to 240, perhaps because the economic depression curtailed mill production and forced many people to look elsewhere for work. Outbreaks of influenza and tuberculosis in the winter of 1892–93 also contributed to decline of the population.

Visiting western Canada in 1890–91, the Countess of Aberdeen viewed First Nations people as "the ghosts of a people of other days . . . destined to die out or to be assimilated by European civilization." Indeed, it was federal government policy to promote the ultimate integration of Native people into an emerging mainstream society. Providing additional land to a people intended for assimilation was difficult to justify, especially on Burrard Inlet where most of the land had already been distributed via pre-emptions, Crown grants and timber limits. Burrard Inlet was to be the site of a great metropolis, and the continued presence of First Nation

A FALSE START 1886–1899

When Vancouver burned to the ground on June 13, 1886, North Shore residents—both Native and non-Native—rushed to the rescue. Alice Crakanthorp remembered:

We were at Moodyville, and I just went out to get the pudding for dinner, and looking out of the door I saw the terrific smoke coming from "Gastown," such a terrific smoke. And then I saw the steamers coming out; the Robert Dunsmuir *and a little boat called the* New Westminster; *they were half way across with the refugees. It must have been about three o'clock when they landed at Moodyville. We went down to see them land; it was tragic to see the people come ashore; their shoes were charred . . . The people were all very tired, and very quiet; some had just the clothing they wore, nothing else, and many did not know where their children were, it was very, very pitiful.*

Although the city had been almost entirely destroyed, Vancouver's frontier spirit rose to the occasion. A new city emerged from the ashes, many of the commercial buildings being rebuilt with fire-resistant brick. Despite its initial setback, Vancouver began to prosper. People flooded into the new city, most of them arriving on the Canadian Pacific Railway (CPR), which began service on July 4. In January 1886, Granville and the Hastings Mill had been home to just two hundred or three hundred people; by the end of the year the city's population had soared to five thousand. Explosions reverberated across the inlet as builders worked to clear sites laden with stumps and logging debris. Houses and business blocks sprouted up daily, and real estate agents seemed to lurk on every corner.

North Shore residents must have viewed the scene that unfolded across the inlet with unbridled interest. Some were well positioned to share in the booty of speculation, having acquired extensive property in the terminal city as well as on the inlet's northern shore. Likewise, a number of Vancouver residents had purchased property on the North Shore, anticipating that development would some day cross the inlet and make its way up the mountain slopes. Late in 1890, those who owned property on the North Shore began to make their move. On December 29, an unobtrusive notice appeared in the *Vancouver Daily World*, announcing a meeting to be held that evening in the Vancouver chambers of Rounsfell and Co. for the purpose of considering "the advisability of forming a municipality, to be known as North Vancouver." All property owners, pre-emptors and residents of the area lying between Point Atkinson lighthouse in the west and Roche Point in the east were invited to attend. Twenty-eight people participated in the meeting and, after some discussion, determined that the time had come for "this important section to take a forward step and become a [distinct] municipality, clear, free, and independent of the District of New Westminster." A committee of six "gentlemen" was formed to take the steps necessary "to bring into existence the municipality of North Vancouver," the appointees being James Cooper Keith, G.G. Mackay, James Wattie, Alan C. McCartney, J.E. Green and B.J. Cornish. Several were destined to play significant, continuing roles in the lives of the North Shore's communities; at the time, however, none of them seems to have been a resident of the area.

The process of incorporation was relatively straightforward. Having prepared a petition, the committee gathered signatures from those with interests in property in the area. Hugh Nelson, who had left the Senate in 1887 to become the province's fourth Lieutenant-Governor, helped to expedite the process. The boundaries of the finalized municipality ended up being much the same as what the committee initially proposed, but with several notable exceptions. The Squamish and Tsleil-Waututh Indian reserves were federal property, held in trust on behalf of their First Nations inhabitants, and could not be included in the new municipality. Moodyville, defined as District Lots 272 and 273, was also excluded. Though the petitioners had initially hoped for the milltown's inclusion, seeing its large industrial plant as a potential source of significant tax revenues, its owners—represented by well-connected Victoria businessman R.P. Rithet—declined the opportunity to have others dip into their collective purse. Despite these deletions from their original vision, the petitioners had considerable cause for celebration when the letters patent for the District of North Vancouver were issued on August 10, 1891.

The district's first election was held twelve days later at Tom Turner's farm near the foot of the future Lonsdale Avenue, formerly the site of his uncle William Bridges' saloon. J.P. Phibbs, owner of a dairy ranch at the mouth of Seymour Creek, was duly elected reeve, and Tom Turner, John Nelmes, Fred Thompson and John "Navvy Jack" Thomas succeeded in their quests to become councillors. Thomas resigned his seat a few months later and Edward Mahon replaced him in a by-election. The newly elected council members soon found themselves in a difficult

position. Theirs was one of the largest municipalities in the province but lacked the lucrative tax base that the Moodyville sawmill might have afforded. Most of the properties within the district were undeveloped and the resident population was small. Many of those who lived within the district's boundaries were squatters who paid no rent or taxes. To invite development, North Vancouver District would require roads and bridges, water works, sanitary sewers, street lighting and a public transportation system. The big question was how all this was to be achieved.

James Cooper Keith, a financier and North Shore land promoter who had been an influential voice on the district's incorporation committee, provided part of the answer, underwriting a $40,000 loan on behalf of the council for the construction of roads. Keith's loan was generous but also served his self-interest: as owner of extensive properties at either end of the proposed east-west road (ultimately named in his honour), he would be one of the principal beneficiaries of the road network. The firm of Williams Bros. and Dawson was quickly engaged to survey the routes. Keith was able to keep an eye on the project by standing for reeve in 1893 and holding that position through 1894. Construction of the road network, which would have run the length of the municipality as well as into the Seymour watershed, was an ambitious undertaking. In their early years, parts of these roads were little more than trails, and their construction did little to encourage rapid settlement. At first, the limited development was mostly situated around the site of Tom Turner's farm. Keith's involvement in both land promotion and politics was typical of the times, when developers with close connections to local government were viewed

Located near the foot of what later became Lonsdale Avenue, Tom Turner's modest house was built by his uncle, William Bridges, as a saloon for the alcohol-starved workers at the Moodyville Sawmill.
City of Vancouver Archives, CVA SGN 1037

more with approval than with suspicion, and when conflicts of interest were often disregarded.

For Keith and other North Shore property owners, the incorporation of the district was one of the more significant events of 1891. But several other events rivalled municipal incorporation in terms of their importance. One was the sale of the Moodyville sawmill and its lands to a consortium of English aristocrats in July. The transaction, brokered by financier Johann Wulffsohn, was quite possibly the largest in the young province's history and was reported to have involved the exchange of about $1 million. A German-born financial whiz, Wulffsohn had come to Vancouver in the summer of 1886, established a private bank with Percival Henry Bewicke of England, and began to purchase land on either side of the inlet. Those

James Cooper Keith was a shareholder in the North Vancouver Land and Improvement Company and member of the City of North Vancouver incorporation committee. Although a resident of Vancouver, Keith served as the District of North Vancouver's second reeve (1893–95).
North Vancouver Museum and Archives, Fonds 106 Series 15 Photo 2

German-born Johann Wulffsohn—shown here in his consular uniform—was a key player in the sale of the Moodyville Mill and its assets to a group of English aristocrats in 1891. Wulffsohn was also instrumental in organizing the North Vancouver Land and Improvement Company.
Photo courtesy Jock Wulffson

who had invested in the mill included the Third Earl of Durham, the Tenth Earl of Chesterfield, Colonel the Hon. Oliver Montague, Arthur Pemberton Heywood-Lonsdale and Edmund Evan-Thomas. One account of the sale also indicated participation by three members of the famed Rothschild family.

Although the list of titled gentlemen was impressive, it was the Heywood-Lonsdale family who were to have a lasting connection with the inlet's north shore. The Heywood family had been prominent gentry in Lancashire since the early 1600s, known for their involvement in the church, banking, the army and the law. Arthur Pemberton Heywood-Lonsdale was not born a Heywood but changed his Lonsdale surname by royal licence in 1877 to please his childless uncle John Pemberton Heywood, a retired banker who owned substantial property in Shropshire and who wished to leave his fortune to a Heywood. When his uncle died in 1877, the freshly renamed Arthur Pemberton Heywood-Lonsdale became a wealthy man.

The newly organized Moodyville Lands and Sawmill Company possessed "a very large capital" and owned 1,786 developable acres on the North Shore (with a water frontage of about three miles) and 9,384 acres of agricultural and forested land elsewhere. The new firm had also inherited rights to 31,488 acres of timber limits at various locations throughout the lower coast. All these developments were hailed by the Vancouver press, which noted that Wulffsohn would serve as managing director of the company. The sale of the mill was the talk of the town, especially when the names and titles of its purchasers became common knowledge. Reports in the Vancouver papers prophesied a doubling of the mill's capacity and the rise of a twin city on the inlet's northern shore. According to the *Vancouver Daily World*, the English investors were "determined to make their estate a valuable one by establishing industries, building streets, operating electric railways, ferries, and railways in that locality." The mill's extensive property, they were certain, was destined "to become a very important suburb of Vancouver, it being to this city what Brooklyn is to New York, Birkenhead to Liverpool, or Oakland to San Francisco."

The firm's certificate of registration enabled it to pursue activities as varied as logging and sawmill operations, farming, wharfage and warehousing, building construction, marine and rail transportation, and the drainage or diversion of rivers and other watercourses. In a letter to *The Times* (of London) a few years earlier, Wulffsohn's partner Percival Bewicke advised the newspaper's readers that Burrard Inlet's timber trade had "entered into a new and more profitable phase, as the British Columbian timber is more sought after in the South American market than the less durable wood in Washington Territory and Oregon. It is not uncommon to see ships with a capacity for carrying from 500,000 to 1,000,000 ft. moored along the jetties of the various mills in Vancouver and its neighbourhood." But Bewicke was also mindful to report that the inlet—home to the most significant British port in the North Pacific—had even greater potential as the site of major urban development. Inlet properties had evolved from being mere sources of timber to land with substantial industrial, commercial and residential potential.

These were heady days for North Shore property owners, with major investments from abroad auguring great days ahead. But 1891 had even more in store: the incorporation of yet another land and development company, the North Vancouver

Arthur Pemberton Heywood-Lonsdale, photographed at his family estate in Shropshire. Heywood-Lonsdale was a major investor in the Moodyville Lands and Sawmill Company, in association with a group of titled English gentlemen.
Courtesy Bob Heywood

Above left: Edward Mahon, sixth son of Sir William Vesey Mahon, photographed at the family estate of Castlegar, County Galway, Ireland.
Photo courtesy Mahon family

Above right: Mahon, a prime figure in the North Vancouver Land and Improvement Company, also owned the Capilano Suspension Bridge from 1910 to 1935. Originally constructed in 1889, the bridge hangs 230 feet above the Capilano River and continues to be one of the most popular tourist attractions in the Greater Vancouver area.
North Vancouver Museum and Archives, 330

Land and Improvement Company. The firm's application for incorporation listed objectives including the purchase, management and sale or lease of real estate but also encompassed a long list of infrastructure improvements:

To erect, construct, take on lease or otherwise acquire and hold and maintain, and in any way dispose of railways, tramways, roads, sewers, drains, pavements, telegraphs, telephone lines, with all necessary equipments, quays, wharfs, docks, canals, piers, harbours, landing places, jetties, shops, stores, bridges, channels, wells, viaducts, aqueducts, gas works, water works, flumes, culverts, warehouses, libraries, institutes, inns, hotels, foundries, factories, shops, churches, chapels, schools, brick kilns, lime kilns, crushing works, iron works, and mills and factories and undertakings of all kinds . . .

In short, the company would have the capacity to build a city. The firm's three founding trustees—Edward Mahon, Harry A. Jones and the omnipresent Johann Wulffsohn—were empowered to guide its affairs for its first three months. Wulffsohn was thus involved in the two companies that between them at one time owned almost all of the future City of North Vancouver, and naturally directed their co-operation and co-ordination. The fact that the August 1891 incorporation of the North Vancouver Land and Improvement Company occurred within days of the district receiving its letters patent is another indication of how closely men of business followed or participated in political developments. J.C. Keith, for instance, served not only on the district's incorporation committee but on the board of the North Vancouver Land and Improvement Company as well. John Balfour Ker was another noted shareholder but the bulk of the company's shares were owned by the Mahon family, represented in British Columbia by district councillor Edward Mahon.

Born into an aristocratic Anglo-Irish family, Edward Mahon received his education at Marlborough College and Oxford. After considering the priesthood or law, Mahon followed the advice of his older brother John and travelled to British Columbia with his younger brother Gilbert. The elder Mahon had visited British Columbia while on a round-the-world tour in the mid-1880s. He had seen Vancouver in its infancy, recognized the importance of the CPR and predicted significant trade with the Orient. Vancouver, he felt, was "going to be a very important city because it was British, and British in the North Pacific, in the centre of the British Empire." Arriving in 1888, Edward and Gilbert, then in their twenties, travelled around the province looking for opportunities in land speculation, development or mining. After spending some time in the province's interior, Edward Mahon returned to the coast later in 1891.

Although the provincial government had announced its intention to place its North Shore timber leases on the market "in small blocks to suit gardeners and others of small means," massive blocks of land had already passed into the hands of speculators. Many of these men had long associations with the North Shore, with Captain William Power prominent among them. By the end of 1886 Power and his syndicate had amassed considerable land holdings on both sides of the inlet, including District Lots 544 to 550. According to the Vancouver press, Power was also thought to have been involved in the sale of the Moodyville Mill. Ever a shrewd businessman, Power bought out his partners and on January 30, 1891, sold his North Vancouver properties to speculator J.C. Keith. In mid-November, Keith sold his newly acquired properties to the Moodyville Lands and Sawmill Company, which in turn sold them to the North Vancouver Land and Improvement Company. Keith was also involved in the conveyance of District Lot 271, having purchased the property from Tom Turner in March 1891 before selling it to the North Vancouver Land and Improvement Company almost a year later. The machinations were complex, with Captain Power and Johann Wulffsohn brokering several of the deals. Two days after the sale of his property to the North Vancouver Land and Improvement Company, Power and his wife set sail, cash in hand, for what the Vancouver News-Advertiser termed "an extended pleasure trip" to California, Philadelphia, the eastern seaboard, England, Germany and Italy.

Captain Power's associates included Moodyville Mill alumni Josias Hughes and Benjamin Springer. Both had found dealing in real estate more lucrative than working for wages, but Springer had greater prominence in business circles than Hughes. While still employed at the mill, Springer had gone into partnership with James van Bramer to purchase land in Vancouver, where he erected several of the city's first brick commercial buildings. After resigning from the mill in 1890,

Springer formed a partnership with Captain Henry Augustus Mellon, dealing in land and other investments as well as insurance. Other North Shore personalities involved in speculation included accountant and postmaster Alfred Codrington King, stevedore Murray Thain, blacksmith Patrick Allen and lighthouse keeper William Erwin.

Power was not alone in divesting himself of real estate in the months following the district's incorporation. Advertisements for North Vancouver acreages quickly began to appear in the Vancouver papers. The Vancouver Loan, Trust, Savings and Guarantee Company (managed by Henry Tracy Ceperley, who was later to partner with the same John Rounsfell who had hosted the first meeting on incorporation) offered "rare bargains" in North Vancouver acreage, while a vendor identified only as "Owner, c/o the *Vancouver Daily World*," advertised several large properties on Seymour Creek, claiming that a new wagon road to the acreages was under construction and that a new electric railway would put them within twenty minutes' travel of the Vancouver city post office. But properties such as these were on the peripheries of the district and in the short term were poor investments. With so much land in their possession—much of it located directly opposite Vancouver and on or near the inlet—it soon became clear that the two land companies would determine the location of the district's core. Both companies were cautious in putting their land on the open market, wanting its value to increase prior to offering it for sale.

Realizing that the newly incorporated district would require an electrical system, and driven by the optimism of the time, a group of investors formed the North Vancouver Electric Company in 1892. Still others saw the need for transportation systems, and two separate companies—the Burrard Inlet Railway and Ferry Company and the Burrard Inlet Tunnel and Bridge Company—were formed to address the need. Though neither railway realized its goals, their early activities helped determine the location of the future city's core. Williams Bros. and Dawson had started their survey from the point on the waterfront where District Lot 271 met District Lot 274. This was also the point where an old skid road reached the inlet, not far from Tom Turner's farm. From here a proposed railway line would run up the hillside to Keith Road before turning west. The District of North Vancouver's decision to locate a ferry wharf where the two district lots met on the waterfront confirmed a growing consensus that this was where the core of a future town would lie.

Incorporated under a federal statute, the Burrard Inlet Tunnel and Bridge Company, owned for the most part by Vancouver MLA and publisher Francis Carter-Cotton, had a massive mandate, having been authorized to build a tunnel at Burrard Inlet's First Narrows as well as a bridge over the Second Narrows. The two proposed crossings were required to provide for every conceivable type of traffic: traditional railways, electric street railways, vehicular traffic and pedestrians. The railway system was intended to connect with the CPR, thereby providing a circular route around the inner harbour.

Though the vision might have been right, the timing was wrong. In 1892, economic recession struck the lower coast, making it clear that Vancouver's early prosperity had largely been due to the arrival of the CPR and rampant speculation in land. The terminal city's early growth could not be sustained and significant development in adjacent municipalities was simply out of the question. The Moodyville sawmill continued to ship to export markets under the direction of manager James Henry Ramsdell, but trends in the global economy cast a dark shadow over the future of even that venerable enterprise. Growth on the North Shore stagnated during much of the 1890s and real estate agents on both sides of the inlet suffered as a consequence. Although a few lots were sold, some were only imaginary. During his round-the-world honeymoon in 1892, author Rudyard Kipling and his wife stopped to visit the inlet:

> . . . with an eye to the future we bought, or thought we had, twenty acres of a wilderness called North Vancouver. But there was a catch in the thing, as we found many years later when after paying taxes on it for ever so long, we discovered it belonged to someone else. All the consolation we got from the smiling people of Vancouver was: "You bought that from Steve, did you? Ah-ah, Steve! You hadn't ought to ha' bought from Steve. No! Not from Steve." And then did the good Steve cure us of speculating in real estate.

Speculators, real estate agents and land companies may have lost the power to influence events on the North Shore, but the authority of the Oblates continued to grow. In 1893, the local Indian agent extolled their influence in his report to the Department of Indian Affairs:

> The Squamish Mission (Burrard Inlet) is one of the most progressive and also the most advanced band of Indians in the agency. A great many of the men are employed in the different lumber mills in Vancouver, and the remainder are engaged in catching fish for the Vancouver markets, where they find ready sale for all they can catch. These Indians have good houses, well furnished, and live as comfortably as most white people do.

Oblate influence on the Mission Reserve appears to have reached its apex in the 1890s, when Durieu and his colleagues used their Squamish converts as examples to others, replacing traditional ceremonials with activities more suited to their purpose. Under Oblate direction, brass bands were formed at both the Sechelt and the Mission reserves and taken to perform at religious events at various locations in the Lower Mainland. These events included the dedication of Oblate churches on reserves throughout the Fraser Valley. Squamish converts were also taken to perform in the impressive passion plays presented at St. Mary's Mission, the central Fraser Valley site of an Oblate school for First Nations children since the 1860s.

Like the provincial and federal governments, the Oblates felt that adherence to traditional culture made it difficult for First Nations to adjust to the modern world of the white man. It came to be generally accepted by church and government that children had to be separated from the "negative" influences of their parents before they could be effectively educated and it was with this in mind that the province's residential school system was expanded through the 1880s and 1890s. To further their aims, the Oblates constructed a residential school in North Vancouver in

The Oblates of Mary Immaculate established brass bands on Native reserves throughout the province. The Douglas Reserve brass band posed in front of St. Paul's Church on the Mission Reserve c. 1889.
City of Vancouver Archives, IN P139.1

The French-styled buildings of St. Paul's Indian Residential School, built in 1899 on West Keith Road, just north of the Mission Reserve.

North Vancouver Museum and Archives, 11417

1899. The new facility, named St. Paul's, was located on West Keith Road close to the Mission Reserve, it being federal policy that residential schools be built near but not on Indian reserves. Although the school was to be run by French-speaking nuns who had to teach Squamish-speaking children in English, the local Indian agent was pleased with the development. In June 1899 the agent reported:

> *Only a few of these Indians have ever received any education, no school accommodation having been provided for them. This want is now being partly supplied, the Roman Catholic bishop having built a school adjoining the Mission Reserve on Burrard Inlet during the last spring, which is now open with four sisters in charge as teachers, having quite a number of pupils, but for want of funds they are unable to provide for one-fourth of the children who are anxious to attend.*

Details of the physical and instructional nature of the new facility were revealed by the school's first principal, Father E.M. Bunoz, in a letter to the Superintendent of Indian Affairs in July 1900. St. Paul's School, he reported, was a co-educational facility situated on a twenty-one-acre property owned by the Sisters of the Instruction of the Child Jesus. Its grounds were partly wooded, but a vegetable garden had been cleared and planted by the school's boys, thereby providing "a plentiful supply of vegetables for use of the school, besides giving plenty of healthy exercise to both boys and girls." Subsequent reports from the principal revealed a strictly regimented program of instruction that began with religious training at 5 a.m.:

St. Paul's Indian Residential
School Soccer Team 1908.
The team includes members
of the Joe, Andrew, Paull,
Pierre, Campbell, Julian,
Baker, Isaac, Dominic,
Thomas and George families.
North Vancouver Museum and
Archives, 4840

All the pupils attend service every morning and prayers are said in common. The pupils are constantly reminded of their duties toward God, their neighbours and themselves, and of the necessity of cleanliness, purity of body and mind. To make our teaching effective, a continual supervision is exercised and all infractions are punished, the usual mode of punishment being to make those guilty do some extra work during recreation hours.

Prior to 1920 enrolment in residential schools was not compulsory, but parents were placed under heavy pressure by the priests as well as the Indian agents. The school's principal sent glowing annual reports to Ottawa, but after several years of operation, statistics indicated that few St. Paul's students had moved beyond a very elementary education. Writing his autobiography *Khot-la-cha* in 1994, Chief Simon Baker—who spent his early years on the Mission Reserve and who grew up on the Capilano Reserve—questioned both the morality and the usefulness of a residential school education:

There is a lot of feeling of hate about the days when people were controlled by the church and by the school. At the school, they were forbidden, like in a lot of other schools, to speak the Squamish language. They had to learn English and also had to learn lots of Latin words. What good anyone ever did with Latin, I don't know.

When they purchased their extensive property just north of the reserve, the Sisters of the Instruction of the Child Jesus may have thought they had acquired a site far removed from any outside influences. In 1899, this was more or less true, as hardly any development had occurred in the district since its incorporation in 1891. Residents, landowners and district council did what little they could to spur development. An embryonic settlement was beginning to emerge adjacent to Tom Turner's farm but it was largely inaccessible. The existing ferry service was run by the Union Steamship Company, a firm formed in 1889 when the Moodyville Ferry Company merged with the Burrard Inlet Towing Company. In 1894, the company's small steamer, the *Senator*, was still on the Moodyville–Vancouver run but no ferries ran between Vancouver and Tom Turner's farm. The situation prompted a "mass meeting" in March 1894 to discuss the situation and to review potential solutions. These included a municipally subsidized service contracted to a private operator.

Inevitably, a committee was formed to explore the possibility of a ferry subsidy from the North Vancouver Land and Improvement Company. The company expressed modest interest in the proposal, offering a subsidy of $250. The management of the Moodyville Lands and Sawmill Company was also approached and cabled its English owners for instructions. Proposals from three potential operators were sought and reviewed. The Union Steamship Company was ultimately selected, having proposed putting the now aging *Senator* on a triangle run connecting the two North Shore communities with Vancouver's inner harbour.

Those who had lobbied for an improved cross-harbour service may have been edified by their achievement, but this minor success was not a portent of the future. The recession seemed unstoppable. Torrential rains in January 1895 destroyed the district-built bridges over the Capilano and Seymour rivers, and there was no money to replace them. By 1896, the district's property values had plummeted. Distraught taxpayers lost their investments and were unable to pay taxes. No longer in a position to borrow, and finding itself with diminished revenues, the district was in crisis. Just when it seemed that things could not get worse, the province enforced its Municipal Clauses Act requiring members of council to be *resident* owners. Only one councillor, lighthouse keeper Walter Erwin, met the qualifications. The district drifted without a council for seven long months, awaiting the passage of enabling legislation.

Investors with vast reserves of capital weathered the setbacks, the North Vancouver Land and Improvement Company going so far as to have its land surveyed for subdivision in 1896. Wulffsohn and Bewicke and the Moodyville Lands and Sawmill Company, on the other hand, found themselves in trouble. A decline in the timber trade had forced the mill to close for a number of months in 1893 and 1894. In March 1896, business managers Wulffsohn and Bewicke resigned and were replaced by Robert Ward and Company, who in turn replaced the competent and popular mill manager James Henry Ramsdell with John S. Woods. Wulffsohn and Bewicke had invested heavily in the mill, had made poorly secured loans, and had seen the value of their speculative investments around the inlet fall substantially. Their brokerage firm was thus obliged to go into receivership. The report of the Official Receiver noted that unsecured losses to the firm's creditors totalled $24,223 and losses to its shareholders totalled a further $85,833. The Moodyville Lands and Sawmill Company fared no better. Although the demand for lumber had risen dramatically in 1896, the company's profits had generally been unimpressive. This, coupled with the death of Arthur Pemberton Heywood-Lonsdale in February 1897, ultimately forced the company into receivership.

Whatever uncertainty may have existed at the Moodyville Mill seems to have had little impact on the strategy of the North Vancouver Land and Improvement Company. Sometime around the turn of the century, the company developed city plans influenced by Britain's Garden City movement and the City Beautiful movement then enjoying favour in the United States. The two movements mixed social reform with urban design. Their advocates hoped to develop new cities or to rehabilitate existing ones according to standards that would eliminate ugliness, crime and squalor. The Garden City movement, articulated in a seminal book by British reformer Ebenezer Howard in 1898, called for the creation of planned new cities that offered the best of both country and city. These self-contained communities would be green and peaceful but also offer opportunities for work in clean, efficient factories. In such an environment, Howard postulated, inhabitants would develop high moral standards and possess a strong sense of community identity and pride. The City Beautiful movement had much in common with its British equivalent, suggesting that living in a sanitary, landscaped environment would inspire even the poor to live respectable, virtuous lives that would lead inevitably to productivity and happiness.

This 1912 plan for the city of North Vancouver, showing the intended circle of parks, appears to have been influenced by the British Garden City and American City Beautiful movements.
North Vancouver Museum and Archives, Map 126

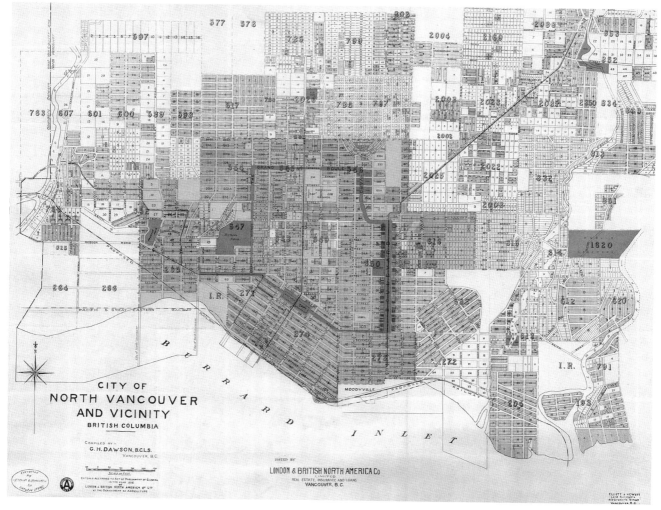

The names of those who developed the master plan for what became the North Vancouver townsite remain elusive. What is unmistakable, however, is how much the plan owed to the Garden City and City Beautiful movements. The new settlement was to be laid out on a regular grid, with the slope of the land requiring doglegged streets in its central area. A network of parks and boulevards was to circle much of the community, including formal civic spaces and playing fields as well as passive parks. Commercial and industrial development would locate along the waterfront and a range of housing options would be available farther up the slope.

The one function the townsite's planners did not provide for was a cemetery. District council had already addressed the matter following an outbreak of smallpox in March 1893. Although no residents of the district appeared to have succumbed to the disease, the need for a municipal burial ground was suddenly apparent. Council favoured acquiring a site in the Seymour River area and authorized Councillor McCartney, a professional surveyor, to investigate a potential site. With a mandate from council, McCartney approached the province with an eye to obtaining title to District Lot 1620, a sixty-acre site between Lynn Creek and the Seymour River. The property offered several advantages. It was high, well-drained and close to the townsite but largely beyond the view of the living. McCartney's negotiations went well and within a matter of months the district owned the property. According to the surviving records, a remarkable thirteen years were to pass before the cemetery received its first burial: Roy Allan Blackburn, who died of tuberculosis in 1907 at age twenty-two.

In the late 1890s, however, North Vancouverites were thinking more of temporal life than of the afterlife. The economy may not have been booming, but the depression appeared to be waning. In 1897, the North Vancouver Land and Improvement Company began to open up its lands up the hill for purchase. During 1897 and 1898, five brave families purchased twenty acres near what later was to become the corner of Fifteenth Street and Lonsdale Avenue, presumably intending to build homes on part of the land while holding the remaining lots for resale at a profit. Although North Shore residential properties were undoubtedly cheaper than comparable lots across the inlet, their development would face obstacles. Construction of the lower portion of Lonsdale Avenue had begun, but the road was decidedly primitive. Rodger Burnes, whose father purchased a series of lots on Lonsdale Avenue in 1898, remembered the situation:

> This was a cheap road to build, but it was also a cheap road to travel on, as I well knew in later years. It was just wide enough for a wagon, and was not straight, nor was it graded in any way, but it was a means of getting in supplies and served the purpose for a few years. The contract called for the road to be built as far as Eighth Street. From there it followed Dawson's survey to Fifteenth. But the last portion was not graded and had to be puncheoned, or timbered, for some distance.

The North Vancouver Land and Improvement Company knew that if its venture were to succeed, a streetcar system would be required to access the shore's steep slopes. Although its articles of incorporation permitted the firm to build and operate

*A turn-of-the-century
view of Lonsdale Avenue,
recently cut through the
second-growth forest that
still covered much of the
townsite.*

*North Vancouver Museum and
Archives, 1912-2-p1*

a street railway system, in 1897 the economic situation was still too uncertain for the considerable capital that would be required. As the nineteenth century drew to a close, the project was still very much a dream. Electricity, running water and a sewer system were equally elusive goals. Though most of the families who had purchased property in the North Vancouver Land and Improvement Company's "townsite" had built houses, some were quite modest and served more as weekend retreats than year-round homes. Rodger Burnes recalled the small cluster of residents who built nearby as "not many and not too friendly." There were few children in the area, so Burnes and his sisters made friends "out of the big trees that were all about . . . We called the trees by name and had many that were two-headed giants to us."

J.B. Cornish had built a small house on his property and puttered around its grounds on weekends, spending the rest of the week in Vancouver. Arthur Bramah Diplock lived next door, his two sons forming with young Burnes the nucleus of the Anglican church choir a few years later. William Keene served as the district's municipal clerk from 1897 to 1902 and is remembered for his sizeable orchard and in later years a dairy operation. Alfred Edward Crickmay, another property owner, was Keene's brother-in-law and worked as a customs broker in North Vancouver. Arnold Evan Kealy, the last of the founding five, was perhaps the most interesting. Active in real estate circles, he became a district councillor in 1903 and reeve in 1905. In the early 1900s, Kealy became a leading advocate for civic incorporation at the expense of the already existing district. Each of these early settlers had been born in England and each was a staunch supporter of the Anglican Church.

The William Keene family's house on St. George's Avenue at Fifteenth Street, c. 1898. The modest scale of the house—set in a landscape of blackened stumps—was typical of the time.

North Vancouver Museum and Archives, 4066

Although men and women of other backgrounds and religious persuasions were to move into the area, the community's general direction was set; for decades those who wielded power there were white, Anglo-Saxon and Protestant.

For several years, however, few new settlers of any description made their way to the townsite. A.D. Nye purchased a one-acre lot in 1898. Captain Lawrence Kickham built a house on Second Avenue toward the end of the same year. Although the *Senator* provided regular service between Vancouver and the townsite, settlers landing at the foot of Lonsdale Avenue faced a long and hazardous trek to their properties up the hill. But in July 1897 all citizens in the area were undoubtedly encouraged by the news from the north: gold had been discovered in the Klondike. Within weeks, thousands of gold seekers stopped in Vancouver to purchase supplies and book passage to the Yukon. The inlet's economy surged. North Vancouver property owners once again looked to the future with optimism and ambition.

FROM TOWNSITE TO CITY 1900–1905

The turn of the century was a time for both celebration and reflection. Prime Minister Wilfrid Laurier's claim that the twentieth century would belong to Canada was taken as no idle boast. In 1900 the Canadian west, once months away from Europe, could be reached in less than a fortnight. Encouraged by the prospect of free land, thousands of eastern European settlers streamed onto the Canadian prairies. Homesteads, villages and towns popped up almost overnight. A vast array of Britons also crossed the sea: mill workers, agricultural labourers, artisans and gentry. Most were drawn by the prospect of a brighter future and many saw that future in British Columbia.

By 1900, many such people had made their way to the westernmost province. Four in particular were to have a considerable impact upon North Vancouver—Edward Mahon, Joseph McFarland, Alfred St. George Hamersley and J.P. Fell. Edward Mahon had settled in Vancouver in 1891, co-founding the firm of Mahon, McFarland, and Mahon with his elder brother John and real estate and insurance agent Joseph McFarland. The firm dealt in real estate, particularly the properties of the North Vancouver Land and Improvement Company (which also happened to be owned by the Mahon family). The formidably named Colonel Alfred St. George Hamersley had arrived on the inlet in 1887, a year after McFarland. Hamersley was every inch the British Victorian gentleman. His upward course had taken him to colonial New Zealand and eventually Vancouver, where he became city solicitor in 1870. James Pemberton Fell was the last of the four to reach the inlet, passing through Vancouver in 1897 on his way to the Klondike. He too was a well-born English gentleman, his mother a member of the Lonsdale family.

Despite their extensive interest in North Shore properties, only one of these men ever lived in North Vancouver, and then only for a very short time. Mahon, McFarland, Hamersley and Fell all took up residence in impressive homes in Vancouver's prestigious West End. And who could blame them? In 1900, North Vancouver was more promise than fact. The district was a vast landmass covered by ancient forests, stumps and slash, with only an occasional cluster of dwellings. Amenities were few and the municipal infrastructure was largely undeveloped. The bridges lost to the floods of 1895 remained mostly in ruins, severely hampering travel across the district. Vancouver, in contrast, appeared to have everything a progressive new city could desire: paved roads, running water, sewers, sidewalks, street lighting, streetcars and shops in abundance.

In 1900, Vancouver's population was nearing thirty thousand, a remarkable number given that the city was only fourteen years old. That same year, the *British Columbia Directory* listed just seventy-two households in the much older community of Moodyville and made no mention at all of the handful of households in the neighbouring District of North Vancouver. But the district would grow suddenly over the next five years, in part due to the demise of the very community that had given the North Shore its start. Years of alleged mismanagement and the decline of the timber trade had resulted in the closure of the Moodyville Mill in December 1901. With little reason to remain in the now quiet mill community, much of its multiracial population began to disperse. The Lonsdale Estate—which had inherited the assets of the Moodyville Lands and Sawmill Company—began to consider other options for its vast land holdings. Arthur Pemberton Heywood-Lonsdale's son Henry was now administering the estate, with his cousin J.P. Fell acting as his agent in British Columbia.

The mill was located in District Lot 273, one of the Lonsdale Estate's easternmost properties. Although the estate's properties to the west showed considerable promise for new residential, commercial and industrial purposes, these were long-term prospects offering little immediate financial return. The Lonsdale Estate thus elected to sell the Moodyville Mill and the area that surrounded it. In the winter of 1901–02 rumours abounded about its buyer. The list of suggested purchasers included Puget Sound lumber magnate Frederick Weyerhaeuser and Great Northern Railway promoter James J. Hill. One elaborate rumour had the two industrialists joining seven other investors to buy the mill, then moving Hastings Mill to Moodyville in order to make room in Vancouver for the terminus of the Great Northern Railway.

But much of the speculation overlooked the name of John Hendry, a businessman then involved in both railways and the timber trade, and owner of the Hastings Mill since 1889. Hendry knew the Moodyville Mill well: he had served a term as its night foreman and had also supervised its re-equipping after the fire of 1873.

Henry Heywood-Lonsdale co-owned, with James Pemberton Fell, the Lonsdale Estate, a vast collection of acreage around Burrard Inlet and elsewhere in the Lower Mainland.

Courtesy Bob Heywood

The intervening years had treated Hendry well. By the early 1900s, he and a small group of business partners had formed the British Columbia Mills, Timber, and Trading Company, one of the largest lumber concerns on Canada's west coast. Hendry's purchase of the Hastings and Moodyville sawmills reflected more than an interest in lumber. As a quintessential nineteenth-century capitalist, he had interests in politics, railways, the timber trade and business in general. By the early

Alfred St. George Hamersley, one-time solicitor for the City of Vancouver and prominent personality in the evolving townsite. Hamersley's purchase and subdivision of District Lot 274 in 1902–03 led to the rapid settlement and development of the townsite's Lower Lonsdale area.

North Vancouver Museum and Archives, 4583

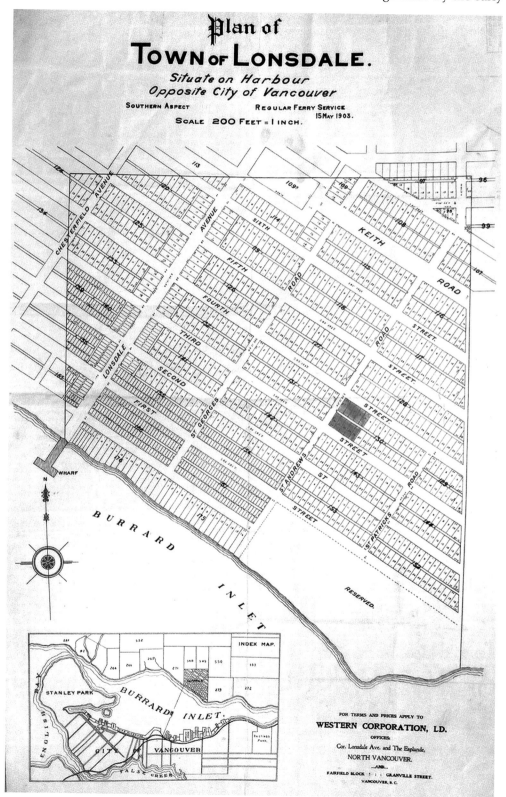

Map of the "Town of Lonsdale," today's Lower Lonsdale area of the City of North Vancouver, subdivided and sold by Alfred St. George Hamersley beginning in 1903.

City of Vancouver Archives, Map 686

1900s, he had also acquired a significant share of the New Westminster Southern Railway Company, a minor regional line.

Hendry's overriding ambition, however, was to connect "his" railway with James J. Hill's Great Northern Railway to the south and to extend the system northward into British Columbia's interior. Construction of the railway's first 23.5 miles of track, between Liverpool (now north Surrey) on the Fraser River and the American border near Blaine took several years to complete. John Hendry held the Moodyville site in hope that its lower levels, at least, might prove useful for his projected railway or a relocated Hastings Mill. Aside from this hope, the closure of the Moodyville mill had resulted in a major loss of population and many buildings sat empty. The one-room school continued to serve all the students of North Vancouver District until the district built its own school in 1902. By 1906, Moodyville ceased to be listed in the *British Columbia Directory*, its residents instead being subsumed under North Vancouver despite the fact that it was not part of the district.

Although it would be some years before Hendry advanced his railway dream, the first ten years of the twentieth century were good ones for Alfred St. George Hamersley, the North Vancouver Land and Improvement Company and the Lonsdale Estate. By early 1903, Hamersley had bought a large property from the Lonsdale Estate in District Lot 274. Working quickly, Hamersley had the parcel surveyed and subdivided, naming the area the "Town of Lonsdale," though it still remained part of the district. Lots soon appeared on the market, with sales conducted through several Vancouver-based real estate firms. By late 1903, land was being sold, lots were being cleared, homes were being built and an up-to-date infrastructure was being created. Within a year, a small but thriving commercial core began to develop

Principal Land Owners, North Vancouver townsite, c. 1903. The map does not show the individual ownership of the few residential and commercial lots sold by the North Vancouver Land and Improvement Company and Alfred St. George Hamersley by this date.

Map by Perry Beck, City of North Vancouver

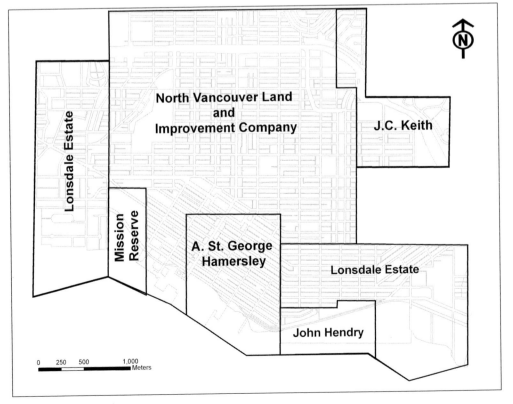

on Lonsdale Avenue close to the ferry terminal.

Thanks to Hamersley and the large land companies, the townsite was becoming an area of suburban homes—a retreat far from the hubbub of the heavily industrialized south shore. North Vancouver residents and property owners could see a new community taking shape around them, one destined to emulate an English garden suburb rather than a ragtag mill town. The townsite's supporters felt satisfaction as each new house was built, as gardens were planted and as roads began to penetrate the bush. Spirits were also buoyed by improvements to the ferry service. The service offered by the Union Steamship Company had proved unsatisfactory, so the district determined to establish a system of its own. A new vessel was ordered and put into service in 1900. Initially named SS *North Vancouver* and known more simply as the *Norvan*, the new vessel was considerably larger than the aging *Senator*.

Although it was superior to any of its predecessors, the *Norvan* did not fully solve the ferry problem. By the early 1900s, traffic on the inlet had become so congested that the *North Vancouver* could not always keep to its schedule. It didn't help that Captains Parsons and Smith had some trouble handling the steering; the wharves on either side of the inlet took a dreadful beating as the two mariners attempted to dock. Captain Jack Gosse, who assumed command of the *North Vancouver* after Smith, was rather more successful. Boys such as Rodger Burnes were fond of the ferry's genial master: "I got to know Captain Gosse very well as I was travelling on the ferry going to school in Vancouver at the time he came to the

Ferry North Vancouver, *later* **North Vancouver Ferry No. 1, launched in 1900.**

North Vancouver Museum and Archives, 5451

The Little Ferry "North Vancouver"
Vancouver B.C.

ship. He would let me ride in the pilothouse and hear all the talk about the ships in the harbour. He would also let me steer the boat while he collected fares. This was a great privilege, I felt."

Taking the helm of the cross-harbour ferry was an experience enjoyed solely in good weather, for navigation became extremely challenging in foggy weather. A frequent hazard on the inlet, fog was exacerbated by the widespread use of wood, sawdust and coal in residential furnaces. Experienced masters used the "echo system" to find their way to the landings on either side of the inlet, but this was more difficult on the north side than on the south, there being fewer substantial buildings to throw back the sound of the whistle. District council solved the problem in 1904 by hiring Joe Bustemente, a one-armed Chilean who lived in a shack on the waterfront near the ferry wharf. His job was to stand on the wharf each morning and to blow a trumpet or horn to guide the *Norvan*'s captain to the wharf.

When the *North Vancouver* was launched in 1900, district council felt that the ferry would meet the needs of the small community for many years to come. But within a year or two the service was already inadequate. The wave of population growth that had begun would continue into the next decade. Would-be residents jostled commuters on the ferry as they crossed the harbour to scout out a lot, purchase a house or look for a business opportunity.

Pete Larson was among the first of a series of entrepreneurs attracted to the neighbourhood, establishing his Hotel North Vancouver on Esplanade in 1902, on a slope within easy walk of the ferry dock. Larson became a familiar figure not only to his guests, but to the wider community as well. His hotel, with its capacious grounds and nearby pavilion, became a surrogate public park—the site of public gatherings and a destination for pleasure seekers from Vancouver. The large covered veranda of the sprawling three-storey building afforded excellent views of activities on its grounds and on the beach nearby as well as of the city across the inlet.

Arthur Diplock was another businessman who saw the area's potential. Diplock moved to the townsite in 1900 and established the Western Corporation in October 1902. His associates included piano dealer William W. Montelius, bookseller Wentworth Sarel, lawyer A. Dunbar Taylor and the omnipresent J.C. Keith. Arnold Evan Kealy served as the company's secretary. Diplock and his partners responded to the housing boom by forming a multi-faceted business involved in real estate, house construction, general contracting, sawmills, road works, land clearing, sales of coal and lumber, and house rentals. The company developed its own extensive facilities at various points in the townsite including wharves, warehouses, coal bunkers and lumber sheds as well as a business office near the foot of Lonsdale Avenue.

Located two miles from the wharf, east of what would become the Grand Boulevard between Fifteenth and Seventeenth, the Western Corporation's large sawmill cut logs felled on nearby properties, thereby relieving property owners of having to clear their land themselves. Ownership of its own sawmill and access to unharvested timber were central to the firm's success. By 1907, large sections of the townsite had been cleared and the company was able to boast:

Land covered but a year ago with brush and forest is now supplying tomatoes and other fruits and vegetables earlier in the year than they can be produced elsewhere in the district for the ready Vancouver market at a handsome profit [while] the tired businessman is enabled to employ his leisure with the growing of flowers and fancy horticulture.

Looking back, it seems remarkable that serious consideration was ever given to North Vancouver becoming a centre of agriculture. Its altitude invited late and early frosts, and the area's share of rich, alluvial soils was meagre to say the least.

The construction of Larson's imposing hotel and the Western Corporation's Syndicate Block in 1903 motivated others to follow their example, including the District of North Vancouver. More than a decade had passed since incorporation, but in 1902 the district's affairs were still administered from rented premises in Vancouver. As the townsite's population grew, the arrangement had become physically and politically untenable. Council accordingly built a hall of its own on the northeast corner of Lonsdale and First. The private sector was equally active, and a number of wood-frame commercial premises were built in Lower Lonsdale the following year. The Beasley Block, featuring the offices of druggist Marcus McDowell and physician Dr. H. Dyer, opened in 1904. A number of specialty shops also appeared including R.H. Evans' bakery in the Wright Block, James Murray's tea rooms, P. Burns' butcher shop and Birt Campbell's barbershop. The latter

Building and road construction on Lonsdale Avenue, 1905. The Syndicate Block, built by the Western Corporation to kick-start development in the townsite, is in the centre of the photograph.
City of Vancouver Archives, CVA 677-703

establishment was deemed very much up to date, its patrons conducting much of the bustling new community's business while enjoying the ragtime tunes that poured from Mr. Campbell's hand-wound gramophone.

More amenities arrived in 1905: the D.E. Thompson Block, D.G. Dick's real estate office, W.A. Russell's grocery store (in competition with J.A. McMillan's grocery store in the Syndicate Block), W.P. Hogg's restaurant, the Walden Brothers' hardware store, H.A. Shaw's real estate office and Mrs. Shaw's dry goods store. The retail businesses that clustered near the foot of Lonsdale Avenue met the day-to-day needs of residents. North Vancouver, however, was still a relatively small community, and specialized goods were often only available by shopping in Vancouver. Travelling across the inlet in pursuit of the latest fashions became a popular Saturday evening diversion for many a young North Shore woman. The frequent ferry service made such recreation easy and as Rodger Burnes recalled, "A separate ladies' cabin near the stern of the vessel . . . closed to male travellers" provided all the privacy the young shoppers might desire.

John Hendry's connections with North Vancouver dated back to 1874, when he supervised the reconstruction of the Moodyville Sawmill. Hendry went on to own the BC Mills Timber and Trading Company, one of the largest sawmill enterprises in the province. North Vancouver boosters hoped in vain that his Vancouver, Westminster and Yukon Railway would connect their city with the province's resource-rich interior.
Surrey Museum and Archives

As confidence in the townsite's future continued to grow, people once again began to talk of a railway. Ten years had passed since the completion of Hendry's line between Blaine and Liverpool. In 1901, Hendry secured a charter for what was to prove an even greater dream, his Vancouver, Westminster and Yukon Railway (VW&Y). Hendry's charter authorized the company to build a line from Vancouver to Dawson City by way of the Squamish Valley, Hazelton and Teslin Lake. Getting to the Squamish Valley required that the line cross Burrard Inlet at the Second Narrows and follow the north shore of the inlet through the District of North Vancouver. Property owners in the district, especially those who owned land in the townsite, could not have been more delighted. The idea seemed logical if not predestined, and the rhetoric in the press did much to fuel the optimism. North Vancouver, boosters unceasingly proclaimed, had a far longer coastline than Vancouver and had deeper water. Furthermore, unlike the south shore, the North Vancouver waterfront was not controlled by the monopolistic Canadian Pacific Railway.

Most members of North Vancouver's district council were strong supporters of Hendry's proposed railway. On occasion, however, dissenting voices rose above those of the railway's advocates. An all-candidates meeting held before the 1903 municipal election resulted in "some rather heated passes between the parties," with councillor William May complaining that a "bylaw granting [municipal tax] exemption to the Vancouver, Westminster & Yukon Railway had never been discussed in Council." Candidate John Balfour Ker, on the other hand, asserted that the railway was of utmost importance to the district, with the capacity "to make a town of North Vancouver in three years." Ker was a key figure in the North Vancouver Land and Improvement Company, a firm that stood to make millions if the railway became a fact. The perception that the district's affairs were being run to the benefit of the large landowners who lived on the south side of the inlet was by no means reduced by the fact that the district's offices had only just been moved to North Vancouver.

One of the leading advocates of the railway was publisher George Bartley, who founded the *Express* newspaper in North Vancouver in August 1905. Bartley had previously established the *Independent* in Vancouver, a paper identified with the province's growing labour movement. But Bartley found himself supporting the ambitions of one of British Columbia's leading capitalists when his leading article of the inaugural issue of the *Express* fuelled support for Hendry's great dream. The scheme also enjoyed support from local Member of Parliament Robert George MacPherson, who concurred that North Vancouver would become Vancouver's twin. When asked why he was so confident about the townsite's future, MacPherson answered:

Why, because North Vancouver is located on Burrard Inlet, and all railroads coming to the Canadian Pacific coast must find their way to this great harbour. The VW&Y would mean to North Vancouver what the CPR is to Vancouver, as it would open up some of the richest and greatest areas of BC lands—the immense heritage in the north of us, all of which is tributary to North Vancouver.

Hendry, MacPherson and a host of others envisioned the agricultural, forest and mineral wealth of the Cariboo, Chilcotin, Omineca, Okanagan and Kootenay districts all flowing to North Vancouver, and those who invested in North Shore lands enjoying unimaginable levels of prosperity. Whatever doubts existed were largely allayed when survey parties began their work, determining a route from the Second Narrows in the east to Howe Sound in the west.

In local transportation, the district was restrained from expanding its overtaxed ferry service by competing demands on the public purse and a poor credit rating.

*Ferry **St. George**, launched in 1904 and named for Alfred St. George Hamersley, president of the ferry company. The vessel was later known as **North Vancouver Ferry No. 2**.*

North Vancouver Museum and Archives, 3820

Anxious to sell lots in the new townsite, Alfred St. George Hamersley proposed forming a company to provide a cross-inlet ferry service. Taxpayers, eager to rid themselves of a liability, eagerly embraced his offer. The North Vancouver Ferry and Power Company thus acquired the *North Vancouver* on a lease basis and within a year placed a new ferry into service as well. Christened the *St. George* in 1904 in honour of its owner, and later renamed *North Vancouver Ferry No. 2*, the vessel was double-ended and able to accommodate several hundred passengers as well as a dozen teams with wagons. It had two pilothouses and a propeller at either end. As with the *North Vancouver* (which continued in service as *North Vancouver Ferry No. 1*), the *St. George* contained separate lounges for male and female passengers, and First Nations of both genders were informally relegated to a space of their own.

What the *St. George* was lacking, however, was a way for the local wharfinger to communicate with businesses whose freight had been deposited at the dock.

With frontier ingenuity, ticket agent J. Piers devised a novel system, sounding a horn to announce deliveries: two toots for J.A. McMillan's grocery store, three for Pete Larson's hotel, a long and a short and two shorts for the local newspaper, and two longs for McKenzie's butcher shop. Although lacking in sophistication, the system worked remarkably well. By 1905, however, council began to plan a district-wide telephone system.

The district also began to develop its electrical infrastructure and land-based transportation system. Council issued a call for proposals for lighting, power and street railway services, ultimately resulting in an agreement with the British Columbia Electric Railway Company (BCER). The development of a street railway (streetcar) system was a particularly important aspect of the proposal call, for streetcar systems were obligatory features of any successful turn-of-the-century town. Street railway systems offered the middle and working classes a chance to purchase affordable homes from which they could cheaply commute to work. Given

Community volunteers organized a "work bee" to clear Victoria Park, 1905 or 1907.
North Vancouver Museum and Archives, 2421

North Vancouver's location and challenging topography, prior to the construction of a bridge and the proliferation of the private automobile, a street railway system was vital to what newspaperman George Bartley had dubbed "the ambitious city" in the inaugural edition of the *Express* in 1905.

In North Vancouver, the BCER's proposal called for a fifty-year monopoly, with "the initial length of track to be built to be about five miles, starting from the foot of Lonsdale Avenue, and continuing along said avenue to Nineteenth Street with branches therefrom as may be mutually arranged between the Council and the Company." Given the magnitude of the undertaking, the company's managing director Johannes Buntzen sought the approbation of his superiors in London, telling them where North Vancouver was located and advising that the deal would offer a guaranteed profit: "Any possible loss on the railway portion during the first two or three years should easily be covered by the profit on street lighting, private lighting and commercial power sold."

Other important developments also occurred in the townsite in 1905. The first of these was the clearing and levelling of the first in a series of parks and other green spaces ultimately intended to encircle the community. Early in 1905, district council received a tantalizing offer from the North Vancouver Land and Improvement Company. The firm proposed donating the northern half of a future park to the district, subject to Hamersley donating the southern half. The result was a formal park two blocks long in the heart of the townsite's emerging residential area. Lacking the finances to develop the park, district council turned to community volunteers, who formed a "work bee" in the manner of the time.

By 1906 the foot of Lonsdale Avenue had power poles in place and a streetcar system under construction.
North Vancouver Museum and Archives, 1456

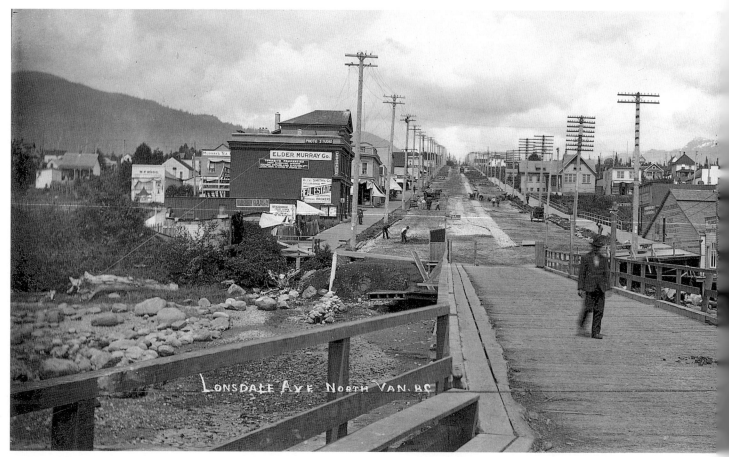

Victoria Park was not the only public open space made possible through the largesse of the large land companies. In the spring of 1905, Hamersley took a portion of District Lot 274 at the foot of St. David's Avenue and set about transforming what had formerly been Nyman's dairy ranch into an attractive picnic ground. A wharf and float were constructed, sand was spread along the beach, and change rooms were built along with a refreshment booth and sports field. Dubbed "Lonsdale Gardens," the park attracted both locals and visitors from across the inlet until the site was redeveloped for industrial purposes some years later. The community's premier park, also acquired from the North Vancouver Land and Improvement Company, began to be developed about the same time: Mahon Park would become the site of community events as well as a number of recreational facilities.

In March 1905, land was purchased for a fire hall for the townsite's volunteer firefighters, a transaction that gave property owners some sense of reassurance. Forest fires had been recorded on the North Shore as early as the 1860s. Moody had pointed the finger at his Squamish neighbours, but in hindsight lightning strikes or logging activity seem more likely explanations. A major fire had swept across the townsite in September 1898, narrowly missing the homes of the few families who had only just finished building. Another important addition to the municipal infrastructure was a water system. The townsite drew its supply from an intake located in the upper reaches of Lynn Creek, a project the previous council had initiated by going on foot to inspect the intended source. As Rodger Burnes recalled, few of the councillors were physically fit. The route was difficult, and to restore themselves the councillors stopped periodically to take a swig from a bottle they carried with them labelled "Mosquito Lotion":

> *After the inspection was over, the return trip was commenced, when one of the councillors said that the water should be tested. But no container was at hand till the empty bottle was thought of. So the bottle was filled, taken back to North Vancouver, and handed over to the analyst and tested. Yes, the water was pure and good, but it contained a trace of, of all things, alcohol.*

By mid-1905, the water system was connected to one hundred homes, and fifteen fire hydrants had been installed along its length. As the district's services increased, it hired a waterworks foreman and a fire chief, and divided the previously combined position of road foreman and policeman into two.

Work on the electric and street railway system began by the end of the year. Gigantic poles were felled from nearby forests to carry the system's power lines across the Second Narrows. The construction of the BCER's car barn was well under way by January 1906. That same month, the BCER engaged the Western Corporation to supply hundreds of fir poles to carry the overhead wires the system would require. The selection of an electrical service provider had been a relatively straightforward process, but finalizing routes for the street railway system soon embroiled the community in controversy. The 1905 council had agreed on one set of routes, but the 1906 council chose another. Individual residents had opinions of their own, often reflecting their own property interests. One plan called for a relatively short line of track running in a loop around the townsite's core. This met some opposition, as the district's outlying areas—the Lynn and Capilano valleys in particular—would have had no service.

Although most ratepayers recognized the importance of a central route travelling up Lonsdale Avenue from the ferry terminal, they disagreed on whether the east-west lines should run along First or Third Streets. While council's 1906 proposal favoured First, supporters of the Third Street route met in February 1906 in what the *Express* termed a "large gathering of interested speculators." Upwards of seventy people crammed into the council chamber but it soon became clear that there was no chairman and no agenda, and many in attendance were unaware of the meeting's purpose. When the meeting progressed, a succession of speakers including former reeve and major landholder J.C. Keith voiced suspicions about the proposed change of route. In the end, council endorsed the First Street option with minor revisions suggested by the North Vancouver Land and Improvement Company, which owned land along the route.

As work continued on the streetcar system, the Western Corporation extended its dock at the foot of Lonsdale Avenue to assist in the transport of steel from Vancouver. Western's busy sawmill provided much of the lumber required for the construction of both homes and business blocks. Like the firm's operations in the forest, its mill was wholly modern, using electric rather than steam power. It was a vast establishment, with offices, bunkhouses, a cookhouse, stables and a kiln. Like its predecessor at Moodyville, the business employed a culturally diverse

The Western Corporation's Syndicate Block housed J.A. McMillan's grocery store, the offices of the Express *and upstairs, the North Vancouver Club.*

City of Vancouver Archives, CVA Out P1057

staff housed in segregated bunkhouses, including a large number of Japanese and Chinese workers. The Western Corporation also employed large numbers of Sikhs, some said to be veterans of the British Indian Army. The mill later acquired the rights to extensive stands of timber beyond the townsite. It also established an export trade, conveying its finished lumber down to the inlet on flatcars via the BCER's newly installed streetcar tracks.

A ready supply of inexpensive land, a new series of wharves, a reliable ferry service, an evolving street railway and a vision for a great port city all contributed to the Western Corporation's success. The commercial buildings it designed and built provided premises for key components of a successful town. Its Syndicate Block, built on the northwest corner of Lonsdale Avenue and Esplanade, was the townsite's first commercial building and provided space for a grocery, a post office and the *Express* newspaper, also accommodating a meeting and dance hall on its upper floor. The firm also provided a wealth of opportunities for employment, its workforce eventually swelling to more than eighty employees.

A number of institutional projects, churches foremost among them, were also undertaken independently in the early 1900s. North Vancouver's Anglicans were the first denomination to organize, holding Sunday services in the Central Lonsdale homes of Alfred E. Crickmay and James Burnes as early as 1899. As the congregation grew, services moved to what was later remembered as "Dorman's shack," a modest building constructed of shakes at the corner of Lonsdale Avenue and Thirteenth Street. With the support of the Cornish, Diplock, Keene, Crickmay and Kealy families, a small wood-frame church was erected the following year. St. John's was dedicated in October 1900 and built on land donated by faithful Anglican Edward Mahon. By 1907 the townsite's Anglican population had grown substantially and had to build an extension to increase the church's capacity. Two years later the foundation was laid for a still larger church.

Other denominations followed the Anglican example. Recognizing the growth of the community, the Methodist Church integrated the townsite into its mission system about 1904, almost four decades after Reverend Ebenezer Robson had delivered his first sermon to a small congregation at Moodyville. Despite having retired, Robson continued to visit North Shore Methodists, holding services in both Moodyville and the townsite. In the absence of a Methodist church, services were held in the schoolhouse or homes of local Methodists until the mission chose to withdraw from the North Shore, briefly leaving it to their Presbyterian brethren. Although a Presbyterian minister had visited Moodyville as early as the 1860s, it was not until 1903 that the denomination began to regularize its North Shore missions. In May of that year, Walter L. Nichol, a student of theology at Knox College in Toronto, delivered his first sermon in Dorman's shack, which had been vacated by the Anglicans a few years earlier. Services were later held at Morden's Hall at Lonsdale and Victoria Park, and the new public school at Chesterfield and Fourth, until the congregation purchased a series of lots on Lower Keith Road in January 1904 and opened the first St. Andrew's Presbyterian Church in November.

The townsite's first school was also constructed in these early years. The land boom had brought dozens of young families to the area, many intent on providing their children with a wholesome upbringing. Residency in North Vancouver offered fresh mountain air, rambles in the forest and along the shore, and a physical separation from the perceived filth and crime of the larger city across the inlet. In 1902 district council wrote the province advising of the number of school-age children who had to walk to Moodyville's one-room school, where class sizes were large and a single teacher had to instruct all the grades. The province acknowledged the need for an additional school and authorized the construction of a suitable building nearer the centre of the townsite. The more spacious North Vancouver School (later renamed Central School) was built in 1902–03 at the corner of Chesterfield and Fourth. By 1904 there were forty-four students enrolled, but the inspector of schools reported "a certain laxity in the conduct and management of the school." The situation in Moodyville was far worse. Enrolment there had declined markedly following the closure of the mill and the construction of the new school in the townsite. The inspector was by no means pleased by the progress of the school's senior grade, which following his visit in 1905 he termed "the most irresponsive class of pupils I ever met." The school eventually shut down in 1910.

Land promoters continued to laud the virtues of the townsite and settlers continued to pour in via Hamersley's much improved ferry service. Many arrived with nowhere to live and threw up tents or wooden shacks along the waterfront as they waited for a house to purchase or rent. Real estate agents opened offices on Lonsdale Avenue, enabling them to bypass competitors based in Vancouver. Larger businesses moved in as well. In 1905, the Bank of British North America secured premises in a commercial building recently erected by the North Vancouver Land and Improvement Company. The *Express* was ecstatic: it was one thing to attract real estate agents, but a major coup to capture a bank.

Around this same time, Captain Charles H. Cates, whose family's activities were to become closely identified with Lower Lonsdale, took a close interest in the North Vancouver waterfront. Like Sue Moody, Cates was from Maine, but his expertise lay in marine navigation rather than in the lumber trade. Cates moved to the townsite by 1904, constructed a wharf at the foot of Lonsdale Avenue and started what was to become one of the largest fleets of deep-sea tugs on the continent's west coast. Under the guidance of Cates and his sons Charlie, John H. and Jim, the firm of C.H. Cates and Sons became a West Coast legend.

As the townsite grew, a community began to form. Like-minded men and women met, talked and founded organizations to meet their collective needs and aspirations. Several recreational associations emerged in 1904–07, chief among them the North Vancouver Horticultural Society, the North Vancouver Boating Club and the North Vancouver Athletic Club. The groups held local events that created bonds between residents and forged a sense of community identity and pride. These activities took place on the Horticultural Society's extensive grounds on Lonsdale Avenue at Twenty-first Street as well as on the waterfront near the Hotel North Vancouver. Beginning in 1904, the Horticultural Society's annual fall show brought out the best in North Vancouver's home and agricultural work, with prizes being awarded for the finest displays of flowers, vegetables, livestock, baking, "ladies work," "native work" and children's work.

The Horticultural Society soon became one of the leading organizations in the young city. By 1907, its members had sufficient resources to build a wood-frame

Captain Charles H. Cates, a native of Maine, settled in Moodyville in the 1890s prior to building his wharf and beginning his tow boat business near the foot of Lonsdale Avenue. The Cates family's tugboats have been a fixture on the North Vancouver waterfront since the early 1900s, though the family no longer owns the firm.

North Vancouver Museum and Archives, 923

structure on its property then known as the Alexandra Horticultural Gardens, in honour of the reigning king's consort. Initially known as the Horticultural Hall and later as the Lonsdale Hall, the structure would serve as a popular meeting place for the next six decades. The annual regatta hosted by the North Vancouver Boating Club also became a popular event. The nine races it featured in 1905 included competitions for the district's finest male athletes in skiff, sculls and gigs; a ladies race; a competition between the Western Corporation and the North Vancouver Ferry and Power Company; and an "Indian canoe race." A greasy pole competition, won by BC wrestling champion Rod Renshaw, capped the festivities in the late afternoon.

Even the largely abandoned Moodyville area was making progress, as William Bauer purchased a 156-acre plot in District Lot 273, immediately above the mill site, from the Lonsdale Estate in October 1905 for the sum of $50,000. Two years later, Bauer married Ruby Springer, one of the daughters of Benjamin Springer. Bauer had other associations with the North Shore; he had worked as a surveyor with Alan C. McCartney, one of the members of the original incorporation committee formed in 1890. Bauer's interest in Moodyville was likely encouraged by the renewed activities of John Hendry, his new neighbour to the south.

Talk of a railway heightened in October 1905 when James J. Hill, president of the Great Northern Railway, visited Vancouver and closeted himself in the local railway office with John Hendry. After the meeting, Hill was somewhat evasive on the subject of a North Shore railway, noting that a northern extension of his

Central School (photographed c. 1908) was the city's first purpose-built school, and held students until replaced by Queen Mary School in 1915. The building served as city hall, court house and police building. In 1975 it became Presentation House, home of an art gallery, theatre, and museum and archives. Albert Nye House is on the right.

Vancouver Public Library Special Collections, 5665, Philip Timms photo

The corner of Moody Avenue and Seventh Street, c. 1911. This area of the city was purchased from the Lonsdale Estate by Vancouver businessman William Bauer in 1905. Bauer subsequently subdivided his property and offered individual lots for sale.

City of Vancouver Archives, CVA Dist N83.2

own railway system was "in the hands of Mr. Hendry, who can give you all the information. It is an admirable project, but my connection with it is an indirect one." Speaking a few days later, Member of Parliament Robert G. MacPherson was much less taciturn, linking the VW&Y, the Great Northern Railway and the Grand Trunk Pacific Railway together in a single sentence. It was all very confusing, but the public were left with the impression that since great men were behind the various schemes, and since growth in the townsite continued unabated, something major was bound to happen.

INCORPORATION AND INDOCTRINATION 1905–1909

S omething big was indeed in the offing, but it wasn't a railway. On November 3, 1905, the *Express* ran a prominent notice announcing one of the "mass meetings" that were then part and parcel of civic life. The notice advised ratepayers of a plan to carve a new city out of the central portion of the fifteen-year-old District of North Vancouver. Supporters of the townsite were increasingly referring to it as "the ambitious city," despite the fact that it was part of one of the largest district municipalities in the province. At the meeting, the idea of incorporation was endorsed and a committee of thirteen was established to review the matter further. Another nine were subsequently added.

Unsurprisingly, a number of committee members had close ties to the townsite's major real estate interests. District Reeve Arnold Evan Kealy, also secretary of the Western Corporation, chaired the committee. Three of the district's four councillors—William Morden, Patrick Allen and Edmund Bell—were also committee members. Those who favoured incorporation included district politicians, real estate agents, major landowners and longer-term residents of the North Shore as well as a number of recent arrivals. Some of these men were non-residents and several had significant interests in land. Although they spoke of secession, the term was never officially used. These men viewed properties

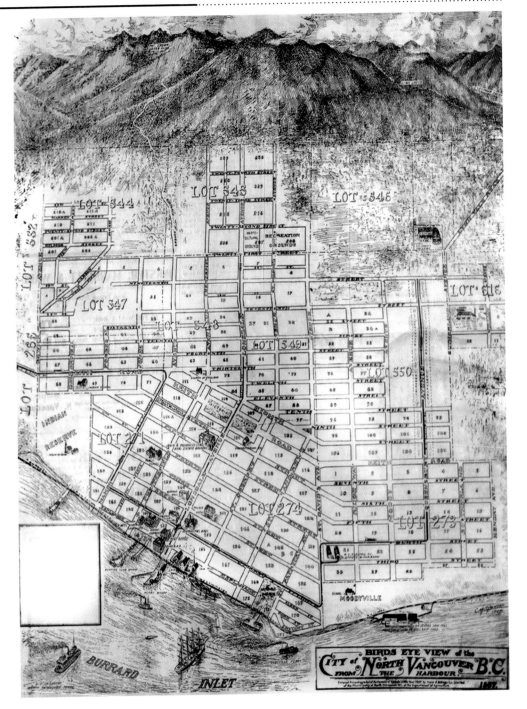

Irwin and Billings map of the townsite, published in the Express *at the time of civic incorporation. Several of the community's early landmarks are visible in the map, as is the community of Moodyville, which initially remained outside the city's borders.*

North Vancouver Museum and Archives

in the townsite as the core of a viable community, and those beyond it as a financial drain. Demands for infrastructure were considerable in both areas, and supporters of the townsite felt it should not be required to finance a sparsely populated rural district with which it had little in common. Furthermore, provincial legislation afforded cities borrowing powers that rural districts did not enjoy.

A second mass meeting took place in early December. Benjamin Cornish, Arthur Diplock and J.J. Woods reported on the interviews they had conducted during the intervening weeks, seeking insights into whether the proposed city should incorporate under the Municipal Clauses Act or under a charter of its own as Vancouver had. Reeve Kealy was an outspoken supporter of a charter, advising,

"The large taxpayers favour a charter. Why do they do this if it's not a good thing, as they are the people who have to pay most of the cost?" The recommendations received from other prominent men were mixed, however, and therefore it was agreed to pose a series of questions to voters in a referendum: whether a city should be incorporated, whether it should be incorporated under a special charter or under the Municipal Clauses Act, and what the new city should be named.

At Larson's hotel a few months later, the second annual banquet of the Western Corporation provided yet another boost for the movement. The formidable guest list included the American consul, the local Member of Parliament, the local Member of the Legislative Assembly and a host of prominent businessmen. MP Robert G. MacPherson led the speakers: "If the Dominion and the provincial government do what they should do, you will hear the whistle of the locomotive here within the next two years. I for my part will do all that lies within my power to assist the VW&Y or any other railway that wishes to come through here."

For proponents of incorporation, everything seemed to be going well. If there were any contrary voices, they were not reported by the media of the day. The district ought to have been concerned, insofar as it stood to lose much of tax base at a time when funds were needed for a municipal infrastructure of incalculable proportions. But with its reeve and council solidly behind the incorporation movement, no one was left to champion the interests of the few farmers and fishermen who lived outside the townsite. The one asset the district possessed from the time of its own incorporation in 1891, however, was its name.

Considerable debate took place regarding an appropriate name for the projected new city, with North Vancouver and Burrard being generally preferred above others such as Northport, Hillmont and Parkhill. Pete Larson, the hotelier, was one of a number of residents who wrote to the *Express*:

Why should we wish to change the name? Surely the name of Vancouver should be good enough for us, with the prefix of North, to indicate our location . . . Our ratepayers, I hope, will not change the name, but one thing I can say, is that so long as I have anything to do with the hotel I conduct, it shall always be known as the "Hotel North Vancouver." Any new name would, to my mind, be absurd.

D.G. Dick took an opposite view: "'Burrard' is a name that every school-child knows . . . so let us give the young city a new name! And we will build a city of such dimensions and splendour that all the earth will rejoice with us in our greatness." Even as the debate raged, the names of the city's principal streets were already being chosen. Several of these honoured the major landowners: Heywood, Lonsdale, Fell and Mahon. Some recognized other men of business—both current and historical—such as Wulffsohn, Bewicke, Hendry and Moody. Others were more obscure: Shavington, Cloverley and Adderley referred to homes and villages in Shropshire owned by the Heywood-Lonsdale family.

In the December 15 referendum, the electors agreed to incorporate under a charter as the City of North Vancouver. However, although the plebiscite had favoured incorporation under a special charter, the committee found this approach would take too long. A subcommittee of the incorporation committee thus decided to seek incorporation under the Municipal Clauses Act, a process expedited by MLA Francis Carter-Cotton. Further delays loomed when an angry John Hendry presented a petition against having his Moodyville mill site included in the proposed city; but the subcommittee agreed to exclude Moodyville and Carter-Cotton negotiated the change to the North Vancouver Incorporation Act, which was passed by the legislature in March 1906.

One issue still stood in the way of the province issuing letters patent to finalize the process: neither the committee nor the province wanted to finalize incorporation until amendments to the Municipal Clauses Act, granting cities the right to tax railway property, were passed in the next legislative session the following year. Hendry's property in Moodyville may have been outside the city's jurisdiction, but the proponents of incorporation were determined that his Vancouver, Westminster, and Yukon Railway would not avoid taxation.

While providing for the creation of the new city, the North Vancouver Incorporation Act also protected the interests of the district. Under its terms, the new City of North Vancouver was required to assume over $170,000 of the debentures issued by the district and to ratify pre-existing electricity, transportation and telephone agreements made by the district. The city, when incorporated, would acquire title to the Municipal Hall, the municipal pound and stable buildings, the water system, the district's wharves and slips, a number of street ends, the ferry system, the street light system and various pieces of equipment. The city would also fall heir to all public parks lying within the townsite as well as title to the as-yet-unused cemetery. Perhaps more importantly, the city would also acquire a number of liabilities including a responsibility for a portion of the local improvement, waterworks and street improvement loans the district had taken out in the preceding six years.

As plans for incorporation proceeded, the townsite continued to develop. By August 10, 1906, twenty-four key intersections had been provided with arc lamp street lights, and their activation just five days later elicited considerable public celebration. Work on the street railway's western line had also begun. Four small streetcars arrived at the Western Corporation's dock near the ferry landing. These were older cars pulled from the company's other systems, but for North Vancouver residents they were the stuff of dreams: the tracks up Lonsdale Avenue would constitute the spine of the future city. The first trial run along the Lonsdale route took place on August 29, 1906, causing considerable excitement not only in the townsite but across the inlet as well. According to the *Vancouver Province*, the general superintendent and chief engineer appeared at the door of the district's council chamber, interrupted the council meeting and extended an invitation to take a ride:

> *. . . it did not take long to finish up the business of the meeting, adjourn, grab a hat, climb aboard the waiting car and be whisked along the street at a good brisk speed . . . Several trips were made up and down the streets from the Municipal Hall to Twenty-first Street and return, after which the crowd adjourned to the well known hostelry of Pete Larson, where light refreshments were served. When the merry party broke up, there were cheers for Mr. Milne, Mr. Jorgeson, and the*

Foot of Lonsdale Avenue, c. 1908, showing what was then a modest ferry wharf. The buildings of the Western Corporation were conveniently located near the entrance to the wharf, enabling visitors to take advantage of the firm's multifaceted range of services.

North Vancouver Museum and Archives, 458

One of North Vancouver's first streetcars, on Lonsdale Avenue north of Esplanade, September 1906. The red ensigns and Union Jacks decorating the car indicate a celebratory mood, the streetcar system only having just been officially inaugurated.

North Vancouver Museum and Archives, 9936

British Columbia Electric Railway Company, and the unanimous opinion of all was that with the completion of the lines that North Vancouver would have an electric car system second to none.

A more official inauguration of the system took place just two days later. It generated its own excitement with two cars derailing during the course of the day.

The acquisition of a telephone service was also a significant indicator of the community's progress. In later years Rodger Burnes recalled how the first telephone cable was stretched across the inlet: "Those telephone people were pretty ingenious. They blew up a football and attached it to a line. The ball was dropped into a [water] main on the North Shore end and pulled out the other side of the Narrows." Recognizing that the market for a telephone system had yet to be developed, district council assisted the service provider, the British Columbia Telephone Company, by waiving its taxes and fees until such time as there were two hundred subscribers. The North Vancouver Land and Improvement Company also struck a deal, allowing the telephone company to remove telephone poles free of charge from District Lot 550, a parcel that had to be cleared in any case to allow its subdivision and sale.

The year 1906 was memorable in other ways as well, including the construction of a shipyard by Alfred "Andy" Wallace of Vancouver. Wallace had moved to Vancouver in February 1891 and worked for a number of shipbuilders before establishing his own operation with two partners two years later. Located in Vancouver's False Creek, the small operation built a variety of craft from fishing boats to tugs, scows, schooners, yachts and ferries. Wallace's customers were equally wide-ranging, varying from individual fishermen to larger corporations, the Union Steamship Company among them. His commissions helped him connect with many of the inlet's movers and shakers, including Johann Wulffsohn, who had interests in the Union Steamship Company, and Alfred St. George Hamersley, president of the North Vancouver Ferry and Power Company.

Wallace's assembly in 1904 of the *St. George*, the ferry company's flagship vessel, may have piqued his interest in North Vancouver as an alternative site for his shipyard. By then, his family owned the firm in its entirety, and through his wife's skilful financial management the Wallaces were able to purchase three

The newly opened Wallace Shipyards, located at the foot of Lonsdale Avenue, c. 1906. Wallace's modest endeavour was to grow into one of the nation's largest shipyards and would play a major role in equipping Canada's merchant marine during the Second World War.
North Vancouver Museum and Archives, 2838

large waterfront properties in District Lot 274, east of Lonsdale Avenue. A number of factors may have influenced the firm's decision to relocate. False Creek was relatively shallow and a series of bridges restricted the movement of larger vessels. The North Vancouver location was larger, was located on the inlet's inner harbour and featured deep water. Additional inducements were the proximity to future rail and port facilities, and inexpensive electrical power from the BCER.

Opened in 1906, the Wallace Shipyard soon became a part of a bustling complex of harbour-based operations. Captain Charles H. Cates had built a wharf near the foot of Lonsdale Avenue in 1904 and was soon to establish a boat repair and towing business in the area as well. Boatbuilder Andy Linton's nearby yard was located west of Cates' tugboat operation. In early 1906 Brackman and Ker, a well-known firm with branches throughout the province, purchased land adjacent to Wallace for the construction of a feed, flour and seed operation. At the time, North Vancouver was being promoted as an ideal location for not only the cultivation of berries and orchard fruits, but also the establishment of poultry and dairy operations.

Other prominent businesses started farther up the hill. John B. Paine's hardware store, eventually to become a Lower Mainland institution, opened its first premises on East First Street. Lorenzo Reda and Carolina Andrus launched their impressive brick Palace Hotel a block to the north. Three storeys high and faced with red brick, the Palace Hotel boasted the province's first rooftop gardens, which in the absence of taller buildings nearby, provided magnificent views of the mountains to the north and the harbour to the south. These accommodations joined the Hotel North Vancouver and the venerable Moodyville Hotel. The latter now-aging establishment, then under the management of Charles Mee, was but a ten-minute tram ride away from the centre of the townsite, and according to the *Express*, afforded an excellent base for users of the recently established gun range near the mouth of Lynn Creek.

Although these hotels offered a range of accommodation for visitors, hopeful settlers without the means to purchase property seem to have been less well served. The *Express* claimed that the peopling of the townsite was hampered by "a dearth of good houses . . . which can be rented at reasonable rates. There are a few vacant shacks, but all the desirable houses, for which an excessive rental is not asked, are all occupied." Publisher George Bartley predicted that faster ferries, coupled with the townsite's streetcar system, would soon place North Vancouver within quicker reach of downtown Vancouver than many suburbs on the other side of the inlet.

Bartley and other promoters of the townsite may have seen "city-building" as a race in 1906, but there were also people in the infant settlement who strove to build community. Before the end of 1906, North Vancouver was home to a Boys' Brigade (a junior militia), a School Debating Society, a Dancing Academy, a Loyal Orange Lodge, an amateur orchestra and an athletic club. A new Masonic Lodge was organized the following year, filling the void left when Moodyville's Mount Hermon Lodge had moved to Vancouver in 1887. Leading organizations in the community in these formative years—membership in which conferred higher social status—were the North Vancouver Board of Trade and the North Vancouver Boating Club. To some residents, the Boating Club's annual ball was *the* event of the social season. Held at Larson's pavilion amid a forest of Union Jacks and bunting,

Paine Hardware, originally established as Paine and McMillan, was a landmark business in North Vancouver's Lower Lonsdale area for eight decades prior to succumbing to fire in 1997. The interior of the company's first store—with merchandise occupying every available space—is shown in this photograph, dated 1908.

North Vancouver Museum and Archives 7516

Harbor View Sanatarium
N. Vancouver B.C.

Alfred St. George Hamersley's large arts and crafts-style home, Langton Lodge, in use as the Harbour View Sanitarium, c. 1914–18.
North Vancouver Museum and Archives, 8935

the ball provided an opportunity for North Shore matrons to show off their latest gowns while they danced the night away with their tuxedoed male companions. Membership in the executive of the Board of Trade conferred similar status, though membership in the full organization was more broad-based. In 1906 Alfred St. George Hamersley headed the board's executive and local businessmen—many of whom did not live on the North Shore—filled out its ranks, Edward Mahon and William A. Bauer prominent among them.

If the rapidly developing townsite possessed a single leading citizen in the years immediately prior to incorporation, it was undoubtedly Alfred St. George Hamersley. Of all the prominent investors in North Vancouver lands, Hamersley alone had chosen to live among the people whose community he was helping to shape. His impressive Arts and Crafts–style home, Langton Lodge, stood at a distance from the townsite's other homes as if his were the local manor house and theirs the village cottages. With its mock Tudor walls set on a granite foundation, Langton Lodge took two years to build. He sold it in 1906 to move back to England, leaving a remarkable legacy for only a three-year residency in the district.

Hamersley was not the only business leader who chose to build in District Lot 274. James A. McNair, the lumberman and land promoter, purchased a large residential property (nine lots, in fact) not far from Victoria Park, where he built a mansion every bit as grand as Hamersley's. Begun in 1906 and completed in 1907,

the house cost a phenomenal $15,000 and featured hardwoods from Australia as well as oak and walnut from eastern North America. Although he owned property on both sides of the inlet, McNair's main interest lay in the manufacture of shingles. As he stood on his covered wraparound porch, McNair could gaze across the inlet and survey his extensive properties, factories and mills. Although his move to the North Shore may have made good business sense, it verged on social suicide to separate himself and his wife from the cream of inlet society. The McNairs rose to the occasion, with Minnie McNair hosting a select group of North Shore women over tea at four o'clock in the afternoon on the third Thursday of every month.

Also in 1906, a number of more accessible community events appeared on the social calendar of the evolving community. April's "grand prize masquerade ball and supper" at Larson's pavilion was hailed as "the largest function of its kind ever held on this side of the inlet," attracting participants from Vancouver as well as from the townsite. The setting aside of May 24 as Empire Day, in honour of the late Queen's birthday, focussed on "patriotic exercises among the children, including patriotic songs, recitations, etc," according to Bartley.

The most memorable event in the year, however, was the townsite's first-ever July 1 Dominion Day celebration. By North Vancouver standards, the crowds were immense, their ranks swelled by a tide of visitors from across the inlet and even from Washington State—the steamer *City of Whatcom* arriving from Bellingham

Pete Larson's Hotel North Vancouver and its pavilion on West Esplanade, July 1, 1907. The well-dressed crowds were there to celebrate both Dominion Day and the creation of the new City of North Vancouver.

North Vancouver Museum and Archives, 5705

with a reported eight hundred passengers. Once again, Larson's hotel was the focus of activity. People brought picnic lunches or dined in the hotel. A brass band performed both popular and patriotic airs from the hotel's bandstand. The program featured races and other athletic events. A smoke-filled balloon ascended high above the crowd, which watched in rapt fascination as its operator parachuted to the ground. The daylong event was concluded with a grand display of fireworks.

Though nominally a celebration of Canadian confederation, Dominion Day was also a celebration of the community's connections to "the mother country." Imperial sentiment swelled unabashedly and publisher George Bartley epitomized its promoters:

> On the shores of the great Pacific Ocean, Canada's natal day will be celebrated in the embryo ambitious city of North Vancouver in such a way as will do proud to an empire whose power and might and majesty are the wonders of storied centuries. Children of this great dominion, we glory in the tradition and history of that proud guard of human progress, we send a message of love across a broad continent and wide sea to the old folks at home, with the assurance that we glory in [their] prowess and courage and proudly boast ourselves, daughters in our mother's house, if mistress in our own.

The vast majority of those who then peopled the townsite traced their origins to Britain. A review of the surnames in the directories for North Vancouver in the early twentieth century reveals just how British the population had become. The trend, established in the early 1900s, appears to have continued well into the century. By 1921, 44 percent of North Vancouver's population of 7,500 people

Chesterfield School Cricket Club, 1920. The school was one of a number of privately operated institutions that operated in North Vancouver while emulating similar schools in England.
City of Vancouver Archives, CVA 99-1355

could claim to have been born in Britain, and 87 percent possessed British roots.

Many elements of British social life were present in turn-of-the-century British Columbia, but others would have to be re-created. Principal among these was an educational system to shape the character and strengthen the identity of middle- and upper-class children. Sending their children—their sons and heirs in particular—to a state-run Canadian school was unpalatable to many British immigrants. Reverend R.S. Marsden therefore found it easy to convince a major landowner to donate a sizeable property near the intersection of Sutherland Avenue and Lynn Valley Road for the construction of a private school for boys. Named in honour of St. John, the school was modelled on the institutions that several of the landowners had attended in Britain. Restrictive fees were set to ensure that only a certain type of boy gained admission. Non-resident "day boys" were also accepted, but boarding was the norm.

St. John's School had close connections with the Anglican Church, the place of worship for many who made up the community's establishment. When the school opened in September 1906, the Bishop of the Diocese of New Westminster and much of his clergy assembled for an age-old ritual. Carrying a processional cross, the school's newly selected "head boy" led a long line of clergy, students, parents and staff around the school and its grounds, both of which the bishop blessed in turn. As the century wore on, a British "public school" education began to appeal to families whose roots were more Canadian than British. Chesterfield School opened shortly after St. John's, but both eventually closed due to the separate departures of their founders for family health reasons. Other schools would take their places in the next decade.

St. John's School for boys, 1906. The privately operated school was located near the intersection of Sutherland Avenue and Lynn Valley Road. Initially run by Rev. Richard Marsden, the school was closely associated with the Anglican church.

North Vancouver Museum and Archives, 13055

Although its population assumed an increasingly British flavour, the fabric of the townsite reflected the architecture of both Britain and North America. When first built, the Hamersleys' house stood alone in the midst of desolation. Langton Lodge might have resembled an English country house, but the landscape that surrounded it was hardly "England's green and pleasant land." Yet the once barren landscape soon began to reforest, and settlers quickened the transformation. Traditional English cottages rose amid dwellings descended from the houses of the American West. American-style white picket fences competed with English hedges and rockeries, and rambling roses and English ivy distracted from the sea of blackened stumps. The design of the townsite's public parks was more ambiguous, coupling formal, rectangular squares with tamed tracts of semi-romantic woodland. That the parks also served as firebreaks was an added bonus.

Built to the west of Lonsdale Avenue for the North Vancouver Land and Improvement Company in 1906, Ottawa Gardens offered a pleasant green frontage for what the company hoped would become a prestigious residential enclave. Victoria Park was larger, spanning Lonsdale Avenue between Upper and Lower Keith Roads and was intended for active as well as passive recreation. Alexandra Park, farther up the hill, had grounds for athletic activities and also featured the

Although it was never built to the full width described in this 1908 plan, the Grand Boulevard remains the widest landscaped city street in British Columbia.

North Vancouver Museum and Archives, pamphlet 1908-2

Horticultural Society's exhibition building. The Grand Boulevard, the clearing of which also began in 1906, was the largest of the parks and proudly touted as "the most prominent feature of the new city."

Designed in part as a firebreak between Lynn Valley and the city of North Vancouver, the development soon became the showpiece of the entire North Shore. According to its developers, the North Vancouver Land and Improvement Company, the Grand Boulevard would be to North Vancouver "what the Champs Elysées is to Paris, what Unter Den Linden is to Berlin, and more than Rotten Row is to London." Almost a mile in length and a phenomenal 346 feet wide, the Grand Boulevard and its adjacent park encompassed some forty-five acres and afforded magnificent views of Burrard Inlet and the city of Vancouver. To control development, restrictive covenants on properties fronting the boulevard limited new construction to residential buildings with a construction value of $4,000 or more.

The North Vancouver Land and Improvement Company published several documents to promote its property in the Grand Boulevard area. The plans bear no signature, making it difficult to determine the boulevard's designer. However, the similarity of the plans to those for Boston's Commonwealth Avenue suggest a connection with American landscape architect Frederick Law Olmstead or his designer sons John Charles and Frederick Law Jr. Land promoter Edward Mahon is known to have possessed a plan of Boston's Commonwealth Avenue, which was built about the same time.

In the eyes its promoters, the Grand Boulevard was to be the inlet's premier residential area. To achieve its objectives, however, the North Vancouver Land and Improvement Company would have to compete with the land-rich and heavily capitalized Canadian Pacific Railway. The CPR had ambitions of its own on the south side of the inlet. In 1907, the railway announced plans for an elite subdivision to be called Shaughnessy Heights. When its lots were put on the market two years later, would-be buyers lined up for blocks. Doing battle with the CPR's real estate interests would be no minor campaign.

People who bought and built along the Grand Boulevard may well have anticipated significant growth around the inlet. On a clear day, individual buildings stood out amid the chaos of Vancouver's rapidly growing skyline. If the terminal city were growing, surely North Vancouver could as well. The 1906 visit of the Royal Commission on Grain provided yet another source of optimism. Starting in the 1890s, Clifford Sifton, Minister of the Interior in the Laurier government, had encouraged the peopling of the Canadian prairies by settlers from Eastern Europe. The harvest was ready and West Coast ports lobbied to share in the export trade. If a bridge and a railway were to be built across the Second Narrows, grain-laden ships would be sailing from *both* sides of the inlet.

Improved transportation within the district, at least, was coming to fruition. The first part of the eastern streetcar line, running from Lonsdale Avenue to the intersection of Queensbury Avenue and Keith Road, opened in January 1907. By Valentine's Day, the route had been extended northward along Queensbury Avenue to a terminus at Nineteenth Street. The initial portion of the company's western line also opened to the public early in January 1907, after some controversy as to

*Mayor Arnold Kealy,
c. 1907. While reeve of the
District of North Vancouver,
Kealy headed a committee
of councillors and other
influential citizens to carve a
new city out of the already
existing district.*
North Vancouver Museum and
Archives, 4817

whether it should proceed north on Forbes Avenue, the eastern boundary of the Mission Reserve, rather than on the more heavily populated Mahon Avenue. It was no coincidence that the latter route was ultimately chosen: Mahon Avenue formed the western boundary of the Lonsdale Estate's prestigious Ottawa Gardens subdivision. The system reached its most extensive configuration in December 1910 with the completion of the Lynn Valley and Capilano Extensions. The latter line came within a mile of popular recreational area Capilano Canyon.

The BCER's North Vancouver trackage had exceeded 10.3 miles, a veritable triumph of technology over topography. Despite some initial glitches, by 1907 the streetcar system was in operation. The clatter of wheels along its rails and the sound of streetcar bells would become as familiar to North Vancouver residents as the sight of the ferries coming and going at the foot of Lonsdale Avenue or the sound of the foghorn at Point Atkinson echoing across and up the inlet.

The other highly anticipated event of 1907 was the issuing of the letters patent finalizing the incorporation of the City of North Vancouver, which happened on May 13. The only political controversy to emerge since John Hendry's petition the previous year was related not to incorporation but rather to the close relationship of the Western Corporation and district officials. Writing to the *Vancouver World* early in 1907, a correspondent signing as "Veritas," observed that the secretary, legal advisor and auditor of the Western Corporation were the reeve, legal advisor and auditor of the District of North Vancouver. The writer went on to claim improprieties, maintaining that the Western Corporation had benefited substantially from the relationship at the ratepayers' expense. Upon investigation, the *World* declared the charges "unfounded," and George Bartley reiterated these findings in the *Express*.

District Reeve (and Western Corporation secretary) Arnold Kealy had no problem being acclaimed the first mayor of the City of North Vancouver upon incorporation on June 1. If this were not enough, his wife had given birth to a son

*City fathers and invited
dignitaries pose in front
of City Hall on July 1,
1907. J.C. Keith and the
North Vancouver Land and
Improvement Company's
Edward Mahon flank the
more formally attired
Mayor Arnold Kealy (centre,
seated).*
North Vancouver Museum and
Archives, p96

the day after incorporation became official. He was thus not only "the first father of the new city," but "the first father of the first boy born in the new city." At a "mass meeting" on June 8, a group of voters (male British subjects aged twenty-one and over) convened to elect the city's first council: Alexander Smith, William J. Dick, William Irwin, Alfred Crickmay, William F. Emery and Dr. A. McKay Jordan. As three of these men plus the mayor were sitting members of district council, the district had to hold mid-term elections to replace them. The newly elected aldermen were sworn in by Mayor Kealy—who was also a local magistrate—on June 10 and the city's first council held its inaugural meeting two days later.

A committee of residents had long been at work to plan the second annual Dominion Day celebrations, and it took little extra effort to add a celebration of incorporation to the July 1 agenda. The event was a huge success, with thousands taxing the capacity of the three ferries carrying visitors from across the inlet. Official estimates placed the total attendance at somewhere between eighteen thousand and twenty thousand, no mean feat for a city of less than two thousand. There was something for everyone: aquatic sports, a hose reel race, field events and a band concert. Politicians proliferated. A military band played appropriate tunes. Bunting hung from city hall and Union Jacks fluttered in the breeze. Mayor Arnold Kealy officiated, and began by offering the community's thanks to Francis Carter-Cotton, "the official dry nurse of the new city." Carter-Cotton called upon the population to develop a sense of pride "that would forever stand in the way of establishing slums or so-called Chinese quarters." After the official opening of the athletic grounds and a professional boxing match, a formal banquet at the Hotel North Vancouver assembled a veritable who's who of North Vancouver business and society, augmented by politicians, diplomats and captains of industry from the inlet's southern shore.

Anyone who had known the townsite just five years earlier would have revelled in its progress. In 1902, the district had possessed a mere 20 miles of roads, ¾ of a mile of sidewalk, 400 feet of bridges and 75 settlers. By 1907, there were 39.5 miles of roads, 4 miles of sidewalk, 5 miles of tramways, 51 telephones and a complete waterworks and electrical system serving a population of over 1,500. Conscious of its newfound responsibility for the safety of this public, the recently installed city council quickly organized what was to become a highly efficient fire department consisting of two halls: one down the slopes at Fourth Street and St. George's Avenue, and the other up the hill in the 100 block of East Thirteenth Street.

The new council also attended to the matter of policing, appointing Arthur Davies as its first police chief along with a number of constables and a jailer-caretaker. Within six months the memorable Pete Stewart had also been hired, soon rising to the position of sergeant. Assuming the post of chief in 1910, Stewart remained with the force until his retirement in 1932. When he died a decade later, the community united in paying tribute to a man "whose character and sterling qualities were beyond reproach." Many young men had particular reason to remember the chief, having been called into his office for a fatherly chat rather than sent to the cells below.

With emergency services in order, residents and business owners could go about their business with a certain degree of confidence. The city's progress continued

City of North Vancouver

1867   1907

GRAND JOINT

CELEBRAT'N

OF DOMINION DAY AND

Incorporation of the City

The Greatest Demonstration of the Year

MONDAY, JULY 1st

AQUATIC AND FIELD SPORTS

See Full Programme in This Issue

$2,500 in Prizes

G. J. Phillippo,   M. S. McDowell,

July 1, 1907 was a dual celebration in the Ambitious City, marking the 40th Anniversary of Canadian Confederation as well as the incorporation of the City of North Vancouver.

North Vancouver Museum and Archives

North Vancouver City Hall, originally built as the District's Hall in 1903–04, is decked out with red, white and blue in celebration of both Dominion Day and the creation of the city. The Palace Hotel, top right, is similarly decorated.

North Vancouver Museum and Archives, 2844

unabated. By the end of 1907, Andy Wallace could point toward a newly launched tugboat while Captain Cates surveyed his boat repair facility and sawmill nearby. Hotelier Pete Larson, ever on the lookout for an expanded clientele, commenced screening films in his pavilion every winter evening. The Anglican Church had been enlarged, a baseball club had been formed at Moodyville and additional lots had been opened for purchase. Development followed the streetcar lines, with lots in District Lot 550, site of the Grand Boulevard, selling for $600 to $700 each; lots facing Ottawa Gardens commanded a healthy $1,000. Lots in lesser locations continued to be sold for as little as $100. Speculation was greatest around the streetcar lines, Robert Ward & Company having sold 150 lots in District Lot 265 in just one and a half hours in June 1907.

The flood of promotional material continued to flow out of the North Vancouver Land and Improvement Company. According to the company, if location were everything the infant city had no rivals. North Vancouver was "on an almost direct line from Liverpool, through Montreal or New York, to the ports of China." Railways, the promoters continued to maintain, had their eyes on the inlet. Construction of the VW&Y Railway was deemed to be imminent: "As the railway company's charter extension expires on or about the 16th of May, 1910, there need be little doubt that every effort will be made to complete by that date the five miles of road necessary to connect North Vancouver with the railroad systems of the South." The construction of a bridge at the Second Narrows would guarantee success. A

connection with the Grand Trunk Pacific Railway was also claimed to be only a few years away.

Although few questioned the type of city that North Vancouver would become, there were contradictions in the oratory. George Bartley and many others shared John Hendry's dream of a city with a heavily industrialized waterfront: a railway would increase property values and offer a windfall to those who speculated in land. Mayor Kealy had publicly predicted a city with a population numbering in the millions. Yet at the same time, people spoke of the townsite as a city of families and homes—an idyllic garden city suburb with green rolling lawns, productive fruit orchards and flowers in abundance. Theirs would be a peaceful community with crisp, clean air, serving as a gateway to the pristine wilderness that lay beyond. Journalist I.A.R. MacLean captured this vision well:

The thermometer rarely drops to zero, and grass is green the year round. Ocean breezes bring a fresh coolness throughout the long summers, and the seasons are

Firefighters stand ready with horse-drawn equipment outside No. 2. Fire Hall on East Thirteenth Street, near St. George's Avenue. Horses could not easily travel quickly up the city's steeper slopes so the city initially maintained two fire halls. When mechanized transport replaced horse power, the fire department downsized to a single hall, and the No. 2 Hall was renamed No. 1 Fire Hall.

North Vancouver Museum and Archives, 4419

The arrival of the SS Lonsdale at Cates Pier in 1909 was a memorable event: the first ocean-going steamship to dock in the city. The successful berthing proved the harbour could accommodate deep-draught vessels.

North Vancouver Museum and Archives, 287

a continual delight. Her sunny southern slopes coax out trees and flowers and fruits two weeks earlier than they appear on the opposite shore, and the extreme elevation ensures a high standard of health. In front of the city's lawns is spread the shining blue of the Inlet, with ships, big and little, plying up and down, and beyond the peninsula of Vancouver and Stanley Park, the heave and swell of the western ocean . . . North Vancouver [will have] the right to be classed, in days to come, with the beautiful cities of the world.

Those who advocated for an industrial metropolis on the inlet's north shore were undoubtedly pleased when the SS *Lonsdale* berthed at Captain Charles H. Cates' dock in September 1909. The aptly named *Lonsdale* was the first steel ocean-going steamship to berth in the ambitious city and her arrival proved once and for all that the North Vancouver harbour was sufficiently deep to accommodate vessels of considerable size. Owing to the early freezing of the Yukon River, the Klondike-bound ship had been forced to winter in the inlet. City council and the board of trade hosted a "grand banquet" in honour of the officers and the steamship company. It was the sort of occasion with which the community had long since become accustomed. Speaker after speaker, each dressed in formal evening wear, rose to his feet to comment on the significance of the vessel's visit. There was a toast to the king, accolades to the company and comments on the greatness of the British Empire. But in the spirit of the times in North Vancouver, it was the tributes to the foresight, enterprise and confidence of the city's business and political leaders that dominated the rhetoric.

6

BOOM AND BUST
1909–1912

Amid all the civic celebration, there was little mention of the Squamish people who lived just next door. How were they to fit into the new civic order? The Mission Reserve was not part of the city, but the city surrounded it on three sides. George Bartley considered the presence of the reserve to be a hindrance to development: "The fact that Moodyville on the one hand and the Indian village on the other, causes breaks in the continuity of our town, is tending to narrow the ideas of some men as to where our possibilities lie."

Despite the boasts of the Oblates, life on the Mission Reserve was far from idyllic. Many of the Squamish there commuted to jobs as longshoremen on the Vancouver wharves. Some women, such as painter Emily Carr's friend Sophie Frank, wove baskets and peddled them door to door, sometimes accepting old clothes in payment. Poverty and disease were common. The rows of little white crosses in the churchyard testified to high rates of infant and child mortality. The reserve's whitewashed little cottages appeared picturesque from the outside, but their interiors were another matter: overcrowded, sparsely furnished and devastatingly cold in winter. Family life was fractured by children being sent to residential schools. For some, only alcohol seemed to offer any solace. Emily Carr, who first met Sophie Frank in 1907, left a rare account of Squamish life at the time: "Every year Sophie had a new baby. Almost every year she buried one. Her little graves were dotted all over the cemetery. I never knew more than three of her twenty-one children to be alive at one time. By the time she was in her early fifties every child was dead and Sophie had cried her eyes dry. Then she took to drink."

Although some Squamish people found themselves immobilized in the face of cultural change, there were also those who rose above to work for a better future for their people. Chief Snatt had fought for Native rights in the 1860s. Another man, named Sahp-luk, would continue the fight some fifty years later. Born in Squamish in 1850, Sahp-luk came to the inlet as a youth to work in the Moodyville Sawmill. Bishop Paul Durieu was quick to notice Sahp-luk as a natural-born leader, and made him the church-appointed chief of the Capilano Reserve. By the early 1900s, Chief Joe Capilano, as he became known, had become a champion of Native rights, travelling up and down the coast to solicit support for the cause. It was a chance remark in a local newspaper office that catapulted him to international notice, when an editor who was tired of Capilano's litany of complaints suggested he go see the king.

Capilano took the suggestion literally, and on August 29, 1906, departed with chiefs from Cowichan and Bonaparte to seek the sovereign's support. Capilano and his fellow chiefs became the toast of London. Newspaper reporters had a field day, escorting them to each of the major sites. Capilano was largely unimpressed, reserving his energies for his anticipated meeting with the king. Lord Strathcona, who as Donald Smith had helped build the Canadian Pacific Railway, was now Canadian High Commissioner in London and agreed to arrange an audience.

Chief Joe Capilano (fifth from left with robe over arm) and other Native leaders gathered on the North Vancouver ferry wharf prior to embarking for Ottawa to press their claims with Prime Minister Sir Wilfrid Laurier, May 1908. William Nahanee is at the extreme right.
North Vancouver Museum and Archives, 2575

176. - Mission Village. No. Vancouver. B.C.

Mission Reserve and St. Paul's Roman Catholic Church, c. 1912. Growth in the church's congregation had required an expansion of the church in 1911, at which time two towers replaced the smaller, lone tower on the original building.

City of Vancouver Archives, CVA SGN 52

In later years Capilano took considerable delight in recounting what had happened. Having seen Westminster Abbey and the other great buildings of London, Buckingham Palace had little effect on him. Escorted into the royal presence, Capilano received the respect that one chief owed to another:

The great white Chief he big man, the biggest man in the world and he step off platform and come down room to me and take my hand and shake it, and then he lead me to Queen and say we his friends from British Columbia, Queen . . . she very beautiful and so kind she make me feel water in my eyes . . . Then we talk with King and at end he shake my right hand hard and with his left hand pat my left shoulder three times so and say, "Chief we see this matter righted, but it may take a long time, five years perhaps." . . . King, he received me like brother chief and very kind.

Capilano returned to the inlet full of hope, speaking of how the king had promised the reinstatement of First Nations hunting lands. In June 1908, Joe accompanied two dozen other Natives to Ottawa to seek a meeting with the Governor General, vowing they would wait a year if required. In the end, Prime Minister Sir Wilfrid Laurier met with them, agreeing to take up their complaints with the Department of Indian Affairs. Chief Joe Capilano died on March 11, 1910, his "brother chief" King Edward VII only two months later. Both went to their graves amid great pomp and circumstance, the question of Native rights still unresolved.

On the day of Capilano's death the *Express* reported a proposal from the Mission Reserve to exchange land for an extension of Third Street through the reserve for access to city services. Under the terms of their proposal, which replaced earlier demands of $10,000 per acre, the reserve would receive twelve water taps, a fire

The Mission Reserve as seen from its cemetery, before 1910. The proliferation of Latin crosses offered mute testament to the influence of the Oblates of Mary Immaculate in the spiritual life of the Squamish people.
North Vancouver Museum and Archives, 5779

hydrant, three thousand feet of hose, a series of street lights, lighting in the church, a series of sidewalks and a sewer system. The road was built and became a key component in the North Shore's east-west system of arterial streets. Its subsequent widening was a question with which a later generation of Squamish leaders would be forced to wrestle.

Capilano's passing left a tangible void, but within a decade other leaders—such as the Mission Reserve's Andy Paull—rose to take his place. Born in 1892, Paull had attended St. Paul's Residential School in North Vancouver prior to working as a longshoreman. Paull then studied law as an employee of a Vancouver legal firm and worked as an interpreter for the McKenna-McBride Commission, a joint federal-provincial body empowered to study the allocation of reserves in the province. As secretary of the Allied Indian Tribes of British Columbia, Paull helped to organize the hop-pickers of the Fraser Valley and assisted in the formation of an agency to promote and facilitate Native employment. By the late 1920s, at a time when about one-third of all coastal fishermen were Native, he helped to establish the Pacific Coast Native Fishermen's Association. Native politics on the North Shore reflected divisions that existed provincially and nationally during a period of transition for Canadian First Nations. Some, like Paull and Joe Capilano's son Chief Mathias Joe, supported the revival of traditions such as the potlatch. Others, such as Chief Jimmy Harry of the Seymour Reserve and Chiefs Tom, Harry, Charley, Joseph and Edward of the Mission Reserve, called for its demise.

The early twentieth century had seen a major turnover in the North Shore's population, as much of the multiracial society of Moodyville dispersed with the closure of the sawmill. The new European, mostly British, population that made its way across the harbour knew little of the Kanaka, Chilean, Chinese and Squamish people who had once been so familiar in the area. Some saw the Squamish as curious reminders of a bygone age, enjoying the occasional exhibit of native handicrafts or cheering Squamish oarsmen on as they raced against the Sechelt in the annual regatta. Safely out of sight and under the seemingly benevolent watch of the Roman Catholic priests, the Squamish could largely be ignored, despite occasional outbursts from the Joe Capilanos of the world.

Although having an Indian reserve nearby discomfited some, it was the Japanese, Chinese and Sikhs who seemed to pose the greater threat to the European identity of the new city. In Vancouver, working-class discontent with East Asian immigration came to a head on September 7, 1907. A peaceful but largely anti-Asian Labour Day parade ended with a series of anti-Asian speeches. Upon dispersal, an angry mob formed and surged into Chinatown, breaking windows as it went. The crowd then marched into the Japanese quarter, where it was soundly pummelled. MP Robert MacPherson summarized the event by decreeing, "British Columbia is to be a white man's country." Five weeks later, over one hundred North Vancouver residents attended a meeting to found their own Asiatic Exclusion League. Mayor Kealy opened the meeting by observing, "The people of British Columbia are nearest the Orient and we therefore feel it most. There are many sides, but the majority acknowledge that this must be a white man's country." Councillor Jordan asserted "that the time had arrived when the people of British Columbia had to say to the East and also to the Far West that we want no more Oriental labour here."

North Vancouver wanted to profit from trade with Asia, but there was no way that many of its residents would accept Asians in their community. When the ill-fated *Komagata Maru*, a tramp steamer laden with would-be immigrants from the Punjab, anchored in the harbour in 1914, North Vancouver city council passed a motion "protesting against the admission to Canada of Hindus aboard the *Komagata Maru* now in the harbour, and calling upon the government for strict enforcement of the order prohibiting further immigration of labourers at the present time." The

Opposite: The city's Japanese Gardens, located near the intersection of Lonsdale Avenue and Twenty-Third Street, were a community anomaly. The attraction featured a Japanese tea house, stone lanterns, and a 108-foot high observation tower built around an even higher tree.
North Vancouver Museum and Archives,4360

Despite the anti-Asian sentiment prevailing in the early 1900s, affluent West Coast families often engaged Chinese servants. Alfred St. George Hamersley employed Jin, a Chinese cook, shown here serving tea at Langton Lodge.
North Vancouver Museum and Archives, 8762

North Shore Press voiced the opinion of many when it declared:

> The temper of the public in British Columbia is strongly in favour of the total exclusion from Canada of all immigrants who cannot assimilate with the Canadian people and who will not be prepared in due course to renounce their allegiance to the land from which they came in order to become Canadians for all time.

Despite such sentiments, many Asians continued to make their homes in North Vancouver. Sikhs from the Punjab continued to work at the Western Corporation's sawmill near the city's northeast corner. The Sikhs had a largely self-contained community, and other residents were only likely to encounter them as they made their way to and from the ferry landing. The Chinese were more visible, but as their numbers were small, and they filled needed positions in the community, most of the racism they encountered was more often subtle than overt. Wealthy families such as the Hamersleys and Dyers sometimes kept a Chinese cook or gardener, as British servants were impossible to retain given the upward social mobility that life on the West Coast afforded.

Given the racism prevailing at the time, the construction of a Japanese teahouse not far from the Horticultural Hall was no small miracle. Built under the direction of Reverend Goro Kaburagi, publisher of Vancouver's Japanese-language newspaper, the construction of a spiral staircase around a 225-foot-high fir tree on the site was sensational. Constructed by contractor Matt Martinson, the staircase led to a "look-out house" 108 feet above the ground, where visitors could gaze in wonder at the mountains and sea before them.

Chinese fish and produce dealers were a common sight in early North Vancouver as they peddled their wares from house to house. A memorable few established more permanent operations that evolved into the corner stores familiar to generations of North Vancouver residents. Merchant Lim Gong was possibly the most familiar, living in the city for half a century. According to Charlie Cates, Lim arrived penniless and without any knowledge of English. After working for others and opening unsuccessful laundries in Yaletown, New Westminster and at the corner of Third and Mahon, Lim opened a small store on Second. There, Cates recalled, "He was in his element. He was kind to everyone, especially the children. He always had Chinese candies or fruits or delicacies for the children when they came to see him." Evidently prospering, Lim opened a larger store at the corner of Second and Chesterfield. He became a familiar figure as he hauled his hand truck, laden with supplies, up the hill from the ferry. Despite his isolation from a larger Chinese population, Lim retained his affection for ancient Asian customs. Whenever Chinese New Year came, Lim would set up a table weighted down with Asian foods, which he encouraged his customers to sample. Despite his close relationship with many in the neighbourhood, Lim was also the victim of racist remarks and actions. As Cates remembered, he "invariably turned the other cheek and returned good for evil." When he died in 1951, scores of people attended his funeral, taking away an envelope containing a coin and candy "to remove the bitter taste of sorrow."

The world of big business also had its success stories, with a number of financial institutions establishing branches in the city in 1910 and 1911. These

Grocer Lim Gong was a familiar figure in North Vancouver for over half a century. Residents such as Charlie Cates remembered him for his generous and forgiving nature.

City of Vancouver Archives, CVA Bu P. 670 N.553

included the Bank of Hamilton, the Royal Bank and the Bank of Commerce. For North Vancouver residents, having access to a bank in one's own community was not just a convenience, it was a sign of a coming of age. The Bank of Hamilton building was the most impressive of the three, with brick and concrete walls and neo-classical details. Speculator J.C. Keith built his own commercial structure just south of the Bank of Hamilton. Initially named the Keith Block, accounting for the large letter "K" carved above its sandstone entrance, the building was later known as the Aberdeen Block. The initial tenants included the federal post office and the British Columbia Electric Railway Company. Keith also applied his name to another building in 1911: located at the southwest corner of Lonsdale and First his second commercial block provided temporary quarters for the Bank of Hamilton while its own building was still under construction.

With their several floors of rentable office space, new buildings such as these increased opportunities for medical, legal and financial professionals to locate in Lower Lonsdale. They also provided opportunities for employment for existing residents, making the area less of a bedroom community and more of a self-contained city. The establishment of several new industries contributed to the city's internal cohesion. Following a fire in his Vancouver shipyard in May 1910, Andy Wallace decided to close the facility and consolidate his shipbuilding enterprises at the foot

East side of Lonsdale Avenue between Esplanade and First, c. 1913. The now benched First Street is clearly visible above the Bank of Hamilton and the Aberdeen Block.

North Vancouver Museum and Archives, 3964

of Lonsdale Avenue. In 1911, McDougall-Jenkins Engineering Works absorbed the Albion Iron Works to become North Shore Iron Works, an enterprise that located at the foot of St. Patrick's Avenue. Purchased from its founders by Francis Carter-Cotton, the publisher of the *Vancouver News-Advertiser*, the firm described itself as "shipbuilders, boilermakers, iron and brass founders, and general engineers." By 1912, the company was a major employer with a staff of several dozen men.

But the North Vancouver business life was not without tragedy. Despite its prominent and powerful role only a couple years earlier, the Western Corporation collapsed and went into receivership in October 1909. Its timber operation was renewed as the Seymour Lumber Company, but in May 1912 its sawmill and a portion of its timber lots burned down. The company folded and 120 workers found themselves unemployed.

Council, meanwhile, was forced to address challenges that accompanied the city's rapid growth. Commercial activity had more or less emerged along Lonsdale Avenue or near the waterfront, but as time wore on it began to follow the residential growth steadily climbing the North Shore's lower slopes. Council was confronted by the question of how to establish grades for the city's evolving road network. The issue was complex, but largely centred on the determinations of whether east-west streets should be benched (levelled) to provide a flat bed for future streetcar routes, and what constituted a safe grade for streetcars running up and down the city's

north-south streets. Given the technical nature of the matter, council commissioned a written report from a committee that included its engineer George S. Hanes and city engineers from Vancouver and Seattle.

After receiving the engineers' report, council elected not to accept it. In the days that followed, the unlikely subject of road grades became the most heated topic in the new city's short history. George Morden reported how "knots of ratepayers were engaged at every street corner discussing the popular subject of grades . . . The gesticulating manifested evidenced the burning nature of the grades question." A petition circulated deploring council's "breach of faith" and demanding the resignation of "the entire board of aldermen." In the face of controversy, council relented and adopted engineer Hanes' vision for a series of benched streets. The city's engineer was just as fastidious in his work on its water supply system. Gerry Brewer, city manager from 1987 to 1993, reflected on Hanes' "genius" in ensuring the city had multiple sources of water, and the backup plan of a tunnel to the artificial water body Rice Lake: "They protected the city from ever running out of water." The fire department was also considerably bolstered, boasting some 4,700 feet of hose and 222 fire hydrants by the end of 1912. Three years later, the department's staff transformed a battered motorized taxi from the Cariboo into the city's first fire truck.

Builders at the time were grateful that the issues of grades, water supply and

Lower Lonsdale c. 1910. Three years after its incorporation, the city's business core boasted elegant street lights, paved sidewalks, and a sophisticated streetcar system. An abundance of real estate offices such as Eve and Lawson's (note the large rooftop sign on the left) drove a boom in land sales that has not been equalled since.
City of Vancouver Archives, CVA Out P82

fire protection were being addressed. The growth of the city's waterfront industries had created a demand for additional housing. Modest apartment blocks began to rise in the Lower Lonsdale area. Two- and three-storey apartment blocks such as the Harbour Manor and the Mount Crown Block were typical of the new buildings, many of their suites accommodating single men. Families, however, generally strove for something more. With an abundance of relatively inexpensive land and well-paying employment opportunities, thousands were able to take out mortgages to buy or build single-family homes.

H.J. Haslett offered property "in all districts of North Vancouver," vowing, "A great Transcontinental Railroad is on the eve of building into North Vancouver. This is a sweeping statement to make, but nevertheless it will be proved up to the hilt, and with greater celerity than the average man anticipates." The British-American Trust Company lauded its North Vancouver properties as the only location for "the Ideal Home." Its aptly named View Avenue lots were bound to rise in value, given that "construction will start on the Burrard Inlet Bridge and Tunnel Company's scheme immediately." Promoters' audacity knew no bounds. Dozens of bird's-eye views and maps were published, often showing forests not yet felled, buildings not yet built, railways not yet constructed, and bridges that were more fantasy than fact. Views were distorted and perspectives foreshortened. Tracts of wilderness located miles from civilization were drawn as if they were the centres of the known world. The messages were clear: "buy here, buy now, and buy from me."

Indicative of the times, an amateur theatrical group called "the Queeries" satirized "all the pioneering problems of the north shore: the ferries, the tramcars, the telephone system," and "the black bears that came down from Grouse Mountain during the night and nosed off the lids of our garbage cans," but reserved its greatest scorn for the real estate boom. The Queeries invented a character named "Lottie" and sang about her varied forays into land speculation:

Now Lottie has lots and lots of lots,
In lots and lots of likely spots;
In Cedar Cottage she's two for sale,
And in Lulu Island and Kerrisdale;
In Fairview, Burnaby, Shaughnessy Heights,
And in Kitsilano, she now has sites;
In Newport, Hollyburn, English Bay,
And in North Vancouver and Point Grey . . .

Some in the real estate business were men of integrity, J.P. Fell and Edward Mahon being among them. Mahon once reassured his son that it was possible to be in real estate *and* remain honest. At Mahon's funeral in 1937, his son was assured by one of his father's business rivals that Mahon was the most ethical man he had ever met. There were others, however, who were far less scrupulous, their exaggerated promises forcing prices higher and higher while increasing the debt loads of the unfortunates who believed them. Some questioned the sustainability of the pre-war boom. In October 1910, the newly founded *Lonsdale Spectator* advised that the boom may have slowed:

Real estate in North Vancouver during the past month has been very quiet. We gather this from the fact that all the dealers report that business is picking up. When a real estate man tells you that things are improving, you may know that there is lots of room for improvement.

The *Spectator* also recognized the dangers of speculation, advising its readers, "A repetition of the boom is not desired by local dealers, and a quiet, steady return to normal conditions will be welcomed." The paper went on to attribute much of the speculation to real estate agents and investors on the southern side of the inlet: "Many small lots far out have been thrown on the market by hard-up owners, but it is satisfactory to note that most, if not all, of these are in tracts marketed by wild-cat subdividers in Vancouver." The paper was not far wrong. By 1912 upward of thirty real estate firms were promoting property on the North Shore, and many were based in Vancouver.

One of the more impressive buildings to be built in the pre-war boom was the St. Alice Hotel. Built for Antonio Gallia in 1911–12, the St. Alice was a five-storey brick-faced structure on West Second. The building's height and design were so distinctive that it became a point of navigation for sailors. It also appears to have attracted an eclectic clientele, ranging from travelling salesmen to professionals and cabinet ministers. A Scottish woman who styled herself as Lady Elizabeth Campbell was prominent among the guests. Campbell often puzzled the staff with admonishments and instructions to maids and others such as, "You washed all the spirit out of that dress!" or, "I am going to take a bath and I will sing, but the minute I stop singing, come in!" On another occasion, she wandered about the hotel wearing nothing but a "dress" fashioned from her bedroom's lace curtains, only to be ushered back upstairs by the owner's wife.

Miss Mina Dawson established North Vancouver's first public hospital with her sisters Jennie and Margaret in 1908. The hospital initially accommodated up to six patients and was located in a house on Fifteenth Street near St. Andrew's Avenue, not far from today's Lions Gate Hospital.

North Vancouver Museum and Archives 5549

Some in the ambitious city were no doubt impressed by the lists of prominent hotel visitors, eccentric or not, that were dutifully published in the local press. But there were more significant signs that the city was beginning to mature. Steel letterboxes were installed in key locations throughout the city with home delivery of mail being established about the same time. In 1913, the former district hall was renovated to accommodate a relocated post office. Recognizing the need to ensure public health, the city and the district contracted with three sisters—Mina and Jennie Dawson and the widowed Mrs. Stevenson—for the provision of hospital services. Their new six-bed facility, located in a house on Fifteenth near St. Andrew's Avenue, opened in 1908 with a monthly subsidy of $25 from the two municipalities. Additional revenues were generated through fees paid by patients.

With physical health attended to, residents of the city turned their attention to matters of a spiritual nature. In 1909–10 the Oblates added twin towers and transepts to the church at the Mission Reserve to accommodate a growing Squamish population. At the turn of the century, the Roman Catholic population of the townsite remained small, largely confined to the Chilean squatters who lived along the foreshore. But by 1910 the non-Native Roman Catholic population had grown enough to warrant the construction of a church, St. Edmund's. The Oblates also built a Roman Catholic school for non-Natives adjacent to the church in 1911, and a rectory in 1913. All three facilities stood near Mission Reserve, enabling the

Oblate priests to conveniently serve both communities.

The Protestants were also active. The city's first Methodist church had opened in 1907 only to be replaced by a more commodious structure in 1910. A second Anglican church, dedicated to St. Agnes, opened in the city's east end that same year, an architectural testimony to a growing population of immigrants from England. Although the Presbyterian mission to the settlement at Moodyville had ended three years earlier, an impressive new church complete with tower, spire and mullioned windows opened in the city in 1912. Located on the northeast corner of St. George's Avenue and East Tenth, the church's first service was apparently in Gaelic.

Given its proliferating churches, few doubted that North Vancouver was destined to remain a predominantly Christian city. Churchgoing was commonplace and Sunday was generally regarded as a day of rest. The federal Lord's Day Act ensured Christian behaviour on what was a day sacred to a majority, but by no means all, of the British Columbian population. Working on the Sabbath was frowned upon, and Sunday shopping was quite illegal. The idea of holding professional sports matches on Sundays had been floated as early as 1903, but opposition from district council and property owners had stopped the proposition dead in its tracks. The proposal re-emerged in July 1907, but it too died a quick death. As the *Vancouver Daily World* reported:

> There will be no Sunday baseball in North Vancouver. When queried regarding the announcement that the directors of [Vancouver's] Recreation Park would make an effort to play their Sunday games at North Vancouver, [Mayor Arnold] Kealy was somewhat wroth. "What do they take us for? Do they think that North Vancouver is to be made a dumping ground for what Vancouver will not stand for? First it was prize-fighting and gambling and now it is Sunday baseball. There will be no Sunday baseball in North Vancouver. You can rest assured of that."

Despite the city's opposition, one promoter, A.J. Picton-Warlow, decided to take his chances. Sub-leasing the North Vancouver Athletic Association's Recreation Park, Picton-Warlow organized a baseball game guaranteed to overflow the stands. The match, between the Vancouver Beavers and Washington State's Aberdeen Black Cats, was scheduled for Sunday, May 2, 1909. The ferries and the trams did a roaring trade, with thousands of spectators crossing the inlet to view the forbidden event. Years later, BC Electric traffic inspector Bert Hughes recalled how the streetcar system was taxed beyond capacity: "The crowds were so large that we had 'em riding on the sides and roof of the cars. They were hanging onto everything but the trolley pole and we aren't sure they didn't do that too."

Those not fortunate enough to secure a place on the trams trudged the two miles from the ferry landing to Recreation Park on foot. Once settled in their seats, the crowd received a warning that the game was unlawful and that all in attendance were liable to a fine of forty dollars. The crowd—estimated at between 3,500 and 4,000 and thus larger than the entire population of the city—greeted the warning with what was described as "a derisive shout." The game went on and after one hour and forty minutes of play the Vancouver team was victorious.

Religious conservatives were outraged. Council met the following day, the

Vancouver Province describing their proceedings as "the most disorderly yet held in North Vancouver." Newspapers on both sides of the inlet were flooded with letters to the editor. Churches and other local organizations held meetings and passed resolutions denouncing the offence. Few doubted that the law had been broken, but a courageous few felt the law was too restrictive. City alderman Samuel Schultz had a unique perspective: as a Jew, he considered Saturday rather than Sunday to be the Sabbath, so no wrongdoing had occurred. But once again, the views of the Christian majority prevailed. Picton-Warlow pled guilty and Magistrate Arnold Kealy imposed a five-dollar fine.

Thankfully, the politicians of the day weren't too caught up in a baseball game to pursue more important opportunities for the city. When the province established a commission to search for a permanent site for the University of British Columbia, North Vancouver City and District took up the challenge and established a committee to develop a brief. The committee identified two potential sites: one to the west of the Capilano River, the other to the east of the Seymour River. The committee also suggested that the four Indian reserves might soon come on the market, and that one of these might serve the university equally well. Indeed, the committee was of the opinion that the commissioners could choose any site they wanted, and the two municipalities would do anything necessary to acquire it.

When the site commissioners visited the city in June 1910, the committee touched on all the possibilities and lauded the North Shore's numerous advantages. Speaking on behalf of the district, Reeve McNaught openly mused on the university concept as "not merely a matter of buildings and courses of study, but its real object was to make manly men who would be of the greatest possible value to the state." In the end it was all for naught; the commissioners recommended a site at Point Grey to the province. Once again North Vancouver had to sit on the sidelines while Vancouver basked in the glow of another victory.

Even without a university, by 1910 North Vancouver had possessed or was in pursuit of many of the attributes of a successful British city. What seemed to be lacking to some was a military presence, to assist in the defence of the empire and help create the leaders of tomorrow. That uniformed young men and a resident brass band would add distinction to community events was an incidental bonus. Two men—Alexander Philip and Donald Cameron—both of whom had military experience dating from their British youth, took the first step in the summer of 1910 when they petitioned for a militia unit to be located on the North Shore. A public meeting on the subject was held, and a decision was made to request authority to raise a company of field engineers. The petition proved successful, and the first enrolment, of thirty men, took place in May 1912, with Major J.P. Fell as officer commanding.

The timing was perfect. Designated the Sixth Field Company of Canadian Engineers, the unit was sufficiently well organized to provide an honour guard just four months later for the visit of the Governor General, the Duke of Connaught. In 1913, the engineers saw their first active service. Nanaimo-area miners were in the midst of a strike and the Sixth Field Company was among the militia units called out to maintain the peace. Coming from a community in which trade unions were conspicuous by their absence, the unit's men reportedly had little sympathy for

North Vancouver's pre-war boom years resulted in the construction of several imposing churches to serve a growing population of both renters and homeowners. Photographed shortly after 1912, St. Andrew's Presbyterian Church (now St. Andrew's United) still stands on the corner of East Tenth Street and St. George's Avenue.

North Vancouver Museum and Archives 11422

The Sixth Field Company's band was one of the few musical ensembles in North Vancouver during the city's early years. The band performed at community and military functions and was photographed practising in Mahon Park in March 1918.

North Vancouver Museum and Archives 9441

the strikers. The development of the North Shore's Scouting movement paralleled that of the Sixth Field Company. Both were organized in 1910–11 and both traced their origins to British military traditions. Two troops of Scouts appear to have been organized in the city prior to the First World War: one in Upper Lonsdale that met at Lonsdale School, and one in Lower Lonsdale that met at Chesterfield School. In 1911 local Boy Scouts hosted a visit by the esteemed Major-General Baden-Powell, founder of the Scouting movement.

Ethnic and fraternal organizations also developed in the city. The now obscure Ambition Lodge of the Good Templars was in operation as early as 1907, its twice-monthly gatherings featuring not only business meetings but basket socials and "ladies' nail-driving contests" as well. NorWest Aerie No. 1794 of the Fraternal Order of Eagles—"a fraternity of the common man"—acquired its charter that same year. The Knights of Pythias, an order dedicated to the cause of peace, built a facility of their own on Fourth at Chesterfield in 1908. The St. Andrew's and Caledonian Society, organized in 1909, became increasingly active in the community, serving the city's large Scottish population. In 1910 a Masonic lodge was re-established on the North Shore when a new branch of the organization (Burrard Lodge No. 50) was formed and a new temple was built to house it. Located on Lonsdale Avenue between Tenth and Eleventh, the new temple was one of the first non-residential buildings in the Central Lonsdale Area.

The pre-war years also witnessed the growth of the Sons of England Benefit Society, a fraternal organization whose membership reflected the large English population that had come to the area. Not to be outdone, the city's Irish population organized a branch of the Ancient Order of Hibernians. A local branch of the Loyal Orange Lodge was founded to safeguard the Protestant faith, promote the English language and uphold the nation's constitutional monarchy.

Gathering of members of Loyal Orange Lodge No. 1840 in North Vancouver, July 12, 1908. The lodge was one of a number of race- and religion-based organizations that flourished in North Vancouver in the early 1900s.

North Vancouver Museum and Archives, P3

Residents with artistic and intellectual interests were also taken care of. The North Vancouver City Band enlivened many a community event, its musical prowess and tailored uniforms causing the Vancouver dailies to mistake them for "the splendid band of the Royal Marines." In September 1909, Mayor Arnold Kealy presided at the inaugural meeting of the North Vancouver Operatic Society in the parlours of the North Vancouver Piano Company and School of Music. Not long afterward, the North Shore Literary and Debating Society began to offer its members a monthly regimen of lectures and debates. The tone was civilized and the discussions surprising liberal. A debate between a Miss Peers and a Mr. Boult in November 1913 resulted in the audience voting by a margin of two to one in favour of granting the franchise to women. Even non-Europeans were greeted with civility; when Reverend Goro Kaburagi spoke to the group on the subject of Japanese immigration, members readily agreed to have him back to talk again.

The education of the community's youth was also a major concern for the city. As young families streamed into the community, the City of North Vancouver School District, founded at the same time as the city, focussed its attention on the development of schools. Overcrowding at Central School (Chesterfield and Fourth) necessitated new facilities. Lonsdale School, an impressive new wood-frame structure near Twenty-second and Lonsdale in the city's north end, opened in April 1911. In the spring of 1912 the school district opened Ridgeway School, a

The impressive Second Renaissance Revival style Ridgeway School, shortly after its construction in 1912.

North Vancouver Museum and Archives, 6762

brick and sandstone structure built in the Second Renaissance Revival style. With
its grand entrance columns, decorative porticoes and soaring cupola, Ridgeway
School was the equal of similar buildings erected on the south side of the inlet. In
June 1914, tenders were opened for a new Central School, ultimately to be named
Queen Mary. Like Ridgeway, Queen Mary was an architectural wonder, its three-
storey brick-and-stone facade, Palladian details and central cupola a fitting tribute
to the king's consort.

New private institutions included the Lynn College for Boys, also known
as Wykeham School, which took up quarters in a spacious mansion in Ottawa
Gardens in 1913. Misses O.M. Butler and V.G. Gradwell had opened their North
Vancouver School for Girls at the corner of Lonsdale and Seventeenth in 1909. The
school's promotional materials promised prospective students "special attention
to morals, conduct, and discipline." In 1914 Miss Melville Green re-established the
school in the mansion vacated by the failed Lynn College for Boys, and six years
later the school relocated to the North Lonsdale home of the late Judge Schultz.
Under the principalship of Miss Ella Philip, the school offered its students a full
range of studies, singling out music, painting and dancing as subjects appropriate
for residents' daughters. Another school, which had appropriated the Chesterfield
name, became known as Vancouver Residential Schools in 1914.

Two new private schools—Kingsley and North Shore College—opened just
outside the city in North Lonsdale shortly after the First World War. Lacking the
depth of history of a Rugby or a Winchester, these newly created schools were
quick to establish traditions of their own such as coats of arms, striped school
ties and the "old school song." Located in the Bank of Hamilton Building, B.C.
Hilliam's Conservatory of Music offered additional opportunities for tuition: in
pianoforte, voice and composition. The enterprise was a springboard for Hilliam,
who later achieved fleeting fame as a lyricist, composer and musical director on
Broadway, and later as part of the musical comedy team of *Flotsam and Jetsam* on
BBC Radio.

By early 1911, the city even had its own gentlemen's club. Located on Lonsdale
Avenue just north of Esplanade, the North Vancouver Club aimed to rival similar
organizations on the south shore, offering its members the chance to sit and read
English illustrated magazines as they puffed on their cigars. The club's premises
included a billiard room, a reading room, a silence room, a strangers room, a card
room and a bar. The decor was impressive, featuring traditional wooden panelling,
heavy carpets, a large fireplace and a stained glass skylight. Those seeking more
modest diversions could visit the newly opened Gem Theatre to watch a silent film.
With developments such as these, *Lonsdale Spectator* editor Jack Loutet and his
associates were increasingly content: "With the club and a show to go to in the
evenings, North Vancouver is a much more attractive place for a home seeker than
it was a short time ago."

As 1911 drew to a close, the tiny Gem Theatre receded in importance when the
much larger Lonsdale Theatre opened up the hill. Residents could now take pride
in a vaudeville house that rivalled the best of the theatres across the inlet. Erected
on the west side of Lonsdale Avenue between Fifteenth and Sixteenth, the Lonsdale
was an opulent structure with orchestra, balcony and box seating. Its opening

ceremony was both a civic and imperial occasion, featuring the raising of the Union Jack on the theatre's rooftop by Mayor William McNeish.

Although the young city's political and professional leaders could frequent the North Vancouver Club, those who still owned the majority of the townsite participated in an entirely different set of organizations located across the inlet. Men such as Mahon, Fell, McFarland and Keith lived not on the North Shore but in Vancouver. Most had offices in what was then the downtown core—on Hastings or Cordova Streets—maintained memberships in Vancouver's own gentlemen's clubs, and lived either in the West End or in Shaughnessy.

None of the land companies ever succeeded in their attempts to create elite residential areas to rival Shaughnessy. The Grand Boulevard failed to attract the well-healed clientele its promoters had hoped for. Although a dozen or so wealthier families built in the area, many lots remained unsold or undeveloped for decades to come. Despite ex-trooper T.S. Nye's efforts to develop District Lot 2026 as "the acme of high-class residential sections," and even build his own twenty-three-room mansion as an example, the results of his "North Lonsdale" development were mixed at best. Instead, this area lying just outside the city's boundaries, near the end of the Lonsdale Avenue streetcar line, became home to a mixture of white-collar

Lonsdale Theatre opening night, December 11, 1911. With its two-tiered balcony and elegant plaster decoration, North Vancouver's new theatre rivalled many of the vaudeville houses then being built elsewhere in the province.
North Vancouver Museum and Archives, 1471

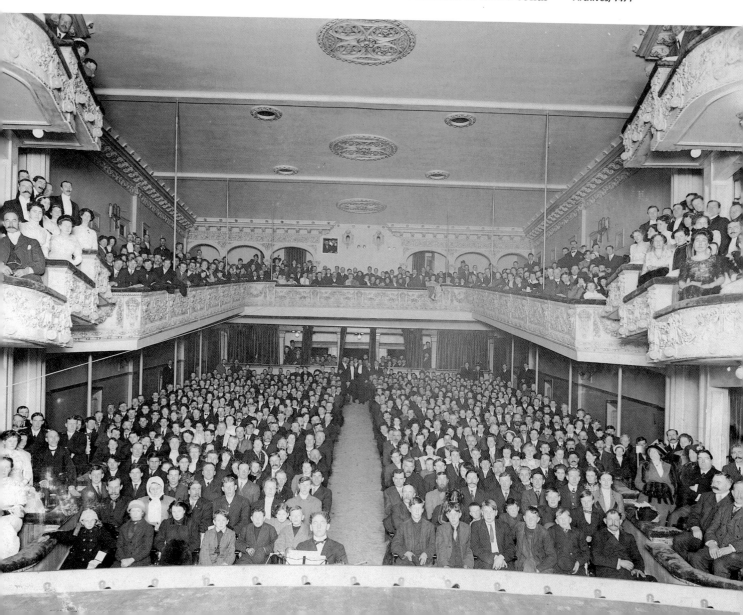

workers and English eccentrics such as the Monteiths, who lived in a "thatched cottage" where they eked out a living raising goats and bees.

By 1910, even the most optimistic North Vancouverite had given up on John Hendry's railway dream, hope instead shifting to the recently revived Burrard Inlet Tunnel and Bridge Company. Once again, entrepreneur J.C. Keith was at the table, seated with fellow directors D.W. McLean, Lambert Bond and J.Y. McNaught, reeve of the district. When the company was formally reconstituted early in 1910, Edward Mahon joined the board and was subsequently elected president. A meeting of ratepayers, from both the city and the district, was held at Larson's Pavilion in July 1910 to discuss the project in detail. By this time J.P. Fell and timber baron James A. McNair had also joined the board. Representatives of the company outlined the history and plan for the bridge project and requested municipal support through the purchase of stock in the company. The district was requested to purchase $250,000 worth of stock, and the city $100,000. A referendum in the city approved the investment by an overwhelming majority, 279 to 3.

In November 1910, it was announced that the bridge and railway would be constructed the following year "without let or hindrance." Confidence in the project was so high that district ratepayers presented Reeve McNaught with a gold watch "as a token of appreciation . . . for his efforts in promoting the bridge." Yet some were beginning to view the project with suspicion, wondering if taxpayers were subsidizing an initiative that would primarily benefit the large land companies. Advertisements began to appear in the *Vancouver World*:

> *Bridge bylaws, Turn Them Down!*
> *They are the schemes of interested property owners.*
> *They mean the useless expenditure of public monies*
> *and $50,000 extra taxation yearly!*
> *They are not needed for some years to come.*
> *GRAFT! THINK, MR. VOTER!! BEWARE!!*

The invective appears to have had little impact. By mid-1912 the City of Vancouver had invested $200,000 in the company's stock, a consulting engineer had been hired and the federal government had pledged a grant of $350,000. Sir Richard McBride's provincial government announced its support of the project early the following year. But controversy continued to pursue the initiative. In an apparent effort to maintain public trust, the company's board was again reorganized, the representatives of the land companies being replaced by councillors from either side of the inlet.

Progress was slow. As if on cue, the Canadian Pacific Railway developed a proposal of its own to bridge the inlet. Its plans called for a bridge across the North Arm and an extension of its tracks from Port Moody through Roche Point to North Vancouver. North Vancouver embraced the plans with caution, fearing too much of the harbour front might be acquired by the railway and the monopoly the company enjoyed on the south shore might be repeated on the north. In any event, with assistance from the Tunnel and Bridge Company, the North Shore municipalities hatched plans of their own.

The Tunnel and Bridge Company issued shares to John Hendry in return for his charter to build a crossing at the Second Narrows. Once knowledge of the deal became public, hopes renewed and speculation in lands close to the projected bridge began in earnest. Public optimism about the project was no doubt fed by the fact that J.C. Keith's Howe Sound and Northern Railway had recently completed a short railway line from the head of Howe Sound into the Cheakamus River Valley. Though it was only eleven miles long, it was eleven miles longer than Hendry's aborted project and had the potential to connect Lillooet with the North Shore.

Also of significance, it appeared that Keith's little railway was about to be taken over by the larger, provincially chartered Pacific Great Eastern Railway (PGE). Incorporated on February 27, 1912, the PGE was largely funded by British interests and intended to connect Prince George with North Vancouver, with additional lines extending to New Westminster and Vancouver. The railway's very name inspired confidence, evoking images of Britain's long-established and respected Great Eastern Railway. With the PGE's southern terminus in North Vancouver, a planned connection with the Grand Trunk Pacific Railway at Fort George would ultimately link Burrard Inlet with the resource-rich northern interior, the developing port of Prince Rupert, and the growing cities of the prairies. Bridges and railways had once again come to the fore and it seemed once again that North Vancouver had genuine cause for optimism.

7 AMBITION POSTPONED 1913–1919

Residents of North Vancouver looked at 1913 with confidence, believing that both a railway and a bridge across the Second Narrows were about to become realities. All eyes were on the waterfront. Vancouver Member of Parliament H.H. Stevens had recently persuaded the federal government to establish the Vancouver Harbour Commission. Enabling legislation was passed on May 16, 1913, granting the new commission extensive powers to regulate and control navigation, works and operations within the port. The commission was also mandated to oversee "the proper development and administration of the port," and licensed "to impose rates, fees, and dues for revenue purposes." One of its three charter members was Francis Carter-Cotton, a man with considerable experience in North Shore business and political life. With Carter-Cotton at the helm, North Shore ambition stirred once again.

The city's optimism was only natural. Across the inlet the CPR had established a highly successful trade with Asia, its famous trio of white *Empresses* plying the North Pacific laden with passengers and freight. Other steamship companies jostled to join in the burgeoning trade, but in the absence of a bridge and railway to the North Shore, all had chosen to locate in Vancouver. Nevertheless, with construction of the Panama Canal well under way, many North Vancouver residents saw only potential. The real estate slowdown many had predicted began in 1912. By the summer of 1913 the western world was in the depths of an economic depression the likes of which had not been seen since the early 1890s.

Despite the economic downturn, residents put on a brave face. Some even continued to fan the flames of civic ambition. In February 1913, Harry Bridgman, president of the North Vancouver Board of Trade and employee of the Lonsdale Estate, suggested that the infant city extend its borders to encompass much of the district municipality from which it had seceded a mere six years earlier. Had the idea been approved, the city would have expanded its boundaries west to the Capilano River, east to the Seymour River or Lynn Creek, and up the mountainside as far as the district's northern extremity. New cities would have been created from what remained: one in West Vancouver (West Vancouver had been incorporated as a district municipality in 1912, it too having been carved out of the District of North Vancouver), and the other comprising an area along the North Arm of Burrard Inlet. Although Bridgman's proposal was endorsed by the board of trade, it died an early death—in no small measure due to the worsening economic situation.

For some citizens the only hope left was railway construction. The local paper was full of stories about rights-of-way and bridges. The federal Board of Railway Commissioners had granted the CPR a right-of-way from the North Arm of Burrard Inlet through the district and west as far as Hendry Avenue, where it appeared that the new line would connect with the PGE. The CPR had one year in which to begin construction, or the right-of-way would be forfeited. In July 1913, the local press reported that the PGE had begun construction of its North Shore line and that J.P.

Opening ceremonies of the PGE's North Shore Line (in West Vancouver), January 1, 1914.

North Vancouver Museum and Archives, P11

Fell had sold a half-mile of foreshore to the railway for port and industrial purposes. *North Shore Press* editor George Morden was nothing short of ecstatic:

> *The event is so 'big with possibilities' and so replete with certainties as to benefits to follow that the mind hesitates to depict what it really means to the North Shore . . . The markets of the world will be made available to the twenty miles of magnificent waterfront which is the chiefest asset of the North Shore.*

Under a new name, new editor and new investors, the *North Shore Press* carried on in the tradition of George Bartley, relentlessly promoting the potential of the North Shore. The owners' motives, however, were not entirely altruistic. As Morden disclosed some years later, "Several shareholders in North Shore Press Limited originally invested in the business for the reason that they had large holdings of property on the North Shore and considered part ownership in a newspaper published locally as a desirable means of serving their property interests."

By early August, demolition began on what remained of the old Moodyville Sawmill to accommodate construction of the PGE. Furthermore, the railway had secured rights-of-way through both the Mission and Capilano reserves. The Squamish people had requested fair market value—estimated at $100,000—for these lands and were instead offered only $6,000. In the end, the demands of the Squamish were overruled by the federal government. To add insult to injury,

November 12, 1913—A crowd gathers at the foot of Chesterfield Avenue to witness the arrival of the first PGE railway engine in North Vancouver.

North Vancouver Museum and Archives, 6901

the government granted the railway a four-hundred-foot wide strip of land on the Capilano Reserve on which to build a station.

Real estate agent A.S. Billings had recently returned from a visit to the province's northern interior, all but proclaiming it the Promised Land. North Vancouver, he advised, was finally on the threshold of greatness. Before the year was out a small railway station stood near the foot of Lonsdale Avenue and construction of the railway line—from North Vancouver to Dundarave—was all but complete. Six months later the line reached Whytecliff, but the planned extension to Squamish was nowhere in sight. The prospect of a bridge across the inlet was fading with every passing month. While the line from Squamish into the interior reached Clinton in 1916, the interior line failed to connect with the North Shore Division. The PGE collapsed in 1918 and and was acquired by the province. A subsequent investigation by a legislative committee revealed appalling financial irregularities. According to the committee, the railway's principals and contractors had lined their own pockets with public funds while providing kickbacks to the coffers of the provincial Conservative Party. Provincial railways minister John Oliver reflected the public's anger, vowing to make "British Columbia a very unsatisfactory place of residence for scoundrels who make a livelihood and become millionaires at the expense of the common people."

In time the PGE became a provincial joke, its initials suggesting insults ranging from "Please Go Easy" and "Prince George Eventually" to "Past God's Endurance." A writer for the *Toronto Globe* was even less charitable, dubbing the railway "the big white elephant of the coast . . . a railway without a beginning or an end." For North Vancouver, the experience with the railway had been a major disappointment. Its construction had been of little direct benefit to city residents, with the bulk of its workforce and supplies having come from the other side of the inlet. The North Shore Division was resurrected when the province took over the railway, but the line never paid its own way, serving more as a tourist line than anything else. The line was closed in 1928 in the face of continuing annual deficits. The ambitious city became a little less ambitious.

Although a transcontinental railway had yet to reach the city, North Vancouver's residents could turn their hopes elsewhere. In 1914 plans were unveiled for a massive industrial plant costing up to $6 million—in those days an astounding sum. The Dominion Shipbuilding, Engineering, and Drydock Company secured rights to property west of Lynn Creek near the old Moodyville Sawmill site. The company's plans called for a dry dock capable of servicing any vessel then afloat. Its graving dock was to be a thousand feet long and one hundred feet wide at its gates, while its cranes were to be capable of lifting one hundred tons. Up to seven thousand workers would be employed on the site, a number only slightly less than the total population then living on the entire North Shore.

In June 1914 the company's officials, the mayor and council, and over five hundred spectators gathered at the property for a sod-turning ceremony. The atmosphere was electric as speaker after speaker lauded the virtues of the project. Mr. A. Frey, the company's fiscal agent, reassured the crowd that the company had the best of intentions: "We are not asking any favours; we have got the money and are going to have a shipbuilding plant in one of the greatest cities of the American

James Pemberton Fell, British Columbia representative of the Lonsdale Estate, in the uniform of an officer of the Canadian Engineers. Fell helped organize the city's Sixth Field Company of Canadian Engineers and distinguished himself on active service during the First World War.

Courtesy Michael Fell

continent . . . we want you to forget being skeptical and boost and assist us. It makes no difference to you, so long as our intentions are good and we are spending money." It was too good to be true. After some initial work on the site in the fall of 1914, the project was abandoned, its promoters having failed to attract the federal subsidy required to make it feasible. The silver spade acting mayor George W. Vance had used to turn the sod was consigned to a dusty shelf, the home of so many other broken promises and shattered dreams.

Residents took comfort by focussing on the city's progress in other areas, such as athletics, the arts, education and surprisingly, waterworks. But it was in organized sports that city residents found their greatest comfort. The North Vancouver field hockey team won the Mainland League's championship in 1914 just as it had every year since its establishment in 1911. The city's Caledonian soccer club also brought laurels to the North Shore when it captured the Mainland Amateur Football Association's trophy in May 1914. The city's infrastructure continued to undergo improvements. By mid-1914, voters in both the city and the district had approved the purchase of District Lots 856 and 857, the site of what was to become the Rice Lake Reservoir. Other large initiatives were also contemplated, not the least of which was the extension of the city's boundaries to include District Lot 272, a key piece of waterfront land just east of what had formerly been the Moodyville Sawmill.

Despite such developments, the economy failed to recover and the storm clouds continued to form. The construction of the long-awaited span at the Second

Men of the Sixth Field Company train at Larson's pavilion, 1914.

North Vancouver Museum and Archives, 2507

Narrows seemed all but certain in 1914 when Sir John Wolfe-Barry's $2,225,000 design, favoured by the Burrard Inlet Tunnel and Bridge Company, went to tender—the company having rejected a $1,500,000 bascule-style proposal endorsed by the premier. The Canadian Bridge Company won the bidding, but delays occurred and the project ground to a halt with the onslaught of troubles overseas.

In early August the British Empire was at war. There was no question about where Canada would stand, Sir Wilfrid Laurier once having summed up the feelings of the nation, "When Great Britain is at war, Canada is at war!" Like Canadians from coast to coast, North Vancouverites rallied to do their bit. The formation of the Sixth Field Company of Canadian Engineers appeared to have come at an opportune time. Construction of its vast, brick armoury adjacent to Mahon Park had already been tendered. A cadet corps had been organized the year before. Open to boys aged twelve to eighteen years, the unit was intended to provide instruction in field engineering, infantry drill, musketry and other military skills.

The Sixth Field Company was quick to mobilize its existing members, and started recruiting others within days of the start of hostilities. The North Vancouver Civilian Rifle Association rushed its rifle range to completion, and with assistance from the Sixth Field Company prepared the formation of a home guard to augment the militia. A War Relief Committee was struck to assist families who had lost their principal wage-earner to the forces. The committee acknowledged that the war might not be "over by Christmas," as so many had prophesied: "Relief throughout the winter, and perhaps for a whole year, may prove humanely necessary." The

Men of the Sixth Field Company camp and train in trench warfare at the company's drill hall on Mahon Avenue, 1916. The neatly constructed demonstration trenches built in North Vancouver bore little resemblance to the cold, wet and rat-infested trenches that recruits would experience on reaching the Western Front.

North Vancouver Museum and Archives, 9474

first contingent of Canadian Engineers left the city on August 25, 1914, under the command of Major J.P. Fell. Friends, family and elected officials gathered at the ferry wharf to see the contingent off, as district reeve William May urged the volunteers "to win glory and victory for the empire." Fell spent the fall and winter posted in England, in December 1914 training with his troops through the incessant rain and mud of Salisbury Plain. Even so, the soggy Wiltshire landscape was nothing compared to the living hell the Sixth Field Company would eventually face in the sodden fields of Flanders.

Fell did not forget his business obligations in Canada. When his business manager in Vancouver, Harry Bridgman, informed Fell that he had been elected reeve of the district, Fell wrote back with advice verging on a stern command: "Your office work comes first & requires regular attention every day. Depute others for as much of the regular Council work as you can." In writing to his cousin Henry Heywood-Lonsdale, Fell expressed fears that the United States might enter the war on the German side and warned that the family could expect little revenue from its British Columbian investments: "I have instructed Bridgman at the office to sit tight, collect what he can, pay only what he must, contract no new liabilities & start no new work & generally prepare to ride out a financial storm." When Fell returned to North Vancouver while on leave in July 1916, he received a hero's welcome. City council made him guest of honour at the annual Dominion Day celebrations. Rather than bask in the adulation, Fell called upon residents to rally to the cause:

This war is going on until Germany is smashed. Whether it is four months or four years depends largely on the number of men and the amount of munitions that can be put into the field. In Flanders, Fritz does not always fight like a gentleman, but it must be recognized that he is a stubborn and courageous foe. It will take all the men we can get to best him . . . Until Kaiserism is dead and damned, we will not stop fighting, but we must have men and munitions.

Despite early predictions, five Christmases were to pass before the boys came home. In the meantime, group after group trained at the drill hall—as the armoury was popularly known—until some 4,176 men had passed through the unit en route to the war. Prior to departing, many took steps to ensure their legacies. In 1914–15, the city's birthrate was reported as the highest in the nation. A large number of men who left the drill hall were posted to engineering units filling a variety of combatant and non-combatant roles overseas: harness making, blacksmithing, doing carpentry, framing, laying communications wires and handling workhorses. Prospective recruits were promised they would not be required to dig trenches or build roads themselves, but rather they would train and supervise infantrymen to do the work. The reality of wartime engineering proved different, with recruits shoring up collapsing trenches, building bridges while under fire, and digging tunnels and placing mines under enemy lines. Other Sixth Field Company recruits were transferred to other branches of the army, finding themselves slogging in the infantry or loading heavy artillery guns.

The company worked successfully to foster an esprit de corps. A draft of engineers leaving North Vancouver in March 1916 adopted the name "BC Beavers,"

OFFICERS & N.C.O's. 6TH FIELD Co. C. E.

T. ROW:- DR McCARLEY, LT. S.A.CUNLIF... LT. S.A.LAKE, MAJ. WARD, O.C., LT. J.B.HOLDCROFT, (ADJ.) LT. R.F. McINTOSH, LT. F.R.DYKE.
ROW:- SGT. W. B. FLEMING, CORP ... SON, CORP SPENCE, SGT.-MAJ. J. GILL, Q.M.S. J. ELDER, SGT. A.M. LAWSON.
THIRD ... ELL, SGT. DOUGLAS, CORP BUTLER,

a reference to the hard-working rodent that appeared on their badges. The group, under the command of Captain Percy Ward, also adopted its own marching ditty:

We're Canadian Engineers
And we want the world to know it.
We're fine and fit
And we think we're it,
And we're going abroad to show it.

North Shore recruits were both coaxed and coerced, the Sixth Field Company's promotional material characterizing its members as possessing:

. . . not only the brains, but the physique, the dash, the courage, and the resourcefulness that everywhere characterize the typical Canadian . . . we belong to an Empire that has stood for freedom and today is fighting with all her mighty force for that most precious of all priceless things, Liberty . . . The man who can, but will not fight is unworthy to be called a Canadian, much less a subject of the British Empire.

Officers and non-commissioned officers of the Sixth Field Company of Canadian Engineers. Records indicate that at least 4,176 men enlisted in the unit during the years 1914 to 1918.

North Vancouver Museum and Archives, 9505

Recalcitrant recruits were not the only men to be viewed with scorn. When one "selfish, unpatriotic wholesaler" made a "cruel attempt to force a soldier out of business," the community took issue. According to the *North Shore Press*, grocer J.H. English had answered the call of his country and was on his way to the front, only to have one of his suppliers attempt to foreclose his business. An unnamed advertiser came to his family's aid, urging "the sincere and earnest support of every loyal Britisher in North Vancouver . . . it is a matter of patriotism to keep this soldier's business [running]." Patriotism was the order of the day as males of all ages, backgrounds and conditions attempted to enlist. Most early recruits were British-born or at least had British ancestry. There were labourers and gentlemen; Europeans and Natives. The majority were men in their twenties, but there were also older men, some even of retirement age. At the other end of the spectrum were boys of sixteen or seventeen who lied about their age.

Those who remained behind did whatever they could to support "their boys": knitting countless pairs of socks, sending food parcels, subscribing to victory bonds and raising funds to assist the impoverished families of soldiers overseas. There were concerts aplenty, each reaching their climax as the audience rose to sing "Land of Hope and Glory," "Rule Britannia" and "God Save the King." Local physicians donated their services to the financially distressed families of absent servicemen. Primary school children packed firewood to earn a few cents, which they dutifully donated to the war effort. Students in the public school system were swept up in the patriotic fervour. Schoolyard war manoeuvres featured the wooden-gun-wielding boys hauling each other around on stretchers and being bandaged up by girls wearing Red Cross bands.

The war years took their toll on the home front as well as overseas. Friends and relatives of serving soldiers lived in constant fear, awaiting the fateful knock on the door that signalled the arrival of a life-altering telegram. For many, poring over the lists of dead, missing, and wounded in the regions' daily papers became a much-dreaded duty. In the face of the pervading gloom, North Vancouver residents sought diversions whenever or wherever they could. The formal opening of the city's premier sports ground at Mahon Park was one such opportunity. The opening of the sports ground, with its one-thousand-seat grandstand, was a milestone for the community. Newspaper editor George Morden dubbed the event "an epoch in the history of North Vancouver" and city council declared June 5, 1915, a half-day civic holiday. The crowds were immense, with fully one-third of the city's population gathering to listen to speeches, watch the races and listen to the North Vancouver City Band. For some, the highlight of the day may well have been the alderman's race, while others would have preferred the baseball game and dance that followed.

The conflict overseas helped to ease the effects of the city's economic depression. North Vancouver's pre-war workforce included many artisans who had harnessed their skills building houses, churches and commercial blocks. The economic downturn of 1913 had spelled imminent disaster for many, but the call to arms took hundreds into the army. Many of those who remained found work, as industrial plants on either side of the inlet retooled to make new products. Wallace Shipyards and North Shore Iron Works soon acquired contracts to manufacture

332.

munitions, including shells for the 18 pounders that formed the backbone of the British and Canadian field artilleries. As the war progressed, German submarine action inflicted crippling losses on Allied shipping. The Imperial Munitions Board thus contracted with Wallace Shipyards for the construction of a number of merchant vessels including six auxiliary wooden schooners, the first of which was the *Mabel Brown*. Wooden schooners may have seemed an unlikely choice for wartime shipping, but steel was in short supply and wood was locally abundant. The schooners were not intended for the war zone, but rather to replace West Coast ships diverted to the North Atlantic. With the *Mabel Brown* nearing completion, Wallace secured an even more challenging project, the contract for *War Dog*, a 3,000-ton, 315-foot-long steel steamer with 1,300 horsepower engines. Contracts for two additional freighters, *War Power* and *War Storm*, followed.

The construction of these ships led to an expansion of the industrial facilities now lining the city's waterfront. Although the Wallace Shipyards chose to use its core facility east of the ferry wharf for the construction of the steel-hulled vessels, it built wooden ships in a new facility on the foreshore west of the Mission Reserve. Wallace purchased the property from the Lonsdale Estate in 1916, much to the delight of the local press, which labelled the event "a sunbeam in the darkness." Finding the site, dubbed No. 2 Yard, too large for his immediate needs, Wallace leased a portion to the William Lyall Shipbuilding Company, which ultimately built twenty-seven wooden ships there. When the war ended in 1918, Lyall's continued to build ships on the site, ultimately relinquishing it when its lease expired in 1920.

Wallace Shipyards was busy throughout the war, but its contracts were not always lucrative. There is no record of the firm being accused of profiteering as so many others were, the firm having lost money in the construction of the *Mabel Brown* series of ships. Andy Wallace had entered the war with little infrastructure and knowledge from which to build a ship with steel. By 1918, his firm had expanded considerably, had developed its own foundry and engine works, and had secured contracts for an additional six steel-hulled freighters. Wallace Shipyards and the City of North Vancouver became increasingly conjoined, sparring on occasion when one party attempted to wrest concessions from the other. Though innovative in some respects, Andy Wallace's operation was traditional in others. Like employers in other areas of wartime business, at least one of Wallace's rivals had added females to its workforce. Wallace wrote to inform Canada's Deputy Minister of Marine in March 1918 that his firm had "come to the conclusion that at the present time it is not practicable to employ women in any of the branches of the trade."

Wallace was able to prevent females from joining his ranks, but unable to prevent gradual unionization. In 1916, Lodge 194 of the International Brotherhood of Boilermakers, Iron Ship Builders, Blacksmiths, Forgers and Helpers secured its first contract with the firm, providing for a nine-hour day and wages for inside workers of fifty cents an hour. The shipyard was not a closed shop, but lodge members were nonetheless given preference in hiring. A similar agreement was signed between the lodge and the neighbouring North Shore Iron Works at the same time.

Despite the resistance of North Vancouver's leading employer, the war did provide some benefits to local women, including the right to vote. The question of female suffrage had been a topic of growing interest throughout the empire beginning with the founding of the Women's Social and Political Union in Manchester in 1903. The issue had reached the North Shore shortly before the outbreak of war but failed to elicit the same sort of drama associated with the debate in Britain. In 1913 Mayor George Hanes, the former city engineer, lent his support to the movement by stating categorically, "I believe in votes for women." In 1914 his successor Mayor W.J. Irwin chaired the first meeting of the city's suffragists, taking care to note that he was undecided on an issue on which he was "not conversant." In 1916, the provincial Liberal Party had made votes for women and prohibition two of the pillars of its election campaign. In the ensuing referendum both measures were approved. Women acquired the provincial franchise along with the right to stand for provincial office.

In 1917, the federal government enacted similar legislation, proffering the right to vote to war nurses and the immediate female relatives of servicemen in hopes of shoring up support for a conscription-supporting Unionist government. A national election was scheduled for December 17, 1917. Regardless of the fact that voting was extended only to women most directly associated with the war effort, pro-conscription *North Shore Press* editor George Morden still feared women "unversed in the wily tactics of the unscrupulous politician" might vote the wrong way. In the end, Burrard constituency voted solidly for the pro-conscription Unionist candidate. In British Columbia, the same referendum that had approved female suffrage also forbade the sale of alcoholic beverages, save for medicinal purposes with the consent of a physician. Four decades after his passing, Sue Moody's North Shore was dry once more . . . in theory. Distilleries appeared in many an isolated location, and a surprising number of British Columbian doctors suddenly discovered the redeeming effects of alcoholic beverages, dispensing 315,177 prescriptions in 1919 alone.

The war went on, with North Vancouver residents keenly following it progress. Though the hostilities were thousands of miles away, the reality of war struck home frequently. There were shortages and rationing, and toward the end of 1918 an influenza pandemic. Inaccurately dubbed the Spanish Flu, the pandemic carried away more lives in eighteen months than the war had done in four years. Homes were quarantined, churches were closed and public assemblies were strongly discouraged. In desperation, many people resorted to folk remedies, consuming vast quantities of cinnamon, onions and garlic while fumigating their homes with formaldehyde lamps.

The city's small health-care facilities were hard pressed to deal with the crisis. By 1910 the Dawson sisters' small hospital, its capacity failing to accommodate the burgeoning population, required replacement. A new fifteen-bed facility had opened on Twelfth east of Lonsdale Avenue in September 1910, but in time it too proved inadequate. Two doctors subsequently leased the old Hamersley mansion, and operated it as the Harbour View Sanitarium. At the time of the influenza epidemic the sanitarium was closed. Some patients had no alternative but to seek care in Vancouver, no easy task in a community without a single ambulance. Without adequate vaccines, facilities and health-care staff, the North Vancouver death rates for 1918 and 1919 were 50 percent higher than for 1917. Even after the soldiers returned from overseas, death continued to stalk North Vancouver homes well into 1920. Wealth and position were no protection. In March 1920 alone the disease claimed the lives of Fred Macdonald, local manager of the PGE; Dr. William E. Newcombe, the city's former medical health officer; and—within hours of each other—magistrate David G. Dick and his wife Mary.

The *North Shore Press* reported that when the war finally ended on November 11, 1918 both sides of the inlet joined in a common celebration. Not wanting to wait until 11 a.m. local time to start the festivities, Mayor George W. Vance visited the drill hall in the darkness of the early morning. There, he gathered his troops together and led an impromptu but enthusiastic procession to the ferry landing, flags waving as the regimental band struggled to be heard above the din of singing and shouting engineers. Once at the wharf, the mayor "hustled out Captain Falke and the crew of the No. 2 ferry, and with a large number of citizens, the big ferry steamed across the inlet, and the local contingent lent its quota to the wild celebration which was in full sway in Vancouver." Residents of both cities paraded up and down Hastings and Granville Streets, making "all the noise it was possible to make with the available instruments." In the evening, the crowd returned to North Vancouver. When darkness arrived, the gathering lit a gigantic bonfire in Victoria Park, where "every burst of flame brought forth a chorus of shouting." By

Miss Canada Contest. North Vancouver. July 1st 1918.

The "Miss Canada" contest, held in Mahon Park on Dominion Day 1918 gave North Vancouver residents an opportunity to demonstrate their patriotism.

North Vancouver Museum and Archives, 2860

this time the regimental band was not in attendance, its members pleading utter exhaustion having already played for most of the day.

There were accolades for the survivors and laments for the slain. It was difficult to measure the size of the city's sacrifice, as some residents had enlisted in units other than the engineers, and many who joined the engineers had come from elsewhere. According to some estimates, over two hundred of those who had joined the Sixth Field Company were never to return, and the city's overall losses were never fully tallied. Some families suffered unimaginable sorrow. Wentworth Sarel, a director in the Western Corporation, had to contend with his sons Charles and Ian enlisting early on in the war and dying a few months later only eighteen days apart.

Amid all the sadness there was considerable pride. The three North Shore municipalities (including West Vancouver) had exceeded their quota for the sale of Victory Bonds by over 100 percent and were awarded a flag to commemorate the achievement. The banner, presented on behalf of the Governor General, was framed and hung with reverence in North Vancouver City Hall. There was also adulation for returning heroes: recipients of the Military Medal, the Military Cross, the Distinguished Service Order and the Belgian *Croix de Guerre*. Some families had greatly exceeded expectations, such as former city treasurer J.J. Woods and his three sons who all went overseas. In addition, Mrs. Woods worked with the North Vancouver Red Cross, and their daughter Nora made hospital supplies for the Tipperary Girls' Club. The family of Donald Cameron, co-founder of the Sixth Field Company, was equally remarkable. His seven sons enlisted for service overseas

while he and his wife worked at home "in every patriotic movement on the North Shore."

Although the war had been fought in the name of democracy and freedom, equality remained an elusive goal. Soldiers of British origin received far greater recognition than those of non-European backgrounds, such as brothers Ralph and Herbert ("Jumbo") Nahu of mixed Kanaka and Squamish ancestry. Ralph, curiously enough, had enlisted in a local battalion of Irish Fusiliers, and Herbert in the 131st (New Westminster) Battalion. Herbert sustained wounds in the leg, throat and skull, but it was not until his obituary was written in 1957 that mainstream society paid appropriate tribute to his sacrifices.

Although veterans' affairs were not within the purview of local government, North Vancouver city council did what it could. "Tag days" were authorized to enable the Disabled Veterans' Association to fundraise for its members. Council met with representatives of the local branch of the Great War Veterans' Association

Remembrance Day service at the newly unveiled cenotaph in Victoria Park, November 11, 1923.
North Vancouver Museum and Archives, 8933

(GWVA) to explore "what should be done for the support of widows and orphans of soldiers killed during the war, and also any proposals which they consider might be more effective in helping returned men to become reinstated in civil life as self-supporting and self-respecting citizens."

Council, the GWVA and the community at large also committed to honouring the city's "fallen heroes." There was general agreement that a physical memorial was in order, but not on the form and purpose of the memorial. Some residents advocated the erection of a cenotaph, and others supported the construction of a hospital ward (and ultimately, a new North Shore Memorial Hospital). In the end it was decided to undertake both projects, but to defer the hospital to a later date. All the major organizations in the city were invited to a meeting to explore how the cenotaph might be funded; in the interim, a "committee of ladies" under the supervision of Eva Grahame was formed to undertake door-to-door fundraising of the entire North Shore, and council agreed to provide a site in Victoria Park. Local architects Blackadder and Mackay supplied the design and the completed monument was unveiled on November 11, 1923.

The nascent trade union movement had subordinated many of its aspirations to the loftier objective of winning the war, with workplace harmony encouraged through legislation. In early 1918, the federal government had outlawed both strikes and lockouts, though unions were still permitted the right to organize. The legislation was not successful. A one-day strike on the waterfront in August 1918 had led many to question the patriotism of the strikers. With peace achieved, the gloves were off again. The cost of living across Canada had risen by 30 percent between 1916 and 1917 alone, and in British Columbia the rate was greater than the national average. Union membership increased by close to 400 percent in the years between 1914 and 1919. As wartime production wound down, workers were let go, and returned soldiers added to the jobless rate. Before the decade was out over 20 percent of the province's workforce was unemployed.

PROMISES AND PROBLEMS 1920–1929

With the war behind them city residents had hoped for a return to prosperity, but fate dictated otherwise. A recession hit North America in 1920–21, with conditions in North Vancouver reflecting those in the province as a whole. Many property owners defaulted on their taxes. In April 1921 the city offered some three hundred and ninety lots for sale, their values ranging from $75 to $2,000. Most were vacant, having been bought at the height of pre-war speculation. The situation reflected badly on the city. The *North Shore Press* called on "residents to show their faith in North Vancouver by getting a stake in the town." The city's loss of tax revenues placed council and its employees in a difficult position. A salary schedule adopted on February 9, 1920, provided most staff with substantial wage increases. The city's firemen, however, found the settlement unacceptable and went on strike five days later. Council fired the entire department and hired a replacement chief. The new chief, Bill Murphy, was directed to fill the empty positions; a conciliatory council allowed the terminated men to apply for reinstatement.

Shipyard and sawmill workers also lived in uncertainty, never sure of when a layoff might occur. The longshoremen's nascent unions, such as the Vancouver local of the International Longshoremen's Association, were continually assailed by returned soldiers seeking to break up the closed shop situation that prevailed at the time. Ed Nahanee, a Squamish longshoreman with mixed Kanaka and Native blood, recalled a time of violence and union-busting: "One time the union guys had taken a stand in the union hall, armed with clubs and whatever we could find. There were swarms of soldiers storming the doors, and on the roof of one of the warehouses three machine guns were trained on us by the RCMP, so close I could practically see down their barrels."

Events in 1923 were particularly bitter. Largely influenced by developments in the United States, the British Columbia Shipping Federation resolved to break the unions. In October 1923, the BC branch of the International Longshoremen's Association voted 1,300 to 100 to walk off the job. The ensuing strike, which featured a small army of armed guards protecting an even larger army of strike-breakers, crippled the union and resulted in many of its members never working on the inlet's docks again. Years later, longshoreman Jimmy Greer remembered the strike and recalled how it affected ILA members on both sides of the inlet:

The Empress of Japan was used to house strike-breakers. The ILA members kept their picket lines going right through June to December, when the officials could see no win in the future and told the members so . . . I think there was a raid on the Great Northern Dock by ILA members and there was some fighting with the strike-breakers on the dock. Out of the 1923 strike a new organization was formed—the ILHA, Independent Lumber Handlers Association—mainly by the North Shore members of the ILA plus others who worked lumber ships. Some of the men who started the ILHA were Andy Paull, Ambrose Reid, Herbert ("Jumbo") Nahu, Gus Band and Jack Fisher.

Strikes notwithstanding, as the decade wore on, the province's economy improved. Property values in the city of North Vancouver slowly recovered, but the pre-war boom years were never to be repeated. Wallace Shipyards continued to provide work but many employees of the enterprise resided on the other side of the inlet. The outbreak of the war had certainly helped the firm. In 1914 the shipyard's workforce had totalled 172. Five years later it totalled 1,067. Wallace periodically landed contracts to replace smaller vessels lost during the war, and the shipyard's workforce tended to rise and fall as a result. Recognizing the importance of the shipyard to North Vancouver's economic well-being, city council kept a close eye on Wallace's corporate health. In 1916 city council initiated a series of agreements with the shipyard, trading water and a low tax assessment for guarantees regarding hiring practices. An agreement dated December 24, 1920, required the firm to hire "not less than forty white workmen, in addition to the respective numbers the Company has already . . . agreed to employ, all of whom shall be permanent

residents of the said City of North Vancouver."

Similar agreements were made with other firms. With much of the North Vancouver population commuting to jobs across the inlet and local sites for industrial activity still largely undeveloped, civic spirits were lifted whenever a major employer chose to locate in the city. The E.C. Walsh Lumber Company opened its waterfront sawmill in September 1919. Employing over sixty men, the mill shipped lumber by ship and rail throughout the world and offered North Shore residents a ready source of building materials in their own front yard. Rumours of other ventures were greeted with equal enthusiasm though many, such as a proposal from the Coast Range Steel Company to build a steel plant employing over four thousand men, never came to fruition.

By the end of the war Andy Wallace had recognized how shipbuilding was changing. There would be increased demand for steel-hulled ships and wooden vessels would become a thing of the past. Although Wallace had built a number of steel-hulled freighters late in the war, the firm's big break came with a contract to build a replacement for the ill-fated *Princess Sophia* for the CPR. The contract for the new vessel, the *Princess Louise*, promised to propel Wallace into the big leagues of the shipbuilding industry. Due to wartime shipping losses to German submarines, the railway company's traditional British suppliers had more orders than they could handle. Firms such as Wallace's were the interim beneficiaries of a temporarily increased demand for new ships. Once the need for replacement ships had been satisfied, companies such as the CPR returned to their former suppliers.

Still, the *Princess Louise* was a high point in Wallace's corporate history. The $1.5-million vessel was wholly made in British Columbia, and promised to open new doors for the North Vancouver shipyard. The *North Shore Press* was confident about Wallace's future and suggested that the project would "demonstrate to the entire shipbuilding world that just as artistic and highly finished vessels can be turned out in this province as in any of the biggest and best known yards in Europe." Andy Wallace was equally proud of the achievement: "The building of the *Louise* was a great undertaking for a small firm such as ours. Switching from tramp steamers to passenger liners is a feat which I doubt yards in the Old Country are capable of."

As much as Andy Wallace might have hoped "in future to build a ship as big as the *Empress of Asia*," it was the construction of a dry dock on his North Vancouver property that ensured the firm's long-term viability. Schemes for a dry dock had appeared in the local newspaper for years. No less than six proposals ranging in value up to a phenomenal $6 million were touted in the decade prior to the end of the war. In 1919 the federal government contemplated providing a subsidy to an appropriate project, and in October three separate proposals were filed for a dry dock on Burrard Inlet. Ottawa approved plans prepared on behalf of John Coughlan and Sons, owners of a shipyard and steel fabrication company on the south side of the inlet. In September 1921, Wallace was brought into the project. The graving dry dock originally proposed by Coughlan had become a floating dry dock, and Wallace Shipyards became the Burrard Dry Dock Company a few weeks later.

North Vancouverites had long since learned not to count their railways and bridges before they were built and many must have been wary of the dry dock project as well. Their distrust proved well placed. The December 6, 1921, federal election swept the Conservatives out of power and the new Liberal government cancelled its participation in the project. Considerable lobbying by the inlet's business interests followed, and in spring 1923 the project was reinstated. The new dry dock was opened on August 11, 1925, by the same federal Minister of Public Works who had cancelled the project four years earlier.

One year later, the *Vancouver Morning Star* was able to report that 149 vessels had been served by the dry dock, 30 of which would not have been able to use the port were it not for the presence of the new facility. A new pier, machine shop, blacksmith shop and other facilities were also added to the site. The completion of the dry dock resulted in the creation of an additional 250 jobs. Although the facilities ceased to attract construction projects on the scale of the *Princess Louise*, the success of the dry dock ensured the firm's survival through the 1920s and 1930s. The construction of smaller vessels such as two fireboats for the City of Vancouver, and the *St. Roch* to serve the RCMP's Arctic detachments, also contributed to the firm's success.

The expansion of Wallace's facilities gave new hope to the city's struggling economy. So did the construction of a second dry dock and shipbuilding facility. In 1925–26, Arthur C. Burdick and his two brothers purchased a large waterfront property on the western side of Lonsdale Avenue. The Burdick family had previously operated a boat-repair yard in Vancouver's False Creek: Vancouver Drydock and Salvage. Their North Vancouver operation opened as the Pacific Salvage Company

A ship undergoes repairs in the newly commissioned Burrard Dry Dock at the foot of Lonsdale Avenue, 1926.
North Vancouver Museum and Archives, 27-8B

and in its initial years focussed on ship repairs and small boat construction. For North Vancouver council, the Burdicks' arrival couldn't have come at a better time. More local jobs meant more families buying property, building houses, purchasing goods and services, and paying taxes to the city. But Burrard Dry Dock remained the largest employer on the North Shore. The firm's expansion increased the value of its property and with it, the amount of taxes payable to the city. The fates of the company and city became increasingly interlinked.

Burrard's expansion and its competitor's arrival were not entirely straightforward. Canadian and international steel and boilermakers' unions vied with each other and with longer established craftsmen's unions as they attempted to recruit the shipyard's workers. Yet whenever there was job action, *all* Burrard's workers responded as a body, ignoring stipulations of the labour code. Alex Young, who started work for Wallace in 1918 or 1919, recalled the unions' relations with Andy Wallace's sons Hubert and Clarence well:

The one thing that we did in those days that paid off, when a dispute arose we all walked off the job. That was it. We went back when we got what we demanded, and I'd say 99 cases out of 100 we got what we wanted when we walked off the job. I was in more strikes, I'll bet you, in a couple of years than the average guy in his lifetime. We always had a strike, but we didn't declare a strike—we just walked off the job, everybody who was on it. We walked off the job until they asked us what the trouble was. Then we would go tell them. Then we'd get it corrected and go back to work . . . We never had long strikes. Didn't need them, so long as every man walked out. Even those who weren't in our Union, they walked out with us.

Despite the workers' emerging clout, Andy Wallace maintained a paternalistic style of management. Young recalled observing Wallace in his final years as he made his way around the shipyard:

I was in the yard when the father was there. He walked around the yard all day long with his big fat belly and his hands in his hip pockets. One day this pipefitter was kneeling down doing something. He had a big mop of blond hair and it was hanging over his face and the old man put his hand in his pocket and gave him 50 cents and chased him away right there and then. He says, "Go out and get a haircut and don't come back until you get it cut!"

The opening of the dry dock may have promised a rosy future, but the city's economic health continued to be challenged by transportation considerations. Though discussion about a bridge at the Second Narrows was periodically revived, it was extinguished just as quickly. Residents became increasingly skeptical about a crossing ever being built. They wanted both a bridge and an upgraded ferry system and it did not seem to matter which of the two alternatives came first.

By 1920 the city's ferries were overtaxed, aging and operating at a loss. In June, council raised ferry fares for the first time since before the war. Consideration was given to charging non-resident passengers at a higher rate. Transportation issues were to dominate the public agenda throughout the 1920s. The city's steep grades

Alfred ("Andy") Wallace, photographed in the 1920s, opened his North Vancouver shipyard at the foot of Lonsdale Avenue in 1906. Wallace maintained a paternalistic style of management throughout his career, despite the growth of trade unions in the years following the First World War.

North Vancouver Museum and Archives 8090

had long been a challenge, and the prospect of a motorcar or tram hurtling down the hillside was a constant concern. Council addressed the issue in part in February 1923 when it approved a bylaw requiring motor vehicles to park on Lonsdale Avenue's lower slopes at right angles to the grade with both rear tires touching the curb. When the British Columbia Electric Railway proposed introducing "one man cars" on its North Shore runs, city council disapproved for safety reasons.

The bridge question resurfaced in May 1920 when Vancouver Mayor Robert H. Gale revealed that the Harbour Commission was investigating the feasibility of constructing a dam across the Second Narrows. The structure would enable the Canadian Northern Railway to connect with the Pacific Great Eastern. "The damming of the Second Narrows would in a short period of time cause the upper pool to become a fresh water harbour, and would further be of value in that this would prove ideal for ridding ships of barnacles after they had passed in to the upper reaches through a set of locks." The scheme, like so many others, came to naught.

North Shore hopes were raised again in 1920 when the federal Minister of Marine and Fisheries promised to provide the city with a new car ferry and landing. When word was received the following year that the project would not be proceeding, council appealed to no avail. And in April 1921, the provincial government confirmed it could not "recommend the inclusion of $400,000, or indeed, any sum in the estimates of the current year" in support of a bridge at the Second Narrows. There were plenty of parties to blame: federal ministers, the provincial government and the Vancouver Harbour Board. The North Vancouver Board of Trade smelled a rat:

> Due to the fact that the project has been thrown from pillar to post and the commencement of work on the project postponed on so many occasions, the members of the Board of Trade generally are inclined to think that this constitutes a deliberate attempt on the part of the Harbour Board to curtail progress as regard harbour improvements and developments on the north shore.

The board of trade formed a special committee to prepare a formal protest to the Vancouver Harbour Board. Despite the board of trade's concerns about developing the waterfront, some residents preferred the status quo. Prohibition had ended in British Columbia, but it was still in place in Washington State. Ocean-going vessels such as the fabled rumrunner *Malahat* were said to be picking up illicit rum and whiskey in Canada and delivering it under the cover of darkness to dealers across the border. Too much scrutiny could spoil a good thing for those who supplied the rumrunners from the foot of Bewicke Avenue.

For North Vancouver city council, the efficient transport of goods and people was a far greater concern. By May 1921 the ferries were carrying over a quarter million passengers per month. That same month, the federal Minister of Transportation advised council that the government had not abandoned the concept of a new car ferry; it had only postponed action on the project. By this point council was not particularly enthused, and began discussions with the district around joint ownership and operation of the ferry system.

The city's elected officials were between a rock and a hard place. Raising ferry fares would act against economic development. But not raising fares would increase the city's deficit. A bylaw to charge non-residents a higher fare was duly passed, but failed to receive provincial approval. Negotiations with the district collapsed. The two jurisdictions each sponsored mass meetings in the Knights of Pythias Hall to explain their positions. Money bylaws to support the ferry service, in 1922 and 1923, failed to secure the required levels of support. Despite the failure of initiatives to improve the system, ferry employees did their utmost to maximize revenues. Alex Young recalled one occasion when fiscal diligence blinded good judgment:

When you were boarding the ferry and the ferry was pulling out, you could always run down the ramp and catch it right at the end of the dock. But this guy, just as he went to jump, the ferry slid out about three or four feet and he landed in the chuck. However, he managed to grab a toehold and he held on until they fished him out. When they got him on board, and he's soaking, of course, the ferry mate that took the tickets came over, and the first thing he asked him was, "Hey, where's your ticket?" After he nearly drowned—and they wanted his ferry ticket!

North Vancouver's May Queen and her entourage, Ottawa Gardens, 1929.

North Vancouver Museum and Archives, 8247

The 1920s saw many of the city's most important organizations emerge as leaders in community life. Most of the community's larger churches continued to grow. North Vancouver's first Girl Guide Company was formed in 1922, receiving its flag and standard from the Pauline Johnson Chapter of the Imperial Order of Daughters of the Empire (IODE). The city's first Brownie pack was founded the following year when Mrs. McTaggart-Cowan accepted the role of "Brown Owl." The Great War Veterans' Association held a seemingly endless series of "smokers"—male-only gatherings featuring tobacco, liquor and gambling—to benefit its members.

The local Benevolent and Protective Order of Elks (the "Brother Bills") supported a range of community activities, including an annual boat trip and picnic, and the organization of the city's May Day celebrations. The latter event was held on or near May 24 (then known as Empire Day) and coupled traditional English May Day celebrations with expressions of loyalty to the Crown. The lodge's 1923 event was particularly memorable. The city was hung with flags and bunting, and a prize was offered for the "best dressed window." On the day itself, members of the Navy League, Boy Scouts, Girl Guides, Elks, North Shore police and the Elks band, and hundreds of local schoolchildren, formed a parade from Victoria Park up Lonsdale and on to Mahon Park via Fifteenth. The newly chosen May Queen, Ethel Marshall, followed with her entourage, seated in the same horse-drawn carriage King George V had used during his West Coast visit as Duke of York in 1901.

By 1923, adult male residents could join one of a number of fraternal organizations: the Masons, Elks, Ancient Order of Foresters, Knights of Pythias or Independent Order of Odd Fellows. Their wives might join the Order of the Royal Purple, Order of the Eastern Star, the Rebekahs or the now largely forgotten Women's Benefit Association of the Maccabees. Several service clubs were also founded that contributed substantially to the city's physical infrastructure through fundraising or labour. In the absence of a public recreation department in 1921, the city's just-founded Kiwanis Club mustered volunteers to enhance the bathing beach at the foot of St. Patrick's Avenue, the former Lonsdale Gardens. That same year, community members petitioned for the establishment of a local branch of the YMCA.

Not content to rest on its laurels, the Kiwanis Club started to raise funds for the North Shore's first ambulance in 1922. Remarkably, the vehicle was in the city's hands by the end of May. However, little thought had been given to where the ambulance should be housed or who would operate it. Council initially thought that the vehicle might be administered by the fire department. When this proved impractical it was suggested that the ambulance be posted to city hall. This too proved infeasible, one councillor thinking he might have to drive it. In the end, council wrote to the board of police commissioners with the request that they "take charge of the ambulance for a small consideration."

Race-based organizations flourished, reflecting the predominantly British nature of the post-war community. Although the Sons of England ceased to advertise its meetings in the local paper, the St. Andrew's and Caledonian Society remained a major force in the community, organizing the Dominion Day observances. The society's annual Burns Night supper and dance attracted both crowds and headlines, with many non-Scots joining in the festivities. A local branch of the British-Israel Society was meeting in the city by the mid-1920s, its members united by the belief that the Anglo-Saxon and Celtic races numbered among God's chosen people. A local post of the Native Sons of British Columbia was organized in 1923, with membership being open to select adult males born in the province. While men with a bit of Native blood in their primarily Caucasian veins might be welcomed, those of Asian ancestry were not. Racial and gender restrictions also apparently applied to membership in the North Shore's Old Timers Association. Formed in 1925 for individuals who had settled in the community prior to 1906, the association consisted solely of men of British origin.

Loosely modelled on a similar organization in London, the formidably named Savage Club was founded in 1920 for the promotion of "social and intellectual harmony rooted in unanimous adherence to British ideals," among other goals. Each of its initial twenty-two members was an adult male of British ancestry. At its founding meeting it was moved "that ladies not be admitted to membership." Prior to the war, in 1911, 74.2 percent of the city's population claimed British origins. Indeed, the city was *almost* as British as the Vancouver Island community of Victoria where British residents then formed 74.8 percent of the population. By the early 1920s, the percentage of the North Vancouver population with British roots, 87.4, exceeded that of the island city, where the rate was 84.7.

In the 1920s North Vancouver seemed destined to become the white man's city that its founders had foretold. Although the city may have had Chinese residents, they were few in number and virtually all were single males. With a new Chinese Immigration Act proclaimed in 1923, the entry of additional Chinese immigrants was effectively halted. For many in the ambitious city, it seemed the Chinese population would gradually fall rather than increase. Relegated to working out of sight in sawmills, laundries and kitchens, the Chinese appeared more curiosity than threat. Murdoch Grahame, whose father served as the city's jailer in the 1920s, recalled the situation:

> *The Chinese men seemed to live in any wee shack on a lot, or back of a laundry or shop and a lot of opium smoking went on. There would be a real hush, hush round our house, as my father would come in and say, "A raid on the Chinese tonight." Off the police would go and raid these places and take the men to jail ... Then my father would feel sorry for these chaps in cells and he would slip them a bit of whatever it was that they used. But they would get out and do the same thing again.*

British Columbians had lobbied long and hard to convince Ottawa to draft the Chinese Immigration Act. They were also determined to stop immigration from Japan. In the early 1920s, former city engineer and mayor George S. Hanes, then serving as North Vancouver's MLA, introduced legislation to halt the "Asiatic inflow" once and for all. Hanes presented two bills to the house, one calling for the termination of the 1913 Treaty of Commerce and Navigation between the British king and the Japanese emperor, the other urging the federal government "to totally restrict the immigration of Asiatics into this province, keeping in view the wishes of the people of British Columbia that this province be reserved for people of the European race."

A number of sports-related organizations also emerged, several of which attracted a growing population of young men. By 1923 these associations included the North Shore Cricket Club, Junior Cricket Club, North Vancouver Lawn Tennis Club, North Shore Junior Football League and North Shore Amateur Athletic Association. There were also opportunities for older men. The North Vancouver Lawn Bowling Club formed in 1923, luring city mayor Dugald Donaghy and district reeve Jack Loutet to serve as honorary president and vice-president, respectively. Prior to the club's foundation, bowlers had met just east of the Horticultural Hall, playing on a makeshift green later described as "a one-way affair, full of bumps and ruts, and known as the 'cow patch.'" Once organized, members of the club acquired a lease of land from the Horticultural Society, established a proper green and converted a shed into a makeshift clubhouse. In 1924 a ladies auxiliary was formed to assist members at social events. The ladies formed a club of their own just two years later.

Prior to the Amateur Athletic Association being founded, sports teams had approached the city separately regarding their individual needs. The new body proposed co-ordinating their requests and lobbying for all. Playing fields required upgrades and competing schedules had to be addressed. Equally importantly, the Amateur Athletic Association promised to become a vehicle capable of putting North Vancouver athletes on the map. As George Morden put it, the organization would promote "the pep and go get 'em spirit that makes sports go in any community."

Baseball and soccer were the two most popular sports at the time. The Wallace Shipyards had organized its own baseball and soccer teams as early as 1918, their successes on the inlet's sports fields helping to create a sense of community not only among the firm's employees but also throughout the city. When Wallace's soccer team won the Mainland Cup in 1920 and went on to compete for the provincial trophy

Opening Day, North Vancouver Lawn Bowling Club, 1930. The organization's first clubhouse stood near the site of its current facility, on Lonsdale Avenue south of Twenty-Third Street.
North Vancouver Museum and Archives, 7655

in 1920, the achievement was a source of considerable civic pride. The creation of the North Shore Baseball League was also a welcomed development. Half a dozen teams—sponsored by groups such as the Elks, the Sixth Field Company, and the St. Andrew's and Caledonian Society—eagerly joined the new organization and all developed strong local followings. While soccer also continued to be popular, the rise of baseball demonstrated a significant incursion of American culture into the predominantly British community. The use of the American term "soccer" rather than "football" was a further indication of the phenomenon.

In spring 1920, all the North Shore's public schools came together for their first-ever sports meet. Soon afterwards—and perhaps for the first time—substantial numbers of city residents had an opportunity to see their Squamish neighbours in a new light. The Squamish team joined the North Shore Baseball League shortly after its inception, their level of play and sportsmanship impressing all who saw them in action. When Andy Paull and his "Squamish nine" won the league championship, the team was credited with having attracted "an unexpectedly large number of fans" and winning many supporters. The Squamish Junior Soccer team also attracted significant support, having surprised most observers with their enthusiasm and skill.

The development of organized sports was paralleled by advances in the arts

Andy Paull and his senior "B" baseball champions, 1929. Paull's players included members of the Baker, Joseph, Nahanee, Band, Lindsay, Sargent, Galligher, and Mack families.

North Vancouver Museum and Archives, 4843

and entertainment. The city's theatres offered residents opportunities to view the latest silent movies from Hollywood as well as the occasional live vaudevillian performance. When the Empire Theatre reopened in August 1921, its new manager treated city residents to the "mammoth photo spectacle: *Before the White Man Came*," featuring Chief White Elk, "the noted Indian Tenor, Dramatic Reader and College Graduate." For many city residents, the highlight of White Elk's visit was his highly publicized appearance on the "top-most point of the theatre, where he sang to an enraptured audience." Ironically, in the racially segregated society of the day, Natives from the nearby Mission Reserve were forced to keep their distance from White Elk. Speaking in 2006, Squamish elder Lila Johnston recalled her mother's memories of the theatre: "They weren't allowed to sit down below. They had to sit upstairs because they were Native. And even on the ferry they couldn't sit downstairs. They had to go upstairs."

The educational infrastructure also continued to be addressed. The city's first high school class had been formed in 1910, and over the next fourteen years high school students had been shuffled between buildings. Although there was strong recognition that a purpose-built high school was highly desirable (ratepayers voted 67 percent in favour of a $67,000 building in 1923), economic realities dictated the form of the school that ultimately opened in January 1924. With its wood-frame construction, hollow tile veneer and stuccoed exterior, the new structure was a far cry from Ridgeway or Queen Mary schools, both built during the city's pre-war boom. Despite its appearance, the new high school won a reputation for being eminently functional. Located at Twenty-third and St. George's, North Van High opened to considerable acclaim, the provincial Minister of Education applauding its facilities for manual instruction and home economics.

A substantial amount of the city's community-building was championed by women. Men were meant to be the breadwinners in the family; women, when not raising children, might be allowed to volunteer in the community. North Vancouver

North Vancouver High School, built in 1923 to the designs of architects Benzie and Bow, was the city's first purpose-built high school.
North Vancouver Museum and Archives, p151

NORTH VANCOUVER HIGH SCHOOL
North Van, B.C.

resident Robin Williams remembered his father's views on the role of women in society:

> *His was a common attitude among the men of his time. Having babies, raising children, managing a household, these were all women's work. Likewise in the social dimension, participation in church, school, and community was in the category of "doing good," best left to women, so long, that is, as men had the say-so in matters of power and property.*

Doing good encompassed a range of causes, literacy being prominent among them. Beginning in the early 1920s, Agnes Wheeler and Violet Johnson oversaw the chartering of the North Vancouver Public Library Association. The organization received no civic support. Members donated books of their own to form the collection, augmenting it with purchases made from the proceeds of innumerable afternoon teas and card parties. The library occupied whatever quarters it could find, one of its homes being a room above a butcher's shop. It was not until 1949 that the association was able to secure its first permanent facility in Lower Lonsdale, and even then the city council declined to contribute toward its operation.

Other women chose to better the community through other causes. The Women's Christian Temperance Union continued to assemble in the city despite the repeal of prohibition in 1921. Parent Teacher Associations were founded at several of the city's schools in 1920, the successors to a less than successful inter-school committee of parents. The Ladies' Auxiliary of the Army and Navy Veterans of Canada offered support to returned servicemen and their families. In the 1920s, the entirely female Victorian Order of Nurses (whose North Vancouver branch was founded in 1912) conducted about 1,500 home visits per year, many of them to address the needs of returned soldiers. A Women's Auxiliary to the North Vancouver General Hospital was founded in 1921, the *North Shore Press* reporting "Mrs. Harry Bridgman, Mrs. Jack Loutet and Mrs. J.A. McMillan" prominent among its initial members. Identifying females by their husbands' first names was not unique to North Vancouver. The province's women may have acquired the right to vote, but they remained hidden in their husbands' shadows.

It was a rare female indeed who could rise to a notable position in what had always been a male-dominated society. Clarice Williams was one of these, opening shop in the mid-1920s as the first female chiropractor on the North Shore. Mary Meredith was another. Meredith had a long-standing interest in the education of mentally handicapped children and accordingly opened St. Christopher's School on East Fifteenth Street in the early 1930s. Emily Gulland was also interested in private education. Founder and headmistress of the Crosby School for Girls, Gulland made female education the focus of much of her working life. She established her school in Victoria about 1922 and moved it to a house in North Vancouver in 1926. Her venture was successful enough to relocate the school to the former Luther Watts Doney mansion on the Grand Boulevard in the 1930s. There, Gulland and her staff worked with a small number of students spanning the years from kindergarten to junior matriculation. The school's aims included training girls "to become worthy citizens of the future, capable of understanding and fulfilling their civic duties, and,

Miss Emily Gulland, photographed in 1910, established her Crosby School for Girls in Victoria c. 1922 and moved it to North Vancouver in 1926. Like the many boys' schools that had preceded it, Gulland's was a private venture with a focus on building students' characters.

North Vancouver Museum and Archives 4899

if the need arise, qualified to assume positions of leadership and responsibility." At the same time, however, Gulland's stated curriculum appeared to focus on traditionally female—in the eyes of many at the time—subjects such as art, music, languages and gardening.

Jessie Cant was perhaps the most prominent female educator of them all. The Scottish-born Cant had been trained as a teacher and arrived in the city in 1911. In 1920, Cant's interest in public education and the welfare of women propelled her into local politics, winning a seat as a school trustee. She stood for election to the school board in 1920. In 1924, her fellow trustees chose her as their chair, no small achievement for a woman at the time. That same year saw her appointed as judge of the juvenile court of the city. Despite Cant's success at the polls, many years were to pass before a woman was elected to council, and still more before a woman became mayor. Women may have been trusted as volunteers for the Red Cross and other charitable organizations, but real power remained with the men of the community. Even within the realm of health, women were often consigned to the sidelines as the major decisions were made by men.

Nowhere was this demonstrated more clearly than in the ongoing hospital debate. When the Dawson sisters had built their second hospital in 1910, the city was home to fewer than five thousand inhabitants. By 1921 the population had increased by over 55 percent, but the number of hospital beds in what was now the district-owned hospital had not kept pace. When the three North Shore councils began a series of monthly joint meetings in January 1919, hospital services were high on the agenda. By July, representatives of the district had conducted a study of their own and came to the conclusion that "the three nurses are graduates and judge that they know more concerning the requirements of patients than the average woman" as well as the more questionable belief that sterilizing surgical instruments on the facility's kitchen stove was acceptable practice. In the eyes

Meeting of the North Vancouver School Board, Mrs Jessie Cant, chair, c. 1924. The province's women took an active interest in causes such as education, but it was unusual for them to stand successfully for office, much less to be elected to positions of such prominence.
North Vancouver Museum and Archives, 5347

of the district's all-male council, there was nothing wrong with the hospital that couldn't be corrected with an additional subsidy of $500 per year.

The community's women took a different view. Under the presidency of Ruth Clements, the North Vancouver Red Cross Society secured the donation of thirty hospital beds and placed them in storage as they waited for the city fathers to get behind a new facility. It was not until the North Shore's doctors began to speak openly about mismanagement and filth at the hospital that the two councils began to take notice.

A mass meeting held in March 1920 endorsed a proposal to construct a new, thirty-bed fireproof facility to be located in the city and serve all three North Shore municipalities, and the North Shore Memorial Hospital Society was formed the next month. But the councils rejected the proposal, the society was ignored, more proposals were made and abandoned over the next several years, and West Vancouver dropped out of the discussions. It was not until 1928 that the two remaining governments agreed on a funding formula, acquired voter approval and hired a firm of architects for a wholly new facility. When funding proved inadequate, the Imperial Order of Daughters of the Empire, the Girls' Auxiliary and the Women's Auxiliary raised the funds for furnishings and equipment. When the state-of-the-art three-storey hospital opened on May 29, 1929, the city was exultant. The North Vancouver General Hospital, the provincial secretary declared, was the "best for its size in the province," while the president of the British Columbia Hospital Association observed that "In hospital matters in general, the North Shore is very much to the fore."

For many North Shore residents, the debate on hospital services was but one indicator of an ongoing civic malaise: surely having one local government rather than two would lead to more efficient decision-making. After considerable discussion at

North Vancouver General Hospital, 1929. When government funding proved inadequate, North Vancouver women's organizations raised enough money to help equip the state-of-the-art hospital.

North Vancouver Museum and Archives, p283

its November 1923 meeting, the board of trade dispatched a committee to investigate the pros and cons of the city amalgamating with the district. With one mayor, one council, a single staff and a single hall, the advantages of amalgamation seemed self-evident. But the idea was forgotten when, once again, North Vancouver's attentions were taken up by the bridge issue.

North Shore officials revived the Second Narrows initiative in April 1922 when council reviewed a proposal for a bridge from the American Iron Products Company of New York. All three North Shore councils approved the initiative, but negotiations with the firm collapsed. Just when it seemed again that the bridge would never be built, two Canadian firms—the Northern Construction Company and J.W. Stewart—offered a proposal of their own. Federal and provincial grants were re-secured, the necessary municipal bylaws were passed, and on July 25, 1923, a contract for construction was finally signed. The bridge would accommodate both cars and trains. The final design, by engineer William Smaill, reflected both compromises and improvements. The swing span formerly proposed became a bascule span. The deck and approaches were raised, and the load capacity was increased in the vehicle lanes.

The signing of the contract was cause for great celebration. Over four hundred citizens from the three North Shore municipalities gathered in the Knights of Pythias Hall to recognize the occasion. Numerous dignitaries rose to compliment each other's efforts and to comment on the significance of the contract. Hyperbole was rampant. Dr. W.H. Sutherland, the provincial Minister of Public Works, asserted, "Within the next few years the North Shore is bound to advance very rapidly and I believe we will see the time when a stranger entering the harbour will wonder which is Vancouver and which is its northern suburb." Although the assembly contained many distinguished citizens, the event maintained a community feel, the banquet having been cooked by local housewives while ladies from the local St. Andrew's and Caledonian Society waited the tables. Song sheets were provided and the evening concluded on a decidedly folksy note as guests belted out a series of popular tunes.

Construction of the bridge began on September 13, 1923, a date the *North Shore Press* trumpeted as "the most important date in local history." After so many years of promises and false starts, for some, the event defied belief. According to the local press, "One old timer undertook to break the glad news to a disbelieving friend on Lonsdale Avenue. Walking up to the friend he said, 'Well, they have started work on the bridge at last.' 'Huh,' replied the friend. 'I know one funnier than that!'"

When the bridge finally opened on November 7, 1925, the controversy and disappointment that had long hounded the project faded into memory. Hundreds of people gathered on both sides of the inlet to take in the festivities. A parade of cars assembled in downtown Vancouver, made its way along Hastings Street, and stopped at the southern end of the bridge. According to the *Vancouver Province*, Dr. Sutherland made a short speech before cutting "the silken strand which barred the approach. As the ribbon parted, a signal rocket was fired and the bascule span was lowered amid the cheers of the throng, shrill blasts of steamboat whistles and sounding of automobile horns." Dr. Sutherland and the other dignitaries then made toward their cars to lead a mile-long parade of automobiles across the inlet.

The first Second Narrows Bridge under construction, April 1925. Its completion was the fulfillment of a decades-old dream.

North Vancouver Museum and Archives, 9736

APR. 28. 25.

"Indians in war paint and native dress stood up in their canoes and shouted the war cries of their tribe," while "those on board pleasure craft passing and re-passing beneath the bridge added their cheers to the clamour and the roar of the motors of the seaplane circling overhead." Having crossed the bridge, the procession made its way along Third past Lonsdale Avenue and down Keith Road to the Drill Hall. There, in true British spirit, participants were served tea amid the strains of the Sixth Field Company's brass band.

The three North Shore municipalities, residents felt, were poised for a period of unprecedented growth and prosperity. The benefits were to be threefold: more residential construction, industrial development and outdoor recreation. A booklet published to commemorate the bridge captured the tenor of the time. With so many mountains, forests and valleys at its back, North Vancouver was destined to become an important centre for outdoor recreation.

Adjacent to mountains and forests, North Vancouver was destined to become an important centre for outdoor pursuits. A climbing party including Don Munday of the BC Mountaineering Club ascends the Lions.

North Vancouver Museum and Archives, 6315

The North Shore had long been the object of day trips from the inlet's southern shore. Pete Larson's Dominion Day celebrations had helped in this regard. Periodic improvements in the cross-inlet ferry system, coupled with North Vancouver's own reliable streetcar system and the construction of the North Shore Division of the PGE furthered the ambitious city's reputation as the gateway to the wilderness. Work by Don and Phyllis Munday and other members of the BC Mountaineering Club, and the opening of the Grouse Mountain Highway and Scenic Resort in 1926, popularized climbing in the North Shore mountains. Ken Gostick was typical of the young people who considered a trip from Vancouver to the North Shore mountains a tremendous adventure: "The Cub Scout leader used to take us over on the ferry. We'd get on the streetcar and go out to the top at Lynn Valley and then headed over to the Seymour River. He hiked and we swam and did everything kids do." Construction of the bridge had made the North Shore even more accessible for day trips such as these. And importantly, the city was replete with residential and industrial potential only a bridge could foster.

The Board of Harbour Commissioners had long been criticized for concentrating its efforts on the south shore of the inlet. Industries located in North Vancouver had developed their facilities without material aid from the Harbour Commissioners. For many harbour-based industries, fire was a constant worry. In August 1923 alone, the Hobson Shingle Mill and the McNair Shingle Mill were both destroyed by fire. The latter fire was spectacular, attracting a crowd of over four thousand spectators, many of whom narrowly missed injury when a sixty-gallon chemical tank exploded and ascended three hundred feet into the air before landing dangerously close to the onlookers. The *North Shore Press* was quick to point the finger of blame at the Harbour Commissioners, who had yet to fund a fireboat to serve the inlet. Many considered the lack of a co-ordinated approach to fire suppression "a standing reproach to the harbour of Burrard Inlet." The completion of the Second Narrows Bridge, however, resulted in a series of events that the North Shore municipalities could only applaud. In January 1925 provincial legislation extended the city's boundaries to include Moodyville. That same year the Harbour Board acquired title to two thousand feet of waterfrontage west of the foot of St. David's Avenue, in District Lot 274, and a similar amount of waterfrontage to the east in District Lot 273.

The city's waterfront entered a period of unprecedented change. As the Harbour Board noted, construction of the bridge had rendered the area east of Burrard Dry Dock ripe for development. As parts of the area's foreshore were extremely shallow, much of the Moodyville hillside was scraped away and re-deposited as fill on the tidal flats. About fifteen acres of land were reclaimed, all highly suitable for industrial and commercial purposes. Low Level Road was constructed parallel to the new railway line. The concrete road was built at the city's expense, the ratepayers having approved borrowing $150,000 for various road and waterworks projects. A number of industries soon expressed interest in locating in the new lands. By late 1927 Randall, Gee, and Mitchell Ltd. announced their intention to lease land for the construction of a concrete grain elevator. Another firm, the Canadian Transport Company, decided to lease the five-hundred-foot long Japan Wharf and adjoining sheds to support a lumber export business. Yet another firm

The Midland Pacific Grain elevator, built on reclaimed land east of the site of Moodyville, c. 1930.

North Vancouver Museum and Archives, 9683

was exploring opportunities for a manufacturing plant, but it was the grain elevator that attracted the most discussion.

The construction of Vancouver's first grain elevator had begun in 1913, shortly after the creation of the Vancouver Harbour Board. North Vancouver's own grain elevator, owned and operated by the Midland Pacific Elevator, opened in 1928. The new facility was smaller than Vancouver's, having an initial capacity of 500,000 bushels but capable of expansion to three times that amount. Its capacity was only 5 percent of the harbour's total capacity, but this was an impressive start for an unproven area of the harbour. Midland's elevator proved an instant success, prompting the construction of a one-million-bushel addition the following year.

With these new feathers in their caps, North Shore industrialists cast a covetous eye on the inlet's four First Nations reserves. Many North Vancouver residents considered the Mission Reserve an obstacle to industrial development and an inefficient use of valuable waterfront. City council actively advocated for the removal of the Squamish from their reserve early in 1922, with support from municipal and provincial bureaucrats. In December 1920 the provincial travelling health officer and the city's medical health officer had visited the reserve and prepared a written report, which noted:

> *Conditions are better than on some reserves I have visited but I have yet to see an Indian Reserve where sanitary conditions are satisfactory . . . I think the only satisfactory solution is the removal of the Indians to some remote point from large centres of white population and this can be done only by the Federal authority by agreement with the Indians.*

Press reports offered no details of the alleged health infractions and although the board of trade and council periodically approached the federal government to relocate the Squamish—who do not appear to have been consulted in the matter—the reserves remained where they were.

Squamish councillors may well have wondered what effect the bridge would have on their reserves. Four transcontinental railways had secured running rights over the span: the Canadian Pacific Railway, Canadian National Railways, the Great Northern Railway and the now obscure Chicago, Milwaukee & St. Louis Railway. Once completed, the Terminal Railway proposed by the Harbour Board would connect the railways on the south side of the inlet with the Pacific Great Eastern Railway, which served points as far away as Horseshoe Bay. Although the bridge opened to motor vehicles toward the end of 1925, the acquisition of a right of way to the PGE's terminus at the foot of Lonsdale Avenue was no easy matter. The question of jurisdiction over the foreshore and over the adjacent water lots was at the core of the problem. The city, the province, the federal government and private

On April 24, 1929, bystanders crowded along the tracks to witness the opening of Vancouver Harbour Commission's railway tunnel below Esplanade. The tunnel allowed trains to pass through the heart of the city without negative impacts on business or residents.

North Vancouver Museum and Archives, 11298

property owners each claimed some measure of authority. The Wallace family in particular opposed any infringement on their property, and were able to influence the decision makers. In 1927, construction began on a railway tunnel south of Esplanade but it was not until the spring of 1929 that the line was completed. The first passenger train from Vancouver arrived to popular acclaim on April 26, 1929.

Over four thousand spectators gathered for the event, presided over by Governor General Lord Willingdon. The $200,000, 1,500-foot-long reinforced concrete tunnel was generally regarded as a miracle of modern engineering. Mayor George Morden was ecstatic. In his remarks Morden recognized the creative work of George Hanes, the city engineer, who routed the railway in such a way that it didn't infringe on the properties adjacent to Esplanade and avoided a level crossing at the foot of Lonsdale Avenue. The provincial government, he declared, ought now to complete the railway line to Prince George. Mayor Malkin of Vancouver dared to think of the day when amalgamation would see North Vancouver and Vancouver as a single political entity, with a population twenty years hence of over one million people.

For many, the heady days of the late 1920s were reminiscent of the pre-war boom. The bridge having only just been completed, the city's population surpassed ten thousand people by 1927. The growth of the city, and of its waterfront industries in particular, prompted the adoption of the city's first zoning bylaw as well as the creation of its first Town Planning Commission. The *North Shore Press* felt sufficiently confident of the ambitious city's future to issue a "prosperity supplement" in May 1927 and cited the recent opening of the Second Narrows Bridge as "the first real break" the aspiring city had had in its "quarter century struggle" to achieve its rightful destiny. Other noteworthy developments named in the special edition included the construction of the highway up Grouse Mountain and the purchase by the Board of Harbour Commissioners of "extensive tracts of city waterfront property" in the eastern part of the city. Extensive industrial, wharfing and warehousing developments were predicted as the inevitable outcome of this significant investment in the city.

The major local industries of the day included the Burrard Dry Dock, Vancouver Drydock and Salvage, a Home Oil depot and cracking plant, and a number of waterfront sawmills. The Vancouver Creosoting Company, Capilano Timber Company and North Vancouver Sawmills all operated in the district, but they too offered jobs to the city's growing population. The harbour was also booming. Official reports noted that 328 deep-sea vessels had visited the inlet in 1919. By 1928, the number had increased to 1,344. If the economy continued to be sound, the North Shore would finally become the industrial centre so many had been hoping for.

It was not to be. The PGE closed its North Shore Division in 1928, just months before the completion of the railway from Vancouver. The company's financial difficulties and the challenge of building and operating in areas of steep grades had proved insurmountable. The railway's tracks remained in place for the time being, but the prospect of connecting North Vancouver to the much-vaunted riches of the province's interior was called into question. The recently completed bridge encountered problems of its own. On March 10, 1927, the American steamer *Eurana*, her hold filled with a cargo of lumber destined for New York, hit a section

Tug *Lorne* and the Pacific Gatherer *at Second Narrows Bridge, September 1930. Since its opening the bridge had been struck twenty times, but it was the Pacific Gatherer's collision with the ill-fated span that put the bridge out of commission until repairs were completed in 1934.*

North Vancouver Museum and Archives, 15597

Below: Installation of vertical lift span to replace the bascule at Second Narrows bridge, May 29, 1934.

North Vancouver Museum and Archives, 7969

of the bridge. The ship was jammed into the span, prompting fears that the bridge would break apart as the ship forced it upward under the force of the rising tide. Quick work on the part of salvage engineers released the ship and the western lane of the bridge was soon re-opened to traffic. The bridge was repaired at a cost of $30,000, but the incident was an omen of misfortunes to come. A year later the freighter *Norwich City* also collided with the bridge, necessitating repairs to both span and ship.

By April 24, 1929 the bridge had been struck an additional twenty times, many of the accidents having been attributed to treacherous currents in the narrows. Damage ranged anywhere from $400 to $100,000, the latter sum having been required to repair the extensive damage inflicted by the *Losmar* on April 24, 1930. On September 19, 1930 the bridge was hit once again. This time the offending vessel was a log carrier, the *Pacific Gatherer*. The tug-drawn hulk, which was in ballast, was caught by the current and forced into the span, wedging itself under the same section previously hit by the *Eurana*. According to the *Vancouver Province*:

> The span was hurled about fifteen feet off its south piers by the first impact. Jammed solidly underneath the structure, and defying all efforts of the tug to move it, the carrier slowly but surely forced the bridge span out of position. About an hour later, as the tide rose, the span gave a tremendous heave, lurched eastward, slithered off the piers, and . . . with a final scream of breaking bolts and twisted steel . . . crashed into the water.

With the Second Narrows Bridge closed, line-ups for the ferry stretched well up Lonsdale Avenue. The situation eased in 1934 when the bridge re-opened.
City of Vancouver Archives, BR P75.2

Lying eighty feet under the water, there was little hope of recovering the sunken section of the bridge. Officials of the Burrard Inlet Tunnel and Bridge Company—the owners of the span—predicted a closure of up to three months. In fact, four years were to pass before the bridge was repaired. The company declared bankruptcy in 1932, and ownership of the span passed to the federal government in 1933. It was not until November 1934 that the bridge re-opened, this time with a centre lift-span carefully placed to avoid the currents that had caused so much grief.

THE PRODIGAL CITY 1930–1939

9

The loss of its bridge was a major blow to the ambitious city, but the worldwide economic depression of 1929–33 was a far greater setback. Curiously, the *North Shore Press* initially ignored the event, its first issue after the stock market crash instead focussing on plans by Stuart Cameron and Company for a $25,000 plant east of St. George's Avenue on the city's waterfront. The following issue confidently suggested that a link to the northern portion of the PGE might well be completed in the coming year, with North Vancouver as the southern terminus. Three weeks later the paper's twin headlines proclaimed the CNR's faith in the British Columbian economy and a lobby in favour of a ferry service across Howe Sound.

But reality soon set in. On December 6, 1929, a story announced the formation by district council of a committee to address a growth in unemployment. More importantly, the paper reported an impending joint meeting of ratepayers in the district and the city to discuss the potential of amalgamating the two jurisdictions, a move partly spurred on by the deteriorating economic situation. As Christmas approached, it became increasingly

clear that many North Shore families were facing severe hardship. The Elks'
Christmas Cheer Committee issued a frantic appeal for help in distributing 250
hampers prepared for needy families, the Girl Guides and Boy Scouts prepared toys
for children who would otherwise go without, and the North Shore Press Gifts in
Kind Fund gathered clothing to help families face the winter yet to come.

The economic situation was indeed becoming desperate. In Canada, corporate
profits had reached $396 million in 1929. Four years later, the nation's corporate
losses totalled $98 million. Canadian exports shrank by 50 percent between 1929 and
1933. With much of its workforce employed in resource-based industries and with
prices for exports plummeting, North Vancouverites, like other British Columbians,
were particularly susceptible to economic hardship. By 1933, per capita incomes
in British Columbia had decreased by 47 percent while the unemployment rate
hovered around 30 percent. Wages were cut and families found it increasingly
difficult to make ends meet. Family assets began to disappear. Women pawned
their wedding rings. Homeowners defaulted on their mortgages and their savings
eroded until disappearing altogether.

In 1930, the financial statements of the North Vancouver Land and Improvement
Company recorded annual sales of only $1,508. With land holdings valued at
$420,940 and $1,422.36 cash in hand, the company was as challenged as many
of the homeowners with whom it dealt. Edward Mahon, one of the company's
principals, weathered the storm quite well. Despite his wealth, Mahon and his
family had always lived a modest life, never owning an automobile and generally
travelling by streetcar. It seems unlikely Mahon had anticipated the stock market
crash, but his sale in 1928 of his West End home to the builders of what would
become Vancouver's Marine Building could not have been better timed. J.P. Fell,
co-owner of the Lonsdale Estate, remained in his Shaughnessy home and if he
economized in the face of the new reality it was not very obvious. As Fell's son
Michael recalled of his parents:

> They obviously had enough to live very comfortably—even during the Depression
> years. As a boy, I remember that we had a cook, housekeeper, chauffeur, gardener,
> and nanny for me (when I was small). My parents entertained extensively; my
> father especially loved to be host at dinner parties. The clubs that my father
> belonged to included at least the Vancouver Club and the Shaughnessy Golf Club.
> My father played polo (when he was hale and hearty), and kept polo ponies and
> a groom to look after them. At the same time, I was (I think) aware that he was
> by no means the richest of the social group that he consorted with.

For those of lesser means, the Depression was devastating. Wage earners
suddenly lost their jobs and much of their self-esteem. People became increasingly
dependent on government relief and private charity. Soup kitchens became
commonplace. A barter economy began to appear, with people often trading labour
for food and other necessities. One North Shore physician, Dr. Emile Therrien,
later related how he had provided clinical services in return for what could only be
described as unorthodox commodities:

I recall in those years getting paid off with chicken manure, goats' milk, people doing odd jobs around my place, eggs, you name it. And there was no vet on the North Shore then and I neutered cats, splinted legs on canaries, deloused and dewormed dogs. There were only eight doctors on the North Shore then. People were reticent to come to a doctor because they couldn't afford it. And they were more reticent to go into hospital because of the high cost.

University enrolments fell, students no longer able to pay their fees. Youths aged sixteen and over left the family home to fend for themselves, lest their continued presence at home disqualify their families from relief. Many became itinerant workers, taking odd jobs wherever they could, or drifting toward the relief camps scattered through the province. There they lived on wartime rations, donned war surplus clothing, and slept cheek by jowl in tarpaper shacks.

No one, it seemed, had any money. Free vegetable seeds were supplied to the registered unemployed. Families took to growing their own produce and supplemented their meals with locally procured fish and game. Eva Hallaway, born in North Vancouver to Italian immigrant parents, recalled how city lots were turned into miniature farms: "We had all the boulevard in garden and all the back, and we had goats, chickens, and rabbits. You had to count the rabbits every morning! It was quite common . . . We were raised on goat's milk. It was horrible!"

Hungry families needed to jig for salmon and beg their butchers for soup bones. Some relied on handouts from charity organizations. Jigging for salmon was a risky business that put many a city resident in trouble with the law. Despite the danger, boys like Robin Williams revelled in their forays to the Capilano River: "It was illegal to jig for salmon as they moved upstream in the shallow waters of the river, good for a ten-dollar fine or a couple of days in jail. But times were so hard during the Depression that many North Shore families wouldn't have had any meat to eat without salmon from the river and an occasional deer."

For families on the Mission Reserve, the effects of the Depression were severe. With cutbacks in the forest industry and reduced levels of exports, men who had earned a living in the forests, on the docks and in the mills returned to more traditional pursuits. A century and a half after first encountering Europeans, the Squamish people remained accomplished fishermen. Entire families travelled the coast, living in bunkhouses or on their boats, the men working the nets while their wives laboured in the canneries.

Although many families abandoned their homes in North Vancouver to seek opportunities elsewhere, others such as Robin Williams' family had been forced to sell their homes in Vancouver in favour of less expensive habitations on the North Shore. Williams remembered the family's move to the abandoned Nye house in Upper Lonsdale well and contrasted life amid "Shaughnessy's manicured boulevards, fortress-like mansions, and aloof society" with his freer life in North Vancouver: "There was no end of places to explore and play within easy distance of the old mansion, nor a shortage of adventurous boys nearby. We were all in the same boat more or less financially, so we developed friendships rapidly and based upon common interests rather than a division between the haves and the have-nots."

For women living in North Vancouver during the Depression, working at the switchboard in the telephone exchange was a rare employment opportunity.

North Vancouver Museum and Archives, 4208

Many children were oblivious of the economic situation and continued to enjoy the outdoor opportunities that the North Shore provided. On the Mission Reserve, kids played football and baseball in the open space behind the church and amused themselves on the nearby beach. As Lila Johnston recalled, "We did a lot of climbing up the steeple . . . a lot of playing hide and go seek, kick the can, skip rope, swim all summer. Mom would never see us because we'd have a piece of homemade bread and stayed out there all day long. We'd never get back until four or five in the afternoon in the summer."

For adult females, life was rather more challenging. Robin Williams recalled gender-based discrimination in hiring practices:

> *A woman primary school teacher with twenty years experience received $1,360 per year in 1931, but was cut to only $1,030 by 1933. Not until ten years later, when World War Two was well under way, did she get back to where she was in 1931. If she was a married woman she took double punishment; first for being female, second for being married. The theory behind the two pay scales was that men were "heads of families" and that a married woman was not the main breadwinner, both wrong assumptions in many cases.*

Eager high school students faced a rude awakening upon graduation. Upper Lonsdale resident Jim Galozo recalled the constraints of the 1930s: "It wasn't easy. I graduated from Vancouver Technical School in 1932. It wasn't until 1940 that I

started working in a decent, recognized, full-time job. I survived the eight-year period from 1932 to 1940 by doing part time work, such as chopping wood or picking berries, fruit, or hops in the Fraser Valley." Dora (Curry) Stacey had similar memories:

> Jobs were scarce and boys and girls would pound the pavement for months looking for work that just wasn't there. Some were willing to work for nothing just to gain experience. No one would even look at you unless you had Junior Matriculation. Those days were the worst in history for unemployment. People waited for hours in bread lines to get a free meal.

In some areas of the country, unemployment had led to social unrest. Fearing that the province's disenchanted youth might well engage in destructive behaviour, Minister of Education Dr. G.M. Weir took action. His Provincial Recreation Programme, more popularly known as "Pro-Rec," was unveiled in 1934 with the stated intent of combating "the demoralizing influence of enforced idleness." Offering opportunities in areas such as callisthenics, team sports, track and field events, swimming meets, gymnastics and dancing, the program was an instant success. The province provided instructors and basic equipment, while local communities were expected to supply the necessary sports fields, courts and indoor facilities. Fraternal, community and church-owned halls became transformed into rudimentary gymnasia overnight. Originally intended for youth aged sixteen to twenty-one, the program was opened up to any resident of the province in 1936. The Pro-Rec initiative found a welcoming home in the Horticultural Hall, where for the next two decades instructors offered programs in callisthenics, badminton and other indoor sports.

The threat of social unrest triggered responses in residents themselves. The North and West Vancouver Council of Women formed in 1930 to work "for the betterment of conditions pertaining to the family, the community, and the state." Members could join either as individuals or through affiliated organizations such as the Women Conservatives, the Women Liberals, the Lady Laurier League and the Women's Christian Temperance Union. Over the years, the council co-ordinated much of the works of its affiliated groups, but also took on projects of its own, including the conversion of an old house into a kindergarten, organizing services for senior citizens and advocacy on behalf of abused children.

Other volunteers addressed the needs of itinerant seamen. With sailors wandering through the town with nothing constructive to do, residents with a social conscience met to consider the formation of a North Vancouver Missions to Seamen. The initiative had originally been proposed during the 1920s but had failed to get off the ground. The *North Shore Press* was highly supportive of the proposal:

These seamen land upon our shores without friends or acquaintances, with nowhere to go, knowing not what to do with their leisure time while the vessel is in dock. They are men, who, because of the nature of their calling are deprived of that home life and influence which is dear to the landsman. They are men, who in the main, appreciate the provisions that are made at very many ports in the world for their welfare and entertainment . . . Any port that is known among the rank and file of the men who sail the seven seas as a port that has at heart the welfare of the seamen of the merchant service, has made for itself an enviable reputation that those men will carry to all parts of the world.

The city's Seamen's Institute opened in 1935, much of the impetus having come from the Men's Club of St. John's Anglican Church and the local branch of Toc H, a service organization established in Flanders during the First World War. The response from visiting sailors was immediate and intense, resulting in the Institute renting increasingly large quarters until securing a permanent home at First and St. George's in 1936.

The Depression placed enormous strain on both families and individuals who lived in North Vancouver, but its effect was no less stressful on the city itself. The city stagnated. As the economy worsened, successive councils were faced with the difficult task of balancing the civic budget. Desperate for cash, city council decided in October 1930 to tax not only land, but improvements as well. The result was catastrophic. Property owners unable to pay their taxes lost their homes to the city. Although it soon became land-rich, the city remained cash-poor. By the end of 1932, the city had fallen heir to properties with an assessed value of $723,692. These were properties from which no tax revenues would be forthcoming. Further, arrears of taxes for the years 1930–32 totalled $217,711. In 1932, the city's total tax levy amounted to $414,366. Much of this amount was simply not collectible. Civic expenditures continued to outstrip revenues and the city was soon in the position of no longer being able to honour its bonds.

In January 1933, incoming mayor George Morden expressed relief in noting that the provincial government had not chosen to intervene in the city's affairs. The provincial government had other ideas. Unbeknownst to council, the province had already decided to terminate the elected officials in the city and to replace them with an appointee. On January 24, 1933, the Lieutenant-Governor-in-Council abolished the elected mayor and council and approved the appointment of Charles Edward Tisdall, a former mayor of Vancouver, as commissioner of the city. Tisdall, who had also been appointed commissioner of the district in 1932, assumed a weighty portfolio, having been granted "all powers and authority heretofore vested in or exercisable by the Mayor, the Council, the Board of Police Commissioners, the Board of School Trustees, the Municipal Clerk, and the other officers of The Corporation of City of North Vancouver."

Tisdall's first priority was to reduce the city's expenditures while seeking new sources of revenue. Within a week, Tisdall dismissed all city officials paid a monthly salary, and cut teachers' and ferry workers' salaries by 10 percent. The district hall and school board offices were closed and their staffs relocated to city hall. Nothing was untouchable. Tisdall's successor G.D.G. Tate abolished the city's police force in October 1934 and contracted with the province's police force to undertake its work. Although such measures may have appeared heavy-handed, Tisdall and his successors also exhibited compassion and conciliation. Water rates were forgiven on properties rented to families unable to pay their rent. A dismissed schoolteacher was "given first call for substitute work and first consideration when a vacancy occurs" and former elected officials found new work sitting on the hospital board.

The new commissioner also took steps to increase the revenues. The date when penalties were imposed for the non-payment of taxes was brought forward, and concerted efforts were made to collect monies owed. By mid-August 1933, the City of North Vancouver's revenues had increased by 14 percent compared with the same period in 1932. The same could not be said of the district, where revenues decreased by 29 percent in the same time period. Tisdall encouraged the need for collaborative action to address a range of public needs. Recognizing the importance of preserving the public transportation system, he supported the BCER's renewed proposal for one-man streetcars. At his instigation, discussions were held with the hospital board, the Red Cross and the Victorian Order of Nurses to find ways to provide medical and dental services to the city's destitute unemployed.

Providing for the unemployed and their families was no small undertaking. By mid-1933, the worst year of the Depression, over 1,600 city residents were on relief. For many of the unemployed, socialism and communism became appealing

Charles E. Tisdall, first Commissioner of the City of North Vancouver, had a long career in public life, also serving as a parks commissioner, alderman and mayor in the City of Vancouver as well as a member of the province's legislative assembly.
North Vancouver Museum and Archives, 7874

alternatives to the seemingly discredited capitalist system in which the North Shore had so long placed its faith. When a group of 150 unemployed men appeared at city hall to lay their demands before the commissioner, Tisdall received a representative committee, heard them out, and dissuaded them from crossing the inlet to join a larger demonstration.

But Tisdall had a more difficult time controlling conversations and debates that raged beyond his reach. As Robin Williams recalled, "Arguments, theories, and remedies were bandied about in families, among friends, neighbours, occupation groups, church members, and to some extent . . . the public schools." Each year, every elementary school pupil in North Vancouver was encouraged to write an essay or story about the perils of Bolshevism. There was a monetary prize for the best essay in support of the capitalist system provided by the Royal Canadian Legion, an organization that had morphed from the Great War Veterans Association and a number of other bodies in 1925. In the end, Tisdall and his successors preserved the peace. Although some city residents may have joined in the riot of the unemployed in Vancouver in 1938, the streets of North Vancouver remained largely protest-free.

Tisdall took steps to encourage new businesses to locate on the North Shore. When the M.B. King Lumber Company expressed interest in establishing a sawmill at the foot of Fell Avenue in March 1933, Tisdall underwrote the firm's costs in connecting to the city's water system. The arrival of the sawmill was a major coup for Tisdall and just what the city needed at a time of high unemployment. Over time, the King family's mill became the stuff of local legend with King's sons Donald and Graeme eventually joining its management. Long-time employee Alf Donati recalled a benevolent style of management where he was referred to affectionately as "blacksmith," while another long-term staff member, George Atchison, was called "Old George." According to Donati:

> The company was proud that it was able to hire many young people during summer holidays and on weekends, which assisted greatly in furthering their education. As a result, there were many families who had two or three generations employed at the same time.

Malcolm King appears to have been the antithesis of the stern captains of industry so typical of the time. The story of how unemployed carriage setter James Polk obtained his job at the mill is a case in point. After lingering around the mill's time clock for a while, Polk was approached by an unassuming man who asked what he was doing. Polk replied, "Looking for a job," and then continued, "No need you hanging around, the old bastard that owns this mill will never hire you." The unassuming man was Malcolm King, and despite his faux pas Polk was put to work that morning.

It was the presence of the Wallace family's shipyard and dry dock that continued to put bread on the table for many North Vancouver residents. As if choosing to avoid the economic tumult to come, Andy Wallace had died in his Vancouver home on January 1, 1929. His sons Clarence and Hubert took his place at the helm of the family business. In the depressed economy of the 1930s, however, the future of even the Wallaces' enterprise was uncertain. British and eastern Canadian firms underbid the local firm on a succession of shipbuilding contracts. With major financial losses in every year from 1925 to 1936, save for 1927, the collapse of the firm often seemed imminent. Yet somehow the Wallaces hung on, securing the occasional shipbuilding contract and repairing the many vessels that had struck the Second Narrows Bridge with appalling regularity.

Wallaces' payroll rose and fell dramatically as contracts came and went. It was a frustrating situation for both management and labour. As Jim Galozo recalled in later years, would-be workers went to almost any length to secure even a single day's employment:

> *Jobs were hard to come by in the early thirties. There would be a surge of work here in North Vancouver whenever a ship would go on dry dock to have its hull scraped of barnacles and painted. There was no set crew at the site to do this menial unskilled work. Those men seeking to be chosen to do the job would line up side by side and the foreman, Big Jim, would travel the length of the line and choose his crew at random . . . We would often know that a ship was being dry-docked by the noise created by the pumps as they raised the dry dock. The sound was audible as far away as Lynn Valley, North Lonsdale and Capilano. One winter morning after a snowfall I heard the pumps at work, and rushed down to the dry dock expecting to find a ship waiting. You can imagine my disappointment when I found that the dock had been lowered into the waters of Burrard Inlet only to rid the deck of its burden of snow!*

The sad state of the city's economy was a significant challenge for those who sought to revive its former spirit of unabashed optimism. Gloom hung over the ambitious city well into the 1930s. The deaths in early 1936 of King George V, for whom so many North Shore residents had fought two decades before, and of Charles Tisdall did nothing to boost the city's sagging spirits.

As the 1930s wore on the economic situation and the mood of the community both began to improve. A much-respected former mayor, George Washington Vance, assumed the commissioner's chair in 1936. As conditions permitted, Vance restored selected city services. The city's sporting life also provided hope. When North Shore United captured the dominion's soccer championships in Winnipeg in August 1938, the *North Shore Press* was jubilant: "It was a series that wrote soccer history. In point of fact, it was a soccer marathon that for sheer exemplification of the never-say-die spirit, will live on in memory if for no other reason than it will give teams of the future something really worthwhile at which to shoot."

The team returned to a hero's welcome, with what seemed to many to be the entire population of the North Shore meeting them at the CPR station in Vancouver. The team was feted at a civic banquet hosted by Vance. According to the *North Shore Press*, Vance had been gratified "to find that eight of the members of the team were local boys born and bred on the North Shore." One of the team's star players was twenty-three-year-old Jimmy Spencer. That season, Spencer had scored forty-nine goals in league play and another six in a quarter-final match. For North Vancouverites, Spencer and soccer became virtually synonymous. Although he

George W. Vance was one of the City of North Vancouver's most distinguished citizens, serving as mayor from 1917 to 1921 and as commissioner from 1936 until his death in 1944. It was largely through his efforts that the city's financial health improved, making a return to elected government possible before the end of the Second World War.

North Vancouver Museum and Archives, 6925

North Shore United Soccer Team, national champions, 1938. Jimmy Spencer, fourth from right in the first row, was one of the team's high scorers and declined an opportunity to play professionally in the United Kingdom.

North Vancouver Museum and Archives, 13874

declined offers to play for English professional teams such as Wolverhampton and Derby County, Spencer played and coached locally, eventually turning his talents to refereeing juvenile soccer. Spencer joined the city's fire department in 1936 and became its chief in 1958. By the time he retired in the early 1970s, the name Spencer had become a much-respected household word.

Victories on the sports field greatly enhanced community identity and spirit. So did activities at the North Shore's schools. Dick Hallaway began his education at Ridgeway School before pursuing secondary schooling at North Shore College. In the 1930s and 1940s, instruction at the college reflected the same sporting and academic traditions that Reverend Marsden had brought to St. John's School a generation earlier. Dayboys and boarders both wore the school's distinctive uniform and tie, two elements of a comprehensive scheme to build school spirit. Participation in team sports was rigorously encouraged. As Hallaway recalled:

The discipline was certainly very strict . . . it was a long day. You had to play sports unless you had a medical certificate. Our day started at ten past nine . . . We went till ten o'clock and we didn't go back into school till one o'clock. We played sports after that, either rugby, cricket, soccer, boxing—that type of stuff. And then we went into school from one to three o'clock, then out for fifteen minutes then back till quarter to five. Then you went home. And you had two hours of prep every night . . . homework in other words . . . They made you work. You were there to work; there was no question about it!

Staff of North Vancouver High School c. 1936. Principal Mickey McDougall, one of the community's legendary figures, stands in the top left. McDougall nurtured a long-serving and much-remembered staff of teachers, many of whom were also active in community affairs.

North Vancouver Museum and Archives, 3901

Students at North Shore College generally came from British families, and as Hallaway remembered, "some of them were kind of class conscious." Though attracting a wider clientele, North Vancouver High School, the city's only public secondary school, also fostered a sense of kinship among its students. Indeed, the 1930s were in many ways the school's golden years, one of those rare times when conditions were ripe for both scholastic and athletic success. More importantly, however, the 1930s was a period in which the school became a focus for community, with students and residents at large sharing pride in its achievements.

Much of the school's success was due to one remarkable man, Wilfrid R. "Mickey" McDougall. For many who grew up in the ambitious city, McDougall *was* North Van High. A teacher in the school beginning in the early 1920s, McDougall went on to serve as its principal until the mid-1950s. With McDougall at the helm, students were encouraged to find their gifts and pursue their dreams. Students with personal or family problems received his personal attention. New teachers were advised, "By the time boys get to high school, they're too old for physical punishment to do any good. We have to use psychology." And McDougall was the greatest psychologist of them all. Speaking of McDougall in 1997, Robin Williams recounted how:

> *He made it his business to know and follow every student's progress. He kept his hand in as a teacher. He was careful in choosing his teaching staff and seeing that he got the most out of them to enrich the school's program. He involved the parents in the school and the school in the community. He could be charming. He could be gruff. He could be gentle. He could be tough. But whatever he did was always pointed in the same direction; to get every student to rise to his best, that North Van High gave its best, and that all pulled together to make North Vancouver a quality community.*

Teachers taught well and worked cheerfully after school to support an enviable set of extramural activities, particularly in music and sports. There were also opportunities for students in journalism, chemistry, woodworking and other activities. But it was in organized sports that the school excelled. Where baseball and soccer had been the pre-eminent sports in elementary school, Canadian football and rugby were preferred in high school. With only one rival high school on the North Shore (in West Vancouver), North Van High's school teams traversed the inlet most Saturday mornings to do battle with Vancouver and Burnaby's best. Victorious teams came home to triumphant welcomes as the school's girls' pep team cried out the school cheer: "We don't quarrel, We don't fight! We're the gang that's alright! North Van High! North Van High!"

Despite the school's extraordinary reputation, however, there were youth who McDougall and his staff simply could not persuade to stay in school. In the 1930s, attending high school was not compulsory and many North Shore families lacked the financial wherewithal to educate their children beyond grade eight. Robin Williams described the dilemma faced by families at the time:

Families were large, it not being uncommon for families to consist of four to nine children. Attendance at high school was expensive, what with appropriate clothes, books, carfare, et cetera. Many families could not get by without the earnings of minor children, especially large ones or those with an unemployed or absent father. Thus, most of North Vancouver's grade school children never went on to high school, and many who started had to drop out before completing grade 12, a situation made particularly acute in the 1930s.

First North Vancouver High School Orchestra, September 1931, Wilma Morden, instructor. Principal Mickey McDougall championed a wide range of extra-curricular activities for students at his high school.
North Vancouver Museum and Archives, 5094

Ironically, the threat of conflict overseas would cause prosperity to return to North Vancouver. The 1920s and '30s had seen the rise of fascist regimes in several European states, but the expansionist ambitions of Mussolini's Italy and Hitler's Germany posed the greatest menace. The British Empire's shipyards braced themselves, ready for the contracts they hoped would come. Although the Canadian government had shown scant interest in building up its navy, attitudes began to change as the 1930s drew to a close. In 1936, the government doubled the navy's budget and Burrard Dry Dock secured a contract to build the minesweeper HMCS *Comox*, the first warship to be built in British Columbia. Two years later, North Vancouver residents turned out in the thousands to witness the historic launch. Mrs. John W. de Beque Farris, wife of a prominent Vancouver lawyer and senator, presided at the ceremony, breaking the traditional bottle of champagne on the vessel's bow. Although impressed by the warship, Mrs. Farris no doubt expressed the feelings of many in saying, "My only hope is that this ship could sweep the world clean of the spirit of war as efficiently as she will sweep our sea lanes clear of enemy mines."

Launch of HMCS Comox *at Burrard Dry Dock, 1938. With Hitler and Mussolini flexing their muscles in Europe, those who attended the launch were increasingly aware of the possibility of war.*
North Vancouver Museum and Archives, 27-2428

HMCS Comox *was the first, but by no means the last, warship to be built in British Columbia.*

North Vancouver Museum and Archives, 27-2439

His Majesty's latest Canadian warship had been built with a minimum of strife between Burrard's management and its workforce. When the Vancouver waterfront descended into chaos in June 1935, the situation in North Vancouver remained calm. The inlet seemed to keep significant strikes and lockouts safely at bay. Still, the longshore strike and lockout was discomfiting. In an effort to dissociate North Shore workers from what appeared to be a more militant group across the inlet, the North Vancouver Board of Trade suggested the formation of a North Shore local of the longshoremen's union. According to George Morden, North Shore workers would benefit by no longer having to report to union offices in Vancouver before being assigned to jobs in their own community.

North Shore union members remained unimpressed. The labour unrest of 1935 ended with perhaps greater acrimony than the strike of 1923. Labour leaders were arrested and imprisoned. Some received lashings. The strikers went back to work, but many were embittered for life. Sam Engler found himself "punished" by being assigned to work in a predominantly First Nations crew in North Vancouver, but he later recalled, "I don't think I ever worked with a finer group of people. And there was a very harmonious relationship. Now you take old Dan George. I can remember him . . . Louis Miranda. The Newman boys. And fellows like Joe Johnson and all those."

As the decade drew to a close North Shore residents experienced further cause for optimism. In 1932 the British Pacific Properties Company, representing the wealthy Anglo-Irish Guinness family, had concluded an agreement with the District of West Vancouver to purchase some 4,700 acres of land in an area subsequently known as the British Properties. The land had cost the company just $75,000, or $18.75 per acre. The terms of the sale compelled the company to provide much of the infrastructure of a new residential development, including roads, bridges, water lines, water tanks and a school. Intending to attract high-income Anglo-Saxon residents, the company also agreed to build a golf course. Construction of the Capilano Golf and Country Club, with its picturesque neo-Elizabethan clubhouse, began shortly afterward and opened in 1936.

Having acquired vast tracts of well-situated land, most of it with breathtaking views, the Guinness interests faced the same problems the North Vancouver land companies had faced decades before. The company's residential lots may have been highly desirable, but getting to them remained extremely difficult. West Vancouver had a ferry system of its own but lacked the streetcar system enjoyed by North Vancouver residents. With even the working classes increasingly owning their own automobiles, public transportation was hardly an option for well-healed residents. What was required was a bridge, the crossing at the Second Narrows being too far away to serve the westernmost municipality. The much-maligned bridge at the Second Narrows had been put back into service in the fall of 1934, a development that proved a mixed blessing. Although the bridge provided an alternative to travel by ferry, ownership had passed to the National Harbours Board and the toll revenues that had formerly gone to the city now went to Ottawa instead.

Talk of a bridge at the First Narrows had begun in the late 1920s—several years prior to the Guinness family acquiring its West Vancouver properties. A referendum had failed in 1927, but a second referendum experienced greater success in 1933. Construction on what became known as the Lions Gate Bridge—named after the Lions, the twin peaks that guard the entrance to the inner harbour—began in early 1937 and was completed by November the following year. Although the two North Vancouver governments had little direct involvement in the project, both were to reap many of its benefits, the second crossing providing an alternate route for vehicles travelling across the inlet. For many, the completion of the bridge was far more than an improvement in the transportation system; it offered fresh hope for the entire north shore of the inlet.

There were other signs that North Vancouver's circumstances were beginning to change. In the summer of 1939, Commissioner Vance noted a significant increase in both the number and value of building permits issued by the city but warned that ferry revenues had plummeted in the face of competition from the new Lions Gate Bridge. Vance also announced a plan for a combination gymnasium and auditorium, a facility that would be jointly funded by the province, the city and community donors. Vance's statement was timely, coming at a time when organized sports were high in the public consciousness. The North Vancouver Lawn Bowling Club had just won the provincial championship while the city's curlers had narrowly missed securing their own provincial championship.

George Morden at the *North Shore Press* revelled in the city's athletic achievements: "If the record of past years were collated, many readers would be astonished at the extent to which young persons of both sexes of this community have attained prominence or have won local or national trophies in Lacrosse, Football, Baseball, Cricket, Tennis or other fields of athletic sport." According to Morden, the Great Depression and the loss of an elected council had had a detrimental effect on the city's residents and the proposed facility might well renew

The lacrosse team at St. Paul's Church, on the Mission Reserve, included members of the Paull, George and Baker families—three of the North Shore's most prominent Native families.
North Vancouver Museum and Archives, 4799

their sagging spirits: "This city would benefit from a revival of community spirit. The establishing of this auditorium and gymnasium will provide a rallying point in this respect."

Morden's reference to lacrosse was reflective of the community's newfound interest in the sport. In the depths of the Depression, Simon Baker and other Squamish Natives began to play box lacrosse. The game was an ancient one, tracing its origins to the tribes of central Canada. In 1932 Baker, his relatives and friends had little money and lacrosse proved to be an enjoyable diversion:

> We had nothing else to do but play lacrosse behind the church. We used to practice and practice and that's how we became famous in lacrosse. We used to pass that ball, push it in circles real fast. We were good stick handlers. That's how come we used to beat them guys, and the best part of it was that we all talked Indian and when we hollered in our language the white man would look, and when he looked the other way, we were gone. They used to really swear at us Indians for talking in our own language. 1932 was the first year we won the BC championship, but then we broke up because we couldn't get enough money from a sponsor.
>
> In 1932, it was mostly all the Bakers playing. There was Henry "Hawkeye" Baker, Ray, Dominic, Frank, my brother Bill and myself. Bobby didn't play. He played field lacrosse before he got hurt. Also, there was Louie Lewis, Gus Band, Stan Joseph, Chief Moses Joseph, Freddie and Joe Johnson, Ducky Mack, and a few others. That was the family. We were all related. When we won the championship we had four non-Indians playing with us.

Playing in the Lower Mainland's intercity league, the team's existence was sometimes tenuous. Aging and injured players left from time to time and sponsorships were not easy to secure. In 1933 and 1934 the North Shore Indians lost their franchise and a half-dozen players moved to join the New Westminster Salmonbellies. In 1935, however, team manager Andy Paull reinvigorated the team, which went on to win the British Columbia championships. Although the team subsequently lost its Senior "A" franchise, its Senior "B" team maintained the sport on the North Shore, eventually winning the league's President's Cup. Given its meagre resources, the North Shore Indians' succession of victories was remarkable. The team's achievements were all the more noteworthy in light of its members' working lives. Remembering the team of the 1930s, longshoreman Sam Engler observed:

One of the amazing things, as I look back, is that there were a number of men in the gang who were Lacrosse players. And you know how hard we had to work in those days. It was a backbreaking job packing lumber all day long . . . Yet in those gangs there would be four or five Lacrosse players. Those guys would work like slaves all day, packing lumber, and they would go out and play Lacrosse at night. They were one of the best Lacrosse teams that ever played on a Lacrosse floor. The record will show that any time the Indians were playing, the old Auditorium would be packed to rafters because they were wonderful Lacrosse players.

The crowning of King George VI in 1937 had a remarkable effect in drawing residents together. Children in music classes belted out patriotic airs, while those studying art happily coloured the flags of the Empire. Imperial fervour even extended to physical education classes, with students learning the traditional dances of England, Scotland, Ireland and Wales. Community spirit was also advanced in other ways. In the summer of 1939, a group of city residents met to develop plans for what eventually became the North Shore Neighbourhood House. The new facility was loosely modelled on Vancouver's Alexandra Neighbourhood House, which traced its own origins to the settlement house movement of Victorian Britain.

In North America, the movement expanded to serve a wider population than in Britain, but the principle of community development held true. Unlike the recreation centres of a later age, community volunteers, rather than local government, directed operations. Mr. and Mrs. Hugh Beattie were at the helm of the movement, having opened their home to the children of the neighbourhood for a number of activities. Their daughter Anne Silva later remembered children gathering to build model planes, dance, complete jigsaw puzzles, sew and do "whatever took their fancies." Attendance grew, quickly exceeding the home's capacity and a search was launched for a larger facility. Roy Hunter, locally renowned for his scrounging abilities, agreed to see what he could find. The city-owned Bellmont apartment building—a three-storey structure on East First said by some to have been used as a brothel—was an obvious candidate. According to Silva:

It didn't take long for Mr. Hunter to locate a building and to talk the city into letting the group have that city-owned building for one dollar a year provided they would repair it, and how it needed repairing! It was an old, condemned building . . . The foundations were rotting as were old mattresses, pillows, and rags that were discarded inside the building. The roof leaked and made the piles of rubbish inside into a sodden musty mess that the rats had claimed for their own.

Under Hunter's guidance, the building was leased and repaired with most of the work being done by volunteers. The project was a model of residents working together in a time of adversity, and its operation was similarly community-driven. As the *North Shore Press* enthusiastically reported:

The Neighbourhood House provides a place of meeting for both parents and the children . . . If a group of ladies wished to quilt, hook rugs, or play cards, that's the thing they'll do; and they use the premises of the Neighbourhood House to meet. Do they want tea? Fine—but bring it. The stove and water and dishes will be there to use—just leave 'em whole and leave 'em washed.

And what about the youngsters? . . . Kids will always form gangs at the teen age: swell, bring in the gang, call it a club and set them going. Any adult who is an enthusiast . . . will gladly assume leadership of a bunch of likely youngsters who form a club to follow their favourite hobby.

The city's Roman Catholics were also proud of their accomplishments, having converted the lower floor of St. Edmund's Rectory into two high school classrooms in 1932. For Catholics wishing their children to receive a Catholic education, the make-do facility was an utter necessity. When the school doubled in size in 1938, parents were ecstatic.

As the decade drew to a close, however, accomplishments such as these were quickly overshadowed. Indeed, if the 1930s had begun with a whimper—the onset of the Great Depression giving North Vancouver residents little cause for either optimism or celebration—they ended with a bang. Not only had the Second Narrows

King George VI and Queen Elizabeth, May 1939. North Vancouver residents turned out by the thousands to witness the royal couple's brief drive through the city.
North Vancouver Museum and Archives, 11330

Bridge been upgraded and brought back into service, but a second crossing had also been built at Lions Gate. Events in Europe suggested that the Empire was about to go to war again and the mother country sought to reaffirm its ties with Canada. In mid-May 1939, the recently crowned king and queen set sail for North America. After a triumphant tour of eastern Canada and the Prairies, the royal couple finally arrived on the West Coast on May 29. British Columbia—still the most British of all the provinces—embraced its sovereigns with unrestrained enthusiasm; it was after all, the first visit to Canada of a reigning monarch.

Every community the royal couple visited vowed to do the Empire proud. On the south side of the inlet, the CNR and CPR rushed the long-stalled Hotel Vancouver to completion, its royal suite soon being occupied by the king and queen. Plans were made for the visitors to travel by car across the Second Narrows Bridge, along the north shore of the inlet through both the city and the district, then back to Vancouver via the Lions Gate Bridge. Between 75,000 and 100,000 people, many of them wearing their Sunday best, lined the route. Over three thousand schoolchildren waved tiny Union Jacks. Veterans of the Northwest Rebellion, the South African War and the Great War were given pride of place. Mr. Christie Cao, wheeled to his place in a hospital cot, was duly saluted by His Majesty.

No stop had been scheduled for the city, but it was hoped that the procession might pause at the Capilano Reserve where Native people from throughout the coast were holding what the press termed a "pow wow." One-hundred-year-old Mrs. Mary Agnes Capilano, the much-revered widow of the chief who had visited the king's grandfather in London, had been seated on an improvised throne. A carpet had been prepared to be placed across the road in the event of the royal procession stopping at the site. Being behind schedule, the cars only slowed to acknowledge the Native assembly, but this was apparently enough to give considerable pleasure to many in the crowd. Mary Capilano, however, was devastated. As her grandson Simon Baker recalled, "This was the only time we could present my grandmother to the Queen, but the car drove past us. Everybody was crowding in front of us so they wouldn't stop. It was terrible for my grandmother."

Mary Capilano's son, Chief Mathias Joe, however, was reported to be jubilant. His words reflecting an idealistic belief that the sovereign could somehow protect Native rights:

When he comes, Indians and whites will have their own King in their own country. My father visited his grandfather, King Edward, in his home in England in 1906. He was his friend. The King's law is my law. He makes me feel strong.

August Jack Khatsahlahno was equally pleased with his encounter with royalty:

I am awfully glad their Majesties have come to see our country. You can see the whole crowd of my people are here to welcome them to our land. Our Squamish tribe joins with the others in its loyalty to the Great White King from over the water.

The royal visit had lasted a mere thirty minutes. The *North Shore Press* summarized the views of the populace. The visit had been "all too brief, but despite that, it was appreciated beyond all word description. It was ample . . . to create deep down in every citizen's heart" a "feeling of . . . commitment" that would bind Canada to the mother country throughout the impending global conflagration. With its growing port facilities, improved transportation system, and massive shipyard and dry dock facilities, few doubted that North Vancouver would once again do its bit for king and country.

Squamish pole erected in honour of the royal visit, May 1939. The Squamish people hoped for a more prominent role in the visit of the king and queen than organizers were prepared to allow. Even so, the royal couple met an enthusiastic reception as they passed the Mission and Capilano Reserves.

North Vancouver Museum and Archives, 15194

OUTBREAK OF WAR 1939–1941

War broke out a mere three months after the royal couple's departure. Canada also entered the fray, but this time the circumstances were different. The British Empire was evolving into the Commonwealth and Britain's declaration of war by no means put Canada at war. In 1939, most English-speaking Canadians traced their ancestry to the British Isles, but Canada's external affairs were no longer directed from London. Canadian parliamentarians reviewed the situation and issued their own declaration of war one week after Britain did. In reflecting on the situation, newspaper editor George Morden noted Canada's imperial obligations, but his rhetoric had little in common with the sabre rattling so evident in August 1914. It would be a long and difficult war, but Canada was better prepared than ever. North Vancouver residents braced themselves for the challenges yet to come.

North Vancouver's Sixth Field Company was among the first of the community's organizations to swing into action. Under the command of Major T.H. Jermyn, a resident

Lt. Col. T.H. Jermyn, officer commanding, Sixth Field Company of Canadian Engineers, 1943.

North Vancouver Museum and Archives, 2521

of the city since 1910, recruitment and training began in earnest. Jermyn's ascent to the leadership of the regiment—which began when he enrolled as a cadet in 1916—indicated just how much the nation had changed since the First World War. Jermyn's most noted predecessor, J.P. Fell, was an English aristocrat of the old school whose assumption of the regiment's leadership was as much a function of birth as it was of ability. Jermyn had been born in rural Alberta and was educated in North Vancouver's public schools. Although he went on to university, he apprenticed as a machinist and up to the time of mobilization he worked as much with his hands as with his mind.

Jermyn's first contingent left North Vancouver in 1940 to construct an army camp in Debert, Nova Scotia. Having completed their work there, the Engineers embarked for England in June 1941, arriving in Aldershot on July 1. After a period of re-organization, the troops were sent to construct the Hedleigh detention camp before returning to camp for further training and drill. Three long years were to pass before the Engineers were sent into action, a period of time characterized by both anxiety and boredom.

No. 3 Company, Canadian Women's Training Corps, at the ARP demonstration at Mahon Park, May 18, 1941.

North Vancouver Museum and Archives, 9416

A generation earlier, North Shore women had been able to join the forces only as nurses. During the second global clash, the Canadian government authorized the formation of army, navy and air force units exclusively for women. Residents who enlisted in the Canadian Women's Army Corps, Women's Royal Canadian Naval Service and Royal Canadian Air Force Women's Division might work as cooks or nurses, but they also had the opportunity to work in roles once the exclusive domain of men: draughtsmen, radio operators, electricians, radiographers, mechanics and motor transport drivers.

Local authorities were quick to respond to the menace of war. By early September, a number of Lower Mainland municipalities formed a "metropolitan group" to co-ordinate a regional response to wartime dangers such as fire, accidents and sabotage. The city's fire department began to plan for a voluntary aid detachment consisting of men and women with first aid and nursing certificates. The local chapter of the Canadian Red Cross—largely composed of women—established its headquarters on West Esplanade. Plans were announced for the circulation of sewing, knitting and other patterns to enable volunteers to craft "pneumonia

Above: North Vancouver Kinsman Curtis Malcolm promotes his club's "Milk for Britain" campaign, 1940s. The Great Depression that began in 1929 had shown residents how to work together. The Second World War proved an even greater force for building community.
North Vancouver Museum and Archives, 6527K

jackets, hospital bed gowns, bandages, binders, bed pans, and pillow cases," all in aid of the war effort. Residents were encouraged to join the armed forces and Commissioner Vance guaranteed any city employee who enlisted a position upon return. Men and women holding valid military identification were given free passage on cross-inlet ferries, as were women doing secretarial work for the armed forces. He also supported the efforts of the Army and Navy Veterans in Canada to raise funds for the purchase of military ambulances overseas. The organization's "tag days" were to become common events as the war wore on.

The community's service clubs also rallied to the cause. The Kinsmen Club was but four years old at the outbreak of the war, having received its charter in 1935. Its "apple days" and carnivals raised funds for initiatives such as "Food for Britain" and "Milk for Britain." The North Shore Council of Women—renamed when the North

Students at Queen Mary School during a simulated gas attack, c. 1941. Teaching students first aid, drill and other wartime skills helped instill a sense of duty and co-operation among North Vancouver's school-age children.

North Vancouver Museum and Archives, 732

Vancouver and West Vancouver chapters amalgamated in 1937—also gathered its forces. In 1938, the Council had begun to plan for the evacuation of British and European children to safe homes in Canada. The program was implemented and by the end of the war over one thousand children had been brought to the safety of Canada's West Coast.

Many residents reflected on what the war might mean for business. If the experiences of the Great War of 1914 to 1918 were anything to go by, the second war would result in increased demand for both raw and manufactured materials, more employment opportunities, and newfound money rippling through the economy. In North Vancouver the opportunities were obvious. The war effort would require lumber, munitions and ships, and North Vancouver industries were now well equipped and ready to meet the test. In October 1939, the British and Canadian governments announced a need for thirty vessels, each of which would cost $1,250,000 to build. The contracts would be spread equitably among all Canadian shipyards with the capacity to build the vessels. The Burrard Dry Dock's Clarence Wallace was delighted with the news and advised that his yards were "prepared to accept contracts for any vessels up to 12,000 tons." Over at North Van Ship Repairs (as Vancouver Drydock and Salvage Company had become), Arthur Burdick was also pleased. By the fall of 1939 Burdick's firm had two berths, one on either side of an impressive machine shop. Each berth was capable of accommodating vessels up to 275 feet in length. Subsequent modifications to the plant permitted the construction of ships up to 400 feet long.

If the community's adults viewed the war with circumspection and pragmatism, many of its young people saw adventure. According to Robin Williams, the talk on the high school playground had little to do with construction, population growth or finance:

I remember that first day at school after Britain declared war. All over the soccer field boys gathered in excited knots. "At last we're going to teach that maniac Hitler a lesson, and his strutting puppet Mussolini. We'll teach them a thing or two!" Another chimed in, "My dad was in World War I. When I get to be eighteen, I'm going to join the airforce. Mr. Freedman says maybe we're going to start a cadet corps and learn Morse code." There was talk that Wallace's shipyard might start building ships for the war, and maybe there'd be summer jobs for us in the shipyard. It all sounded so good. Excitement. Adventure. Duty. A Righteous Cause. We all wanted to do something, as if starting the first day of high school wasn't enough to get our adrenalin going.

Fears of an enemy attack on domestic soil resulted in the creation of local Air Raid Precaution (ARP) organizations throughout the Lower Mainland. Given the importance of protecting the shipyards, the ARP received particular attention in North Vancouver. Participants were expected to assist in operating air raid shelters, advising civilians, maintaining lists of people living in local houses, assisting with rescues and other emergencies, and monitoring government-imposed blackouts. Residents too young or too old to enlist in the armed forces took pride in their ARP affiliation, which permitted them to wear tin hats and armbands emblazoned with

the ARP logo. A few accounts, however, suggest that some participants had motives other than the purely paramilitary. Some fifty years later, one unidentified North Vancouver woman—an adolescent in the 1940s—admitted that her participation in the ARP had provided an opportunity for social recreation: "If the truth were known most of us in Junior High joined the ARP as an excuse to go out in the evening after supper."

One of the ARP's more important tasks was the enforcement of the wartime blackout. The blackout had been initiated to make potential targets less visible in the event of an attack by enemy aircraft at night. Former ARP member George Lewis remembered some of the problems associated with the blackout:

At home we had all our windows fitted with blackout blinds made out of tar paper, with little or no regard for the fire hazard. On one occasion there was a full scale "alert" with every area covered for possible glimmers of light. My tour of inspection detected only one infraction and it was readily seen from our headquarters in the school. The whole house was a blaze of light. Judge of my surprise when it turned out to be the home of a prominent member of the ARP hierarchy. Needless to say, my report never got further than the nearest wastepaper basket.

There were others in the hierarchy who took their duties more seriously. One was G.R. Bates, a veteran of the First World War and chief warden for the entire North Shore. Bates recruited a number of citizens to serve under him including realtor Noel Copping, who took charge of the area encompassed by the city. By May 1941, Bates and his assistants had recruited and trained some eight hundred volunteers. A public demonstration of their skills was held at Mahon Park. The

turnout was immense. According to press reports, several thousand spectators packed the grandstand and overflowed to the edges of the park. The event was as much an exercise in community-building as it was a demonstration of wartime preparedness. About one dozen organizations were represented, several of which had never worked together before. All shared a common purpose and joined together not just for the day, but for several years to come. The groups were diverse and included the North Shore's Boy Scouts, Girl Guides, Women's Ambulance Corps, St. John's Ambulance Nursing Division, Canadian Women's Training Corps, Legion of Frontiersmen, Canadian Engineers and volunteer firemen.

If the ARP was not enough, wartime needs provided the authorities with other diversions for teenagers. Public school air cadets were charged with collecting paper, tin foil, glass, string and other materials needed for the war effort. Privately operated schools were just as energetic as they tried to prepare their students for every eventuality. Dick Hallaway recollected his wartime experiences at North Shore College: "We had a cadet corps there . . . and instead of rifles we had bits of inch-and-a-half dowelling and we had somebody come up from the armouries here on Fell Avenue and we marched around and thought we were winning the war!" Few citizens were more determined than North Vancouver High School principal Mickey McDougall in encouraging the city's youth to do their bit. As Robin Williams, president of the school's student council in his senior year, recalled over five decades later:

> McDougall was very keen on North Van High doing all it could for the war effort. We had contests between home room classes as to which could sell the most savings stamps toward purchase of a war bond. Vancouver's high schools competed against each other for the same purpose, and now and again North Vancouver would win first place and publicity in the **Province** or **Sun**. The girls knit hundreds of socks, scarfs, and sweaters for distribution by the Red Cross and marched around in Katie Reynolds' girls' cadet corps. And of course all the boys were expected to take part in either an army or air force cadet corps.

The war had begun with great excitement, yet full-scale combat was slow to develop. It was not until April 1940 that the federal government organized a Department of Munitions and Supply to manage the production of war material; aircraft, trucks, tanks, munitions and ships being its major area of concern. North Vancouver's industries rose to the occasion and secured a succession of significant contracts. Burrard and North Van Ship Repairs were the prime beneficiaries, building 4 corvettes, 17 minesweepers, and 161 Victory-class merchant vessels between them. The city's two shipyards also undertook a number of conversions and repaired numerous vessels damaged at sea.

For Burrard Dry Dock, converting its facilities to wartime production was no small task. The challenge faced by North Van Ship Repairs was considerably larger. The firm was a subsidiary of the Pacific Salvage Company, an enterprise founded in Vancouver decades prior to the outbreak of the war. During its early years, the firm focussed—as its very name suggested—on ship repairs. It also built small wooden ships, including several of the ferries on the Vancouver–West Vancouver run.

During the Second World War, the community's children were encouraged to undertake projects to further the war effort, such as this poster for War Savings Bonds designed by North Vancouver High School student Sydney (McLean) Baker in 1942.

North Vancouver Museum and Archives, 5205

Converting its facilities from a small-craft yard to the wartime production of large steel ships was a major challenge, but Arthur Burdick and his yard superintendent Don Service soon proved up to the task. Burrard opened a second yard on the south shore of the inlet to focus on the manufacture of steel hulls. North Van Ship Repairs quickly converted its plant for the construction of large steel-hulled vessels, including both minesweepers and cargo ships. A growing number of contracts resulted in the firm developing four more berths, each capable of turning out a ten-thousand-ton cargo ship. At peak wartime production, the firm was able to launch one large ship every sixteen days.

Much of the work in the shipyards was labour-intensive. Individual workers often had very specific and limited roles. In the absence of the mechanized processes that later became the norm, several staff were needed to perform tasks later performed by one. Yards on both sides of the inlet were often hard pressed to complete their contracts on schedule and the demand for staff was constant. Shipyards vied with each other to attract both tradesmen and labourers. Work went on night and day. Robin Williams remembered the scene:

Aerial view of Burrard Dry Dock's shipyards and Lower Lonsdale, 1944. During the war, Burrard was responsible for the construction of scores of Victory Ships, several of which are shown berthed at the wharves.
North Vancouver Museum and Archives, 27-8H

By the summer of 1941, these shipyards employed several thousand men and several hundred women working three shifts. Some were highly skilled, experienced shipbuilders and metalworkers, most just adaptable workers from other trades, and even farmers from the prairies who came into the yards for the steady work, better pay and to be more useful to the war effort.

By late 1941, other significant businesses had located along the waterfront. The electrically operated Glaspie Sawmill, located at the foot of St. Patrick's Avenue, was known to be one of the most modern lumber mills in western Canada. The neighbouring L&K Lumber Company, occupying a section of waterfront between St. Andrew's and St. Patrick's Avenues, was also deemed to be extremely well equipped and productive. The Pacific Coast Handles Company stood nearby, at the foot of Queensbury Avenue and was noted for its production and export of handles for axes, brooms and other hand tools. Evans, Coleman, and Evans, an old Vancouver firm, took over the Stuart Cameron property at the foot of St. George's Avenue and thereby extended their building-material, cement and coal business to include the North Shore. There were also smaller enterprises, such as the numerous shingle mills that lined the shoreline. Of these, Horne Brothers' mill located at the foot of Forbes Avenue was perhaps the most memorable.

Smoke from the mills and from the coal and sawdust burning furnaces that heated the city's homes created terrible fogs. Murray Dykeman recalled how the fogs affected visibility:

I remember the war years and after, of riding up and down Lonsdale on my bike and the reason I went there was you could see the streetcar tracks, the ties, beside you on the road. You couldn't see anything from the curb . . . You instinctively used that and kept your ears open. But I can remember fog so thick I couldn't see Fifth Street from Sixth. And that happened a lot. That occurred in the fall and right through to the spring.

Vancouver, with its heavily industrialized waterfront and tens of thousands of sawdust-burning furnaces, also contributed to the problem. The mills of shingle king James McNair were some of the worst offenders. The heavy fogs often led to accidents, including a fog-shrouded car crash in early 1942 that claimed the life of McNair himself.

Still, after so many years of deprivation and living hand to mouth, North Vancouver residents were ready to put up with the inconvenience of fog. Long-empty houses and underutilized hotel rooms were quickly rented out to shipyard workers and their families. Unemployment became a thing of the past. Shopkeepers rejoiced as their cash registers began to fill and professionals were once again paid in cash, rather than in butter, fruit or vegetables. As prosperity returned, a few brave retailers began to enter what had previously been a highly challenged market. Ken Gostick was one of these few, opening a "five to a dollar" store in Central Lonsdale in 1942. His family friend Bob Orr was building a series of stores in Central Lonsdale and Gostick jumped at the chance to establish a business of his own. Although Wartime Housing Ltd. had built hundreds of new houses nearer the inlet, little appeared to have been constructed in Central Lonsdale. As Gostick recalled, "I don't think a store had been opened in North Vancouver in ten years."

Gostick arrived at a time when Central Lonsdale was well on its way to superseding Lower Lonsdale as the city's business and professional core. Establishing his store on Lonsdale Avenue between Thirteenth and Fourteenth, Gostick joined a cluster of other small businesses: Harbottle's ice cream parlour, Paterson's confectionery store, a radio shop, Pearson's hardware store, Crowhurst's Garage and Hare's drygoods. The Odeon Theatre stood nearby, but as Gostick later recalled, "The other side of the street, from Fouteenth to Fifteenth up to Crowhurst's, that was just bush—vacant property." Properties to the south were similarly undeveloped. Gostick remembered, "Between Thirteenth and Fourteenth Street, downtown, there was nothing, just nothing. Bush with the odd building. Just below Twelfth Street there was the Mason's Hall and Webb's drugstore, a few houses, but mostly bush."

In a community where only a minority of elementary school students went on to complete high school, a well-paying job on the waterfront was often more attractive to young men than studying Latin or trigonometry. While Robin Williams stayed in school, many of his contemporaries—especially those from blue-collar families—did not:

McDougall had a hard time keeping boys in school during the war years. With both shipyards operating in high gear, jobs were easy to come by, and with overtime, a high school student could earn as much a month as a teacher's salary. Despite doing everything he could to make staying in school attractive and exciting, many boys dropped out, among them Gerry Green who got a chance to learn drafting

Three generations of the Miller family walk to work at Burrard Dry Dock: George, Harry Jr., and Harry Sr., August 1944. During the Second World War, jobs in the city's shipyards were easy to acquire.
North Vancouver Museum and Archives, 12302

in the shipyards, Harvey Marshall to learn steam engineering in the merchant marine, and many others who seized the opportunities opened up by the wartime shortage of manpower.

Williams himself succumbed to the lure of employment in the shipyards, securing a series of summer jobs that allowed him to stay in school while increasing his savings. Then, as now, knowing a high-ranking employee proved to be an asset:

> *Building ships took a lot of kidpower too, for jobs like rivet-passer, chalk boy, and helpers for various trades like draftsmen, pattern-makers, fitters, shipwrights, drillers, blacksmiths, tinsmiths, machinists and steamfitters. And these shipyard jobs paid better than lumber mill or other woodworking places like Vancouver Creosoting, 29-plus [cents] an hour and time and a half for overtime, so every kid in North Van hoped to get a shipyard job.*
>
> *I was lucky. One of my best friends was Murray Williams whose dad was a bigshot at North Van Ship Repair, an old time shipbuilder from the Clyde in Scotland. So one day I asked Murray's dad about a summer job and he said in his Scottish brogue, "Why sure, laddy. Show up at the personnel office at seven sharp tomorrow and I'll see if I can get you on."*

Propagandists portrayed working in the shipyards as a patriotic duty. Trooper E. C. "Bim" Clark had worked at Burrard as an apprentice helper prior to enlisting. In 1943, Clark was wounded while fighting in Italy. The *Wallace Shipbuilder* was only too happy to publish a portion of a letter to his former supervisor Jock Logan:

> *When I was in the Yard, Jock, I didn't think much of the importance of getting those Merchant Ships of ours out fast, but I've seen a lot of them down here and every one is carrying a cargo that is vital to the winning of the war. They bring us the equipment we need and it sure takes plenty of ships. I've thought about that quite a lot lately and if it wasn't for skilled workmen like yourself and others and their Helpers, we'd never get the equipment we need so badly. You've been through two wars, Jock, but the job you're doing now is sure essential.*

Striving toward victory became a national preoccupation. Images of Winston Churchill, his right hand forming the famous "V for victory" sign, appeared in the local press. As the war progressed, the shipyards became fertile ground for a number of victory-related national initiatives. Employees and their families were encouraged to plant "Victory Gardens." Household gardens intended to relieve wartime shortages of food had long been common elsewhere in the world, but augmenting the country's food supply through domestic plantings was initially discouraged by the federal government. City dwellers, it was felt, knew little about horticulture and might waste seeds. The steel in the hand tools they would require might find better use in armaments. By early 1943, however, a shortage of food among Canada's allies resulted in a reversal of policy. Within a year of the program being approved, the Vancouver papers reported that 209,200 Victory Gardens had been planted nationwide and that their average production was 550 pounds of vegetables. Further, there were 15 percent more home vegetable gardeners in 1943 than in 1942, and 24 percent more than two years before.

Shipyard workers were even more supportive of the nation's nine successive "War Loan" and "Victory Loan" campaigns. Some were likely encouraged by government-issued posters, one of which featured an attractive female munitions worker who declared, "I'm making bombs and buying bonds!" Others may have been motivated by patriotism. Many came out to see the king's younger brother, the Duke of Kent, during his visit to the shipyards in August 1941. Still others may have warmed to appearances by Hollywood celebrities such as actress Susan Hayward, bandleader Phil Harris, and comedian Jack Benny with his Vancouver-born wife Mary Livingstone and sidekick Rochester.

So many shipyard workers commuted by ferry from Vancouver that some sailings became dangerously overcrowded. An alarmed Commissioner Vance repeatedly dealt with claims for damages from passengers who were jostled, trodden under

The Duke of Kent with Clarence and Hubert Wallace at Burrard Dry Dock, August 1941. The duke was the younger brother of King George VI and had travelled to Burrard Inlet to promote solidarity with the mother country in its darkest hour of need.

North Vancouver Museum and Archives, 1193

foot or the victims of falls. In February 1941, 94 percent of ratepayers voted in favour of yet another boat construction bylaw. Two weeks after the vote the city tendered a contract for its *No. 5 Ferry*. Neither Burrard nor North Van Ship Repairs bid on the contract, preoccupied as they were with other projects. The contract in the amount of $111,499 went instead to West Coast Salvage and Repair. Recognizing that the new vessel would not be delivered until late in November, Vance rented the MV *Hollyburn* from the District of West Vancouver as an interim measure.

The influx of so many shipyard workers had other repercussions. The demand for housing was entirely without precedent. Writing in the *Wallace Shipbuilder*, columnist Pat Wallace described the situation:

> *They flocked here in thousands to join the shipyard battalion. They brought their families. They found jobs. But no homes. Families were jammed together in one room. Others were separated. Some lived in store fronts with no bathroom facilities. Not the most ideal home conditions for men on whom rests the responsibility of providing the "tools to finish the job."*

Standardized wartime housing under construction in "Skunk Hollow," 1942.

North Vancouver Museum and Archives, 10997

Sensing an opportunity, entrepreneur Mark Cosgrove approached Vance with a proposal to build "cheap buildings of a temporary nature for shipyard workers on the North Shore, on property to be leased from the City," each house to consist of a "combined living and dining room and kitchenette, one bedroom, shower bath and toilet, and to rent at $25.00 per month." The Commissioner greeted the proposal with caution and referred it to the board of trade for comment. Within the week he was able to advise the would-be developer that the city did not favour this type of house.

Cosgrove had recognized a very real need but its solution was left to others. Hundreds of lots to which the city had fallen heir when their owners defaulted on their taxes were finally put to use. In early August 1941, realtor Frank Monahan secured contracts with the City of North Vancouver to purchase over forty lots at 50 percent of their assessed value. In return, Monahan agreed to construct forty houses each valued at $2,250. There was more to come. Later that month, Vance concluded an agreement with Wartime Housing, a federal Crown corporation that ultimately built thirty-two thousand houses across the country. Under the terms of the agreement, Wartime Housing was to build two hundred houses for shipyard workers who could not find housing close to work. The city was to provide the lots at a cost to the company of $1 each. All were to be located in District Lots 273 and 274, within walking distance (or an easy streetcar commute) of the shipyards. Rather than pay property taxes, Wartime Housing agreed to pay the city an annual fee of $24 to $30 based on the value of the house. The company would also pay an annual fee for accessing utilities.

It was further agreed that the company would bear the costs of providing all necessary infrastructure including water, sewers, street lights, sidewalks and road upgrades. At the end of the war, the improvements would become the property and responsibility of the city. Perhaps fearful of what the houses might ultimately look like—some after all were to be located in the shadow of the city's more prestigious residential areas—the commissioner required that the structures "be built in a workmanlike manner." Additional agreements were subsequently completed for the construction of another four hundred houses as well as for two large barrack-like structures for 180 bachelors near the corner of Third and St. George's.

Vancouver architects McCarter and Nairne, whose crowning achievement was Vancouver's art deco-style Marine Building, were selected as supervising architects. The firm's modest wood-frame houses bore absolutely no resemblance to their brick and steel skyscraper, but they were nonetheless destined to become landmarks in their own right. Officially labelled with alphanumeric descriptors such as H-1 or H-12, the houses were more popularly known by terms such as "cracker boxes," "small fours" or "big sixes," the numbers referring to the number of rooms they contained.

Vance also facilitated construction in the district. Before the war was over, Wartime Housing had built extensively east of the Capilano Indian Reserve where newly built streets were named in honour of wartime leaders, including Winston Churchill, Franklin Roosevelt and Canadian general Andy McNaughton. Despite the monotony of their standardized designs, all of these modestly proportioned houses were occupied soon after their completion. Jim Galozo remembered the houses: "The architecture of the wartime houses was repeated over and over and over . . . One of the features of the larger homes with bedrooms on a second floor was the stairway just inside the front door, which provided a great escape in case of fire."

The city's wartime houses were built in several stages, but the resultant change to the landscape was both rapid and dramatic. Anne Silva recalled seeing many

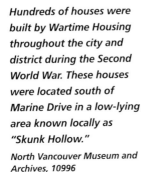

Hundreds of houses were built by Wartime Housing throughout the city and district during the Second World War. These houses were located south of Marine Drive in a low-lying area known locally as "Skunk Hollow."

North Vancouver Museum and Archives, 10996

vacant lots and houses in North Vancouver before she went north for the 1941 fishing season. On her return, she crossed the inlet by the Second Narrows Bridge, ascended Third Street hill and at Queensbury found herself in the midst of Wartime Housing:

> *What a shock—seeing all those Wartime Houses! They were very small and very numerous; one on each fifty-foot lot and sometimes as many as twenty-six to the block. At that time they were still unpainted and to me they looked like chicken houses. They seemed to spring up like toadstools and covered most of the vacant city-owned land between St. George's and Queensbury from Second Street to Sixth Street. This was the first big housing development project in North Vancouver and it completely changed our town. Gone were the days of vacant lots and houses, that September in 1941.*

The project was not without its critics. Local MLA Dorothy Steeves, a member of the Co-operative Commonwealth Federation (CCF, the predecessor of the New Democratic Party), was highly vocal in her negative assessment of the development. Rising in the provincial legislature, Steeves berated what she saw as "rows and rows of shabbily built wooden boxes" that were already reducing the value of neighbouring properties. The houses themselves were "very, very tiny" and would result in "ready-made slums." The MLA perceived an insidious deal between Wartime Housing and the city, describing the federal official in charge of the project as "a contractor in stone and steel. He is one of our famous dollar-a-year men. This dollar-a-year business is going to cost us a lot of money before the war is over. It is certainly a headache for North Vancouver . . . Somebody is making money out of this deal!"

Vance's contention that the additional residents would be good for business was borne out when a plague of door-to-door salesmen descended on residents who had only just moved in. Anne Silva related how wooden sidewalks facilitated their activities:

> *The 500-block of East Fourth Street was so swampy that Central Mortgage installed wooden sidewalks on each side of the street. All houses had wooden sidewalks from the street to the front steps and around the house to the back door. Through the first six months of our tenancy not a day passed without peddlers at the door. Sometimes they were at the front and back doors at the same time.*

With the shipyards working full tilt, the demand for housing continued unabated. Jim Galozo recalled the situation: "The homes were occupied as soon as they were built, often by families from the Canadian prairies. These people had no problem in getting work as both skilled and unskilled workers were needed. One story tells of one overzealous applicant who, in being interviewed, claimed excitedly that he had worked in the shipyards in Regina!" In 1943, Wartime Housing constructed another set of houses north of First between Chesterfield and Forbes. Even these were not enough. Additional houses were built on the city's outskirts between Marine Drive and the waterfront. It was not until a final set of houses rose north of

Marine Drive between Mosquito Creek and Hamilton Avenue that the demand for workers' housing was finally fully addressed.

During the course of the war, the city's population changed. North Vancouver ceased to be the predominantly middle-class city many had hoped for. Blue-collar workers settled by the hundreds. The city's British character also faded; its newer residents might converse in English, but many spoke with unfamiliar accents. A 1943–45 analysis of the origins of 7,438 members of Burrard Dry Dock's workforce revealed a level of cultural diversity that exceeded that of Moodyville a half-century earlier. Canadian-born men and women constituted 61 percent of the workforce. British-born workers accounted for a further 21 percent. Americans, the next most populous nationality, formed a distant 4 percent. The remaining 14 percent traced their origins to forty-four other countries in Europe, Africa, Latin America, the Caribbean and Asia.

Recognizing that racial intolerance had deep roots in the westernmost province, North Shore employers took steps to promote what a writer in the *Wallace Shipbuilder* described as "international harmony." The shipyard's publication profiled its multicultural staff in glowing terms:

> *There's a little League of Nations at work in the North Yard . . . all working on the same job—Armament, all working for the same cause—Victory. The job of this international gang is 100 per cent defence—defence of our ships—for they mount plastic armour plate around the bridge and gun platforms. And how do they get along, all these nationalities? Listen to what their Chargehand, George Smith, says: "I've never worked with a better, happier bunch of men. We all get along swell and nobody's taken a poke at anyone else yet!"*

Workforce harmony was paramount in time of war, so the Wallaces took steps to encourage a collegial workplace. Sports teams were organized and connecting with the community was very much encouraged. When Mary Meredith's St. Christopher School required repairs, the shipyard rallied its troops, transforming the "rambling, poorly equipped tumbledown house into a re-modelled and thoroughly modern home." According to the *Wallace Shipbuilder*, this was "not an old-fashioned and-lo-it-came-to-pass kind of miracle. It is a modern miracle of co-operation between workers, foremen, shop stewards, and executives."

The *Wallace Shipbuilder* also recognized the varied origins of its workers by publishing profiles on their backgrounds and adaptations to the Canadian way of life. It also honoured the contributions of Squamish Chief Mathias Joe. Chief Joe, the editor recorded, had deep imperial connections. His father, Chief Joe Capilano, had met King Edward VII. He himself had met King George VI and British Prime Minister Winston Churchill. Chief Joe was a skilled woodcarver and although he might prefer to carve totem poles, he was happy to turn his talents to crafting the spars required on His Majesty's ships: "Cutting spars is not the creative work I like to do best, but it's good work, important work, and I'm proud to be doing it."

The shipyard's managers were not alone in recognizing how the population had changed. Reporter Pat Wallace visited the families who had recently taken up residence in the city's newly constructed wartime housing:

Throughout the war, Burrard Dry Dock strove to build cohesion and morale within its large and diverse workforce. The antics of the firm's male sheet metal shop workers were perhaps a little more over the top than those undertaken by others at the shipyard.
North Vancouver Museum and Archives, 12388

This community is a lesson in working democracy. The people who live in these homes and do their part in the mighty war effort by sending ship after ship down the ways, come from all walks of life. They speak many languages. But, regardless of class, culture, or nationality, they are all soldiers of the home front, with a single purpose. To defeat Hitler. They work harmoniously together in the yards. Off shift, they live just as harmoniously. They understand the meaning of good neighbour policy. Their community spirit is amazing. They have organized many clubs. They are all ardent gardeners—both vegetables and flowers. Their wives sew and knit together for the Red Cross. Their children work as a group in organized play.

The central cog in this neighbourliness is the community clubhouse, run by the unofficial mayor, H.V. Collins. He is the community councillor. He knows all the tenants, and they know him. He finds out their likes and dislikes—their special hobbies—and interests. It's a thriving community of row on row of bright-as-paint homes fronted by green, well-clipped lawns and flower-beds which is not only filling a wartime need, but is the ground-work of that working democracy which must follow this war, if peace is to be won.

Yet while housing for families and bachelors was dealt with in an expeditious fashion, housing for unattached women was not, despite a growing need. By the early 1940s, with an increasing number of men leaving the inlet to join the Armed Forces, young women formed a significant portion of the industrial workforce. Burrard Dry Dock's policy of not hiring female labourers ceased to be sustainable and women were taken on in increasing numbers. Women were also hired at North Van Ship Repairs as well as in the yards on the opposite side of the inlet. When wartime production peaked in 1942, close to 1,500 women were employed in the Lower Mainland's six major shipyards and well over half of these were working in North Vancouver. It was not until mid-1943 that the shipyards began to address the housing needs of the female workforce. On June 11, Burrard Dry Dock announced plans for quarters to accommodate up to four hundred female employees. About the same time, North Van Ship Repairs revealed its intent to construct similar facilities for its female staff, "as soon as the question of priorities is settled."

For those in charge of housing, segregating the genders seems to have been an ongoing practice. Winning the war was hard enough; irregular relationships and unwanted pregnancies did nothing for the cause of freedom. The rules were strict and applied to all. When married men living in the St. Alice and Olympic (as the Palace Hotel had become) hotels wanted to visit their wives, they were forced to smuggle them up to their rooms using a rear staircase. Increased levels of employment, particularly among women, also had repercussions for the recently established North Shore Neighbourhood House. Within months of its foundation, its focus changed from recreation to daycare for children. With both parents working, many children were left to the care of neighbours or were simply being left alone.

In the shipyards, positions held by women were similar to those held by teenagers. Some were passer girls, others worked as rivet heaters and burners, and a talented few rose to the rank of riveter. Working in a shipyard provided women with much-needed cash as well as with a newfound sense of self-esteem. Jonnie Ottewell, who became Jonnie Rankin when she married Vancouver lawyer Harry Rankin, started work at Burrard in 1943 and remained in shipyard work for about

Following pages: Female shipyard workers pose at Burrard Dry Dock, 1945. During the course of the war, hundreds of women from both sides of the inlet worked at both Burrard Dry Dock and North Van Ship Repairs, not as office staff, but as manual labourers. North Vancouver Museum and Archives, 1421

eighteen months. Interviewed in 1979, she recalled how the opportunity to work in wartime industries changed the lives of many women:

> *If you'd been in the Depression and never worked, and then started raising kids at seventeen like I did, it was an entirely different world, believe me, when I went to the shipyards . . . it was an education. Women learned because we had to; you're so dependent all your life on a man's salary, it was a tremendous thing to earn your own money. And a lot of marriages broke up over it because she wasn't going to go back and ask any more.*

During the First World War, Andy Wallace had steadfastly refused to allow women to work in his North Vancouver shipyard. A quarter-century later, his sons worked with an immense, unionized staff that included hundreds of women. These five female employees were active as shop stewards in what was by the 1940s a heavily unionized operation.
North Vancouver Museum and Archives, 8073

Employed as a sheet metal worker's helper at fifty-five cents an hour, Rankin worked on the large cowl vents used for ventilation on the ships under construction.

> *The main mechanic I worked with was Kenny Sherry, a little Cockney born within the sound of Bow Bells. He was a former singing waiter, dance marathon champion from London, England, amateur psychologist and master sheet metal mechanic. Like most of the men, Kenny at first was fanatically against working with a woman, but he accepted his fate.*
>
> *One of our jobs was to hammer the edges of iron screens to fit around a circle bar, which made the faces of the vent. I was terrible at it, always hitting my hands and smashing up the screen. Finally, one day, in exasperation, I just picked up the damn thing and threw it down the hold. But instead of firing me, Kenny used psychology and gave me a job running all over the yard picking up the iron, getting it burned and welded the right size and so on.*

Rankin went on to work for North Van Ship Repairs as a passer girl. It was there that she had her first encounter with organized labour. Prior to the war, labour-management relations in the North Shore's shipyards had generally been cordial. During the war, the situation began to change, with issues such as piecework and dirty work becoming subjects of negotiation.

The unions themselves also began to change as the old craft unions began to be replaced by larger brotherhoods. The Boilermakers' Union, whose international membership numbered around 350,000 at the height of the war, was foremost among them. Unions that had formerly opposed female employment and equal pay for equal work soon reversed themselves, some male members apparently fearing the loss of their own jobs to lower-paid women in the event of post-war layoffs. Jonnie Rankin analyzed the situation at Burrard as she reminisced some thirty-five years later:

> *For thousands of us who came out of the Depression, this was our first job. All of a sudden, the government, which said it didn't have the money to give decent relief or provide jobs, had all the money it needed to develop a war industry. I was already militant and angry over what I had gone through in the Hungry Thirties but ignorant of labour struggles. This sudden contact with trade unionists, ex-Wobblies [IWW], former farmers driven off their land during the drought and*

the Depression, former leaders and organizers of the unemployed, gave me an education that can never be found in books.

According to Robin Williams, while the war led to greater opportunities for women, it "had the opposite effect with prejudice related to race and nationality." He recalled his friend Betty McLeod telling how one teacher at Queen Mary Elementary School required students of German and Italian extraction to stand and be recognized in class, thereby ensuring that their classmates would associate them with the enemy. Jim Galozo, whose father had come to the North Shore in the early 1900s, remembered being taunted at school simply because he had an Italian surname. Fifty years afterward he was able to declare, "I feel more at ease today being Canadian than growing up then." Williams related how the father of Ralph and Hugh Kuntz changed the family's name to Koonts "in an attempt to lessen the anti-German prejudice directed against his children."

Japanese-Canadians suffered worst of all. Anti-Asian sentiment, long bottled up, began to bubble over even before the Japanese entry into the war. On March 4, 1941, the federal government required all ethnic Japanese people living in Canada to register as such. The government's action gave the city's anti-Asian lobby a new sense of legitimacy, and residents who had formerly suppressed their prejudice came into the open, with members of the city's establishment at the forefront. In November 1941 the North Vancouver Board of Trade wrote Commissioner Vance with a request that he "limit trade licenses to Orientals and make [the] necessary amendments to Licensing Bylaws." The commissioner wisely wrote back and advised the petitioners that he was not empowered "to discriminate against Orientals in the matter of trade licenses."

A month later, the Japanese Air Force attacked the American base at Pearl Harbor and Canadians found themselves engaged in a multi-front war. The day after the attack, the commissioner received orders from Military Command to ensure that all windows were blacked out from dusk to dawn. Mass hysteria and pressure from British Columbia's powerful anti-Asian lobby now came to the fore, its rage resounding in the halls of power. "Take them back to Japan," demanded one Liberal MP. "They do not belong here and there is only one solution to the problem. They cannot be assimilated as Canadians for no matter how long the Japanese remain in Canada they will always be Japanese." Some, he maintained, had already "photographed numerous military objectives in recent years."

The federal government issued a series of directives that ultimately resulted in the confiscation of Japanese-Canadian property and the forced evacuation of all Japanese-Canadians living on the coast. Most were sent to internment camps in the province's interior, and others were sent east of the Rocky Mountains. Among the internees were the well-known members of the Yada family, who had run a successful grocery store in the Ridgeway neighbourhood since 1904. Robin Williams and his friends witnessed the events, but were powerless to help their thoroughly *Canadian* Japanese friends. The community failed to come to their defence: "I don't remember anything being said about their absence." Williams recalled the events of the winter of 1941–42 with a sense of deep regret:

North Vancouver had numerous families of Japanese origin, usually occupied in fishing, boat-building or forestry, and many children in public school. Among those at North Van High were Harold Ishii, highly prized hook on the rugby team, Hoshiro Takahashi and Pauline Hiramatsu, all of whom would have graduated along with the rest of us by 1943.

Japanese-Canadians were not the only citizens subject to a registration process. The federal government had passed the National Resources Mobilization Act in June 1940 to identify both people and resources relevant to the war effort. Vance helped to organize a Citizen's Volunteer Committee to assist the federal government with National Registration, offering the Horticultural Hall available for interviews at no charge. In February 1940, Vance accepted yet another appointment, serving as chairman of the North Vancouver ARP organizing committee. At his direction, the city's fire chief and superintendent of works met with the local Indian agent to extend ARP protection to the Mission Reserve.

As unemployment levels plummeted, finding recruits for the Armed Forces became increasingly difficult. On the North Shore many men were exempt from military service, their jobs on the home front being deemed vital to the war effort. Jim Galozo, then working as a saw setter for the L&K Lumber Company, was deemed one of these. The L&K mill had been established to produce the wood fuel and sawdust that heated thousands of homes on the inlet and derived its name from the initials of its founders Lesseur and Kenny. The mill changed hands

The Yada family ran a successful grocery store in the Ridgeway neighbourhood from 1904 until internment. Photograph c. 1915.
North Vancouver Museum and Archives, 9532

circa 1940, by which time production was expanded to produce small amounts of lumber. As Galozo recalled:

> When conscription was introduced in Canada, an order also came from Ottawa that all essential workers were frozen to their jobs. A setter was considered an essential job, and Mr. Lyttle had to fill out monthly reports to the Federal Government to keep me in his mill as a setter. Some of the questions asked of Mr. Lyttle were: "How can this man be replaced?" "How long would it take to train a man for this job?" What a change! Just five years previously I was unwanted.

Maintaining and facilitating the work of the shipyards was particularly important, not just to hasten victory but for the city's economic health as well. Throughout the war, Vance assisted the shipyards in their efforts, leasing them street ends, organizing rail access and providing access to water mains. Hiring, firing and disciplinary action all fell within Vance's purview, whether for the city, district or school district. Although women had achieved wage parity in the shipyards, Vance continued the tradition of gender discrimination in the school system. Where male teachers might be paid $1,210 per month, a woman in a similar position was paid several hundred dollars less.

By December 1941, Commissioner Vance was able to advise the province of modest improvements in the city's financial situation. Costs had been cut and revenues were increasing. New employment opportunities had reduced the city's obligation to pay relief (social assistance) to economically distressed residents. Under veteran chief Bill Murphy, the fire department was a model of efficiency and its record of fire prevention and suppression kept insurance rates low. With the shipyards booming, ferry revenues were up substantially. Increased numbers of property owners were now able to pay their taxes. The war had pulled the city out of a difficult situation. Vance was careful not to appear too optimistic, but his accounts certainly demonstrated improvement.

11 RETURN TO FORM 1942–1949

With thousands of workers engaged to work in North Vancouver's shipyards, traffic on the ferries increased to unprecedented levels. Passengers complained of being overcrowded. Injuries were common, both to people and to property. Commissioner Vance endeavoured to have those responsible for the situation assist in its remediation. On April 20, 1942, Vance issued an ultimatum to the federal government: "If the City is not given help it is the intention of the City to withdraw *No. 3 Ferry*." Vance's challenge produced its intended result. Wartime Merchants Shipping contracted for the services of the ferry *Crosline* and turned the vessel over to the city to assist in the transport of the legions of shipyard workers crossing the inlet on a daily basis.

Regardless of these measures, scarcely a month went by without the commissioner receiving a report about some mishap on the ferries. Grievances ranged from the sublime to the ridiculous. There were very serious physical injuries, such as R. Binnie's finger being crushed, resulting in an amputation, or shipyard worker T. Howard being crushed by a coal truck on *No. 3 Ferry*. But other complaints related to broken umbrellas and runs in stockings.

Although stockings were scarce commodities in wartime Canada, such complaints paled in comparison with the commissioner's other worries. City staff had unionized in 1940. The newly formed North Vancouver Civic Employees Association included both inside and outside workers, ferry and hospital staff, and a growing number of teachers. With a burgeoning population of residents, maintaining law and order became an increasing challenge. Criminal acts and other problem behaviours—long an accepted reality of life on the south shore—became increasingly problematic on the north. Gambling on the ferries, though actively discouraged, reached epidemic proportions. Writing in 1969, ferry captain James Barr related others' impressions of the ferries during the war:

I have it on reliable eyewitness reports that the trips when the ferries were full of shipyard workers were something to be remembered. I cannot help hoping that the

Shipyard workers hustle to catch a ferry at the end of their shift, 1944. During the course of the Second World War, Burrard Dry Dock alone employed over 13,000 men and women in its North Vancouver operations.
North Vancouver Museum and Archives, 27-678

lifebelt racks were then in working order! There were several floating crap games played without any attempt at concealment and considerable sums of money changed hands on the passage across the Inlet. On paydays it was particularly hectic and it was said that the families of some of the unlucky players went pretty hungry at times.

Albert Stock, who worked on the docks from 1928 to 1972, confirmed Captain Barr's information:

The gambling fever on the waterfront was a real bad thing. The same as the shipyards. You would get your pay and by the time the ferry got to the other side your pay would be gone . . . Every chance you got you had your cards out, gambling.

Ron Gibbs, North Vancouver's city clerk from 1945 to 1972, recalled how gambling was common among a range of nationalities:

During the war period, there was a lot of gambling by the Chinese in Vancouver, particularly by fan tan clubs. The chief of police in Vancouver cracked down in the forties and as a result, two fan tan clubs came to North Vancouver City: one at the west side of Lonsdale and one on East First Street, south side. Sergeant Tom Hardman and Corporal Jerry Sharp conducted a raid on the latter. According to Tom, he told Jerry he would go in through the front door and ordered Jerry to block the back door exit. Jerry told me later that the back door crashed open and hordes of Chinese gamblers trampled out and over him. When I tell you Jerry was a big man, about (or over) seven feet tall, you will get a picture of the situation!

Tom and Jerry used to conduct two-man raids on the shipyard workers crossing the harbour on the MS *Crosline*. However, it was difficult for them to get the evidence because as soon as they were sighted, the blanket, which was placed on the deck along with the dice and money, were thrown overboard (except the money)!

The ferries and the police department were by no means the only city services pressured by population growth and wartime exigencies. Families moved into the city's wartime housing almost as quickly as it could be built. Considerable pressure was placed on existing schools and the city's sole medical facility. By early 1943, the situation became untenable. Commissioner Vance wrote repeatedly to Wartime Housing in the hope that he could secure funds to enlarge North Vancouver Hospital, "the present institution not being large enough to cope with the great influx of families and workers who have come to North Vancouver to live on account of so many new houses being built to house war workers." In his second letter to the corporation, Vance was more forceful: "There is not sufficient accommodation, and patients have to be turned away."

With hundreds of new houses being built in the city's southwest sector, existing schools began to experience the pain of overcrowding. Protracted negotiations with Wartime Housing resulted in an agreement for the construction of a permanent ten-room school (later named Westview) at a cost of $70,000. After school, with their parents at work, North Shore children were often left to their own devices, swimming off the log booms near the Midland Grain Elevator in summer and sledding down closed-off city streets in winter. Rather than getting into trouble, children and youth found themselves swept up in the war effort. Admission to the serialized Saturday afternoon screenings at Central Lonsdale's Nova Theatre was free to any patriotic youngster:

Each Saturday they'd have free admission if you brought a can of bacon grease or a ball—let's say about the size of a softball—of foil from cigarettes and packages and string. You'd have to have a pretty good-sized ball of string. They'd have the kids doing that and they'd fill the theatre.

The nearby Lonsdale Theatre was also abuzz with activity. Longer films or double bills were broken up by intermissions and high school students were often called on to perform. As Murray Dykeman recalled:

We went down there and some kids did magic. Somebody maybe played the piano or sang a song or maybe four of us would do a bit of singing—whatever it was—hit parade songs or something like that, just for fun. And the theatre would give the school club or something ten dollars. It was like a money raiser or an entertainment or a publicity venture for young people.

Screenings at the theatre inevitably ended with the audience rising to sing "God Save the King." And as audiences turned to leave, a moving image of the Union Jack wove resolutely across the theatre's screen. Bowling and roller skating had become popular pastimes. Everybody bowled, or so it seemed as a never-ending line of soldiers, sailors, shipyard workers and teens made its way to Derek Inman's Lower Lonsdale bowling alley. Murray Dykeman was one of the lucky lads who secured a job there as a pin boy:

Bowling was the big thing. It was probably the biggest public recreation of the forties, certainly in this town. There were movies up on Lonsdale, but the bowling alley would be going almost twenty-four hours a day. They went till midnight. They started early in the morning because there were shift workers who had an afternoon shift or something at 4 p.m. I remember working there—pins flying like crazy and you jumped up and down, up onto the plank above the pit.

By 1942, the demand for workers for the shipyards was intense. The supply of contracts appeared infinite, but many workers had been seconded to jobs in forestry and mining. Farmers and fishermen had returned to their former employment, and men in the lower pay brackets could not afford the costs of North Shore housing. In June 1943 the shipyards on the inlet had 1,600 jobs ready for the taking. With so much happening at the shipyards, the impact on the city was immense. Whenever a shift changed, hundreds of workers would flood onto Lower Lonsdale, heading for the streetcars or the ferry dock. Others made the short trip up the hill, jamming the Olympic and St. Alice hotels, drinking beer and listening to the big band recordings of Glenn Miller, Benny Goodman and Canada's own Guy Lombardo. Cafés like the Sugar Bowl welcomed more customers than they could comfortably serve. It was sheer pandemonium. In the eyes of many residents, North Vancouver had come into its own; it was no longer a suburb but rather, a city in its own right. Families such as the Dykemans went "over town," (across the inlet) to escape the frenzy: "To me it was its own place because of the activity of the shipyards. Now, in earlier years, in the thirties, it probably was a suburb, but boy, in the forties, the world was happening here and over town was like a treat to get away from all the workmen."

No one expected employment levels at the shipyards to remain at their wartime levels once the conflict was over, but few anticipated just how quickly the end would come. The paint on the newest wartime houses had scarcely finished drying when the inevitable decline began. By the fall of 1943, the Allies had captured Sicily and much of the Italian mainland. There were signs that the Battle of the Atlantic was about to be won, with more Allied ships being built than were being sunk. Orders at the shipyards began to fall. With fewer orders the workforce was cut and female employees were often the first to go. The impact on the ferries was dramatic. With one thousand fewer passengers travelling in the morning, the leased vessels supplementing the city's original fleet were no longer required.

In the spring of 1944, victory in Europe appeared increasingly likely. Months before the D-Day invasion, residents began to make their post-war plans. Commissioner Vance met with Colonel Molson of the federal Veterans Welfare Office to discuss how the city could assist with "the rehabilitation of returned men from the present war." Fully aware of the effects of war, the city looked into the future and set aside additional acreage in the North Vancouver Cemetery for the burial of returned soldiers and their dependents.

The long-awaited invasion came in June 1944. With the enemy on the run, a renewed spirit of optimism percolated through the city. The deprivation endured for so many years was fast becoming a distant memory. Government by commissioner, coupled with wartime industry, was pulling the city out of insolvency. The province's proclamation in early 1943 of the North Vancouver Debt Refunding Act allowed the city to begin the process of paying off its debts. It was time for a return to democratically elected civic government.

On April 17, 1944, Commissioner Vance wrote to the Minister of Municipal Affairs, applying for permission to hold a referendum. The question to be put to the voters was simple: should government by commissioner continue? Vance received the permission he required and the subsequent vote on June 14, 1944, proved decisive. The turnout was low, but 424 voted in the affirmative and 811 voted in the negative. Just three weeks later, an order-in-council was passed authorizing elections to be held for the positions of mayor, six aldermen and seven school trustees. Tragically, Vance failed to witness the results of his leadership, dying while on vacation a scant two months before the return to elected government.

The civic election—the first conducted in the city since 1932—was held on December 14, 1944. Jack Loutet narrowly defeated Roy Hunter for the position of mayor. Dr. Carson Graham, a popular North Shore physician, topped the polls for the school board and its six other members later selected him as chair. Although the city had returned to an elected mayor and council, the district remained under the authority of a government-appointed commissioner. Two sets of staff were now required, rather than the one that had served both jurisdictions during the previous decade.

Ken Gostick, at the time a newly elected city alderman, recalled the difficulty: "Sam Sowden was a retired banker and he, of course, stayed on as commissioner of the district. They had to move out of the city hall and rented a place on Esplanade, and he took the city engineer, the city clerk, the city treasurer, and we were left with no staff. He took all the heads!" Council acted quickly to remedy the situation, advertising for the necessary department heads and hiring well remembered men such as Jack Greenwood as superintendent of works and R.W. Richards as treasurer. The new council adopted a method of administration in which the clerk, superintendent of works and treasurer each wielded similar power. City clerk Ron Gibbs recalled the arrangement: "The three of us in those positions became a sort of troika and we would have meetings. I think it was called the 'reference committee.' The city council referred matters to the reference committee and we would go over the various aspects of it and submit a recommendation to council." The district returned to elected municipal government in 1951.

Governance on the nearby Squamish reserves remained rather murky. Reserve residents were represented by a council composed of both hereditary chiefs and elected councillors, but true power lay with the federally appointed Indian agent. Chief Simon Baker remembered the situation:

> Our Band didn't have much say about how we wanted changes on our reserve. It was all run by an Indian agent who controlled everything. It was like we were little kids and couldn't think for ourselves. But we didn't know any better, we just did what we were told . . . The Indian agent always tried to control things. He wasn't only the chair of our meetings but he was also the treasurer, and we never seemed to get any reports from him.

Years were to pass before the paternalistic system began to fade from view. In the meantime, men and women like Baker did their best to understand the system. They upgraded their educations and spoke to outside experts, learning to ask the questions that would lead to self-government.

When the conflict in Europe finally came to an end in May 1945, the mayor closed city hall and sent a truck equipped with a loud speaker through the streets to advise area residents that a civic holiday had been proclaimed. After six long years of deprivation and loss, one might have expected a great outpouring of pent-up emotion. There was chaos at the foot of Lonsdale Avenue as the sirens in the shipyards joined the whistles on the ferries. Shifts were cancelled and people all but danced in the street. Elsewhere, however, the populace was eerily calm. As the *North Shore Press* observed: "On the whole, it can be said that North Vancouver's populace took the news pretty much in its stride . . . The almost complete absence of noise and fanfare bordered the uncanny—there was something almost eerie about it as if to say, 'Can this really be true?'"

Men and women went back to work, shipyard workers perhaps dealing with conflicting emotions—pleased that the war was over but worried that their jobs might soon come to an end. Later that morning, the city's churches threw open

The Beattie family's dog calmly takes in the news as the war comes to an end in the summer of 1945. The scene at the foot of Lonsdale Avenue, however, was sheer pandemonium.
North Vancouver Museum and Archives, 3710

their doors to large congregations, each of whom gave quiet thanks for the long-sought end to hostilities. At 11 a.m., citizens congregated as if by instinct in Victoria Park at the memorial to the dead of another war. It was not until the evening that residents began to be overcome by the shear joy of the occasion, lighting a huge victory bonfire at Boulevard Park, singing their hearts out and cheering as an effigy of Adolf Hitler was consumed by the flames.

Amid the rejoicing many paused to remember the fallen. Many Sixth Field Company recruits died on the beaches of Normandy, in the infamous Falaise Gap or on the shores of the Scheldt. The unit had fought valiantly at Nijmegan, had leapt the Siegfried Line and penetrated deep into the heart of Germany. Hundreds of other North Shore residents had enlisted in other branches of the army as well as in the air force and navy. Some had died in accidents, others of disease, but of those who died, most were killed in action. There were hundreds of stories, many a mix of heroism and sacrifice. The much-decorated Eddie Nahanee, whose family connections with North Vancouver were far deeper than most, had attempted to join the Canadian army in 1942, only to be rejected due to a suspected heart condition. Undeterred, Nahanee enlisted in the American army, earning the Bronze Star, the Silver Star and the Purple Heart before he died of wounds in 1945.

There was much to be done to prepare for the men and women who would soon be coming home. Many were of a marriageable age and would soon require homes, jobs and training. The federal Liberal government promised a post-war utopia in which every Canadian would have "a wide-open chance to make a real success of his life" through a vigorous program of job creation, business loans, farm improvement loans, family allowances, affordable housing and gratuities to veterans. There would also be capital projects. A new post office was high on the community's list of priorities. The old post office (built as the district's hall in 1903) was likened to "an old gal" who had "begun to sag in the middle." In November 1945 North Shore MP Jimmy Sinclair declared the structure "the most disgraceful public building in BC" and assured city council that the erection of a new post office would "be one of the first projects to be undertaken in British Columbia."

In 1945, the ambitious city's lone public library was just as disgraceful. Though now a quarter-century old, the library still lacked civic support, moving from one rented space to another at the whim of Lower Lonsdale's landlords. In August 1947, however, the city began to take notice and facilitated the library's move to a disused garage at Sixteenth and Lonsdale. In the absence of direct financial support from the city, however, the library continued to rely on public generosity. In 1946–47, Vancouver's Shaughnessy Library donated over five hundred books to augment the North Vancouver library's collections. In 1949 the Wartime Administration Building on Second Street was secured for use by the library. *North Shore Review* columnist Pat Prowd extolled the efforts of Agnes Wheeler, Violet Johnson and other members of the library association: "Cosily ensconced in its new, modern home on Second Street, the literary emporium is there simply because down through the years since 1923 a group of resolute ladies refused to run up the flag of surrender."

Local government also assisted post-war settlers. As the veterans returned, city and district joined hands to promote the North Shore to potential new residents. North Vancouver was portrayed as a land of "happy homes" and as a community with state-of-the-art educational facilities, spacious parks, a quality transportation system, an efficient fire department, modern hospital facilities, beautiful houses and gardens, and extensive recreational opportunities.

Prior to the war, those who lived outside the community had a decidedly different view of the North Shore municipalities. Writing of the North Shore in October 1947, *Vancouver Province* reporter Alan Jessup remarked how North Vancouver had formerly been seen as an odd, laid-back community. It was a place where, "until 15 or 20 years ago, one could really practice escapism, Yogi, nudism, or nearly any thing else." According to Jessup, North Vancouver had been:

> . . . a cross between a spa, a farming community, and a hick town. It had a shipyard and a few waterfront industries and some notable residents, including a covey of retired army colonels, remittance men, and pensioners. Asthmatics and other invalids found the bracing air of the high, fog-free slopes beneficial; there were several nursing homes, boys' schools and an unlimited number of gardeners, rabbit breeders, amateur chicken ranchers and a small army of people who commuted daily "over town," where they explained apologetically [that] they lived in North Vancouver to "get away from it all."

The Second World War began to change the area's reputation. The demand for post-war housing did the rest. Cheap residential lots abounded in both the city and the district and hundreds of eager couples snatched them up. The population began to swell. As new residents swarmed into North Vancouver, the reputation of the community continued to change. Writing in 1947, Jessup noted, "snorting bulldozers and clanking steam shovels are gouging out new home-sites on its sunny slopes and uncovering the real estate pay dirt the old-timers have waited for since 1905. In this new rush and bustle, North Vancouver has gotten over being a municipal poor relation, the countrified backwater often called 'Vancouver's bedroom.'"

New residential subdivisions sprouted in areas such as Lynnmour, Seymour Heights, Capilano, Norgate, Pemberton Heights and North Lonsdale. The city's main artery, Lonsdale Avenue, sometimes seen as a northern extension of Vancouver's Granville Street, became the "main stem" for both city and district. There, the *Vancouver Province* reported "a medical-dental building, two new banks, modiste shops, hardware shops, florists and dry cleaning establishments have sprung up as fast as the building material shortage permits."

The numbers supported the rhetoric. At the time of the 1941 census enumeration there were just 8,500 people living in the city. By 1947, the population stood at 12,500, an increase of 47 percent. In 1946, sales of city-owned land—most of it acquired from taxpayers who had defaulted on their taxes—amounted to $173,742. That same year, 258 building permits had been issued, their total value exceeding $1 million. The district was growing at an even greater rate, having experienced a population increase of 89 percent in the period 1936–1947. In 1946, over $285,000 worth of municipal lands had been sold for development. A total of 444 building permits had been issued that same year, their value exceeding $1.3 million.

As the 1940s drew to a close, *Vancouver Sun* reporter Christy McDevitt characterized North Vancouver as an idyllic post-war town "of quiet, simple people, of modest businessmen, of ambitious politicians, of club-conscious housewives, of boys who are no better and no worse than boys in any other part of the world; of men and women and children who are your neighbours with their dreams, their hopes and their plans." By all accounts, North Vancouver was an ideal community in which to raise a family. There was little crime. Neighbours knew one another. The transportation system was efficient and modern. There was a true sense of community and recreational opportunities abounded. The place possessed all the advantages of a large community but lacked urban woes. After experiencing the pretentiousness of some of the people he knew in Vancouver, Ken Gostick felt a truly welcoming spirit on the North Shore: "It was very close-knit with very down-to-earth people. They'd come through the Depression. The people were just great, real down-to-earth people."

Gostick was one of the many who had watched the city's business district gradually climb the Lonsdale slopes. There, new businesses began to open, filling in the gaps between those established earlier. For some, the area symbolized a new beginning far from what many considered the grime of Lower Lonsdale. With its two theatres and assortment of confectioneries and cafés, Central Lonsdale became particularly attractive for the young. Don Tatterson's confectionery and Harbottle's ice cream parlour both enjoyed a booming trade. Indeed, consuming a "David Harem"—a concoction of ice cream, chocolate syrup, and bananas—became a veritable rite of passage. As Murray Dykeman recalled:

Harbottle's Jersey Products, next door to the art deco Odeon Theatre in the newly developing Central Lonsdale area, became a favourite haunt for residents of all ages.

North Vancouver Museum and Archives, 8971

> *I remember one of the things that was really big time when we became teenage was a David Harem, which was a form of ice cream sundae . . . And that was not horribly expensive, two bits or something. When you became a teenager, when you reached high school, you'd have a David Harem.*

Hamburgers, milkshakes and sodas were also readily available across the street at Jack's Café. For those able to venture farther afield, there was the legendary Tomahawk Café, where operator Chick Chamberlain also offered french fries. For people with more sophisticated tastes, however, Central Lonsdale still had a way to go. Eva Hallaway recalled how the area was yet to come of age:

> *Until the fifties there wasn't a coffee shop when you got out of the theatre. Latterly, in the mid-fifties, Van's coffee shop opened up across the street. Then, across from the theatre at Fourteenth and Lonsdale, was a big apple orchard. And there was no traffic on Lonsdale. And between pictures at the theatre we'd go out in the middle of Lonsdale and play baseball.*

Many teenage boys had part-time jobs delivering newspapers, picking them up from the "shacks" that each of Vancouver's dailies maintained throughout the city. Others worked for Chew Brothers', Gar Lee's and other grocery stores, delivering orders placed by telephone. The remuneration may have been modest, but it supported a lavish lifestyle: "If you had a dollar, you had it made. You could even take a girl to a movie and have a milkshake after at Harbottle's and not have any money left, but boy, you'd have a big time evening!"

Many young men—boys when they had left school to enlist for service overseas—returned to North Van High to complete their educations. Gerry Brewer, who attended the school in the late 1940s, recalled teachers trying to control returned servicemen in much the same manner as they dealt with 15-year-olds who had seldom ventured away from the North Shore: "Their worldliness had a tremendous effect on us as students. I'm sure it must have been a tremendous challenge for the teachers." Few returned servicemen were in any mood to be treated as children. These were "guys who'd been overseas and seen their best friends blown apart." If they were late for school, failed to study their Latin, or took a liquid lunch in the beer parlour of the St. Alice Hotel, the threat of a detention was hardly a deterrent.

For many British Columbians, the post-war years were a time of carefree optimism and a time of new beginnings. With tyranny vanquished overseas, the time had also come for greater equality at home. In 1947, Indo-Canadians and Chinese-Canadians both received the right to vote. Two years later in 1949, the right was extended to Japanese-Canadians, a population vilified by many a few short years before. The same year, the right to vote was extended to include the

Streetcar No. 153 meets a BC Electric Company bus at the foot of Lonsdale Avenue, 1946. BC Electric's "Rails to Rubber" program influenced the transition from streetcar to bus service in North Vancouver—a change welcomed by most passengers.
North Vancouver Museum and Archives, 6453

First Nations population. Squamish Chief Mathias Joe and his wife were the first Natives in the province to cast their ballots. The historic nature of the development did not go unnoticed. Over two hundred North Shore Natives gathered to witness the event. Prior to completing his ballot, Chief Joe paused and remarked, "I do not understand everything about the franchise, but I do know that this slip of paper gives me the right to choose who will lead me and my people. Only God and myself will know which man I choose."

The city's progress was not without irony. Four decades earlier, the district had been thrilled to secure its street railway system. In the mid-1940s, city residents were pleased to see it go. In September 1944—well before the war had ended—the BC Electric Company announced its ambitious "Rails to Rubber" initiative. The project had an estimated value of $50 million, of which $14 million would result in improvements to the company's transportation systems. North Vancouver's busy streetcar system was initially exempt from the conversion, but the threat of competition from the Blue Line Transit Company soon reversed the decision.

On May 14, 1946, an agreement was reached with the city to replace the entire streetcar system with buses, subject to the electors approving the proposal in a plebiscite. The bus company attempted to influence the vote a week before by offering residents free bus rides on all of its North Vancouver streetcar routes. When the vote was held on September 11, comfort and quiet triumphed over tradition; 89 percent of those who cast their ballots voted in favour of the proposition. The company moved quickly. Buses were travelling on Lonsdale Avenue within a week of the vote, their "dazzling red, cream, and aluminum colour scheme" wowing those who watched them pass. The *North Shore Press* was thrilled by their arrival:

True enough, there was a bit of sentiment attached to North Vancouver's old and yet faithful streetcars. The rattle-tee-bang they used to make while proceeding north and south on Lonsdale Avenue has ceased to be and it is missed and perhaps will be for some time to come. In place of that noise is heard nothing but the whurr of

BC Electric Company buses at the bus garage at Third Street and St. David's Avenue, wartime housing in the distance, c. 1947–50.

North Vancouver Museum and Archives, 5470

modern internal combustion motors as the sleek, new buses make their way up and down the grade with no effort at all. They get away faster, save time on the stops, and in many other ways make matters much easier for the citizen who has to daily make his or her way to and from the ferry.

Even as the buses were taking their initial trips, workmen were busy lifting rails and paving the centre section of Lonsdale Avenue. The last scheduled run from the Third Street car barn occurred on April 23, 1947. The journey took on a party atmosphere as officials of the company, city and district joined with pioneer employees such as Bert Giffen in a car filled to overflowing.

With wartime deprivation increasingly just a memory, residents found themselves tempted by the consumer goods that began to appear in the community's stores. Refrigerators began to supplant the ice boxes supplied by firms such as Storey's and Morrow's. The once catchy slogan—"Phone to Morrow's for your ice today"—began to lose its lustre. There was also time to relax. During the war and the Depression that preceded it, family vacations were the stuff of legends. By the late 1940s, however, families began to experience disposable income, a novel situation for many. Weekend trips to Cultus Lake or White Rock became commonplace and children were often sent to summer camp.

In the absence of a civic recreation department, the North Vancouver Community Centre Committee lobbied and fundraised for recreational and cultural facilities. By mid-1945, the committee had amassed $81,229 for a new gymnasium and auditorium. Its members hoped that funds raised through the Kinsmen Club's Dominion Day Carnival would help the committee to add an outdoor pool to its list of desired facilities. Yet despite everyone's best hopes, four long years were to pass before the gymnasium was built. On May 24, 1949, a group of two hundred residents joined Captain John H. Cates, then the local MLA, to attend the unveiling of a commemorative plaque. The auditorium, whose cost had risen to an even $150,000, would not be opened until the following spring, but the crowd

Third Street Garage proprietor Tom Meglaughlin poses with Alan Barr in his 1948–49 Ford convertible. Postwar prosperity and now-affordable automobiles lured young families to North Vancouver's burgeoning suburbs.

North Vancouver Museum and Archives, 10820

was enthusiastic nonetheless. Speaker after speaker lauded the work of Mickey McDougall, "the sparkplug of the enterprise."

In the postwar years, social needs were also addressed with vigour. Long dormant community groups were restored to life while other associations emerged to supplement their efforts. The pre-war years had been dominated by traditional, ritualistic fraternal orders; the postwar years saw the rise of service clubs that appeared better equipped to meet modern needs. Returning servicemen often joined the Kinsmen while the middle-aged affiliated with Rotary or Kiwanis. The Kinsmen were particularly active, organizing the city's annual July 1 parade and carnival and funding the construction of Mahon Park's first outdoor pool.

A new "aerie" of the Fraternal Order of Eagles emerged in 1947 to take the place of the Eagle's original aerie that had succumbed not long after the end of the First World War. Early projects of the revitalized organization included bursaries for North Shore students, sports activities for youth, services for seniors and raising funds for the chronically under-resourced local hospital. By the end of the decade, the Eagles had embraced St. Christopher's School for the Mentally Handicapped as their primary focus, but still found time to work with "Elmer the Safety Elephant" in supporting the North Shore Boys School Patrol.

The North Vancouver Junior Chamber of Commerce was also resurrected when

Kinsmen Carnival Queen Betty Smyth with attendants Jacqueline Kubisiki and Florence Layton, 1945. After the Second World War, service clubs like Kiwanis and the Kinsmen began to replace the older fraternal organizations.

North Vancouver Museum and Archives, 6531

the majority of its members returned from active service. The Jaycees, as they were more popularly known, quickly established a reputation for both energy and action. Events such as their "Timber Rodeo" were designed both as fundraisers and opportunities for positive entertainment. Held at Mahon Park, the rodeo featured a series of logger sports with men such as world champion spar climber Danny Sailor exhibiting their skills. Many people attended—but without purchasing tickets. In typical style, the organization quickly organized another event to raise the funds to cover the rodeo's deficit. The solution was a "smoker." Held at the Sixth Field Company's Armoury, the event featured liquor, tobacco and female strippers. As Ron Gibbs recalled, "In those days it was accepted. If you were hard up for money, you could have a smoker."

The activities of the North Shore Light Opera Society were decidedly less risqué. Founded at the behest of postman Jack McLaren in 1948, the North Shore Light Opera quickly established a reputation for high-quality productions, the quintessentially British operettas of Gilbert and Sullivan forming the core of its artistic repertoire. Its members—all committed amateurs—espoused goals including developing the vocal talents of their colleagues, fostering the public's interest in music and supporting local charities.

Live theatre was equally well served by the North Vancouver Community Players.

Comic operas, such as this production of Gilbert and Sullivan's The Gondoliers *became a staple of the North Vancouver Light Opera Society for over half a century.*
North Vancouver Museum and Archives, 7997

In the late 1940s, North Vancouver was undergoing a major postwar transformation. North Van High students wore bobby socks and saddle shoes. The jive and the jitterbug were popular dances and rock 'n' roll was soon to appear on the horizon.

North Vancouver Museum and Archives, 7004

Founded in 1945–46, the organization began life in association with the North Vancouver Community Centre Committee, then working from facilities at North Vancouver High School. The relationship between the Players and the Community Centre Committee began positively enough, with the Players understanding that the proposed auditorium would feature raked seating and a permanent stage. By the end of the decade the bond had soured, it becoming increasingly feared that the community centre would be more gymnasium than theatre. The Players presented their first production, *Kiss and Tell*, in April 1947 in the city's aging Horticultural Hall. Director J.K. Stansfield presided over a cast of fifteen players. The *North Shore Press* enthused that "the audience was slightly amazed at the ability of home-grown talent," while newly arrived resident A. Donovan Pool, a subsequent supporter of the group, recalled similar sentiments: "For me coming from outside to a then small place, I was utterly amazed."

Later productions were generally well received and North Vancouver audiences soon began to follow the careers of those who trod the local boards. A talented few went on to professional success including a young Dave Broadfoot, whose stage debut in 1948 was hardly propitious. Broadfoot, well known to later generations for starring roles in *Spring Thaw* and *Royal Canadian Air Farce*, received a lukewarm review, though the *North Shore Press* did acknowledge that he showed "some promise and did manage to conquer his stage fright."

With several successes under its belt, the organization decided that its performances would be vastly improved if presented in a real theatre. The Lonsdale Theatre, which had been converted to a bank, was the logical venue. The bank moved out and the Players moved in, their small army of volunteers endeavouring to restore the theatre to its former vaudevillian glory. Several successful productions ensued, despite the cast having to compete with the clanging of the theatre's hot water heating system. The experiment was not to last. Unable to screen films on

Fridays and Saturdays, the theatre owner was losing money on the arrangement and demanded compensation at a level the Players could scarcely afford. The Players returned to perform at the Horticultural Hall, still longing for a suitable venue of their own.

As the 1940s drew to a close, the province and many of its communities were clearly undergoing both physical and social change. Writing in the *Vancouver Sun*, Christy McDevitt reported on the rapid transition he had seen in North Vancouver: "In the past three years this community has stepped out of its mid-Victorian costume and now holds the spotlight as one of British Columbia's most progressive centres. The old mood is gone. This city realizes now that it cannot stand still while the rest of the world moves ahead."

It was exactly the sort of thing that city enthusiasts wanted to hear. The North Shore's sprawling new subdivisions and recently expanded businesses were clear signs of growth and progress. Tradition and introspection had been cast aside by a brash and boastful modernity. According to McDevitt, only a minority regretted "the recent spirit of industry and its attendant increase in population." These were old-timers who derived "a certain nostalgic pleasure in reciting the days of oil lamps, ancient trams, woodland trails, timbered sidewalks, towering shade trees, myriad chicken flocks, sad-eyed goat herds and all the other indications of a bucolic existence that is gradually giving way to civic progress." The majority looked to the future, confident that the ambitious city was finally on the threshold of greatness. For those who promoted the city, there was only one problem: most of the growth McDevitt had cited was in the district.

12 WAITING IN THE WINGS 1950–1959

In 1941 the city's population had totalled 8,914. The district, in comparison, had a population of only 5,931. A decade later, the city's population had reached an impressive 15,687, an increase of 76 percent. In the same period, however, the district's population had grown by a phenomenal 144 percent. With a population of 14,469 it was only a matter of time, perhaps months, before the district would be larger than the city. Some of the district's growth was at the expense of the city. Lured by the more commodious contemporary architecture of neighbourhoods like Capilano Highlands, Norgate and Sandringham Heights, both long-term city residents and young families moved to the district. Still, a population increase of 76 percent was considerable and for many the growth of the city became a matter of civic pride.

As its population increased, the city's character began to change. Hundreds of residents who relocated to the district retained their homes in the city as investments, renting out their older homes at a healthy return. As the decade progressed, transient renters took on a substantial portion of the city's housing mix. The North Shore's changing demographics carried some drawbacks. Peter Speck, long-time publisher of the *North Shore News* newspaper, remembered how the wartime housing to the west of the city had changed in tone:

> Kids from here were tough: the war had been over for some time, the work was drying up, many new families had fallen apart and there were lots of what we now call "social problems." In those days, from a kid's point of view, it meant drinking, gang wars, theft, and bullying. Hot rods were status symbols, and the "in" dress of the day for teenage males was pants, which if memory serves, were called "drapes" or "chinos," which had a narrow ankle, ballooning knees and double-buttoned flies with a great many buttons. If I saw someone wearing one of those and a wallet on a chain, I got out of the way!

With the rise of teen gangs, North Vancouver's police faced an entirely new set of challenges. The force had experienced great change when it moved from a municipally operated entity to a detachment of the British Columbia Police in 1934. In August 1950, the provincial force was dissolved and its various detachments were absorbed into the Royal Canadian Mounted Police.

During the 1950s, Squamish elders such as the Capilano Reserve's Dominic Charlie (centre) helped to pass on aspects of Native culture to his people's younger generation, including J. Baker (left) and Joe Mathias (right). Joe Mathias later became one of the province's leading champions of First Nations rights.

North Vancouver Museum and Archives, 10526

The North Shore
Neighbourhood House
offered a number of
services now considered
the responsibility of the
community's recreation
commission and school
district, such as this
kindergarten class
photographed in 1952 or
1953.

North Vancouver Museum and
Archives, 7876

John Braithwaite, born in Toronto of Barbadian ancestry, arrived in the city in 1956 to take up a position at North Shore Neighbourhood House. Trained in social work, Braithwaite and his agency worked hard to offer constructive alternatives to the gang culture that had infiltrated the North Shore in the 1950s and 1960s. The challenge was immense, with school-based gangs operating throughout the community: "There were all kinds of gangs. There was the Lynn Valley gang . . . You couldn't go up to Lynn Valley. If they saw you there, they'd attack you. That's how bad it was . . . Lower Lonsdale had a gang. There were a number of gangs." As long as the community's young people remained in their own neighbourhoods, peace prevailed. The violation of another gang's space, however, was sure to elicit an angry response. The city's new demographics were reflected in both its social and political life. Gerry Brewer, who began working for the city as a junior draftsman in 1955 and who later became city manager, reflected on the transformation:

> The stability that comes with owner occupancy is significantly challenged when over 50 percent—whatever number it may be—is tenant occupied. They come and they go. Are they committed to the community? Are they aware of community issues? Or are they simply here for three or four years and moving on? So, the politics of the day, the interest in what was being done or not done, sometimes was challenged by people who really had no stake in the community. But they sort of emerged as the local protest groups.

Immigration in the postwar years also changed the city's ethnic makeup. Starting in 1947, federal legislation gradually relaxed the nation's racially restrictive immigration policies. In 1941, 85.7 percent of the city's population claimed British roots. By the time of the 1951 census, the proportion of city residents with British ancestry had fallen to 79.6 percent. Families from the Netherlands, Scandinavia and Eastern Europe—as well as the defeated nations of Germany and Italy—sailed to Canada in search of a better life. Murray Dykeman had fond memories of how the various populations interacted in the city's Lower and Central Lonsdale neighbourhoods:

In my young days, in the forties and fifties, I knew all kinds of Italian families and I feel like we've lost them. They're homogenized in the community now. They were wonderful people, they identified as a community in North Van. It's kind of a nice relationship you can establish with an Italian family, especially if you're a youngster. I always found they kind of adopted you.

For the children and youth of the community, race and ethnicity were often matters of curiosity rather than concern. For many in their parents' generation, however, the arrival of olive-, yellow- or dark-skinned immigrants was rather more serious. Dykeman and other young people learned how to deal with racist comments: "If you were smart you just kept your mouth shut." It was one thing for members of non-visible minorities to keep silent in the face of racism and quite another for those on the receiving side. Speaking in 1970, John Braithwaite reflected on how he was treated as he attempted to rent accommodation not long after his arrival:

Discrimination is here on the North Shore and don't let anybody tell you differently. I have run into blatant discrimination in terms of housing and apartments. I tried to get a place sometime back, right up here on Sixth Street. I went up to the door and when the woman answered she was shocked to see who was standing there. I told her I would like to look at the place, she started to sputter, then finally said she was looking for an older couple.

Ironically, it took a black eastern Canadian to bring North Shore Natives and non-Natives together in activities in the Neighbourhood House. As Braithwaite recalled:

Let's look at the Indians and the whites—the two main cultures here. When I first came out, there was no way I could see that the whites and the Indians were even making an effort to get along. Here I would like to say the Neighbourhood House was one of the first organizations to include Indians on an equal basis. We did not just pay lip service to equality like so many organizations—we made it a practice.

If the coming together of diverse cultures was one of the postwar city's challenges, housing was another. Hundreds of new dwellings had been built for Wartime Housing during the recently ended war. Fears that they might sit vacant as the shipyards geared down proved to be unfounded. Many laid-off workers remained in the community and continued to live in wartime houses. Any vacant houses were quickly snatched up by returning servicemen or young families who chose to settle in the area. The North Vancouver Kiwanis Club purchased forty of the houses for use as seniors' residences, forming Kiwanis Senior Citizens Homes to manage the initiative.

At the end of the war there were few new houses in the city other than those built by Wartime Housing. During the late 1940s and the 1950s, however, the sight of new houses being built became commonplace. The sounds of handsaws and hammers resounded throughout the community. Despite all the activity, some sections of the city remained undeveloped. The farther one went up the slopes and the farther one travelled away from Lonsdale Avenue, the greater the likelihood of encountering undeveloped lots.

Although the shipyards now had a lesser impact on neighbouring properties than during the war, a few Lower Lonsdale businesses nonetheless received a new lease on life. With a hefty demand for building products, firms such as Ocean Cement, Paine Hardware and Rogers Lumber did a roaring trade. These were exceptions, however, for by the early 1950s many small retailers had closed their Lower Lonsdale shops and moved up the hill. Park Royal, a large American-style shopping centre, had opened in West Vancouver in the early 1950s, further eroding the commercial viability of the Lower Lonsdale area. When Roland and Stella Jo Dean purchased No. 7 Lonsdale Avenue a few years later, the city's old downtown core had clearly fallen on hard times: "Everything was boarded up. We couldn't get insurance for the property . . . because they were all wooden structures. If you bought anything in Lower Lonsdale at that time it was a risk."

Lonsdale Avenue looking north from Thirteenth Street, early 1950s. In the 1950s, Central Lonsdale was a community in transition. One side of the street was fully developed, incorporating a state-of-the-art supermarket while the other was still without the curb and gutter of a fully urban environment.

North Vancouver Museum and Archives, 4112

In the 1950s, Lower Lonsdale remained a study in contrasts. The area east of Lonsdale Avenue was one of single-family homes. To the west of Lonsdale Avenue, older three-storey walk-up apartments predominated. Both sections, however, were home to the city's poor. John Braithwaite, who knew the area well from his work as executive director of North Shore Neighbourhood House, recalled how "people always referred to Lower Lonsdale as the poor area, the ghetto. And there were some pretty bad homes."

For the city, the demand for new housing proved a godsend. Having acquired hundreds of houses and lots when owners defaulted on their taxes in the 1930s, the city was sitting on a veritable gold mine. Indeed, in the early 1950s, the City of North Vancouver was the single largest property owner in the city. Lots were sold at fair market value with the proceeds being used to eliminate the city's debt and to create a capital reserve fund, the intent of which was to finance future civic infrastructure. There were roads to be paved and sidewalks to build, not to mention street lights, sewers, water mains, fire halls and recreation centres.

Gerry Brewer remembered the state of North Vancouver's infrastructure in the mid-1950s. Most of the roads were still unpaved; asphalt was something the city could not afford until the mid-1960s: "The creeks were all open channels. The lanes were typically unpaved strips of dirt that were graded periodically to keep them passable. The streets, in most cases, still had open ditches and wooden curbs to delineate the edge of some of the roadways." Speaking in 2006, John Braithwaite recalled a city full of contrasts. Lower Lonsdale was fully urban, but

North Vancouver's upper levels resembled a wilderness:

Coming from Toronto with all the activity, I said, "It's beautiful, but what am I doing in this frontier town?" And when my wife came out, which was only two or three years later, she never unpacked. She didn't unpack for a year! The curbs were wood. Part of the sidewalks was that pea gravel and when you packed it down it became hard . . . Up Lonsdale, up at Twenty-fifth . . . trucks were roaring off that Lonsdale from Grouse Mountain. They were cutting down trees. They were coming off there, like a hundred a day. Logging trucks. I'd never seen a logging truck in my life!

North Vancouver entered the 1950s with a modern style post office at Lonsdale Avenue and First Street, on the site of the first city hall. For residents and political leaders alike, the new building was symbolic of postwar growth and renewal.
North Vancouver Museum and Archives, 12969

Although the city possessed reasonably extensive storm and sanitary sewers, less developed areas were still not serviced. Small creeks meandered through Central Lonsdale, passing through culverts under the roadway. Floods were a constant worry with major inundations occurring in the area, despite its mid-hill location, in 1955, 1956, 1957 and 1959. Larger creeks were particularly worrisome: the city had lost houses and a bridge at Mosquito Creek. A worried council began to focus its attention on developing infrastructure to address the problem.

Many looked to the new decade as a period of continued material progress in the city. Recognizing that growth required direction, the city adopted a new zoning bylaw in 1950, allowing directed higher-density development in the Lonsdale corridor. When the new post office building opened at First and Lonsdale in June 1950, North Shore MP Jimmy Sinclair asserted that the city had "the best post office in British Columbia where it used to have the worst." Alderman and journalist Christy McDevitt looked to the day when the council would open a new city hall, something that would clearly be needed "now that the city was moving so fast."

The 1950s were also a time of political maturation. When civic elections were held in December 1951, Violet Johnson stood for the position of alderman, basing her campaign on the need for better lighting in the city. Johnson placed second in a field of eight otherwise all-male candidates, and council appointed its first female member in history to a number of key positions including the important finance committee.

Library supporter Violet Johnson became the city's first female council member. Her tireless efforts on behalf of library services began in the early 1920s and finally led to the construction of a purpose-built facility as the city's 1958 centennial project.
North Vancouver Museum and Archives, 13645

By the early 1950s, wartime fears had long since been replaced by an infectious air of optimism. For young men like Murray Dykeman, the possibilities seemed endless:

By the time 1950 was here, the world was my oyster. I remember the teachers were telling me that "you can be anything you want." And it was true. Everyone was looking for people, staff, whatever you want to call it. And I thought, what a wonderful time to be alive . . . Before the war, you took your slice, whatever it might be, and that's what you went with.

Amid his euphoria, Dykeman paused to reflect on those who fortune appeared to have blessed less generously: "Sometimes I had a concern about our aboriginals, that they weren't 'in' like I was 'in' . . . There were times when you felt, why do the Indians live on the reserve? I'd go down there sometimes on my bike and wonder why." Speaking in the mid-1990s, Chief Simon Baker remembered the era:

I look at the Squamish Band today and see the houses, many of them even better than those owned by white people in North Vancouver . . . This is good. I always wanted my people to have everything like the white man. We had to fight hard for those things. Young people today don't realize how us old-timers worked in them days, about fifty years ago, to get what we have today.

For most North Shore residents, however, the future seemed rosy. Young people who a generation earlier would never have dreamed of going to university now could, and the employment opportunities were immense. Home ownership became an attainable goal and the acquisition of consumer goods accelerated as never before. Peter Speck recalled the emphasis on modernity: "The 'culture' of the 1950s was about anything else than 'old'—it was about new cars, television, washing machines and refrigerators." Murray Dykeman remembered how once-acceptable technologies were abandoned for others:

Suddenly, everybody needed a new toaster. I remember that being a significant modern appliance. A waffle iron—wow! All my life I'd known my dad making pancakes on a griddle on top of the two-hole burner of the sawdust burner and getting the heat up well. The wringer washer was soon gone—into the garbage, I guess—and we got an automatic clothes washer. The dryer was later, but the washer was a must in every house. And, of course, the kitchen sawdust-burner. It was almost sad to see that go. We put in gas . . . Mother got a gas stove. It took forever to make that damn oven bake like she was used to.

Wedged between the city's waterfront industries, parts of the Mission Reserve still remained undeveloped in 1952.

North Vancouver Museum and Archives, 3592

Dykeman remembered that equally suddenly, it seemed every teenager had a battery-operated transistor radio: "They were quite cheap, I remember $5.95 in the fifties. That was no big deal." AM radio stations were in their heyday, and rock and roll was at the very heart of the popular youth culture of the day: "That was the way kids could go and listen to it, because nobody would put *that* on the family radio, would they?" Buying a car was every teen's dream and the local malt shop or café became a common place to gather. Chick Chamberlain's Tomahawk Barbeque, located just outside the city on Marine Drive, now a growing shopping district, did a roaring trade as it produced what many considered the best hamburgers in town.

Televisions were the marvel of the age, though many families were unable to afford them until the 1960s. Those who acquired them in the 1950s were sometimes overwhelmed by their neighbours' response. Dykeman's parents acquired their first television at an opportune time:

I'll say it arrived on Monday. On Saturday at two o'clock was the "miracle mile" at Empire Stadium. I can remember standing on the steps outside our house looking through the doorway to watch that, because I was busy working, but I came by the house. There were so many people from the neighbours. They filled the front room! They filled the porch, and I was kind of able to hold onto the porch and watch the mile. It was an exciting thing, wow, television!

The new technology was expensive and many residents of both the city and the adjacent reserve had to rely on the generosity of others to watch a television program. Lila Johnston was in her teens when she saw her first television program at neighbour Ralph Atkins' home: "When I first got married there was one TV [on the reserve]. We thought that was the most wonderful thing in the world—to go look at TV and watch Ed Sullivan!"

The older generation, who had lived through the Depression of the 1930s and the rationing of the war years, found it difficult to adjust to an age of newfound wealth. When Murray Dykeman took his parents out to dinner in an upscale restaurant, their reaction was distressing: "I don't think they enjoyed it at all. I shouldn't have let them see the menu. They got all upset because dinner was $5.50 each or something. They were used to the $1.98 blue-plate special of the Depression years. Mother and father were simply in shock."

Older residents knew only too well that the bubble could burst at any time. Although Burrard Inlet's North Shore appeared to be thriving, the prosperity was less than universal. Down on the waterfront the two shipyards struggled. With the war at an end, the demand for ships fell abruptly. Burrard Dry Dock and the Pacific Dry Dock Company—as North Van Ship Repairs had become—both secured fewer contracts and bid too low to secure a reasonable profit. The two firms negotiated. In what was essentially a hostile takeover, Burrard purchased Pacific Dry Dock in May 1951. Burrard attempted to keep both yards running, but in 1954 was forced to consolidate its operations. Pacific Dry Dock closed and its three floating dry docks and other equipment were subsequently relocated to Burrard Dry Dock.

Partly fuelled by the excitement of the British Empire and Commonwealth Games

TELEPHONE:
NORTH 281

CROWHURST MOTORS
15th. & Lonsdale Ave.   North Vancouver, B. C.

Crowhurst Motors at Fifteenth Street and Lonsdale Avenue, 1950s. The Central Lonsdale garage was home to a highly accomplished all-female softball team in the 1950s.
North Vancouver Museum and Archives, 10945

held in Auckland in 1950 and in Vancouver in 1954, organized sports re-emerged as a focus for community life. The Fraternal Order of Eagles and BC boxing legend Tommy Paonessa established the Northwest Eagles Boxing Club in the old Knights of Pythias Hall at Fourth and Chesterfield. Many local youth trained in the facility, some acquiring golden gloves championships. During the 1950s it became common for community businesses to sponsor local teams. Ron Gibbs remembered the Crowhurst Garage softball team well: "The unique thing about that garage was that it was operated by girls—by ladies—and the Crowhurst girls had a very good softball team and they used to beat practically anybody that wanted to play against them."

Outdoor sports took place in the city's parks and school grounds. Indoor sports were offered in the old drill hall and the recently opened Memorial Gymnasium. Soccer remained a popular outdoor activity, but under the direction of Father John Kilty, priest at Upper Lonsdale's Holy Trinity Church, young men's basketball also rose to the fore. Father Kilty, a highly charismatic figure, had little concern whether his players were Catholic or not. Providing a positive experience was all that really mattered. For Kilty, Protestant-Catholic rivalries were largely a thing of the past. Murray Dykeman was one of "Father Kilty's boys" who had fond memories of the team:

He ended up with a whole bunch of non-Catholic boys who heard about his forming a basketball team, including me, my brother-in-law, it goes on and on. As a matter of fact, John Roberts used to call himself the token Catholic. He said, "The only reason I'm on the team is because I was the one guy who belonged to the church!"

[Father Kilty] was just a wonderful strong builder, coach, and mentor. He was good for all of us . . . That was another reason why my dear friends and I had some sense of community by the time we were eighteen.

If sports for adults and youth were popular, those for children were all-consuming. In the early 1950s, hockey had yet to become a national passion and it was baseball that children longed to play. The sport required little in the way of specialized equipment or facilities. Ron Gibbs remembered how the Junior Chamber of Commerce enlisted community support for Little League in North Vancouver:

> We started Little League and before we knew it we had a tiger by the tail. There were so many kids who wanted to play and the community stood up and backed them all the way. There were firms all over the place that backed them and got them uniforms and equipment. One of the strongest ones was a man called Fen Burdett who lived on the Grand Boulevard. He would treat his boys really well. He'd take them to the game and take them to an ice cream parlour afterwards and give them ice cream. That was duplicated and triplicated all over the community.

But most sports-minded North Vancouverites remembered the 1950s as a time when its national- and international-level athletes came home laden with medals and trophies. No one cared whether "their" athletes resided in the city, the district or even West Vancouver. When it came to supporting the North Shore's best, there was only one community. Those who distinguished themselves did so in a variety of sports. Swimmer Kay McNamee competed with distinction in a number of

Above: Dick Williams and Sam Gardiner, British Empire and Commonwealth Games silver medallists in lawn bowling, 1954. The achievements of Williams and Gardiner proved that competitive sports were not just for the young.

North Vancouver Museum and Archives, 4453

Right: Bill Parnell setting a Vancouver and District record for the 880-yard run, in 1945. Parnell went on to distinguish himself in the British Empire Games in Auckland in 1950.

North Vancouver Museum and Archives, 7527

Sprinter Harry Jerome breaks Percy Williams' high school record (220 yd) at Vancouver's Empire Stadium, May 27, 1959. Jerome went on to distinguish himself in a series of Olympic Games and despite his Prairie birth, became one of the city's favourite sons.

North Vancouver Museum and Archives, 5349

international events including the British Empire Games of 1950 and the 1948 and 1952 Olympics. Her brother Gerry swam in the 1952 Olympics and the 1955 Pan American Games. Basil Robinson, a graduate of North Shore College who had been British Columbia's Rhodes Scholar for 1940, captained Canadian cricket teams throughout the decade. North Vancouver's older adults were not to be outdone; lawn bowlers Sam Gardiner and Dick Williams crossed the inlet to compete in the 1954 British Empire and Commonwealth Games held in Vancouver and returned home with a silver medal.

As remarkable as these accomplishments were, it fell to two young runners to achieve enduring fame. The first of these was Bill Parnell, a middle distance runner who broke a number of records at the Vancouver and District high school track meet prior to his departure for the 1950 British Empire Games in Auckland. There he won the mile run in record time and captured the bronze medal in the men's 880-yard run. The second runner was the even more famous Harry Jerome. Jerome was born in Saskatchewan in 1940. His family moved to North Vancouver when Jerome was twelve and settled in the city's Ridgeway neighbourhood. By the time he reached high school Jerome's athletic talents were readily apparent. Those in the know were hardly surprised when he broke Percy Williams' high school record for the 220-yard sprint at the age of eighteen. Shortly afterward, the young sprinter tied the existing world record by running the 100-metre dash in a phenomenal 10.0 seconds. There was more to come, for Jerome was destined to remain at the top of his form well into the 1960s.

As the shipyards took up less of the waterfront, the city encouraged other businesses to fill in the gaps. Waterfront industry returned to its roots as timber-based industries proliferated on the landscape. Shingle mills and tie mills peppered the foreshore. M.B. King Lumber Co., now managed by the founder's sons Donald and Graeme, was in its heyday, shipping lumber to ports in Europe, Australia, the Far East, the Caribbean and the United States. L&K Lumber Co., destroyed by fire on Christmas Eve 1952, relocated from its waterfront property at Moodyville to a new site in the district. As Ron Gibbs recalled, the advent of new industry came with its costs. Taxes from the mills may well have lined the city's coffers, but smoke produced by their inefficient beehive burners led to heavy fogs: "The fog that we used to get in North Vancouver was just something you wouldn't believe. Inevitably, when you parked your car—even up on Fifteenth or somewhere like that—and came out and wiped it off, you'd have little black cinders on it. Everyone was screaming about the pollution from those burners, so eventually they disappeared." The much cleaner Park and Tilford Distilleries purchased a thirty-acre site at Cotton Drive and Brooksbank Avenue in the mid-1950s, cleared it, and began to construct its facility a few years later. Production began in 1960 and continued until the distillery closed in 1982, its plant having become antiquated in a mere twenty-two years.

Although few realized it at the time, developments on the old West Indies Dock (named the Japan Wharf until the Second World War) were to revolutionize shipping not only on the North Shore, but also throughout the world. In 1953, the White Pass and Yukon Corporation, whose facilities were just east of Burrard Dry Dock, devised what may have been the world's first container system for use in its ship-rail-truck service between Burrard Inlet and the Yukon. The corporation's freighter *Clifford J. Rogers* was designed to accept 250 White Pass containers each about eight-feet square, as well as assorted freight on deck. Although the containers were small, the system worked so well that the company replaced them with containers twenty-five-feet long and built a second vessel, the *Frank H. Brown*, to carry them. A third ship, the *Klondike*, was added to the fleet in 1969, by which time the world was beginning to take notice of the new, highly efficient technology.

As the North Shore's population swelled, the three municipalities struggled to keep pace with an ever-growing demand for services whether in road works,

Containers are lowered into the hold of the container ship Clifford J. Rogers, *1956. Containerization of cargoes was pioneered at North Vancouver's White Pass and Yukon Dock in the 1950s. Ships like the* Clifford J. Rogers *were purpose-built for the technology.*

North Vancouver Museum and Archives, 9626

street lighting or sewers. The baby boom that had followed the war placed greater stress on an already overtaxed hospital. All three councils recognized the problem, but finding a solution was difficult. West Vancouver opposed expansion because it wanted a facility of its own, but eventually relented. An addition to the hospital opened in July 1954, increasing capacity from 83 to 140 beds. Recognizing that the hospital's expansion was only a short-term solution, residents of all three municipalities united two months later to form the North and West Vancouver Hospital Society, an organization focussed on building an entirely new facility. A one-day membership campaign held in January 1955 resulted in an additional 7,200 members joining. Discussions progressed and plans for a 285-bed facility were developed. With promises of federal and provincial funding secured in 1957, a borrowing bylaw went to the voters. The *Vancouver Province* reported an overwhelming 90 percent vote in favour of the bylaw. The new facility opened as Lions Gate Hospital in April 1961.

For city residents who remembered the construction of the Second Narrows Bridge in the 1920s, talk of a replacement must have brought back many memories. By the mid-1950s, it was clearly evident that the much-repaired existing bridge was becoming obsolete. It was low and narrow and its lift-span design required both vehicular and train traffic to stop whenever an ocean-going vessel passed through the narrows. With the North Shore population and the ownership of private vehicles both increasing at phenomenal rates, something had to be done. In 1955, the province announced its intention of building a new six-lane high-level bridge to replace the span built in 1925. The new bridge was to be the longest cantilevered bridge in western Canada and the eighth-longest in the world. It would cost between $12 million and $15 million to build and construction would take about three years to complete. The announcement was music to the ears of North Vancouver residents and businesses alike.

The prospect of a new bridge was particularly appealing to the city, whose ferry

The newly opened Lions Gate Hospital with the old North Vancouver General Hospital to its east, 1960s. The construction of the hospital was the culmination of a decades-old community dream. Built by the North and West Vancouver Hospital Society, the hospital is now operated by the province's Vancouver Coastal Health Authority.

North Vancouver Museum and Archives, 13463

"Aw, come on, Henry... if we don't try it in the next two weeks, we'll never know..."

The cancellation of the cross-inlet ferry service was noted by cartoonist Len Norris in the Vancouver Sun, *August 22, 1958.*

Vancouver Sun

revenues were in serious decline. The hordes of workers who had once travelled the ferries to reach the shipyards had faded into history. Post-war prosperity had enabled thousands of residents to purchase motor vehicles. Commuters without cars of their own took advantage of BC Electric's frequent inter-city bus service. The writing was on the wall; the ferry system had ceased to be financially viable.

Despite the financial realities, residents viewed the loss of the ferries with mixed emotions. Captain James Barr recalled that "people generally were saddened to think of the passing of the ferries." For Rodger Burnes, "who had spent almost a lifetime travelling to work and to school on the ferries, this was a loss that was heartbreaking." The last ferry sailed on August 30, 1958. When Captain Simpson tied his *No. 4 Ferry* at the North Vancouver dock following his final sailing, he simply remarked, "Well, that's it." Within months, the fleet was dispersed. *Ferry No. 5* remained at the foot of Lonsdale, destined to become the fabled Seven Seas seafood restaurant.

Work on the new bridge was well under way. Because its northern approaches would be located in the district, the city stood to benefit without having to pay any of the direct costs of the project. Nothing quite like it had been built in the province before and residents on both sides of the inlet followed its progress with keen interest. Some were no doubt watching on June 17, 1958, when two sections of the partially completed span fell into the inlet. Fireman Dick Hallaway was at home when the bridge collapsed and remembered hearing "just kind of a roar . . . I didn't know what it was. I hadn't got a clue, but I knew it was something." Hallaway grabbed one of his children's bicycles and raced to the hall:

Rosemary Parsons and Mary Lou Philips pose with a life preserver from the North Vancouver Ferry No. 4.

North Vancouver Museum and Archives, 6799

> *I wasn't on duty but I went back to the fire hall and I took a truck down with inhalator equipment and we were working on some the fellows who had drowned . . . Some of them were taken to hospital. I didn't know how many people were there, really, in the emergency end of it. You know, you're so darn busy you don't really know what's going on.*

Within hours the full extent of the calamity became clear. Eighteen workers had died in the mishap and twenty suffered significant injuries.

The collapse of the bridge was the low point in a year intended for celebration. One hundred years had passed since the creation of the Crown colony, and Premier W.A.C. Bennett encouraged communities to mark the occasion in appropriate ways. Amid the performances and re-enactments there were also capital projects: museums, recreation centres and other public amenities. In the city, the centennial committee recommended the construction of a library. Library advocate Violet Johnson had never lost her tireless resolve. Speaking to the *Town Crier* in 1957, Johnson recalled a public excessively slow to embrace the services that she and her society endeavoured to provide:

> *The library functioned for so long in objectionable quarters that when better ones were found it was practically impossible to interest people to come and see. Once it almost died for want of readers, and yet people wanted a library. They did not realize however that one was growing right before their eyes. They still thought of*

The tragic collapse of the new Second Narrows Bridge on June 17, 1958, reminded many of the bridge it was built to replace. The old span had also been haunted by misfortune, being hit by passing vessels and put out of commission for periods of up to four years. In time, many dubbed it "the bridge of sighs."

North Vancouver Museum and Archives, 10076

the library as "those dirty old books in that old room over the butcher shop," and it took a long time to make them understand that things had improved.

When the new library opened at the corner of Twelfth and Lonsdale in 1958, its supporters were exultant. The construction of the library was a godsend not only for members of the public, but for students as well. During the 1940s and into the early 1950s, elementary school libraries were virtually non-existent in the North Vancouver School District. Jack Loucks, who taught at North Star, Westview, Sutherland and Ridgeway schools prior to becoming a principal, concocted a novel approach to addressing the problem:

Every eight weeks we had a field trip over to the old Vancouver Public Library. We'd take the bus to the ferry, march onto the ferry, and make sure they [the students] behaved themselves on the ferry and we'd march them over to the library and pick up our books. We had ten cards and we were allowed ten books per card, four fiction and six non-fiction. Over all those years that I did that in the different schools we only lost one book.

With a burgeoning population, the city's schools were soon bursting at their seams. A series of new public schools were built to accommodate students in the developing Westview, Cedar Village and Moodyville neighbourhoods. Sutherland Junior High School, opened in the fall of 1950, was one of the first to be built, taking considerable pressure off the overcrowded North Vancouver High School. The North Shore's Roman Catholics were also active, building an elementary school

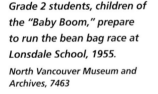

Grade 2 students, children of the "Baby Boom," prepare to run the bean bag race at Lonsdale School, 1955.

North Vancouver Museum and Archives, 7463

in Upper Lonsdale in 1956. Named in honour of the Holy Trinity, the school was staffed by three sisters of the Order of St. Joseph and administered by Father John Kilty.

As the 1950s drew to a close, another Roman Catholic facility was deemed not only a firetrap, but obsolete as well. Now six decades old, St. Paul's Indian Residential School had evolved into a day school. A new generation of parents—many of them alumni of the residential school—were no longer willing to board their children there. Speaking in 2006, Squamish Nation staff member Anjie Dawson recalled her parents' experiences as boarders in the school:

> Both of my parents went and they both had very different experiences . . . my mom always talked about the residential schools . . . She just remembers cleaning and praying, and then breakfast, church, and cleaning and praying, and cleaning and praying, and washing the floors and everything like that, and then lunch. And it was like that every day. There was hardly any academics . . . My mom stayed with the church all her life too and my dad was just the opposite. He never wanted anything to do with the Catholic Church again after. And I think after they came out . . . the hard part for them, well, for all of them, was that they had no parenting skills because they were brought up by nuns.

The residential school system had clearly failed, meeting neither the department's objectives nor Natives' aspirations. In 1959, a new day school was built on West Fifth Street—also named St. Paul's—with the Roman Catholic Church continuing to provide its staff. A century after the creation of the Crown colony, First Nations education remained a troubling business. Most of the province's youth left high school prior to graduation. In 1959, the Department of Indian Affairs reported just three aboriginal students enrolled in the province's universities. Racial stereotyping still endured, the department feeling that Natives might best be directed toward manual labour.

About the same time, the North Shore's Roman Catholics developed plans for a new high school to accommodate their growing population of teenaged students. Consideration was given to locating the school in West Vancouver, but when the Sisters of the Instruction of the Child Jesus offered the site of the old St. Paul's Indian Residential School on West Keith Road, a decision was made to build the school there. Named in honour of St. Thomas Aquinas, the school opened in 1959 with the sisters forming the bulk of its staff. Denece Billesberger was one of the institution's first students and joined the order five years later, ultimately becoming its provincial head. As membership in the order declined, its teaching and administrative duties gradually passed to the laity and the sisters ultimately relinquished the school to the archdiocese in 1975.

13 GROWTH AND CONSOLIDATION 1960–1969

....

When the new Second Narrows Bridge opened in August 1960, the celebrations were understandably muted. Residents throughout the province could not help but wonder what had caused the bridge's collapse and who was responsible. A provincially commissioned inquiry by Chief Justice Sherwood Lett attributed the collapse to an engineering error. The fact that the two men alleged to have been responsible had both perished in the fall struck some skeptics as far too coincidental. To many in the trade union movement the bridge became symbolic of death in the workplace, which was acknowledged in 1994 with the new name of the Ironworkers Memorial Second Narrows Crossing.

The bridge was but a single component of a much larger transportation plan. Rather than dumping traffic onto pre-existing roadways, it would be part of the growing network of provincial highways championed by Premier W.A.C. Bennett and his Minister of Highways "Flying" Phil Gaglardi. Motorists bound for the Horseshoe Bay ferry terminal would no longer be forced to meander along narrow local streets; instead, they would travel at high speeds via a four-lane divided freeway called the Upper Levels Highway. The bridge and the highway were symbolic of a province on the move, but their effect on North Vancouver was devastating.

For many city residents, the march of progress had come literally in their own backyards. Properties were expropriated and houses were demolished. Overnight, residents of the Eastview community found themselves cut off from the rest of the city. The northern portion of the Grand Boulevard, part of the city's historical ring of parks, disappeared under concrete and asphalt. Residents who had been attracted to the northern edges of the city for its peace, quiet and clean mountain air were suddenly beset by the roar of traffic and the stench of exhaust. Gerry Brewer recognized the impact:

It cut the city in half. One could liken it to the Great Wall. Physically, our services were cut in half. You had water mains that went to and sometimes underneath . . . but more importantly, the streets you used to be able to drive through from north to south were no longer able to be utilized, so you had to go to crossing points at either Westview, Lonsdale or Lynn Valley Road . . . The city was told via a couple of quick, quiet meetings, "This is what we're going to do." Bang! The clearing contractors ran. The housing rights-of-way had already been quietly optioned and bought up by the land agents of the provincial highways department, and "Here we come!" . . . It was like putting a railroad through the middle of town, and the hell with you, we're coming through.

Aerial view of the newly completed Second Narrows Bridge, c. 1960. The opening of the new bridge by Premier W.A.C. Bennett was a bittersweet occasion, marred as it was by memories of the structure's collapse while under construction.

North Vancouver Museum and Archives, 4421

NEW SECOND NARROWS BRIDGE VANCOUVER, BRITISH COLUMBIA

The city was experiencing growing pains. There were vacant lots beckoning new development. Deteriorating properties cried out for improvement. Old boardwalks and pea-gravel sidewalks demanded attention. There were roads to be paved and the city's schools and city hall both required upgrading. And when improvements *were* made, they weren't always timed correctly. Gerry Brewer acknowledged, "Sometimes we'd slip up. I remember some sad and angry and laughable meetings where we'd just paved the bloody street and BC Hydro would come in and want to run a six-inch main right down the street." As the population grew, the need for recreation programs and facilities also increased. In the midst of it all, frugal councils and their staffs, remembering the years spent in receivership, adopted a "pay as you go" attitude and provided services only as funds became available. One contribution of additional funds was the unwelcome result of Typhoon Frieda, an "extratropical" storm that ripped through North Vancouver in October 1962. Frieda's relentless winds of up to 129 miles per hour felled many of the oldest trees in Mahon Park as well as in the watershed. Sensing an opportunity, the city went into the logging business and used the profits to upgrade its parks.

While those who lived near the Upper Levels complained of pollution, residents nearer the water benefited—at least momentarily—from cleaner air. Commuter traffic had been diverted up the mountainside and the beehive burners that had once been common along the waterfront were disappearing. The waters of the inlet had been abused for almost a century. Gerry Brewer described just how bad the situation had been:

> *The inlet itself, one must remember, had been a repository for no end of debris and waste materials ever since the development first started on the North Shore. The lumbering, sawmills, the booming grounds, the elevators—they didn't really worry about what went in the water. It just went in the water . . . During the war years, anything not needed and not required at hand was pitched over the side. So the whole subsurface area in that part of the inlet was just littered with anything and everything you could imagine.*

The city was just as guilty as industry. Brewer recalled that sewage "roared straight down the hill into the inlet. There was no suggestion at that age and time that we would do anything otherwise." It was not until the early 1960s that the three North Shore municipalities took collective action. The opening of the Lions Gate Wastewater Treatment Plant in 1961 not only began to address the issue of water pollution, it also permitted the city to increase the number of housing units within its boundaries.

As the city's operations became more complex, its staffing complement grew. Relations with the union changed. Speaking in 2001, retired city clerk Ron Gibbs recalled a time when civic employees and management not only worked together, but also played together. Staff members were represented by the North Vancouver Civic Employees Association. Although he was management, Gibbs was routinely invited to join the association's members for five-pin bowling at Derek Inman's bowling alley. It was not unusual for him to accompany members on picnics to Bowen Island or to bring his wife to the union's annual dance. The bargaining

Family-operated sawmill M.B. King Lumber Company, photographed in 1956, was a fixture on the North Vancouver waterfront for close to 40 years.

North Vancouver Museum and Archives, 11367

process had started out informal and cordial, but this was not to last. As Gibbs remembered:

> I used to be involved in bargaining with them. And we used to have very amicable times every year, two years or whatever it was. I'd say, "Well, what do you boys want—what's the basis of your request this time?" And they would outline them, either the cost of living or something. But one year there was a stranger there. He was a member of a bigger outfit, anyway. So I started with my usual question, "What's the basis for the request or increment?" The guy says, "There is no basis. These are our demands!" So I knew in my heart right then that things had changed.

Labour strife had been a rarity at North Vancouver City Hall. Labour action had occurred in 1958, but after the civic and school district employees began their association with the Canadian Union of Public Employees (CUPE, founded in 1963), regional issues often overshadowed local negotiations. CUPE employees went on strike for the first time in 1966, causing significant community concern.

Employer-employee relations in private industry, such as M.B. King Lumber, had also changed. At its peak, the operation provided employment to 240 workers, many of them long-term employees. M.B. King had died in 1951, but his sons had carried on in their father's easygoing, caring style. Speaking to the *North Shore News* in 2001, Donald King's daughter Gillian recalled, "It was my father who was the one who sort of kept his finger on the pulse of the mill. He could walk in and go up to someone and say, 'Bill, how's Jennifer, is she over the chicken pox?'" Gillian's brother John had similar memories: "He had a really good rapport with the men. When he died that sort of management died with him."

Contract issues were but one of several serious matters confronting Ron Gibbs and his city council. Council meetings were a never-ending circuit of public hearings, budget debates, personnel discussions and policy considerations. The biggest issue that emerged in the 1960s was that of amalgamation. The issue had surfaced as early as 1920, when city alderman W.J. Irwin proposed the reunification of the city and the district. The community's board of trade has raised the issue again in 1944, but Commissioner Vance showed little interest in pursuing the matter. In 1957 council had engaged the firm of Griffiths and Griffiths chartered accountants to investigate the financial implications of merging with the district. The ensuing report suggested that amalgamation might well be feasible, given the economies to be realized with one council, one hall and a single set of staff. Based on the Griffiths' initial findings, city and district councils agreed to proceed with a more detailed study, but after considerable discussion the matter was left to die.

While the two councils dithered, in 1958 the province appointed Hugo Wray, a former reeve of West Vancouver, to undertake a study. Wray's mandate was to consider the potential amalgamation of Greater Vancouver's several municipalities into a single metropolitan city. When his report was circulated in 1960, the City of North Vancouver ranked among its most vociferous opponents. Amalgamation with the district was hard enough to swallow; amalgamation with the municipalities on the south side of the inlet was unthinkable.

"Gracious me! I hadn't thought of it that way before... the two North Vancouvers have been living in sin."

Amid the political rhetoric, the amalgamation issue was also the object of levity. **Vancouver Sun** *cartoonist Len Norris poked fun at the debate in September 1964.*
North Vancouver Museum and Archives, 1968-69 pamphlet

Advocates of amalgamating the city and the district were undeterred. In 1961, the Public Affairs Bureau of the North Vancouver Chamber of Commerce developed a planning process that ultimately determined that amalgamation of the three North Shore municipalities "would not only provide more efficient utilization of existing services, but also considerable financial savings to the taxpayers of these communities." Councils chose to commission a study of their own. Undertaken by Ward and Associates and completed in 1966, the new study recommended a single municipality governed by an eight-member council. Amalgamation, the report argued, would result in an annual savings of $552,000 in 1970, increasing to $789,350 in 1975. The subsequent Stevenson and Kellogg report, initiated by the still-skeptical city, also declared amalgamation as economically advisable and predicted a per capita net saving of $6.37 in 1970 and $8.28 in 1975. It was not what city council wanted to hear. Stung by criticism and hoping to put an end to an irritating topic, council resolved in December 1966 not to "entertain further amalgamation studies for at least ten years."

Provincial Minister of Municipal Affairs Dan Campbell, however, suggested that the province might take unilateral action by forcing amalgamation. In the view of the minister, a preferable course would be for the two municipalities to prepare a draft amalgamation agreement and to present it to the voters in a referendum. In the face of this threat, the city took action by organizing a postcard poll of its electors. The intent of the poll was to request assent for the preparation of an amalgamation agreement, which would be the subject of a referendum at a later date. By the end of June, a total of 5,835 ballots had been returned, of which 3,097 (53 percent) were in favour of amalgamation. In this case, the majority did not rule, as the Municipal Act of the day required a minimum of 60 percent of the voters to approve the proposal. After a second report from Stevenson and Kellogg and the distribution of two separate information leaflets throughout the city and district, the councils each held public meetings on amalgamation, five days apart, in September 1968. District council continued to favour the proposed merger, while in the city four aldermen joined Mayor Carrie Cates in opposition to two in favour.

On September 19, 1968, the voters of both areas had their say in a referendum. The turnout was poor, with less than 50 percent in either jurisdiction bothering to cast a ballot. In the district the vote was resounding, with almost 90 percent of the electors voting in favour. But the Municipal Act required a 60 percent majority in both municipalities, and only 50.5 percent of city voters favoured the proposal. The amalgamation question was laid to rest for the remainder of the decade. Council—and the community—were no doubt relieved by the quiet that followed the storm. There were other matters to deal with, few of which appeared at the time to be anywhere near as controversial as the merger of the two municipalities.

In 1964 Carrie Cates had broken the gender barrier by being elected mayor of the City of North Vancouver. The wife of former MLA and Charles H. Cates & Son principal John Henry Cates, she beat out three male opponents and was re-elected in 1965 and 1967. Building a replacement for the city's aging, overcrowded city hall had long been one of Mayor Cates' main objectives. A new facility would cost the city $1.35 million and could have been funded entirely from the city's extensive capital reserves. All that was required was the approval of the voters. In the weeks prior to the necessary referendum, however, the self-styled Committee for Sound Business Administration began to place advertisements condemning the project in the local papers. The committee, whose members refused to identify themselves, maintained that passing the bylaw would result in significant tax increases. Advertisements placed by the Committee in Favour of Amalgamation of the City and District of North Vancouver tied the project to amalgamation: "Why a new city hall before a decision on amalgamation? There are only four services left to amalgamate: planning, fire, engineering, and administration."

Mayor Cates smelled a rat, declaring to the press that the newly formed committee was composed of small-minded men who "don't want to do anything until they can hand the city over to the district. They seem to be against anything we put up in the city." Council responded by placing its own advertisements urging the passage of the money bylaw. When the question was put to the voters, the bylaw failed by the narrowest of margins. Mayor Cates described the vote as one of non-confidence and accordingly de-emphasized her quest for a new city hall in favour of revitalizing the city's historic downtown core: "Several matters deserve top priority but heading my list and in capital letters is the rehabilitation of Lower Lonsdale. It hurts me when I hear people say it is a forgotten and forsaken area. It is certainly foremost in my heart and mind as I am sure it is in yours."

Mayor Cates might also have referred to the tumbledown appearance of parts of the neighbouring Mission Reserve. Years of tight-fisted management by a series of Indian agents had done little to upgrade the houses on the property. Speaking in 2006, Squamish elders Margaret Locke and Lila Johnston related how they had grown up in little houses with just four rooms: a living room, a kitchen and two small bedrooms. Without indoor plumbing, residents made do with outdoor privies and carried water in buckets from communal taps. Johnston, who grew up in her grandmother's house, remembered how "there was only one tap. Emma Peer— she's the one that had the tap. There was only, maybe, three taps on the reserve." Although electricity had come to the townsite in 1906, houses on the Mission Reserve were not electrified until the middle of the Second World War. Writing in the mid-1990s, Chief Simon Baker recalled the situation on the Squamish reserves: "We lived in shacks with outside toilets. We used coal oil lamps and wood stoves. Most of our clothes were handmade from old clothes given to us by white people. We didn't seem to know that we could have things, the same as the white man . . . All our reserves seemed to be in the same condition."

Baker also related how the situation changed. For years the band's Indian agents had squirreled away revenues received from the sale of gravel and other commodities extracted from reserves. Baker and other council members requested access to the funds and used them to upgrade their people's housing:

> Just at that time they were getting rid of wartime houses. Somebody came and told me, "Gee, Si, we could buy these wartime houses. They come in three sizes, singles, doubles and those with an upstairs, for two hundred, three hundred and four hundred dollars." We figured out how many houses we could get from our money, including the sewer and water. So we got so many houses.

Although improving the housing situation on the Squamish reserves was a major accomplishment, acquiring a semblance of self-government was even greater. The event came unexpectedly when a new Indian agent, Frank Anfield, advised the band council that he would cease to chair its meetings: "You have to pick out one of your councillors to be chairman. I would like . . . to let you people handle your own business. You decide what you want to happen."

The Squamish Band Council chose Baker as its chair. Baker in turn formed committees to address economic development, education and welfare. Within a very few years the band had concluded a series of savvy business agreements with developers in desperate need of land: "By god, things really started moving! We had an economic development committee that I chaired. I was chairman of Kapilano 100, Park Royal Committee. We were working on the leasing of our land to Park Royal. I can say, today, I lived long enough to see the revenue for our people from some of those big leases." According to one observer, the Squamish band's newfound prosperity resulted in a number of residents with Native blood identifying themselves as status Indians, hoping to share in the wealth:

Indian blood . . . wasn't a popular thing to have in those particular days. That's where all the closet Indians, I say closet, became [Indians] as soon as they got a little prosperity. The band started Park Royal and the marina and the other

Dominic Charlie, Stella Jo Dean, and Chief Simon Baker welcome a replica of the SS Beaver **at the foot of Lonsdale Avenue, June 1967. The gathering was part of North Vancouver's memorable "Salute to a Century," a series of community events marking the centennial of Canadian Confederation.**

North Vancouver Museum and Archives, 13144

marina and had some income. Everyone put on a feather. Prior to that they were all hiding in the closet!

There was also progress in the city. The new city hall project may have received a setback, but other civic projects—such as a new recreation facility and a school to relieve the now overcrowded North Vancouver High School—were materially advanced. In 1965, a new gymnasium was added to North Van High and was subsequently named in honour of Mickey McDougall. In the post-war years several new schools were built in both the city and the district, Hamilton Junior High School and Delbrook High School being prominent among them. In 1965, a new high school opened to improve the situation even more. Named in memory of popular physician Dr. Carson Graham, who had died prematurely in 1959, the new facility began as an ordinary high school whose programs focussed on the academically inclined. Within a few years, however, an enlightened administration had developed a curriculum with an emphasis on career preparation for every student in its diverse catchment area.

The *Vancouver Sun* described the school several years later: "It has the same number of people as a small town in BC—Sechelt, say, or Salmo or Stewart. But everyone is in one building. It has the diversity of a city the size of Vancouver. Welders, chefs, actors, mechanics, immigrants, artists, the handicapped, the scholarly, native Indians, carpenters, potters—they're all here." The Canadian-born, immigrants, refugees and Natives all found opportunities to explore their particular interests, whether in information technology, art, car maintenance or business. First Nations students were especially encouraged. "Indian Days" were held annually beginning in 1969. By 1970, an "Indian Senate" had been formed, its members supporting one another while explaining aboriginal culture to the wider population.

Despite being unable to agree on amalgamating their two municipalities, city and district councils had succeeded in coordinating their services in a number of areas. In October 1962 after years of serving both city and district from the confined basement of city hall, the RCMP detachment moved to a new building in the 100 block of East Fourteenth. The two jurisdictions also made progress in recreation. The baby boom of the 1950s and 1960s had created a population hungry for recreational opportunities and the impending 1966 and 1967 centennial celebrations provided an ideal opportunity for the two councils to work together on a suitable initiative. In October 1963, the North Vancouver Centennial Committee (composed entirely of city aldermen and district councillors) recommended the construction of a $1.4 million recreational facility as a joint centennial project. The new complex would be located on city-owned land at Twenty-third and Lonsdale. The old Lonsdale (Horticultural) Hall would be demolished and part of Eastern Avenue would be closed off. A twenty-five-metre indoor swimming pool, a regulation-sized hockey arena with seating for 1,500 spectators, a six-sheet curling rink and a 700-seat auditorium would take their place.

For many residents, the package was irresistible. There was something in it for everyone. Residents who could not afford to join the Capilano or North Shore Winter Clubs or who were unable to travel to them, would be able to skate and curl in centrally located and publicly owned facilities. Those who wanted to swim year-round would no longer have to travel to the Crystal or Killarney pools located across the inlet. Live performances would no longer have to be accommodated in flat-floored halls or decaying movie theatres. Admission and program fees would stay in the community. Even the capital costs seemed to have been addressed. Federal and provincial largesse and a contribution from the district would reduce the cost to city taxpayers to only $490,000.

After some debate, the two councils both agreed to take the question to the voters in a referendum. District electors approved the proposal 4,326 to 2,182. In the city—the proposed location of the new facility—the rate of approval was even higher: 2,565 to 867. Bill Wallace, president of the North Vancouver Memorial Community Centre, was elated and suggested that the time had come for the creation of a joint authority to operate the new recreation centre.

In 1966, North Vancouver's long-dreamt-of recreation centre finally took form, opening in March of that year. Residents were ecstatic. The city and district prided themselves on having built a multi-faceted facility unique in the province. During its first three days of operation, the facility attracted over twenty-five thousand users and visitors. Lieutenant Governor George Pearkes officiated a formal ball to honour the occasion that was attended by over seven hundred people. Amid all the hoopla, celebrants paused to remember the tremendous volunteer effort that had led to the centre's construction; parent-teacher associations and the North Shore Sports Arena Association were prominent contributors. Users flocked to the new facility, and in 1969 a mass meeting of residents at the Centennial Theatre urged the formation of a joint city-district recreation commission. The district accepted the idea quickly, and although the city dallied the North Vancouver Recreation Commission was formed the following year.

The new centre had only just been opened when it was called upon to help address a growing malaise among the community's youth. Neighbourhood-based gangs continued to be a problem and the RCMP detachment was at a loss on how to deal with them. In the opinion of more than a few residents, the force had evolved in quite the wrong way. When the community was smaller, its policemen knew its residents and were regular participants in community events. By the late 1960s, however, constables originally hired by the city and who subsequently served in the British Columbia Police had either retired or been posted elsewhere. In 1966, the RCMP staff sergeant in charge of the North Vancouver detachment refused to participate in local events, allegedly stating, "The RCMP are not part of this community. We are a federal force." Roland Dean recalled the mid-1960s as a time when teen gangs and drugs proliferated among some North Shore youth, making life miserable for a number of residents:

> In the sixties many kid social gangs were becoming delinquent gangs. The locals were known as "greasers" as vandalism around schools and small businesses became common. "Maryjane" [marijuana] had arrived in the late fifties and speed was appearing in the sixties. While a volunteer at the Lonsdale Recreation Centre, I had to participate in the rescue and protection of the management staff from a large group of "greasers" who had invaded the centre. We did not dare call the police as that would have turned the invasion into a riot.

At the Recreation Centre, volunteers and staff knew that the greasers were planning a riot in Edgemont on Halloween 1966. Plans were made to entice the teens away from the riot with free swimming, skating and a teen dance with a well-known band that volunteered their services. However, we were told that the centre had to be closed as the police would handle the riot. The police handled it with shop windows [getting] smashed before the firemen scattered the crowds with high pressure hoses.

The Halloween riot indicated the need for a new approach to local policing, and the detachment astutely responded by replacing the officer-in-charge and adopting a new approach in June 1967. Dean described an entirely different scene at the Canadian centennial celebrations:

Scarlet coated Royal Canadian Mounted Police raised flags, helped with their radios, moved young participants who arrived in wrong places. The officers made many friends that week and seemed much happier. On Halloween 1967, I saw teens greeting constables as friends as they invited the officers to join their parties.

The two municipalities worked more closely and effectively in areas other than policing, as well. Building on the success of the Lower Mainland Regional Planning Board, the province created the Greater Vancouver Regional District (GVRD) in 1965–67, granting it a mandate to coordinate a number of services for what grew to become twenty-one member municipalities. One of the regional district's most enduring accomplishments was the development over a period of two decades of what became the *Livable Region Strategic Plan*. Amended to reflect changing circumstances, the plan focussed on managing growth through protecting green space, building complete communities, stressing a compact metropolitan region and increasing transportation choices. Regional town centres would feature higher-density residential and commercial development well served by mass transit. They would be compact areas in which a high proportion of residents could both work and live, using public rather than private transportation. North Vancouver city's Lower Lonsdale area would ultimately be designated one of eight such centres.

The GVRD's early planning initiatives may not have ignited residents' imaginations, but the year 1967 most certainly did. Canada's centennial was a memorable year throughout the country. There was excitement in the air and people's outlooks began to change. Canada now had a flag of its own. Montreal's Expo '67, with its state-of-the-art technologies and contemporary architecture, helped to eliminate a colonial mindset. The nation's centennial song, "Ca-na-da," the work of composer Bobby Gimby, captured the spirit of the moment. Canadians remained loyal to the Crown but were no longer subservient to Britain. Murray Dykeman reflected on the change: "Singing 'God Save the Queen'—suddenly that wasn't nationalism any more. It got replaced with the maple leaf flag and the anthem, and the young people grabbed onto 'Ca-na-da.' They loved that song. And that separated us. It wasn't disrespect. We just didn't do that anymore."

Gimby's lyrics were sung across the nation, North Vancouver included. Under the guidance of its centennial committee, residents of both city and district joined as a single community to honour the country's anniversary. Co-chairs Stella Jo Dean and John Denley were in the thick of it, tirelessly working to make North Vancouver's "Salute to a Century"—held in the week leading up to July 1—an event to remember. Blessed by good weather, the event captured the same sort of enthusiasm that Pete Larson's Dominion Day festivities had some sixty years before. The festivities were a mix of corn and sophistication, but the levels of participation were immense. A joint mayoral declaration urged citizens to "sing, dance, shout, and rejoice" and thousands of residents did just that. Everyone participated, from Boy Scouts to service clubs, from cadet corps to seniors. The Federal Centennial Commission was awestruck, declaring "North Vancouver's 'Salute to the Century' plans the most ambitious local centennial celebration staged by any community in the country."

There were band concerts, a parade, choral performances, skydiving demonstrations, variety shows and dances. For the community's adult males there was a beard-growing contest with awards to recognize the longest, most unusual, most colourful and even most kissable beard. The highlight for many, however, was the trek to Moodyville. Over five thousand residents took part in the march, trekking in columns from a dozen points to the site of the long-gone sawmill. An additional one thousand celebrants travelled by car. Many participants had dressed in period costume, with Chief Simon Baker and his family prominent among those awarded prizes. Dominic Charlie, the colourful Squamish sage, travelled on foot in a simulated canoe, fell, and quipped, "First time I ever tipped a canoe!"

Amid the celebrations, council and the community considered the question of a third vehicular crossing of the inlet. Like amalgamation, the issue seemed one incapable of rest. Early residents of the North Shore would have been happy with a single bridge and elated to have two; those who lived in the area sixty years later were harder to satisfy. Traffic had increased. With the ferries gone, downtown Vancouver could only be reached by a roundabout half-hour drive. There was nothing to connect downtown Vancouver—the destination of so many commuters—directly with the North Shore.

Federal and provincial politicians were full of promises, especially during election campaigns. Few were more vociferous than BC Highways Minister Phil Gaglardi. In December 1963, Gaglardi made front-page headlines when he advised the *Citizen* that construction of a tunnel to Vancouver might begin in just eighteen months' time. All that was required was the agreement of all the governments concerned plus the sum of $22 million. Elections and politicians came and went and the promised crossing failed to materialize. When the CNR announced the impending construction of a new railway bridge just east of the Second Narrows in 1965, residents took little notice. What they wanted was a vehicular crossing placed somewhere between the existing bridges. Given the magnitude of the project, however, neither city nor district council was in a position to do much more than lobby.

Although the area was governed by two separate councils, residents' reactions to their neighbours' achievements suggested that North Vancouver was a single community. The successes of Bill Parnell, Harry Jerome and others had contributed to a growing sense that North Vancouver athletes were a force to be reckoned with. Despite a succession of injuries, Jerome had earned himself a bronze medal in the 100-metre run in Tokyo's 1964 Olympic Games. Having tied the world record of 9.2 seconds in the 100-yard dash while attending the University of Oregon, the sprinter went on to equal three additional world records before electrifying the North Shore by winning gold at both the British Empire and Commonwealth Games in 1966 and the Pan American Games the following year. Similarly, proud parents, teachers, friends and community leaders assembled at Vancouver's CN Station to cheer Arthur Smith's North Vancouver Schools Band as it returned home with five trophies from the national school bands competition in August 1968. Don Bellamy's White Spot Junior Band played for the occasion.

That same month, changes in the Public Schools Act took effect, drawing North Shore Natives and non-Natives closer to one another. Under the terms of the Act, Natives whose children attended provincial schools were eligible both to vote and run in school trustee elections. Speaking on behalf of his people, Squamish business manager Sam Lewis commented on the historic nature of the event: "Fifteen years ago, it was unthinkable that an Indian would have the chance to hold such official office. This being a democratic country, I am glad we are getting in on the vote for the sake of our children's future." Despite such advances, inequities remained. Paternalistic governments placed limits on Native rights and prejudice was common. Social worker Paul Winn recalled:

> *Discrimination against First Nations people was blatant and inexcusable. They weren't allowed to do many of the things that were a part of the general society. They couldn't buy liquor in a liquor store so they went to one of the two hotels downtown—the St. Alice or the Olympic, but usually the St. Alice. The women were called "squaws" and the men were called "chief," always in a patronizing way.*

Those who had founded the city in the early 1900s had great ambitions for the community's waterfront—including the Squamish reserves—hoping for a massive invasion of rail yards, wharves and factories. It had taken some time, but shipyards, sawmills and other enterprises had come to the North Vancouver waterfront, incrementally taking up property zoned for industrial purposes. Although opportunities remained for further industrial development even in the mid-1960s, an evolving environmental consciousness would turn many residents against the very sort of development their fathers and grandfathers had so avidly pursued. In 1965 the Saskatchewan Wheat Pool announced its intent to build a massive grain-handling facility on the North Vancouver waterfront. The Wheat Pool, a co-operative wholly owned by Saskatchewan wheat farmers, had concluded a lease agreement with the National Harbours Board for land at what had once been the site of the Moodyville Sawmill. Four small firms—North Shore Shingle, Norwood, Vickers Timber and K.S. Maude Industrial Electric—were ordered off the site to make way for what would become the second-largest grain elevator on the northwest coast.

By May 1966, all the necessary approvals had been secured and construction proceeded. Similar facilities had long been operating on the other side of the inlet and few people opposed a plant that would put the city in the forefront of a growing trans-Pacific trade in grain. It was an age when size mattered. The new facility would occupy a footprint 1,200 feet long by 200 feet deep. Its two berths would be able to accommodate ships up to 900 feet long and the elevator would have a capacity of 5.3 million bushels. The total project budget was destined to exceed $21.5 million, $3 million of which would be spent on what was said to be the most complete dust-control system on the continent.

The company's interest in dust control was nothing if not timely. North Vancouver's elevator workers and longshoremen were increasingly aware of the dangers inherent in the transport of grain. Longshoreman John Cordocedo had vivid memories of shovelling grain in the holds of ships berthed at the Midland Grain Terminal:

The Saskatchewan Wheat Pool's grain terminal was built south of the Low Level Road in 1966–68. Residents initally took considerable interest, if not pride, in the state-of-the-art facility (photographed in 2007).
Warren Sommer photo

> *And down at the bottom here, they'd put forty of us shovellers here, forty guys around a feeder, passing it . . . We had masks on and goggles . . . They used to give us candles, they wouldn't even give us lights then, you know, electric lights. After they found out about the explosions they cut out the goddamned candles. So that's how much they cared about us . . . Half the workers didn't realize what they were exposing themselves to. That dust is very combustible.*

When the new elevator opened on June 14, 1968, public curiosity was intense. Anticipating a deluge of the curious, the Wheat Pool organized a series of guided tours, beginning early in the morning and continuing until the official mid-afternoon opening. An enthusiastic press reported how the facility could unload as many as 128 boxcars of grain per day, handling two at a time. Highly sophisticated mesh cleaners would remove any wild oats, seeds, and foreign material well before the wheat reached the ten shipping spouts used to load the grain onto the waiting ships.

The construction of the facility had provided jobs for upwards of four hundred men. When completed, however, the plant was deemed "almost fully automatic." Although few city residents would find employment at the elevator, the Wheat Pool's taxes were estimated at $300,000, making the new facility the city's largest single source of taxes. The construction of the Wheat Pool increased North Vancouver's total taxable assessments by a phenomenal 17.5 percent in just one year. In the eyes of the City of North Vancouver, large-scale industrial development was something to be encouraged, for it clearly had the capacity to reduce the city's traditional dependence on residential property taxes.

The Wheat Pool's elevator was still under construction when the city received a proposal for another development from Neptune Terminals, a privately owned company based in Toronto. By August 1966 Neptune had leased seventy acres of National Harbours Board land at the mouth of Lynn Creek and had acquired an option to lease an additional sixty acres. It also arranged to dredge the harbour to create usable land and space for up to six deep-sea vessels. Neptune's vision was for a bulk dry-cargo storage and loading facility. Initial reports indicated that the operation would ship potash to markets in Asia. Residents of the city's nearby Cloverley neighbourhood began to be concerned. Park and Tilford, the nearby distillery, wondered how the facility would impact its soon-to-be-opened landscape garden:

> We are very concerned over this proposed installation . . . our inquiries reveal that even under the rigidly controlled conditions and using the best of filtering equipment and methods, a considerable quantity of potash will permeate the air in this area. In our case, it may very well have a deleterious effect on a very extensive beautification project we are currently planning.

Despite these apprehensions, the city issued a building permit in June 1967, but required Neptune to address any and all pollution issues once the plant began to ship. Construction began one month later. In July 1968 Neptune loaded its first ship, not with potash, but with ammonium sulphate bound for India. Many observers wondered what other materials the firm planned to ship, and the answer came soon enough. Within the year Neptune announced its intent to ship coal. In early May 1969, council received a 127-name petition opposing such a move. The petitioners were reasonable, not necessarily opposed to a coal terminal, but "concerned with the possibility of serious coal dust pollution that could affect our lives, not only financially through reductions in our property values, but by affecting the very health of our families."

Council recognized that since the project would be on federally owned land, there was little it could do to stop construction. It could, however, seek expert advice on the potential environmental impact of the project, and voted to hire a consultant to undertake such a review. Mayor Carrie Cates was resolute: "We are not going to issue a permit to Neptune until we get assurance from them that they will meet all our requirements." Neptune's spokesman was conciliatory but frank: "We do not want to dirty anyone's house, anyone's hair, or anyone's laundry." The firm offered to post a $1 million performance bond and to have the BC Research Council monitor its activities:

We intend to operate the cleanest bulk handling operations of anywhere in the world. But we are facing a race against time. Unless construction begins immediately, severe penalties will be involved. There is more than $500 million of coal contracts at stake . . . The decision that is made here tonight will affect thousands of people right across Canada.

Council was neither moved nor intimidated. Its members ignored Neptune's pleas and refused to approve the firm's application for a building permit until the project's environmental impacts were more fully understood. The council meeting to study the matter was stormy, so much so that Mayor Cates had to call on the RCMP to clear the public gallery of angry Cloverley-area residents.

By November 1969 the situation was calmer. Neptune had investigated coal dust suppression systems elsewhere and advised that theirs would "become a model of effective dust control procedures for companies around the world." The firm then presented its plans in a brochure sent to twenty thousand North Vancouver property owners and renters. Jim Warne, the chairman of the North Vancouver Anti-Coal Petitioners Committee, was cautiously optimistic: "I think the brochure idea is tremendous and I wish they had done it long ago, but they've been quite quiet about their operations. They certainly seem to have good intentions but we

Aerial view of Neptune Terminals bulk cargo loading facility, c. 1970. Initially built to handle bulk cargoes such as potash, Neptune became the subject of community controversy when plans were announced to load coal and sulphur.
North Vancouver Museum and Archives, 5335

will have to wait and see what happens when the terminal opens in 1970."

Despite the dust from Neptune Terminals, Park and Tilford completed their landmark gardens in January 1969. The attraction was something the community could point to with considerable pride. Designed by Harry Webb of Justice and Webb Landscape Architects, the gardens were laid out in a series of "outdoor rooms," each devoted to particular types of plants. Some may have thought it strange that the company chose to open the facility in the middle of winter, but seasonal presentations like its Christmas light display soon made the garden a regional attraction. By the early 1970s the gardens could claim an annual attendance of over one hundred thousand visitors.

Even as the gardens were completed near the city's eastern border, on the west side of town there were signs that parts of the Lower Lonsdale area were

beginning to enjoy a slight rejuvenation. The small single-family houses that had proliferated east of Lonsdale Avenue began to fall as developers assembled land for three- and four-storey apartments and condominiums. By the late 1960s, high-rise buildings such as the Beacon Hill Apartments and the Kiwanis Towers seniors housing complex, both built at fourteen storeys, also appeared on the landscape.

In the face of all the progress, the city maintained its small-town feel. Despite its new theatre and recreation complex, North Vancouver still lacked many of the urban amenities craved by the young. Sue Macdonald, a recreation programmer who grew up in North Vancouver in the 1950s and 1960s, recalled the city's limitations from a young person's point of view: "North Vancouver really was a hick sort of place . . . When I was in my twenties I went and lived in London, and of course, there was theatre and everything there, and when I came back to North Vancouver it was like, 'I don't want to be here.' It was dead."

Although the city's youth—used to travelling "over town" for more urban entertainments than those available on the North Shore—might not consider new bridges, freeways, grain elevators, distilleries and bulk-loading facilities the stuff of a progressive town, there were many in the city who did. The first bulk freight cars began to travel on the new railway bridge opened by the CNR late in 1968. The crossing, unlike its predecessor, had been built and commissioned with little fanfare. Railway enthusiasts, however, extolled its five-hundred-foot vertical-lift span, touted as the largest in North America and the eighth-largest in the world.

At the end of the decade, the newly built Saskatchewan Wheat Pool elevator possessed the fastest loading rate of any facility in the port. East of the grain elevator, Neptune Terminals prepared for the shipment of coal. Its existing eight-kilometre-long continuous loop track continued to be busy as it handled both outgoing cargoes of potash and incoming shipments of phosphate. The CNR had built new marshalling yards between the Wheat Pool and Neptune Terminals. To accommodate the increase in traffic, the railway built a two-track subway at Brooksbank Avenue and a five-track bridge over Lynn Creek. In time, a new oceanic terminal named "Lynnterm" evolved at the mouth of the creek and became a major facility for the shipment of forest products, steel and machinery. The North Shore waterfront was now all but obscured by the very sort of industries that the city's founders had struggled to acquire some six decades earlier. The ambition of the founders may well have been satisfied, but in the coming years, residents came to wonder if that ambition had been well placed.

Opposite: For decades, North Vancouver residents had waited for a bridge across the Second Narrows. By 1969 there were three. Left to right: new railway bridge (1969), original Second Narrows Bridge (1925), new Second Narrows vehicular bridge (1960). The original bridge was demolished in 1969, shortly after the completion of the railway bridge.

North Vancouver Museum and Archives, 1006

14 COMING FULL CIRCLE 1970–1979

T he postwar decades had been good to North Vancouver. The city's population had more than tripled since VE day, reaching 31,860 by 1971. Significant additions had also been made to the city's infrastructure. Save for the 1958–62 recession, the economy had generally been strong. The city's economy had diversified and the bulk of its workforce no longer relied solely on the shipyard at the foot of Lonsdale Avenue.

By the time of the 1971 census, it was clear that the city and district were taking divergent paths. The district, with its newer, more plentiful and larger single-family homes—many of them located in pleasant mountainside subdivisions—was increasingly upper middle class. The city, with its large supply of older houses and its burgeoning number of three-storey apartments, was home to a different population. Sixty-one percent of residential units in the city were rentals. Furthermore, city residents were less well-off: the average annual income in the district stood at $9,485 compared to $7,148 in the city.

Many of the city's less wealthy residents lived in its yet-to-be-revitalized Lower Lonsdale area where small wartime houses, apartments and tenements remained common. The situation was by no means desperate. When highlighted, however, pockets of poverty in an otherwise prosperous city were a source of considerable embarrassment. Writing in

October 1970, *Citizen* reporter Jack Emberly exposed the squalor of the clearly misnamed Best Apartments:

> *The stench of poverty in North Vancouver is no less rotten and no harder to find than anywhere else although most people don't bother to seek it out and most ignore it when they find it . . . The people who live in the twenty units, or "apartments" here, tell you that this is the end of the road, when you live here you've reached the bottom . . . You can smell their poverty from 20 feet away and the stench of rotting food, uncontained garbage and exposed animal excrement in their dark quarters is enough to make you vomit.*

The apartments were home to an assortment of people, some with physical disabilities and others with unresolved mental conditions. Disabled logger Ed Price described his situation: "I wish the devil I could get something else but it's the rent. This place is not fit for anybody whose been brought up decently. There's

The city's 1973 Dominion Day parade wends its way westward along East Thirteenth Street, past the fire hall on the left and the RCMP building on the right. Dominion Day, now Canada Day, has deep roots in the city, the first celebrations being held prior to incorporation at Pete Larson's Hotel North Vancouver on West Esplanade.
North Vancouver Museum and Archives, 597

no decent language or any home life here at all. Drunken parties go on twenty-four hours a day, every day." The local health inspector attributed the building's problem to the "quality of persons who are the tenants there." The city's fire warden felt the building itself was a hazard. It was eventually demolished, but the redevelopment of its site dealt more with the symptoms of poverty in the city than with its causes.

Although extreme, the situation at the Best Apartments was but one example of how difficult it was for people with limited incomes to secure affordable housing. The condition was nothing new. During the Depression, taking in lodgers had become common practice throughout the city's residential neighbourhoods. During the Second World War, many North Shore residents had accommodated shipyard workers in what were nominally single-family houses. When the population boomed after the war, the construction of illegal basement suites became commonplace. Successive councils debated the issue, but decades passed before definitive action was taken. Speaking in 2002, former councillor and mayor Jack Loucks reflected on how council had finally dealt with the issue:

The ill-named Best Apartments on East Second Street, photographed c. 1974, were built in 1912 as the Goldberg Block.

North Vancouver Museum and Archives, 10643

We had all those secondary suites and they were illegal. But one of the values of them was that they did provide reasonable housing for a lot of people, like a single person with a child who'd rather have a little suite in a house in a single-family area. It would be much safer for them than if they were in an apartment. So we finally did legalize secondary suites, but we laid down certain restrictions as to the size of them—just one in the house—and that the owner should live in the house.

Although secondary suites may have been a concern for council, issues such as substance abuse and teen violence preoccupied the RCMP. Relations between the community and the police improved when Inspector Bob Heywood assumed the position of officer-in-charge in 1970. Heywood had studied police methods throughout the globe and introduced a new approach to policing in which constables worked to build relationships with community members at a number of levels. With the Edgemont riot still fresh in many of their minds, residents expected the police to be proactive. As Heywood remembered:

A couple of years before there had been a significant riot at Halloween . . . There was quite a lot of youth activity. It was a time when . . . there was quite a social change going on in the community. Long hair came into vogue and irritated the hell out of all the parents and everybody. At that time there were difficulties in Lower Lonsdale too. Lower Lonsdale was a little different then. There were a couple of old hotels down there—big beer parlours in the St. Alice and the Olympic.

Heywood's approach was one reminiscent of an earlier age, when chiefs such as Pete Stewart knew their community and how to work with kids at risk. Under Heywood's leadership, North Vancouver was divided into six zones—including two in the city—each with its own non-commissioned officer and team:

They were tasked with analyzing the problems in the community and starting to work with the community to try and find ways to solve these problems and diminish them. They would use traditional things like enforcement and investigation, but they were also to engage the community in an active way and look for ways to impact the behaviour of the people who were causing the problems.

The approach was a new one accompanied by risk: "Nobody else was doing it then. It was an early initiative." Heywood's philosophy was challenged not by council but by the more conservative non-commissioned officers under his command:

The senior NCOs would meet with the senior NCOs of other detachments and complain bitterly about what I was doing and get them to lobby their bosses so that they could lobby Victoria—the senior guys—and bring pressure on me to conform to the old ways of doing things and I didn't know whether I would survive that or not. I spent a lot of sleepless nights over trying to bring about this change.

Although some of his fellow officers had doubts about the new approach, the community could see its effectiveness. Roland Dean commented on how members of the detachment volunteered in the community:

Constables coached soccer and hockey, and worked with Boy Scouts and outdoor groups. The constables met the families and were welcomed . . . Two officers and a police service dog visited each grade five class. On the first visit the officers just

Building relationships with youth: members of the North Vancouver RCMP detachment compete with Windsor Secondary School's Dukes basketball team, 1973. With Inspector Bob Heywood in charge of the detachment in the early 1970s, the RCMP made a significant effort in crime prevention.
North Vancouver Museum and Archives, 2079

talked about their own school days and sports, etc. and the grade fives met the dog. A week later, half the grade five class rode in police cars while the other half visited police headquarters and saw the cells and dispatch office from where they talked to their classmates in the patrol cars. On the third week the half classes changed places. Vandalism around schools almost disappeared.

M.B. King Lumber Company mill at the time of its closure in 1972. Owned by the Fullerton Lumber Company of Minneapolis, the mill's property and its adjacent water lot had become more valuable than the mill itself.
North Vancouver Museum and Archives, 12383

The experiment seemed to work. Though not fully eradicated, hooliganism ceased to be a major worry.

Having addressed one of the community's significant concerns, council turned its attention to a growing list of projects. Since the return to elected government, successive councils had been careful not to borrow. The resale of the city's tax-sale lands had helped to create extensive financial reserves for future initiatives. Industrial development had broadened the city's tax base. But if the development of the city's infrastructure was to continue, the existing tax base could only supply so

much. With this in mind, the city sought ways to increase not only its industrial tax base, but its commercial tax base as well. In hindsight, the move proved prudent, for the massive growth the city had experienced in the 1960s was not to be repeated in the 1970s. Although the city had seen a 34.7 percent increase in its population from 1961 to 1971, population growth from 1971 to 1981 was only 6.6 percent.

The city's zoning bylaw of 1927—reinforced by subsequent bylaws in 1950, 1958 and 1967—had restricted industrial development to a ribbon of land adjoining the inlet. By the early 1970s most of that land had been developed for industrial purposes. If the city's industrial areas were to expand, new locations for industrial activity would have to be found. In a built-up area like North Vancouver, the simple rezoning of commercial or residential land for industrial purposes was clearly not an option. Instead, the solution lay in the creation of new industrial land in the inlet itself.

The closure of the M.B. King Lumber Company's mill early in 1972 had appeared at the time to present such an opportunity. After Donald King's death in 1961, ownership of the mill had passed to the Fullerton Lumber Company of Minneapolis. By purchasing the mill, Fullerton not only acquired the property on which it stood, but the rights to an adjacent water lot as well. By 1970, however, the mill was outdated and acquiring affordable supplies of logs had become problematic. The value of Fullerton's investment no longer lay in the mill, but in the redevelopment possibilities of its site. Early in 1971 the company began to pump sand and gravel from the harbour onto its water lot, thereby creating a vast new development site. Fullerton repeatedly requested that council rezone the site to enable construction of high-rise residential units, but council unrelentingly preferred an industrial use for the property. For the next three decades the property, then known as the Fullerton Fill, sat vacant and undeveloped. When Fullerton finally began to look for industrial buyers for its property it was out of luck. Businesses seeking industrial land saw issues of access and purchased less expensive properties elsewhere in the region.

Not long after the creation of the fill, the federal government's National Harbours Board commissioned the consulting team of Swan Wooster Engineering and CBA Consulting Engineers to propose alternatives for a third crossing of the inlet. The study proposed two alternatives, a bridge or a tunnel, both of which would have negative impacts on the city of Vancouver. Vancouverites were increasingly conscious of urban planning issues and hotly condemned both options. Residents were in the midst of their great "freeway debate" and few were prepared to tolerate highways or approaches through their city's core.

On the North Shore, where support for the project was decidedly greater, elected officials worried about the costs, then estimated at $200 million. An editorial writer in the *Citizen* summarized the situation:

> There's a sort of Alice in Wonderland aura about machinations concerning the proposed third crossing of Burrard Inlet . . . The cost will be nearly $200 million. Ottawa wants to finance its share out of tolls—competing with the two toll-free bridges. Premier Bennett says that BC will not increase its offer of $27 million for approaches; Vancouver apparently won't even consider the suggestion that it ante up $21 million; while North Shore municipalities would be hard-pressed to

contribute anything. That leaves Ottawa in the position of being able to wash its hands of the whole mess. Which is what cynics have been predicting for the past couple of years. At this point, one might expect the second coming before the third crossing.

The proposal died and planners and politicians gradually began to explore other options. In January 1973 the City of Vancouver removed a third crossing from its list of civic priorities altogether. Eight months later, North Vancouver city council took much the same course. Mayor Jack Loucks compared the proposal to both a dead horse and a political football. Council looked to the past for its transportation strategy and elected to focus on the re-establishment of mass transit through a new cross-inlet ferry system.

Even without a third crossing, by the early 1970s the success of West Vancouver's Park Royal Shopping Centre had convinced developers that something similar would also be viable in North Vancouver. The commercial area then developing along Marine Drive, a major east-west traffic artery, seemed a logical location. Not only was sufficient land available, but the area was also flat and able to accommodate extensive parking. Plans for the new Capilano Mall—designed to include a renovated SuperValu store, a Simpsons-Sears department store and a three-storey parking structure—were duly approved, but the project had its problems. Nearby residents had long known the area as "skunk hollow" for good reason: the site of the proposed mall was swampy. Once built in 1973–74, its owners had little choice but to spend considerable sums to stabilize its concrete slabs and prevent its cast columns from cracking.

In the early 1970s, one of the city's older enterprises faced problems of its own. Since the end of the war, the Burrard Dry Dock had known both feast and famine. After the end of the war and its federal contracts, the diminished workforce at the dry dock took on a variety of projects: repairing ships, building barges and equipment for the logging industry, constructing vessels for the province's growing fleet of ferries, and building the occasional naval or coastguard vessel. The shipyard alternately sped and limped along, its aging owners spending less and less time managing its affairs. Family members disagreed on how the firm should be run, resulting in serious discord. One of the two factions within the family finally forced the sale of the company in March 1972. The purchaser was Cornat Industries, a highly diversified company with no previous experience in building ships. Its managers, steeped in contemporary business techniques, struggled with a shipyard workforce whose resistance to change was enormous.

Cornat's managers achieved a number of successes, not the least of which was the remarkable "stretching" of a number of vessels for BC Ferries. The firm's attempts to improve training, project planning and workforce communications met less success. Over time, a portion of the shipyard's workforce became famous, not for the quality of its work but rather for its ability to avoid work. It was not unusual for workers to walk away with the company's tools or to leave their shifts well before quitting time. John Fitzpatrick recalled how workers routinely left for lunch a half-hour early:

At half past eleven you'd be looking at your watch and then if you were working on the vessel you'd try and sneak off on the pretext you were going to the toilet . . . everyone would sneak into the toilet, and as soon as the whistle went you'd be running. We'd hit that intersection at Lonsdale and Esplanade. We didn't care for lights or anything. Just ran across there. We'd run up the hill to the St. Alice, have two or three beers and then run back down. And then they opened the Eagles at 55½ Lonsdale, so that was even better.

Coal piles up at Neptune Terminals' bulk loading facility during a labour dispute among Japanese seamen, c. 1972. The terminal's open air storage led to the escape of considerable coal dust and became a major community issue.

North Vancouver Museum and Archives, 15592

A mile or so east of the shipyard, Neptune Terminals possessed a more compliant workforce. The facility's first load of coal arrived by rail on March 24, 1970. Tests were made of the plant's new $800,000 dust suppression systems and by May 16, Neptune was loading its first cargo of coal into the huge bulk carrier *Reinhard Lorenz Russ*. It looked like the venture would be highly successful. Like the Saskatchewan Wheat Pool project, however, the expanded plant provided little in the way of employment opportunities. Its sophisticated dumping and loading equipment required only a handful of workers.

The city and its residents kept a watchful eye on operations at the plant. Earlier generations might well have rejoiced in the knowledge that the continent's largest coal stacker and re-claimer was under construction in the city's front yard. But by the early 1970s public priorities had begun to change. North Shore residents, many of whom took regular advantage of the area's opportunities for outdoor recreation, were increasingly aware of environmental issues. When Neptune proposed shipping sulphur from the yet-to-be-completed plant, the public's reaction was swift and predictable. Frank Marcino, president of the Cloverley Community Association, summarized the fears of local residents:

> We have had enough trouble with the materials that are being handled now, without adding to the problem. From our observations of sulphur loading at Vancouver Wharves [in the District of North Vancouver], it should be obvious to anyone that this is not the type of product we can tolerate so near to a residential area.

Council responded decisively, proposing a zoning bylaw to prohibit the shipment of sulphur from the Neptune property. Neptune's president labelled the proposal discriminatory: "Zoning bylaws should not be used for controlling pollution." On September 1, council passed the necessary legislation by a vote of five to one. Neptune appealed to the BC Supreme Court, only to be told by Mr. Justice Thomas Dohm that municipalities do "have the power to act in a protective manner to restrict a particular use for the health, safety, and welfare of the public." The bylaw was upheld; sulphur might be shipped from other points in the inlet, but not from the City of North Vancouver. Thwarted in its efforts to launch a sulphur loading facility, Neptune had little choice but to settle on its earlier focus, the export of coal.

There were also developments in city hall. Successive councils had been content to have three parallel department heads—officially known as the "reference committee" but jokingly dubbed "the troika"—reporting to them. Mayor Tom Reid, however, preferred the city manager system currently being adopted across the continent. Under the new system, the three department heads would report to a new city administrator who in turn would be accountable to council. Assistant

"Not too hard to figure out who he's gonna vote for on Saturday!"

Dave Alavoine's cartoons became a much loved feature of the community's weekly paper, the Citizen, *in the 1970s. Politicians like Mayor Tom Reid and Carrie Cates, both advocates for a new city hall, provided ample ammunition for his creative pen.*

North Vancouver Museum and Archives, 1970-16

clerk Ed Raymond was eventually convinced to apply for the job and much to his surprise received the position. In later years, Raymond reflected on his appointment: "Members of staff told me later they had bet on how long I was going to last. Some of them put down two weeks. There wasn't one longer than two years!" Raymond's years as city manager were a period of growth for the civic corporation. For some city staff, the workload was immense. Raymond recalled working from 6 a.m. to midnight until convincing council that the growth of the city required additional staff resources. As municipal life became increasingly complex, specialists were hired to take on tasks such as purchasing and personnel.

The city's membership in the GVRD occasionally resulted in job action driven by regional rather than local issues. When members of the city's striking CUPE local sang a song featuring the city manager in one of its uncomplimentary refrains, Raymond took it all in stride, remembering that the strikers were still city staff. As one city staff member recalled:

Strikes go on, people are standing around, and the weather isn't always good, so Ed would make sure that every once in a while, when he had a moment, he'd make sure they got coffee and doughnuts delivered on the line, say hello

Carrie Cates, Sam Walker, and Frank Goldsworthy assist Mayor Tom Reid in opening the city's new hall and library complex, March 8, 1975. As mayor, the construction of a new city hall had been one of Carrie Cates' greatest dreams, but it fell to Mayor Tom Reid to see the project completed.
North Vancouver Museum and Archives, 4424

to everyone, and exchange a few good words . . . and made sure that everyone understood you've got your role to play, I've got my role to play. It doesn't mean we've got to be acrimonious about it.

Under Raymond's management, the city's infrastructure developed at a remarkable pace. Civic policy decreed that the proceeds of land sales be directed to a capital reserve generally known as the "heritage fund." Interest on the fund—but not the principal—was spent on extensive improvements to the city's underground services. An impressive set of civic amenities was also developed including a new fire hall, city hall and library.

Built in 1975, the new fire hall was constructed next to the old hall, with chief Dick Hallaway and his staff providing considerable input on its design. The technology of fire fighting had changed remarkably since the old hall was built, but one need had remained constant. As Hallaway recalled: "They had a full-sized billiard table [upstairs] in the old fire hall that we didn't know how the heck we were going to get out of there. So we built a little bridge. The fellows got together— we were pretty well out of the old fire hall by then—and we built a bridge from the old fire hall to the new fire hall."

Despite its early ambition, the city had never built a city hall. City staff had been housed in "temporary" quarters in the old Central School for sixty years. By the early 1970s it was abundantly clear that the situation could not continue. As staff grew the old school reached the bursting point. Thousands of new residents had come to the city since the end of the war and prudent financial management had finally placed the city in the position where it could consider borrowing for major capital projects. Even so, selling the idea of a new city hall to the taxpayers was no easy task. Successive referendums were held and each failed to acquire a sufficient majority. It was not until a final referendum was held in 1972 that the project received the go-ahead. The city had been strategic in posing the question to the voters, coupling the proposed new facility with a new building for the public library, dubbing the pair of buildings the "North Vancouver Civic Centre." In reflecting back on the city's referendum strategy, Ed Raymond recalled a conversation with a friend who had opposed the construction of the new city hall: "It was a sly move to include the library in it, now she had to vote for it!"

A prominent Vancouver firm, Downs-Archambault, was hired as architects for the complex. In designing the two buildings, the architects strove not to design a monument, but to create a series of plazas and buildings that was human in scale and blended with its environment. The complex was one of the first government buildings in the province to consider sustainability, long before the term came into everyday use. Though built of concrete and steel, the buildings were clad in West Coast cedar, while the surrounding landscape featured drought-resistant plantings. The new complex opened to critical acclaim on March 8, 1975. The *Citizen* described the Civic Centre as "graphic evidence of the great strides made within the city, particularly in the last few years." The old city hall, in contrast, was called "an architectural monstrosity" and "a civic disgrace." The new facility was both beautiful and functional. It could even serve the purposes of amalgamation, being capable of expansion should the two North Vancouvers ever reunite.

The City of North Vancouver's Civic Centre, completed in 1975, contained both a city hall and a city library and was remarkable, not only for its harmonious design, but also for its commitment to sustainability.

North Vancouver Museum and Archives, 9060

Indeed, talk about amalgamation was in the air once more. This time the debate was initiated by the district, whose council had written to the city in January 1971 with an invitation to join in preparing a new amalgamation agreement. Although agreeing "to discuss the feasibility of joint administration of certain municipal services," city council advised that they did not plan "to negotiate an agreement for amalgamation" in 1971. Sensing a need to solicit public input, however, rookie alderman Jack Loucks proposed a second postcard ballot. The debate was intense. Mayor Tom Reid, seldom a man to mince words, reportedly styled the city as a "reluctant virgin" who had been repeatedly assaulted by the district:

> *We've been taken advantage of. We gave the property for the North Shore Neighbourhood House, the property for the senior citizens homes, Lions Gate Hospital, the land for that which serves the whole North Shore, the Union Board of Health building, the School Board office.*
>
> *On the other side we get no concessions. The district taxes us on the water line going through the district and the watershed. They pay only four percent of the value of the Justice Administration building for the space they rent and that's cheap. It's always been given by the city and taken by the district and that constitutes rape.*

Mayor Reid's pronouncement was persuasive. When the votes were tallied, fully 65 percent of the voters had indicated their opposition to amalgamation. To many, it must have seemed that the matter had finally been laid to rest.

It was not that simple. In October 1972 alderman Stella Jo Dean, then the city's senior council member, entered the mayoralty race against Reid, pledging to push for amalgamation. Aldermen Jim Warne and Chuck Wills, also warm to

"Who needs it? – Besides I'm Captain here!"

The seemingly endless political debate on amalgamation was gently satirized by cartoonist Dave Alavoine in the pages of the weekly Citizen *newspaper. Mayor Tom Reid, shown adrift on a raft, was an outspoken critic of amalgamation.*

North Vancouver Museum and Archives, 1970-16

amalgamation, both decided to join the race as well. The election was held on November 8 and the results were reflective of a divided yet somewhat complacent community. With one in three voters casting a ballot, Reid was gratified by winning the four-way contest with 48 percent of the popular vote: "The votes expressed show people aren't interested in amalgamation. So we should forget about it, and just concentrate on other business." In February 1973, however, North Vancouver MLA Colin Gabelmann entered the fray. Citing the government's forced mergers of Kamloops and Kelowna with their immediate neighbours, Gabelmann was adamant that the two North Vancouvers ought to merge: "It is urgent that the Minister [of Municipal Affairs] consider very quickly the amalgamation of the City and District of North Vancouver. Amalgamation has to come sooner or later—and I would hope it would be sooner. And [the Minister] will have to take a look at West Vancouver. I think we have to merge all into one municipality."

With three relatively new aldermen occupying seats in the council chamber, and the province shaking its stick, the city wrote to the district with the suggestion that discussions be held "with a view to obtaining necessary studies, reports, and formula for amalgamation of the two municipalities." The district agreed in principle and advised that discussions might best occur following the upcoming civic elections. In May 1974 district council wrote to the city requesting a meeting on the cost sharing of recreational facilities as well as on amalgamation. The meeting took place in September, but when the subject of amalgamation was raised, city mayor Tom Reid rose abruptly and left the meeting. Despite his actions, the two councils agreed to establish a joint Amalgamation Study Committee.

The *Citizen* was justifiably skeptical about the two councils' ability to bring the process forward and stated its views in a scathing editorial:

And so the North Vancouver merry-go-round begins anew. There is now no question in our minds at the Citizen *that if the people of the city and the district were permitted to vote on the merger of the two municipalities at this very moment, without any lobbying by self-serving politicians, the union would be endorsed by substantially more than the required 50 percent. But the politicians, particularly those who want to sabotage another referendum or at least delay a vote as long as possible, will now go into the same song-and-dance that we have been accustomed to for so many years.*

The *Citizen* was not far off the mark. The committee met for a period of years, gathered and analyzed information, and reported back to the two councils as it completed various phases of its work. Over the years its membership changed as aldermen came and went or were removed against their will. The committee was disbanded and reactivated, but by the end of the decade it had little to show for its efforts. Amalgamation seemed no more likely in 1979 than it had been in 1970.

Meanwhile, residents of both municipalities with an interest in the community as a whole worked to preserve its history. Hopes for a combined city and district archives had been voiced as early as 1967 when the North Vancouver Chamber of Commerce issued a call to residents to donate their old photographs and documents to a nascent community archives. Local historian Rodger Burnes had volunteered to catalogue the collections, which were to be housed in the city library until a separate facility could be developed. For those who thought historical collections should be housed in old buildings, the city's PGE station seemed a logical choice of facility. The railway had closed the station in 1928 but the structure had somehow endured. Subsequent occupants included Houlden Transfer, a bus station and offices for C.H. Cates and Sons. In 1971, at the behest of museum director Bill Baker and with considerable support from alderman Jack Loucks, the city bought the building, moved it to Mahon Park, and converted it into a museum and archives.

The museum and archives attracted residents and collections from both the city and the district. Silver Harbour Manor, a senior citizen's activity centre located next to the North Vancouver Recreation Centre, was another example of successful inter-municipal co-operation. As John Denley, chairman of the project's fundraising committee remarked on the eve of the building's opening, "Raising the $500,000 to build the Centre was a 'piece of cake' compared to planning to accommodate the close-to-a-thousand interested citizens who have indicated that they will be there [for the opening] on Saturday!" When district resident Karen Magnussen won the Canadian national women's figure skating championships in 1968 and 1970–73, a silver medal at the Winter Olympic Games in 1972, and a gold medal at the world championships in 1973, both municipalities joined in the general rejoicing. Two local boxers who trained at the North West Eagles Boxing Club, Chris Ius and Les Hamilton, also made all of North Vancouver proud by representing Canada at the 1972 Olympic Games in Munich. World heavyweight champion Muhammad Ali trained at the same club in preparation for his Vancouver bout with George Chuvalo in 1972. Ius returned to the Olympics in 1976.

Inter-municipal goodwill also facilitated other initiatives. The creation of the hospital society and the development of Lions Gate Hospital had helped take the politics out of discussions around community health services. In 1965 the old North Vancouver General Hospital had been converted to an activation unit, a facility that enabled recovering patients to leave the hospital and return to their homes. An extended care unit had opened in June 1971. The need for an even more complicated facility, the "northern expansion," had been recognized as early as 1964. Properties were purchased, needs were assessed and plans were drawn up. Inevitably bureaucracy delayed the process, but with all the municipal and provincial hurdles overcome the $20 million facility—which included both ambulatory care and a large parking structure—opened in December 1979.

Earlier generations of city councillors might have given their eye teeth to secure a waterfront industry. For the councils of the 1970s, however, waterfront industries became synonymous with grief. In 1972 fire swept through the Saskatchewan Wheat Pool's waterfront facility, causing about $200,000 damage. This was only the beginning. In March 1973 a massive explosion tore large slabs of concrete from six of Burrard Terminals' (as the former Midland terminal was then known) ninety-foot-high grain elevators, causing over $2 million damage to the plant and its contents. Witnesses' accounts of the blast varied. Burrard employee Jim McEvoy reported how he had been working in a nearby office when the explosion occurred, forcing him to scramble down a fire escape to escape the ensuing fire: "There was pressure everywhere. The office door blew in and the lights went out." The city's RCMP detachment believed there had been four separate explosions, the strength of which was sufficient to rock nearby ships as they sat in their moorings. According to the *Vancouver Province*, "The blast hurled foot-thick sections of reinforced concrete in all directions, down onto the dock and across railway tracks onto Low Level Road adjacent to the plant." The terminal's grain fared no better, the combined power of the blast and firefighters' water turning it into what one observer described as "the world's largest unbaked bread loaf."

Tragedy struck the plant again on October 3, 1975. At 9:55 p.m. the city's fire department responded to what was initially reported as a blaze atop one of Burrard's elevators. As they raced toward the scene, an enormous explosion ripped through the plant, destroying its roof and sending flames hundreds of feet into the air. Fire chief Dick Hallaway recalled the event: "We think it started with a hot bearing or something like that. We got the call on it and were at Second and Lonsdale, responding, and that's when it really blew. It was a long fire. We got the Vancouver fireboat over. We just slowly worked at it and pumped water from the inlet and finally put it out a day and a half later." Despite dispatching all of its equipment to the site of the blast, the city's firemen were hard-pressed to beat the blaze. The hydrant closest to the fire had been knocked out of service and the height of the elevators was well beyond the reach of the ladder truck. Firemen instead focussed their efforts on preventing the blaze from spreading to adjacent structures, their forces augmented as additional men and equipment arrived from the Districts of North and West Vancouver. Even with these reinforcements it was not until the arrival of the City of Vancouver's fireboat and another firefighting vessel, the *Firebird*, that the blaze began to be suppressed.

In the cold light of day the community learned the full impact of the tragedy. Thirty-one-year-old Edward Hooper, who had been working on the plant's top

Smoke billows from a massive fire at the Burrard (Midland Pioneer) Terminals on October 3, 1975. As this was the third fire in North Vancouver's grain terminals in as many years, the federal government commissioned a report on safety standards in the province's grain elevators.

North Vancouver Museum and Archives, 8512

floor, had been killed instantly. Another fifteen men were sent to hospitals on either side of the inlet, Lions Gate Hospital lacking the capacity to deal with such a catastrophe. Four of the fifteen injured men succumbed to their injuries. With two major explosions in the course of just three years, North Vancouver residents joined with Local 333 of the Grain Workers Union in demanding an investigation. The *Citizen* echoed residents' concerns in an editorial entitled "Keep it safe or close it." The weekly placed the blame for the disaster with the Worker's Compensation Board and the Department of Labour: "They have failed miserably in light of Friday's disaster and in many ways we are still in the grip of the Industrial Revolution where in this case human lives are a cheaper commodity than the nation's wheat stores."

The National Harbours Board suggested that a spark from a lathe had ignited the highly explosive grain dust that proliferated in the area, but as much of the evidence had been consumed by the fire, some deemed the findings inconclusive. Federal Minister of Labour John Munro was sufficiently concerned to fly out from Ottawa to survey the situation. The government ultimately commissioned UBC Dean of Law Liam Finn to investigate health and safety standards in all the province's elevators. Finn submitted his report to the minister in October 1976.

Two months later the Pioneer Grain Company, owners of the Burrard elevator, announced plans for a $30 million terminal to replace the destroyed facility. The plant's older concrete silos, which dated from 1928 and had not been affected by the 1975 explosion, were to be incorporated into the new facility. Construction was expected to be complete in about two years' time. Pioneer chairman George Richardson described the planned elevator as state of the art. It would have a storage capacity of four million bushels and be able to unload one hundred rail cars during each eight-hour shift. Its two deep-sea berths would be able to accommodate vessels with up to 55 feet of draft and up to 900 feet long. The proposal also called for a series of silos 161 feet high and a workhouse 258 feet high. The top of the latter structure would be at the same elevation as East Seventh Street, obliterating the views of scores of Ridgeway residents. It was exactly the sort of facility that earlier generations of North Vancouver residents had longed to see built and exactly the sort of thing that a new generation of residents had come to abhor.

By February 1977, the Ridgeway Ratepayers Association rallied to oppose the expansion. Development on the waterfront had become even more menacing in the intervening months, the Saskatchewan Wheat Pool having announced a construction project of its own including a structure 213 feet high. The ratepayers jammed the council chambers. President George Frederick spoke with considerable passion. The city should block the development, he said, for reasons relating to the maintenance of residential property values, public safety, environmental well-being and community aesthetics:

> This development is absolutely incompatible with the area and will destroy its quality. Our homes were here before the grain elevators, and we ask that construction plans be stopped and we want to know where council stands on this . . . If you go down there and look at the development you would realize it contravenes everything you said you were going to do for this city.

Frederick quoted from the city's evolving Official Community Plan, noting how the document allowed for industrial development in *appropriate* locations, with the proviso that residential areas were to be shielded from industrial noise, traffic and pollution. The city would benefit considerably through the additional tax revenues that would flow from the new developments but would face the wrath of a considerable number of voters. In any case, there was little that the city could do to prevent the development, which lay on National Harbours Board property. Decisions regarding the use of that land were a federal responsibility. As long as the development adhered to the city's existing bylaws the city could not stop it. Alderman Frank Marcino expressed the outrage of many as he blamed eastern interests for the way in which the project was being handled: "This project was at a point of no return before we even knew what was happening. The decision to build was made by Pioneer Grain and the National Harbours Board. It seems decisions are made by the wise men in the east on what goes up on our shores below one of our good residential areas."

At Marcino's prompting, council agreed to organize a meeting of the parties in March. It was a raucous assembly, with over two hundred people filling the Ridgeway School gymnasium. Residents cited their objections to the projects, noting how they already had to deal with diminished views, the noise of railcars, grain dust pollution, and periodic invasions of rats and pigeons. The grain companies defended their position, at times struggling to be heard amid a chorus of jeers and boos. Both Pioneer and the Wheat Pool described how they had worked diligently with city staff to ensure compliance with all applicable bylaws. This was the first they had heard of any objections: "We recognize it is an annoyance to live near an industrial area, but we feel it is a little late to say that you don't want us to build." Mayor Reid worked hard to control the meeting, at one point threatening adjournment if audience members continued to shout down the speakers. "That's all you're good for!" shouted one irate resident. The meeting concluded with a statement from the city's solicitor, Rob Orr, who noted that the city had no legal right to withhold a building permit, despite the project's location on federally owned land. Few left the meeting with any sense of comfort, many no doubt wondering what would happen next.

In the face of a determined Harbours Board, the city was largely helpless. By January 1978, construction of the Pioneer elevator had begun in earnest. Residents returned to their daily lives and council went on to deal with other controversies. There was bitterness in the air and few shared the excitement of the community's historians as the excavators' shovels uncovered historical artifacts from the long-forgotten community of Moodyville. Community controversies such as these not only changed the face of the city, they changed the face of its politics. Gerry Brewer recalled the situation:

School teacher and principal Jack Loucks served as the city's mayor from 1978 to 1999. Shown here with one of his favourite books, Loucks was, among other things, a life-long champion of childhood literacy.
Photo courtesy North Shore Outlook

> *In the seventies and eighties we elected people to council, some of whom were there solely for the purpose of stopping something or encouraging something different to happen . . . We had people who got elected from no community involvement—"I'm going to stop that project, elect me"—and they would be found sitting on council wondering, "How did I get here?" And sometimes so ill-prepared that it wasn't fun to watch them swimming upstream and being caught off guard by questions [about which] they had no idea.*

Although some candidates might have been impelled by single issues or even self-interest, others possessed purer motives and aspired to serve a higher public cause. In the judgement of many, retired school principal Jack Loucks was pre-eminent among them. According to Gerry Brewer:

> *He'd been asked to make a contribution by being a member of council. He wasn't championing some particular cause. He wasn't there to stop something from happening . . . It wasn't some desire to get in the front of the parade . . . His effectiveness was that he managed to stay as mayor, stay on top of the game, manage meetings so that they actually worked, so that people felt at the end of the meeting they had been heard, that there had been a fair discussion, and even if they didn't like the outcome, they were always respected. When the cameras came on, he was the last guy to want to be in front.*

Those who had governed the city in 1907 had waxed poetic about the waterfront's potential. Seven decades later the area seemed to bring nothing but trouble. In October 1979, the CNR's railway bridge was hit by a passing vessel and put out of service for a period of months. History seemed to be repeating itself. The one bright spot was at the foot of Lonsdale Avenue, where after a nineteen-year hiatus a cross-inlet ferry service had finally been restored. The service was a provincial one, initiated by the NDP government of Premier Dave Barrett and completed in 1977 during the Social Credit government of Premier Bill Bennett. Seabus—as the service was named—featured two aluminium catamaran-style vessels, the *Burrard Otter* and *Burrard Beaver,* each with a capacity of four hundred passengers and each capable of crossing the inlet in a ten-minute time span. The service was inaugurated on June 17, 1977, and met with considerable success.

The 1970s were also a time when residents increased their interest in cultural matters. With bulk commodities being shipped from the city to Japan, a sister-city relationship with Chiba, a city near Tokyo, was a logical outcome. Agreed upon in 1969 and proclaimed in 1970, the two cities' twinning led to periodic cultural and educational exchanges and ultimately to the development of a Chiba Garden in Lower Lonsdale.

Beginning in 1974, a celebration of Canada's cultural diversity named Folk Fest was held at sites throughout the community. Organized by Stella Jo Dean in her capacity as chair of the Tourism Committee of the North Vancouver Chamber of Commerce, the event soon became a community fixture. Changes in the nation's immigration policy had resulted in greater cultural diversity in the city and Dean was intent on building understanding between Canadian-born and foreign-born residents. Thousands gathered at the Centennial Theatre, the North Vancouver Recreation Centre, St. Edmund's Church and other community venues to view arts and crafts, watch dancers, listen to music and savour the cuisine of cultures that had long been mysterious. The main events were held in the theatre, where

The institution of the cross-inlet Seabus was the first in a series of events that breathed new life into the city's Lower Lonsdale area.
Photo courtesy Translink

the promise of free admission to performances by a dozen or more groups a night packed the house. Dean reflected on the situation: "In those days the fire people didn't care—or I should say they weren't that fussy—about how many people were in the theatre. So we had about 718 people seated and people were sitting up and down the aisles because it was such a novelty."

North Vancouver's Centennial Theatre had opened in 1966, and although the facility proved a success, little had been done to foster other aspects of the arts. The opening of the new Civic Centre provided a golden opportunity. Even as city staff were moving out of their offices in the old city hall, the North Vancouver Arts Council was making plans to move in. The idea of a civic arts centre dated from 1971, when the city and district requested community organizations to suggest projects to mark the one hundredth anniversary of British Columbia entering Canadian Confederation. The concept had been vigorously pushed by the Arts Council and its then-president Anne Macdonald. The city and district, however, chose two other projects: the museum and archives in the old PGE Station and an ecology centre in Lynn Canyon.

It was not until 1976 that the Arts Council's dream for its own facility became a reality. The old school began to be transformed. Offices, courtrooms and the council chamber morphed into spaces for the Arts Council's offices, a gallery and a small theatre, as well as a relocated and expanded museum and archives. Additional

Anne Macdonald Hall was originally built as the first Anglican Church of St. John the Divine and later used as the parish hall. The hall was donated by the church to the North Vancouver Arts Council and moved to the site of Presentation House in time for its opening in 1976.
North Vancouver Museum and Archives, 4688

space came unexpectedly when the congregation of St. John the Divine Anglican Church donated their original building for use as a recital hall. The old church was relocated to a site adjacent to the former school and renamed to honour Anne Macdonald. The renovation of the tired old city hall was a substantial challenge. The well-known architectural firm of Honeyman and Curtis had examined and condemned the building as early as 1930, advising the mayor and council:

> We have inspected your City Hall, and while we were more or less familiar with the building, we were not prepared to find, upon a closer inspection such a rickety condition of affairs, the building has apparently at various times been jacked up, patched up and repaired, until there is not a straight or plumb line in it, with the natural consequence that the doors and windows don't fit and it is neither rain proof or wind proof; and generally speaking, we would strongly advise you not to spend more money on alterations than is absolutely necessary.

Several decades later, Gerry Brewer was far from alone in thinking that the community might well be sending good money after bad. When in mid-renovation Brewer found himself atop the building's roof with fire chief Dick Hallaway fighting a vandal-set fire, he wondered aloud why they were fighting to save "this damned building." Despite the misgivings of those who knew the building in its former role, the renovations continued. A competition was held to name the building, and the community's new cultural facility opened as Presentation House in September 1976. Not long afterward the formidable Ella Parkinson, who had begun as a volunteer for the Arts Council in 1973, assumed its presidency, and later became executive director in 1979. Under Parkinson's guidance—and despite the limitations of its quarters—the Arts Council flourished, taking art into the community, administering a picture loan program and providing support to the community's emerging artists.

The 1970s and 1980s were the golden years of the Miss North Shore pageant. Organized by florist Gertie Todd beginning in 1951, the pageant quickly became a popular community event. Held for seventeen-year-old high school girls, the pageant was loosely modelled on the female beauty contests then popular in the United States. Generally held in the Centennial Theatre, the event judged not only physical appearance, but personality and talent as well. Lenora Baker, a member of the Squamish Nation, was the last Miss North Vancouver, the pageant being renamed Miss North Shore in 1973 to reflect an expanded geographic focus. Winners of the pageant went on to compete in the Miss PNE contest, a province-wide event held at Vancouver's Pacific National Exhibition grounds since 1948. During her time with both Miss North Vancouver and Miss North Shore, Todd focussed on revealing her girls' talents rather than their bodies and assiduously resisted any attempt to turn the pageant into anything less than a wholesome family event. As Todd recalled of her battles with PNE president Erwin Swangard:

> The PNE over here told me you must give them swimsuits . . . I said, "You get out of my face because I'm in a community that is a good, healthy community and if you think I'm going to put on skinny skinnies! . . . I'm going to tell them you're going

to get a hunk of rag around you? No way! . . . You get your own bathing suits, but you're not getting Miss North Shore in a tight, little thing!"

By 1992 the event became a casualty of the feminist movement and was restructured to become the North Shore Youth Contest, an event that judged contestants on communications skills, volunteer effort, scholastic achievement and individual talents and skills.

In its own small way, Todd's defiance of the PNE reflected a change in residents' deference to outside authority. During its early years, the Lonsdale Estate, the North Vancouver Land and Improvement Company, and the British Columbia Electric Railway Company exerted significant influence over the city's development. Beginning in the 1920s successive harbour authorities dictated how the city's waterfront lands were going to develop. In the two ensuing decades commissioners and councils repeatedly went out of their way to accommodate the needs of the city's shipbuilders. The trend had ended by the 1970s; successive battles with Eastern Canadian and Prairie corporate giants had ensured its demise. When in the mid-1970s the provincial government purchased twenty-seven acres of land in Lower Lonsdale, the city was concerned. The province's property encompassed four city blocks and included 1,900 feet of waterfront. Although the government announced its intent to develop a ferry, bus and rail terminal on the site, the remainder of its plans remained sketchy.

The province's lack of communication caused concern at city hall. In April 1975 Mayor Tom Reid complained to the press that all council knew about Victoria's initiative was what they had read in the Vancouver dailies. Several years earlier, council had adopted a "controlled growth" approach to development. City policy called for an ultimate population of about 50,000. To ensure that growth was controlled, the council had encouraged the construction of low-rise apartments rather than high-rise residential towers. Without information from the province, council was stymied and unable to proceed with its own planning initiatives. Although the province gradually involved the city in its planning process, four more years were to pass before details of the initiative became public.

If provincial politicians were elusive, at least one federal representative was not. The country had elected a new prime minister in 1968, the highly charismatic Pierre Elliott Trudeau. With Trudeau in power, a new spirit seemed to pervade the land. North Vancouver played host to the Trudeau saga in 1971 when he married Margaret Sinclair, the daughter of former North Shore MP and federal fisheries minister Jimmy Sinclair, at St. Stephen's Roman Catholic Church in Lynn Valley.

The prime minister paid his first "official" visit to North Vancouver in 1973, attending the opening day ceremonies of the twenty-first annual *Vancouver Sun* Tournament of Soccer Champions. Over 3,500 people jammed Mahon Park's old wooden stadium and the portable bleachers that had been brought to the site for the occasion. There was a carnival atmosphere in the park and dozens of new maple leaf flags fluttered in the breeze. Ever a consummate showman, Trudeau gave a short speech, donned his soccer boots, and kicked the opening ball not once but twice, then joined the crowd to watch the opening match. Five years later, the much-storied stadium lay in ruins, the victim of a spectacular fire in 1978. A

Prime Minister Pierre Elliott Trudeau joins the crowd after opening the Vancouver Sun Tournament of Soccer Champions in Mahon Park on April 28, 1973.

North Vancouver Museum and Archives, 1433

new grandstand was completed the following June. The original stadium had been built of wood; its replacement was constructed of concrete and steel. With just five hundred seats, the new facility was half as large as the original stadium, but its fireproof construction ensured it would last much longer.

When Trudeau returned to the city in July 1977 it was to Presentation House. The prime minister had travelled by Seabus to participate in the opening of a new studio theatre. The visit, however, was not without incident; an unknown woman seized control of the outdoor podium and unfurled a banner protesting the prison regulations then in effect. Angry spectators booed the woman from the stage amid shouts of "We want Pierre, we want Pierre!" Trudeau took the stage and captured the hearts of the crowd, promising not only to look into prison issues, but also to review the federal government's role in the grain elevator controversy. The prime minister applauded North Vancouver's sense of community: "No country can exist with outside force to keep it together. It must be the will of the people. Today you have shown this spirit. You've shown you're concerned with your community, your government and your country."

In the 1970s, however, much of the North Shore remained politically and socially conservative. Prior to 1980 the city had seen only five women elected to its council. Despite the efforts of organizations like the North Shore Council of Women and the North Shore Business and Professional Women's Association, many residents maintained traditional views about female roles in society. It therefore came as a great shock to many when the North Vancouver detachment of the RCMP welcomed its first female recruit not long after the prime minister's visit. Rookie Constable Cathy Robertson had been part of the third troop of female graduates to leave the force's training depot in Regina. A few years later four more women had joined the force. In twenty years time gender had ceased to be an issue. Women accounted for 29 percent of the detachment's strength and fully half of the members on patrol.

The 1970s had placed the city at a crossroads. Gender equity, though by no means achieved, was at least under way. By the time the decade ended, two prominent women—Olympic skiing medallist Nancy Greene and former mayor Carrie Cates—had both received the Freedom of the City. Five men had also accepted the honour: Lieutenant Governor George Pearkes; former mayors Jack Loutet, Frank Goldsworthy and Tom Reid; and former MLA John H. Cates. The Sixth Field Squadron—as the Sixth Field Company had become—was similarly honoured, giving the unit, in theory at least, the ancient right to march through the city "with drums beating, colours flying, and bayonets fixed." Given the controversies the city had seen in the 1970s, the prospect of a military intervention might well have been welcomed by some.

15 BEGINNINGS AND ENDINGS 1980–1989

By the 1980s the neighbouring District of North Vancouver had long since replaced Vancouver as the ambitious city's principal rival. Beginning in the late 1940s the district's growth statistics consistently exceeded those of the city, and by the early 1980s the character of the district's population was clearly different from that of the city. At the time of the 1981 census, 12.4 percent of city families were classed as "low income," compared to only 6.3 percent in the district. Sixty-five percent of the city's dwellings were rented accommodation, compared to 20.6 percent in the district. Average family incomes in the city were $27,477, compared to $40,004 in the district, a difference of almost 46 percent.

The ethnic composition of the city had also begun to change. The Immigration Act of 1967 had introduced a points system tying admission to Canada to job skills and employment opportunities, thereby opening immigration opportunities to people from non-European and non-Commonwealth countries. In 1981 people born in Great Britain and continental Europe accounted for only 19.1 percent of the city's population while those born in Asia formed 3.7 percent. Ten years later the proportion of residents born in

Britain or in Europe had fallen to 15.2 percent. The proportion of residents born in Asia had risen to 8.3 percent. It was a trend that was to continue into the new millennium.

Events over seven thousand miles away had a profound effect on the city. Beginning late in 1978 and concluding in early 1979, the Iranian revolution saw the country's fifty-eight-year-old Pahlavi dynasty swept away in a popular uprising. Most Iranians had great hopes for the revolution, but it quickly became apparent that one autocracy had been replaced by another. Thousands of Iranians fled the country and many settled in North Vancouver.

Iranians were by no means the only immigrants settling in the city at the time. In 1982 the governments of China and the United Kingdom began discussions on the future of Hong Kong. Fearing the worst, over one million Hong Kong residents fled the colony in the years from 1984 to 1997, the year of the historic handover. Those who left generally went to Canada, Australia and the United States, and of those who went to Canada the majority settled in the Vancouver area. Immigrants and refugees from a host of countries found a receptive government in Canada. The nation's policy of multiculturalism, first announced in 1971 and confirmed by the Canadian Multiculturalism Act in 1988, encouraged Canadians to accept cultural pluralism and reversed earlier attempts to force assimilation into English or French society.

A quarter-century after the fall of the Pahlavi Dynasty, opponents of the current Iranian regime protested the killing of political prisoners in their ancestral country. By the time of the 2001 Census enumeration, about 3,200 city residents claimed Iranian ancestry.

North Shore News, *Paul McGrath photo*

For many residents, the increasingly multicultural makeup of the population was exciting, symbolizing the evolution of a more modern, cosmopolitan community. Recognizing that some residents new to the country had limited familiarity with civic regulations around parking, licensing, hours of opening, permits and so forth, city hall responded in a proactive way. Gerry Brewer recalled, "I remember in one case we asked staff to identify . . . all of the second languages many of us were able to speak so if someone came into city hall . . . we could get someone here to translate. And it was fun because a number of library staff had second and third languages." Racial tensions did emerge from time to time with even lifelong residents being subject to abuse. When Lila Johnston and her children left the Mission Reserve to find alternate housing in the city's Lower Lonsdale area they met a less than welcoming reception: "We had to move off the reserve and were up here at Second and Mahon. And they used to say, 'There's those little savages,' or 'Dirty Indians,' or whatever."

Although most residents accepted the newcomers to the North Shore, there were exceptions. In the 1980s columnist Doug Collins, a regular contributor to the *North Shore News*, offered his readers an unremitting cascade of opinion on where the nation appeared to be headed. Collins' rants were often an inflammatory mixture of sarcasm and vitriol. Left or right, no one escaped Collins' wrath. According to Collins, many of the country's woes stemmed from the policies of Pierre Trudeau, "NDP leftwingers" and others with "liberal goggles." But when it came to Canada's acceptance of visible minorities, even Prime Minister Brian Mulroney's Conservative government was roundly condemned:

Anyone who thinks the Baloneyite Tories are going to be tough on liars claiming to be refugees should think again. The same applies to the handling of the immigration

*mess in general. Ottawa plans to go on flooding the country with Third Worldites
. . . If you doubt that, consider the boost in the "family reunification" nonsense
under which more than 50 per cent of immigrants to this country get in simply
because they have a relative here. Nearly all of them come from India, China,
Guyana, etc."*

Although often taken to task for promulgating such outpourings, the *News*
continued to print Collins' writings, attempting to provide balance by also publishing
a column by environmentalist Bob Hunter. For many, Collins' writings were merely
a source of embarrassment, but when the Ku Klux Klan held a recruiting meeting
at the Coach House Restaurant in October 1980, public indignation was immediate
and widespread.

As the city's population grew, its physical fabric continued to change. Small
commercial buildings made way for larger complexes. Old landmarks began to
disappear, the old North Vancouver High School being prominent among them.
The school held its final reunion in May 1979 and by early 1980 the school was
nothing but a memory. As new construction replaced more diminutive or tired
old buildings, the city became increasingly optimistic. The reinstitution of a cross-
inlet ferry service in 1977 and the potential of redeveloping Lower Lonsdale had
generated a sense of excitement in many residents. The city's growth was reflected
on the landscape: by the mid-1980s, 41.5 percent of the city's 17,090 private
dwellings were less than fifteen years old, three-storey apartments having appeared
in significant numbers in the blocks immediately east and west through much of
the length of Lonsdale Avenue.

With the city experiencing a growth spurt, it was more than appropriate that
council approved its first Official Community Plan (OCP) in 1980. The adoption of
the plan, after several years of public input, suggested that the city knew where
it wanted to go and how it was going to get there. It was remarkable that the
city had developed as it had without the guidance of a community plan. The
original townsite plan and the zoning bylaw of 1927—guided by a Town Planning
Commission—had set a direction that subsequent councils had largely followed.
Updated zoning bylaws in 1950, 1958 and 1967 had merely refined the definitions
and delineations of the city's residential, commercial, industrial and public-use
districts and zones. In the early 1980s most of the city's heavy industry was
restricted to a narrow strip along the waterfront. Commercial activity was equally
well defined. Save for a number of corner shops scattered throughout the city's
residential areas, commercial enterprises were largely confined to the Lonsdale
corridor, Marine Drive, the Capilano Mall and the Westview Centre, a strip mall
located in the city's northwest corner.

The new Official Community Plan and its periodic updates reaffirmed the
city's existing land-use patterns but also suggested ways in which the community's
economy and quality of life might be enhanced. Densification would occur in
designated areas, augmenting the city's tax base while improving the health of
the commercial core. The Lower Lonsdale area was singled out for particular
attention. Under the terms of the OCP the area would become the site of higher-
density development. Lower Lonsdale and Central Lonsdale were designated as

mixed-use areas in which both commercial and residential development would be encouraged. Residents would be able to live and work within the bounds of the Lonsdale corridor or commute to work on public transportation.

The new OCP had been developed over a period of several years and had profited from considerable public input. Yet the ink on its pages was barely dry when in December 1981 Chief Joe Mathias claimed the city for his people. "Indians Claim Entire N. Shore," proclaimed the headline in the *North Shore News*. Mathias advised that the territorial claims of the Squamish people were nothing new; their statement of claim had first been released in 1976. Pending talks on the federal constitution had made the matter more urgent. The Squamish claim was an extensive one, encompassing much of Greater Vancouver and extending up Howe Sound. Amid the drama there was reason. Mathias recognized that a century of non-Native settlement could not be reversed, and noted alternate ways for justice to be done: "We are not saying all residents of Vancouver must vacate. We are seeking a just settlement. We have been part of the growth of Vancouver for decades and we now want to share in that growth . . . The settlement might include many elements, including alternate land, financial settlement, and better legislation of Indian self-government."

There was little the city could do about the Squamish land claims. The issue was one that only senior governments were positioned to address. City discussions with the district, however, were an entirely different matter. Even as the city's consultants were developing the OCP, its own politicians once again proposed amalgamation. Rather than authorize a new study themselves, city council sought approval from the voters. When the ballots were counted on November 21, 1981, a total of 2,184 had voted in favour of a new study and 2,491 had voted against. The debate around amalgamation was silenced once again.

Despite residents' rejection of amalgamation, the city increasingly developed a regional perspective. When floods altered the course of Lynn Creek and severely damaged the city's water intake structures in the spring of 1981, council reviewed its options. Since repairs to the system would be expensive and their longevity could not be guaranteed, the city decided to abandon the system and join the Greater Vancouver Water District. Fearing that owners of mineral rights in the creek's headwaters might use their rights to secure cheap timber, and recognizing the recreational value of the area, the city and the district worked with the province to extinguish those rights and turn the headwaters into a park. Lynn Headwaters became a regional park owned and operated by the GVRD. Over time, parts of the park were developed into trails and picnic areas with easy access via Lynn Valley Road.

Having dispensed with discussions around amalgamation, the city prepared to celebrate its seventy-fifth anniversary in early 1982. One of the more memorable legacies of the approaching anniversary was the city's Hose Reel Festival. Begun slightly before the anniversary celebrations at the instigation of North Shore Museum and Archives director Bill Baker, the competition became an annual event. The first Hose Reel Festival featured competing teams pulling antique oak and iron reels around Mahon Park's dusty track, in recognition of the city's early firemen. Pulling the reels was no easy task. As Baker pointed out, each weighed 150 pounds: "You can imagine what it would be like running up Lonsdale with it."

The first annual Hose Reel Race at Mahon Park, featuring teams from each of the three North Shore fire departments, May 15, 1982.

North Vancouver Museum and Archives, 4211, Bill Denniston photo

A worker restores the rose window in St. Paul's Roman Catholic Church on the Mission Reserve, November 1982.

North Vancouver Museum and Archives, 6169, Mary Lafreniere photo

Baker's interest in vintage equipment ultimately led to the return of one of the city's decommissioned streetcars. Built in 1908, *Car No. 153* had been retired when the city's streetcar system was closed in 1947. After thirty-nine years of service the car faced an uncertain future, having been carted off to work at the British Columbia Electric Company's facility at Buntzen Lake prior to being shipped to Chilliwack to accommodate a restaurant. When finally rediscovered by railway enthusiasts, the streetcar was mired in muck and serving as a chicken coop in Ryder Lake. In 1986 the streetcar returned to North Vancouver and underwent a major restoration. Bob Booth, a retired architect and railcar historian, directed the project and shipwrights Carl Anderson and Stephen Ley undertook much of the hands-on work. Four years later, the restoration was largely finished, though returning the vehicle to operate on city streets remained a distant dream.

Residents with an interest in the North Shore's history were equally enthused by the prospect of saving St. Paul's Church. Built in 1868 and enlarged in 1909–10, the Mission Reserve's old Roman Catholic church had fallen on hard times. A consultant's report completed in 1978 documented serious deterioration and the local parish committee requested help from the broader community. By 1979, the parish and the North Vancouver Community Arts Council had banded together to form a joint cross-cultural committee to address the building's restoration. The timing was fortuitous, demonstrating how the Native and non-Native population could work together even as their leaders debated locally about the route of an enhanced Low Level Road, and federally about the place of aboriginal peoples in confederation.

The federal government may have been uncertain about how to deal with First Nations in the nation's ongoing constitutional debate, but it nonetheless recognized the importance of the old Squamish church by declaring it a National Historic Site in 1981. By 1983 the joint committee had raised well over $500,000 to

rehabilitate the building. When the scaffolding was removed, most of the church's original fabric had been restored, with slight modifications to reflect the realities of the twentieth-century liturgy. There were also subtle changes in the building's decoration. Coast Salish motifs replaced the old fleur-de-lys decoration around the building's arches. As it proceeded through its second century of service, the old building would reflect the First Nations origins of its parishioners rather than the French traditions of its pioneer clergy.

There was a certain irony in the Native band's restoration of the Oblate-inspired sanctuary. By the 1980s, Oblate influence among the province's First Nations was very much in decline. The residential school system was widely recognized as a failed attempt to obliterate Native culture and to force assimilation. The government's day-school program was also called into question. The ten-year-old St. Paul's Day School, located on West Fifth near the Mission Reserve, had been closed in 1969 and the government paid the costs of accommodating its 110 grade-one-to-six students in the public school system. The disused school then became the Squamish First Nation's head office until its final transformation in 1993, when it became the Eslha7an Employment and Training Centre.

Native students who went on to high school often chose the publicly operated

Museum and Archives director Bill Baker and others rescued North Vancouver Streetcar No. 153 from Ryder Lake where it had been employed as a chicken coop. The streetcar's superstructure underwent major restoration, but returning the vehicle to active service remained a problematic scheme.
North Vancouver Museum and Archives, 6764, Gary Payne photo

Carson Graham Secondary School over the much closer but church-run St. Thomas Aquinas School. By the 1980s, Carson Graham paid special attention to furthering students' understanding of the province's First Nations and invited Native elders such as Lawrence Baker to visit the school and offer insights into Squamish history and life. Twenty years later, the program continued with visits by Alroy "Bucky" Baker to teach the Squamish language.

The early 1980s were momentous years for the Squamish people in other ways as well. Chief Philip Joe, long active in minor sports and other organizations well beyond his people's reserves, won a seat on the North Vancouver School Board in 1980. He was re-elected in every successive election until 1996. His initial election came thirty-two years after Chief Mathias Joe cast the first Native vote on the North Shore. Philip Joe's election and the restoration of St. Paul's Church suggested positive change on the Mission Reserve.

The area just east of the reserve was on the threshold of even greater change. Successive mayors had long dreamed of somehow revitalizing the city's Lower Lonsdale area. The consolidation of the shipyards, the construction of two vehicular cross-inlet bridges and the proliferation of the automobile had all contributed to the area's decline. Many residents no longer needed Lower Lonsdale. The population had shifted as new housing developments gradually claimed the mountain slopes. Shops and services had opened along the entire length of Central Lonsdale and suburban shopping malls were easily reached by car. Gerry Brewer remembered how Lower Lonsdale hit rock bottom in the late 1970s before rebounding in the early 1980s:

It was in decline but I don't think people recognized it . . . When Ocean Cement moved to the foot of Riverside Drive with their operation, in the district, near the Seymour River, that property sat vacant, looking more like a bomb shelter than anything else for years, as did the west side of Lonsdale where Pacific Salvage Shipyard was. It was only through the efforts of people like Tom Reid that they finally shamed the province into cleaning up the site so it was no longer a hazard for people who would trespass on the property for one reason or another, but also it got rid of a terrible eyesore.

Those who advocated the rehabilitation of Lower Lonsdale may have had differing views of how that revitalization should proceed—some calling for the restoration of the district's historic buildings, others focussing on the need for new construction—but they did agree that something had to be done. Lower Lonsdale was not only historic, but with the advent of Seabus it was once again the very gateway to the city.

Under the terms of the new community plan, the densification of Lower Lonsdale would be encouraged, but in the interests of preserving views and minimizing shadows, any new buildings would be six storeys or less. Historic buildings would be preserved. A healthy street life was envisioned. Restaurants and shops were to be encouraged at street level, with offices and residences rising above. Industrial activity would continue to the east of Lonsdale Avenue, but the parts of the waterfront to the west would become public space. In 1980 the process of redevelopment finally began. Mayor Jack Loucks and Premier Bill Bennett had met with the press in October 1979 to reveal the province's plans. Ralph Hall, the editor of the *Citizen*, was euphoric:

> *It was North Vancouver City's greatest day. And Mayor Jack Loucks, one of the most self-effacing and generous human beings, was exultant but did not want it to show. Premier Bill Bennett, who might seem aloof from afar and who sometimes appears to be inarticulate, was in a warm mood, one to one, where he is at his best.*

Artist's concept of the Lonsdale Quay development as first proposed, 1979. Although the original vision for the redeveloped area called for low-rise development, urban land economics dictated higher density, ultimately leading to the designation of the Lonsdale Corridor as a Regional Town Centre within the Greater Vancouver Regional District.

North Vancouver Museum and Archives, 4816

Lower Lonsdale would be redeveloped to include a new Waterfront Park and a massive residential and commercial project to be known as Lonsdale Quay. The Insurance Corporation of British Columbia (ICBC) would be the anchor tenant in a multi-million dollar development. Over three hundred housing units would be added to the area, creating a new residential neighbourhood. A new facility for the Pacific Marine Training Institute would rise to the west. When completed, the new development would increase the city's tax base by a phenomenal 8 percent. Speaking on behalf of a city tired of playing second fiddle to its neighbour across the inlet, Mayor Loucks was optimistic: "It has been said that Lonsdale Quay will become an extension of Granville Street. I like to think that when the project is complete, Granville Street will become an extension of Lonsdale Avenue."

Over the years, North Vancouver residents had learned to be wary. Businessmen and politicians had made a succession of promises, many of which had never come to pass. But this time, the messenger spoke the truth. Lonsdale Quay would indeed become a place to work, live and play. Shortly after revealing its plans, the province formed a new company to manage the project: the Lonsdale Quay Development Company, a subsidiary of the provincially owned British Columbia Development Corporation.

As the months passed the plans became more specific. There would be office buildings, condominiums, shops and a hotel. Recognizing an opportunity, the city itself began to buy property in the Lower Lonsdale area. Through judicious planning and rezoning measures, residents would not only realize a profit; public amenities could also be provided. Construction proceeded. In May 1980 the *Vancouver Province* advised that tenants had already moved into the low-rise Esplanade Centre and that work was about to begin on three additional components of the overall project: the headquarters building for ICBC, the Pacific Marine Training Institute and a privately financed office building. The development company had called for proposals for an additional two office blocks. By April 1983 ICBC, Pacific Marine Training Institute and BC Rail employees had all moved into new buildings at or near the Quay. In 1982, with the development less than 50 percent complete, the city's tax revenues had swollen by $330,000, an amount significantly more than the $39,000 assessed on the site only four years earlier.

The dream had become reality, so much so that by the end of the year Mayor Jack Loucks was able to predict the imminent designation of the Lonsdale corridor as one of a series of Regional Town Centres within the GVRD. The designation was more than a matter of increased prestige; it would also provide "a higher profile with respect to redevelopment, improved status in relation to transportation needs, and greater opportunities for better promotional possibilities."

There was more to come. A new public market—something the ambitious city had never had—would stand at the heart of the development. According to a February 1984 insert to the *North Shore News*, the Quay would be "a people place" filled with "a festival-like atmosphere, alive with action, spontaneous entertainment, sights and sounds" that would set it apart from the dreary, enclosed shopping malls that had proliferated throughout the Lower Mainland during the last forty years. Furthermore, the market would open in time for Vancouver's Expo 86, the first world exposition to be held in Canada since 1967. According to the development company, Expo's theme of transportation would entice visitors onto Seabus and place North Vancouver on the global stage:

Lonsdale Quay could attract thousands of Expo visitors and bring bonanza business to North Vancouver's retailers and restaurants ... Visitors from places like Saudi Arabia, Kenya, and Kuwait will enjoy some of the best dining and shopping establishments found in the lower mainland—all within walking distance from the ferry terminal . . . Lonsdale Quay is ideally positioned to bring at least a portion of Expo 86's predicted multi-million dollar profits to North Vancouver.

By February 1984, the project's managers had selected Intrawest Corporation to develop the market. Vancouver architect Norman Hotson, whose previous experience included work on the highly successful Granville Island redevelopment project, would head the design team. Intrawest's vice president John Evans advised that the $17 million market project would create "two hundred construction jobs and when completed in August 1985, provide hundreds of permanent new opportunities for small businesses."

By and large, the project lived up to the promises. The area became a transportation hub, with a large bus depot connecting to the cross-harbour Seabus service. Harbour View Park, a massive complex of condominium units, was 50 percent sold prior to its completion. The commissioning of ICBC's new corporate headquarters may not have caused dancing in the streets, but the grand opening in March 1985 of Quayside Plaza, a thirty-thousand-square-foot complex of office, shops and restaurants, was a major community event. The real excitement, however, was reserved for the market, a facility championed by alderman Stella Jo Dean.

Some in the community questioned the appropriateness of a market at the foot of Lonsdale. There was also the question of which of the shops in the area would be able to open on Sundays. Recognizing the obsolescence of the Lord's Day Act but wary of the politics, in the early 1980s the province introduced legislation to permit a limited range of retailers to open their doors on the once-hallowed Sabbath. The debate over Sunday shopping filled the airwaves and daily newspapers. Traditionalists were appalled, forecasting the ruination of family life. One conservative North Shore cleric was utterly indignant, linking Sunday shopping to the "moral revolution and overall spiritual decline" of contemporary society. Unless true Christians spoke up, he declared, "the authorities will continue to pass laws to include abortion, acceptance of homosexuals, Sunday shopping, use of drugs, etc."

Most residents took a more liberal view of the situation, but the city soon found itself caught in a legislative sandwich. Gerry Brewer recalled how retailers strove to comply with successive changes to the law:

The reinstitution of the cross-inlet ferry service and the development of the Lonsdale Quay Market acted as a catalyst for the redevelopment of the Lower Lonsdale area.
Warren Sommer photo (2006)

We had the ridiculous situation where London Drugs were first of all charged for selling certain types of goods in this "drug store," which was disallowed under our bylaws. Then they won the right through court action and legislation to sell these items but only on certain days or times of the day. So then they had portions of the store that had to be screened off by these see-through but locked gates. So for a period of time, you could shop in the store but you couldn't get access to those areas. And I think most people in the community saw the whole issue as just absolutely stupid.

North Shore retailers voiced mixed views on the matter, some of them seeing Sunday shopping as yet another opportunity to sell their wares, others anticipating the loss of precious leisure time. After several false starts the province handed the hot potato to the municipalities, enabling local voters to settle the matter themselves by referendum. City voters went to the polls on November 21, 1981, voting 58 percent in favour of shopping on Sundays. Council approved the necessary bylaw changes just two days later. For larger retailers and the malls in particular, Sunday quickly became the busiest day of the week. The smaller owner-operated businesses of Lower and Central Lonsdale faced greater challenges, unable to justify the costs of extending their hours of operation for what might be limited returns.

As Lower Lonsdale was transformed, however, business began to pick up. To some, the area appeared on the threshold of re-establishing itself as a significant shopping destination, and other areas began to feel threatened. The Central Lonsdale Merchants Association formed in early 1984, its members recognizing how the Quay, an expanded Westlynn Mall, the ever-growing Park Royal Shopping Centre and new commercial developments on Marine Drive might affect business. Their fears may have been well placed. The market, like the rest of the Lonsdale Quay development, was such a resounding success that by 1988 the city was forced to build a pedestrian overpass across West Esplanade.

Much of the new development in the Lower Lonsdale area took place on what had once been the site of North Van Ship Repairs and later Pacific Dry Dock. In the early 1980s it seemed that the area to the east might also be revitalized, not by residential or commercial development but by the construction of more modern shipyard facilities. Burrard Yarrows, as Burrard Dry Dock had become in 1979, was a pale shadow of its former self. Although impressive contracts came its way from time to time, the firm's operations seemed to lack stability. New ferry construction and conversions for BC Ferries and contracts for Canadian Pacific kept the shipyard active throughout most of the 1970s, but internal difficulties and competition from larger, more modern yards in Asia limited its ability to compete on a global stage. By 1980, one in three shipyard workers faced imminent unemployment.

The situation was becoming desperate. Burrard Dry Dock had constructed several icebreakers in the 1950s and another, the *Pierre Radisson,* in the late 1970s. When given the opportunity in the 1980s to bid on three more icebreakers, Burrard Yarrows sharpened its pencils to such an extent that it lost money on three successive contracts. Rather than rescue the shipyard from bankruptcy, contracts with the federal government for the *Terry Fox* and the *Robert Lemeur* pushed the firm closer to the brink. If this was not enough, the shipyard's old dry dock—the object of so much adulation when it opened in the 1920s—was showing significant signs of wear. It was much too small to service the larger vessels that now called regularly in what by then had become the twelfth-largest port on the planet. The shipyard's second dry dock, inherited from North Van Ship Repairs and moved to the Burrard site in the early 1950s, was in even worse condition. With reduced demands for new ship construction, the salvation of the shipyard seemed to lie in ship repairs, an area of business that would require a new dry dock.

The solution did not come cheaply. Burrard Yarrows' consultants suggested a price tag of $28.8 million. Securing the necessary government funding was a protracted but ultimately successful process. By mid-1979 bids had been received from a half-dozen companies for what by then had become a $42 million project. In the end the contract went to a Japanese firm, Mitsubishi Heavy Industries, whose plant was located in Hiroshima. Thirty-five years earlier the Burrard yard had built ships to counter the threat of German and Japanese expansion. Now its very survival depended on the skills and industry of the nation's former enemy.

The new dry dock arrived in August 1981 and strengthened hopes for the shipyard's long-term survival. Within a year the new facility had proved its worth, operating at 75 percent of capacity and becoming the busiest dry dock in the nation. If 50 percent of the firm's activities could be in ship repairs and fifty percent in building new ships, the company's operators hoped, their enterprise might not only survive but also prosper. Their hopes proved misplaced. As ships became increasingly reliable, the demand for repairs in dry docks began to fall. Contracts to build two additional icebreakers, the *Martha L. Black* and the *Henry Larsen,*

Burrard Yarrows' new dry dock arriving in North Vancouver from Japan, August 24, 1981.

North Vancouver Museum and Archives, 27-5

did little to improve the shipyard's viability. The *Larsen* was built at a loss and failed testing both at dockside and during its trials at sea. For Burrard Yarrows the future looked bleak. As they gazed out their windows toward the highly successful Lonsdale Quay development the shipyard's owners began to consider other options for their property.

By the mid-1980s Lonsdale Quay was not only a highly successful development; it had become a focus of community life. Residents and visitors came in droves, enjoying the shops, eating in the restaurants and revelling in the views of the city across the harbour. The Quay's connection with the sea became the object of art as well as commerce. In December 1985 members of the Vancouver Naval Veterans Association joined with the Pacific Marine Training Institute to develop a memorial to seamen. Tom Osborne, a sculptor and veteran of the Royal Navy, had noted a lack of memorials in British Columbia to Canadian sailors. While studying at the institute he was struck by the importance of its site: "It hit me all of a sudden, the North Shore was the place to put the monument. It's where Captain Vancouver first landed, where he was met by the Indians. And Vancouver can say all it wants, but when you want a good view of the city and the sea that surrounds it, you come to the North Shore. What's a more appropriate place for a seaman's monument?"

The seamen's monument was built in the shape of a compass rose, with inscribed bronze plaques placed at each point of the compass. The community embraced it

Artist Doug Senft's controversial iron sculpture in Waterfront Park, photographed in 1987, eventually became a valued component of the park.

North Vancouver Museum and Archives, Fonds 160 photo 84

with enthusiasm. The same could not be said of a sculpture planned for Waterfront Park. In June 1985 plans were revealed for a piece of public art designed as a series of bent steel arches. Those who had bought units in Harbour View Park were outraged, claiming the sculpture both dangerous and ugly. Fears were expressed that children would play on the structure, that it would attract destructive youth and would end up as an expensive eyesore. Council members had entrusted the Arts Council to manage the project and had little desire to become arbiters of public taste. In the end they endorsed the Arts Council's recommendations, much to the relief of its president, Joseph Cantafio, and artist Doug Senft.

As new construction began to reshape the Lower Lonsdale area, several of its most historic buildings faced an uncertain future. In 1977 the city had acquired the old Hamersley mansion, intending it for a yet-to-be-defined public use. After its builder's departure from the community in 1906 the house had seen life as a private hospital, boarding house and rest home. In the early 1980s council was still wrestling with what to do with what alderman Gary Payne referred to "possibly the finest single-family home built in the City of North Vancouver." Council successfully addressed a number of financial challenges and in September 1980 voted to save the building by authorizing its conversion into the Emerald Park Restaurant.

The Hamersley House debate was among the first in a series of heritage-related issues the city addressed in the 1980s, but it was by no means to be the last. Council had no sooner spared the Hamersley House than it doomed the historic Stoker Farm. Located at Twenty-ninth and Lonsdale the Stoker property was one of the city's more interesting anomalies. The land had first been developed by Captain Rupert Archibald, master of the CPR vessel *Empress of China*. Captain Archibald built a seven-room dwelling on the property in 1906–07, naming it Dearne House. Within a year or two the house was raised and greatly expanded. With twenty-eight rooms, the mock Tudor house quickly became a North Shore landmark, its large acreage supporting first a herd of dairy cows and then a chicken farm. By the early 1980s the property's owners decided to sell the property. In the absence of enabling legislation there was little the city could do to ensure the building's

preservation. Despite the herculean efforts of the city's heritage advocates and the community arts council, Dearne House and the farm surrounding it were lost to redevelopment.

Other landmarks disappeared as well. In February 1985 the Anglican Church of St. John the Divine, the "mother church of the North Shore," was all but destroyed by fire. Church authorities deemed its restoration impractical and built a new sanctuary on the site. Two other heritage buildings—the St. Alice and Olympic (formerly the Palace) hotels—had once been symbols of what the city's founders hoped their community might become. By the late 1980s, however, both hotels had long since fallen on hard times, their beer parlours contributing to their unsavoury reputations. Both hostelries had long since become residential hotels and many of their occupants derived their incomes from pensions or social assistance. Heritage advocate Jack Watts recalled the exterior of the St. Alice as having had its architectural integrity severely compromised by a succession of unsympathetic renovations. Within the building, the situation was somewhat different: "The interior was still there—the beer parlour and the pub and all that—in all its old glory."

Dearne House on the Stoker Farm was demolished after considerable public debate in the 1980s. The controversy over the buidling's preservation occurred at an inopportune time, with local governments having little experience with heritage conservation and the provincial heritage management legislation in its infancy.

North Vancouver Museum and Archives, 8605

Public debate focussed not so much on heritage preservation as it did on the height of the building proposed as its replacement. Gerry Brewer remembered how the city had been embarrassed by its inability to prevent or alter the development: "The city got caught with its bylaws down . . . The zoning bylaw of the day had not prescribed a height limitation on that site and a number of other sites and Norm Cressey saw the potential once that building became available for demolition that he could build to whatever height—virtually—he chose." In the face of public opposition to the proposed high-rise structure, the Observatory tower, Brewer and the city considered the possibility of acquiring and restoring the old hotel:

> *While it looked alright from the outside, once we sent our inspection staff inside to have a look at it, the word 'refurbish' wouldn't cover what was required to make it work, to bring it up to anything near code. There were very few dispensations given under the code for heritage buildings, so to bring it up to code would virtually require a rebuild.*

Despite the best efforts of the nascent North Shore Heritage Committee, the two hotels fell to the wrecker's ball in 1989.

For advocates of heritage preservation, the loss of St. John's Church was an unavoidable tragedy but the intentional demolition of both Dearne House and the two hotels was close to heartbreaking. Yet these actions were indicative of the times. The community's heritage was largely undervalued by residents and municipalities had few legislated tools with which to manage their heritage. Progress was the order of the day. Low-income housing may well have been seen as socially worthwhile but non-market housing was difficult to justify in areas where land values were high.

Despite the losses, lessons had been learned. Three separate officially sanctioned heritage advisory committees—one for each municipality—emerged from the ranks of the North Shore Heritage Committee. Some of the community's more significant

The "Observatory Debate" focused both on the demolition of the old St. Alice Hotel and the height of the building proposed as its replacement. A lack of height limitations in the city's bylaws resulted in the construction of a building that towered high above neighbouring structures such as the Barraclough Block, in the foreground.

Warren Sommer photo (2006)

Demolition of North Van Ship Repairs' office building to make way for new development, August 11, 1983.

North Vancouver Museum and Archives, 5076, Ken Smith photo

buildings had been lost, but others would be preserved. As Jack Watts recalled in 2006:

I think because of our work in those early days they're safe, probably because primarily we created an awareness with politicians and people living in the districts and the city. And that's where heritage has gone. Everybody's aware of what it is now and they're more appreciative of trying to incorporate something from the last century in a new development.

The Stoker Farm was put on the market in 1980, sold and redeveloped. Innocuous condominium units soon stood in the place of the noble old farmstead. Any concerns the community might have had about increased traffic were more than allayed in October 1985 by the province's announcement that it was about to build a $15 million eight-lane interchange over the Upper Levels Highway at Lonsdale Avenue. A new overpass was also being considered for the city's Westview area. Social Credit MLA Angus Ree pronounced himself "happy as hell" while Transportation and Highways Minister Alex Fraser denied any relationship between his announcement and an impending provincial election. The Lonsdale overpass opened about one year later, but the Westview project would have to wait until the next decade.

Significant though the debates on the Stoker Farm and the two hotels had been, they were nothing compared to the Park and Tilford controversy. In 1983 Park and Tilford announced their intention of closing their distillery and the gardens that so many had come to love. In the face of a growing market for wine, the demand for distilled liquor had declined and the plant had become redundant. Its gardens produced no revenue and the distillery site was ripe for redevelopment. With their gates closed and no one to look after them, the gardens decayed. Plants were lost to both theft and neglect and the landscape was quickly overgrown. In light of the situation, council authorized staff to negotiate with the property's owners, the Montreal-based Schenley Corporation. The city hoped that one industrial use would succeed the other and that the gardens would be retained.

Schenley proposed a mixed use of the thirty-acre site: ten acres would be reserved for industrial use, four would be preserved as gardens and green space, and the remaining sixteen would become a shopping centre. Following discussions with city staff, plans were dropped for a "fashion oriented centre" competing with the Capilano Mall. The mall had only recently been expanded and was on the verge of becoming completely leased. Plans for a "Festival Market" were also abandoned as such an amenity might compete with the yet-to-be-fully-occupied Lonsdale Quay Market. Instead, the Park and Tilford site would feature a major supermarket, about three-dozen stores and a multi-screen theatre. If council agreed to rezone the site the gardens would be preserved, but council was deeply divided on the issue. Residents were determined to preserve what by then had become *their* gardens. The controversy became intense. There were public meetings and delegations to council, the Cloverley Area Residents Association taking the lead in the fight for the gardens. The matter came to a head in 1987 when council considered a motion to rezone the property subject to the gardens' rehabilitation and protection. Council remained split. It was a moment of high drama when alderman Stella Jo Dean hauled herself from her hospital bed and into a wheelchair and arrived in the chamber to cast the deciding vote. The gardens were saved.

By the time council approved the project's development permit in November 1987, the plans for the site bore little resemblance to Schenley's original proposal. Although a shopping centre and theatre complex would occupy thirteen acres on the southern part of the site, the parcel to the north would become home to a movie studio. Although the studio would not be an industrial use of the property, it would be clean, quiet, and a potential source of jobs for North Vancouver residents.

The construction of a film studio within its boundaries signalled a change in direction for the city. Long accustomed to large and sometimes dirty waterfront industries, residents and council soon found the studio more asset than liability. Conceived by writer-producer Stephen J. Cannell in 1986, the studio was built and ready for production in July 1989. In the years that followed the studio enjoyed considerable success, attracting a string of major film and television productions. Frank Guistra's purchase of the studios and his creation of Lions Gate Entertainment in 1997 further enhanced the facility's profile. By 2004 the company had become the most commercially successful film and television distribution company outside the United States. The firm's resale early in 2006 to the Vancouver-based Bosa Development Corporation, owners of the aptly named Mammoth Studios in Burnaby, promised the enterprise an even greater role in North American film and television production. By then, many of those who had opposed the facility's construction two decades earlier took pride in its accomplishments.

In the mid-1980s, North Vancouver's popular Park and Tilford Gardens, shown shortly after opening in the 1960s, were threatened with redevelopment. The rezoning of the distillery site in 1987 resulted in a project that included the development of a shopping centre and film studio and the preservation of the gardens.
North Vancouver Museum and Archives, 9656

16 RECONSTRUCTION AND RESTORATION 1990–1999

The 1980s had been a memorable decade for the residents of the ambitious city. They had embraced the reinstated cross-harbour ferry service, had revelled in the wholesale redevelopment in the Lower Lonsdale area and had witnessed a continuing influx of immigrants from overseas. After the relative stagnation of the 1970s the rate of population growth had resurged, reaching 8.5 percent from 1981 to 1991, compared to 6.6 percent from 1971 to 1981. Those who had advocated growth in the city were no doubt pleased with what had been accomplished, but the growth of the district had been even more impressive: 15 percent from 1981 to 1991 and 12.9 percent in the preceding ten-year period. While the city developed a new heart in and around the Lonsdale Quay development, the district continued to sprawl. Regardless of where people lived, whether in the city or the district, the city's downtown core— the Lonsdale corridor—continued to be recognized as downtown North Vancouver. Adopted in 1992, a new Official Community Plan confirmed the Lonsdale corridor as a mixed-use, high-density area and introduced policies relating to transportation, green space and heritage. For advocates of heritage conservation still bitter over the losses of the 1980s, the new provisions were not wholly comforting.

But the city took opportunities to redeem itself. In 1993, a prefabricated house manufactured by John Hendry's BC Mills Timber and Trading Company in 1908 was faced with demolition. Originally owned by Captain Henry Pybus, master of the CPR steamship *Empress of Japan*, the Lower Lonsdale house was deemed a "primary building" and as such was an important part of the community's heritage. Rather than allow the unusual structure to be destroyed, the city and its heritage advisory committee worked with the owner, the Sixth Field Company, and the GVRD to have it dismantled and reassembled for public use in Lynn Headwaters Regional Park.

Other buildings in the Lower Lonsdale area presented greater challenges. The old Central School, which subsequently became city hall and then Presentation House, was a case in point. Managed by the Presentation House Cultural Society, the old building had reached the point where it required serious upgrading. Although the rent charged by the city was nominal, the society was left to maintain a building that an architectural review had condemned over sixty years earlier. A representative of the Eighth Avenue Theatre Group offered an unflattering description: "Its roof sags, temperatures inside the building soar to intolerable levels during summer months and leaks in Presentation House walls are causing electrical short-circuits . . . buckets must be placed in the theatre lobby to catch rain that leaks through the roof." In the face of the complaints, the building was repaired, but its odd configuration and aging structure continued to present challenges to tenants.

A block to the east, Lower Lonsdale and the Lonsdale Corridor continued to develop. Low-rise development—featuring a wide array of specialty shops, restaurants, professional offices, financial institutions and other commercial ventures—offered

This prefabricated house, once owned by Captain Henry Pybus, was restored and relocated to Lynn Valley Headwaters Regional Park. Prior to being moved from its original location in Lower Lonsdale, the house achieved brief notoriety as the residence of Richard the Troll, leader of the Rhinoceros Party.

North Vancouver Museum and Archives, Cecil Halsey photo

a comprehensive range of goods and services. Well-maintained streets, sidewalks and street furniture complemented extensive plantings of ornamental trees. Development along the street had been kept to low-rise construction only, allowing sunlight to fall throughout the day. Higher-density residential development in the blocks to the east and west helped keep the corridor's shops viable while allowing residents to walk rather than drive as they went about their business. City hall, the library, Lions Gate Hospital, and the police and fire departments' offices were but a stone's throw away. Other facilities could be easily reached by bus.

As the city increasingly became what it had always longed to be, politicians in the district once again cast a covetous eye in its direction. Even in the 1990s the amalgamation debate would not go away. When district council sent their mayor Murray Dykeman to discuss the matter with city mayor Jack Loucks, the meeting was cordial but the results were predictable. The city was not interested in pursuing the matter. City administrator Gerry Brewer spoke on behalf of his council: "We're really not interested in discussing this further, but there seems to be a continuing district interest in raising the issue. They have been told we're not interested, but they seem unwilling or unable to consider the intent behind the words."

But district council was not alone. In May 1995 the *North Shore News* questioned the logic of the councils' recent decisions to refurbish their municipal halls when efficiencies could be gained from "one good municipal hall." Five months later, just before the province-wide municipal elections, the district suggested the creation of yet another task force to investigate the advantages and disadvantages of union. Many residents observed that the two jurisdictions already shared a number of mutual resources and services. The list was impressive and included the garbage disposal transfer station, the North Shore Union Board of Health, Lions Gate Hospital, and police, recreational and cultural services.

City mayor Jack Loucks was wary: "Listen, the city is not interested in it. We figure the city could only be a real loser in amalgamation." The city's population (about 40,000), annual expenditures and staff were all approximately half that of the district. More importantly, its reserves, also known as the "heritage fund," stood at over $30 million while the district's were $5 million. Although the paper value of the district's land holdings was enormous (a reported $300 million), much of the land was mountainous and would require vast sums to service. City councillor Bill Bell suggested that amalgamation would be "financial folly" for the city: "Amalgamation will only benefit the overtaxed and infrastructure-starved denizens of the district . . . I would be horrified of letting the district councillors decide the fate of North Vancouver City's heritage fund." When city council received the district's proposition it was duly discussed and voted upon. "We respectfully rejected it and it goes into the round file," Bill Bell reported to the press.

Despite their disagreement on amalgamation, the two councils continued to work together on matters of mutual concern. One of the larger projects on their joint agenda was a new building for the RCMP. As the 1990s progressed, both councils agreed on a funding formula, location and design for a new facility. When completed on its East Fourteenth Street site, the building would house not only the RCMP but the North and West Vancouver Emergency Program as well. Ground was broken in August 1995 and the detachment moved into its new $19.5 million facility, named in honour of retired city manager Gerry Brewer, in March 1997. In 2001 the neighbouring plaza was named after former alderman and chair of the Police Liaison Committee of the City and District Stella Jo Dean. The construction of the new police facility was timely, for as North Vancouver's population grew in size and complexity, big-city crime became increasingly common. Serious crime rates were reported as being well below the provincial average, but concerns were raised by incidents such as the execution-style slaying of Mohammed Mirhadi at the Esplanade 6 Cinemas in Lower Lonsdale in February 1997.

The two municipalities also co-operated in honouring the memories of the

Standing Tall: Veteran Jack Bellingham stands at attention at the Remembrance Day observances at Victoria Park.

North Shore News, *Paul McGrath photo*

The Victoria Park Cenotaph was renovated in the 1990s. The improvements to the area around the monument were funded through a mixture of public and private contributions.

North Vancouver Museum and Archives, 1063, Cecil Halsey photo

community's fallen servicemen and women. By the fiftieth anniversary of the end of the Second World War in 1995, the Victoria Park cenotaph required upgrading. The area around it was poorly paved and overgrown—and without lighting, the memorial provided a night-time shelter for illicit activities. Through the efforts of the city, the district, the Royal Canadian Legion and individual residents, over $500,000 was raised to address the issue. The cenotaph was cleaned. An expanded paved area was created as a platform for memorial and associated ceremonies. Benches, lamps and trees were installed. Most importantly, a series of new memorial markers were developed to honour each of the 255 North Vancouverites known to have died in military service: 102 in the First World War, 152 in the Second World War and 1 during the conflict in Korea.

The project was particularly significant for residents who had never been able to visit graves of family members that were overseas or unknown. North Vancouver clerk Merwin Lyonel Woods, who had been killed in action in the First World War a month after his twenty-fourth birthday, was one of over twenty thousand Canadian fatalities whose remains disappeared without a trace. The families of Second World War fatalities who had fought and died in the Battle of the Atlantic, such as North Vancouver stoker James Gilbert Carse, had nowhere to mourn and nowhere to remember. Carse's sister Maggie Carpenter remarked that "Boys lost at sea . . . don't even have graves," as she reflected on how the new memorial markers would rekindle the memories of the community's war dead.

Although refurbishing the cenotaph had required money and collaboration, other projects would require considerably more of both. Not content with the Seabus service, a business lobby group named the Downtown Vancouver Association invited the three North Shore mayors to a meeting in February 1989. Minister of Transportation and Highways Neil Vant had recently announced the Social Credit government's willingness to consider privately funded bridges throughout the province. The three mayors were skeptical, North Vancouver City mayor Jack Loucks proclaiming that any proposal would have to go back to "square two if not square

Canadian National Railway rolling stock on the city's waterfront, James Richardson grain terminal in the distance. Although a branch of the Pacific Great Eastern (PGE) Railway was built from Whytecliffe to North Vancouver in 1913, it was the Canadian National Railway that became the prime line through the city.
North Vancouver Museum and Archives, Cecil Halsey photo

one." The talks led to naught, but in the early 1990s the Ministry of Transportation and Highways initiated yet another study on cross-inlet transportation.

By early 1994 five engineering firms had presented six different alternatives for a tunnel across the inlet. There were deep bored tunnels and immersed tube tunnels. Some firms declined to provide cost estimates; others suggested costs ranging from $300 million to $1.2 billion. Each of the options for a new crossing also included renovations to the aging Lions Gate Bridge. The costs alone were staggering, the politics impossible. In the end the province elected simply to renovate the Lions Gate Bridge and leave the question of a tunnel to some future time and government.

If, like death and taxes, amalgamation and the question of a third crossing were two matters that North Vancouver residents seemed unable to avoid, in the 1990s waterfront industries might well have been a third. From the time of its establishment in 1962, Neptune Terminals had been a source of controversy. Council's efforts to block the storage and loading of coal had been in vain, but efforts to block the shipment of sulphur had proved successful. By 1982 the company's contracts required the construction of a second stacker/reclaimer at a cost of $12 million. Cloverley residents opposed the idea of more noise and dust but the city couldn't stop the company from simply doing more of the same.

Late in 1990 the *Vancouver Sun* revealed plans by Neptune to discharge effluent into the city's sewers. The company had found a legislative loophole: it could not discharge its effluent into the inlet, but it could dump it into the sewers. Greenpeace spokesperson Catherine Stewart was appalled: "This is really outrageous. What's happening is industry is using our sewers for free in order to bypass the regulations set by the ministry, and we as taxpayers are being asked to upgrade the facilities to handle it." A company spokesperson was unrepentant: "In our opinion it's perfectly legal for us to go into sewers. It's the mandate of the GVRD to take industrial sewerage and we see nothing wrong with it." In March 1991 the Vancouver Port Commission approved the construction of a $24 million potash shed on Neptune's waterfront property. The Commission had required the company to adhere to the environmental protection recommendations of an independent review panel. Despite the objections of both council and Cloverley residents, the expansion proceeded.

The actions of the Canadian National Railway became a threat for a much larger population. Despite its best efforts the city had difficulty in monitoring the railway's activities, especially in the transport of dangerous goods. Gerry Brewer recalled the city's frustrations: "The CNR weren't talking to anybody. They did what they wished. And if you didn't like it, they'd do it anyway . . . The railway would have a derail and if they could get away with it they wouldn't tell the city, the fire department, the police department or anyone else."

As the decade progressed, one waterfront controversy seemed to succeed another. One, sadly, revolved around the future of the shipyard founded by Andy Wallace eight decades earlier. Burrard Yarrows had become Versatile Pacific in 1985, but the change of name and the corporate merger of Cornat Industries with Versatile Manufacturing seven years earlier only disguised a worsening situation. In the mid-1980s the federal government announced its intention of building a new, state-of-the-art Polar 8 icebreaker for the Arctic. For the next five years, the financially troubled Versatile Pacific shipyard pursued the $417 million contract only to be advised in early 1990 that the project would not be proceeding. Versatile Pacific's parent company had also run into financial difficulties and sold the enterprise in 1988.

The shipyard's new owners, Shieldings, decided to shut down the North Vancouver facility, sell its assets, and sell or redevelop the property. In mid-1991 Shieldings proposed selling the ten-year-old dry dock and shipping it back to Asia. Mayors Murray Dykeman and Jack Loucks lobbied the federal and provincial governments to save the dry dock and the jobs that went with it. The federal government, which had contributed the lion's share of funding to the dry dock's construction only a decade earlier, agreed to yet another contribution. With additional help from the province and a joint venture company involving Vancouver Shipyards and Allied Shipbuilders, the dry dock was saved. The shipyard however, which had stood at the brink of disaster so many times in the past only to be rescued by a last-minute miracle, was finally lost. On a cloudy night in December 1992 its last ten employees made their way through the snow-covered yard and passed through its gates one final time.

In the months that followed, Versatile Pacific collapsed and it fell to receivers to negotiate the future of the site. The process was slow. In 1996 the city and the Port of Vancouver undertook a joint study of the property. That the port was working in co-operation with local government was a tribute not only to its management but also to the concerted efforts of Jack Loucks, former district mayor Marilyn Baker and her successor Murray Dykeman. By 1999 the city, having witnessed the success of Lonsdale Quay and other developments in Lower Lonsdale, proved amenable to rezoning the shipyard for comprehensive redevelopment. Under the terms of the proposed rezoning much of the site would be redeveloped and several heritage structures would be retained for commercial, civic and cultural uses. A few key pieces of equipment would also be preserved: when councillor Stella Jo Dean

The derelict buildings of the once-proud Burrard Dry Dock, 1990s. Plans for the shipyard's redevelopment took a decade to complete and included provision for the rehabilitation of several historic structures as well as the construction of high-rise condominiums.

North Vancouver Museum and Archives, 15020

urged the donation to the city of a Colby crane and two Gantry cranes recently used on the site, its owners saw little point in resisting. "When Stella Jo Dean asks you for something," joked Seaspan's communications officer, "it's just as easy to say yes and be done with it." Under the terms of the agreement, portions of the site not designated for retention, plus property on the north side of Esplanade, would be developed with eight hundred high-rise housing units and about 300,000 square feet of commercial space. A series of walkways, piers and plazas would ensure public access to an area of waterfront all but forbidden to visitors throughout the preceding ninety-three years.

The old *No. 5 Ferry*—operated since 1959 as the Seven Seas restaurant—also seemed doomed. Since opening, the restaurant and its huge rooftop neon sign had become much-revered local landmarks. By 1992, however, the ship's owner was in arrears for rent, taxes and utilities. Although a lower rent was subsequently negotiated, concerns arose about the vessel's seaworthiness. The city requested a $150,000 bond from the owners in the event that the vessel sank or had to be towed away. The surety was not forthcoming and in February 1999 council decided with what one member described as "a heavy heart" not only to rescind the restaurant's business licence but also to require its owner to remove it from its moorings.

FastCat ferry under construction east of Burrard Dry Dock, November 1997. A decade after their construction, the three catamaran ferries commissioned by Premier Glen Clark's government lay berthed where they had been built.

North Vancouver Museum and Archives, 13166

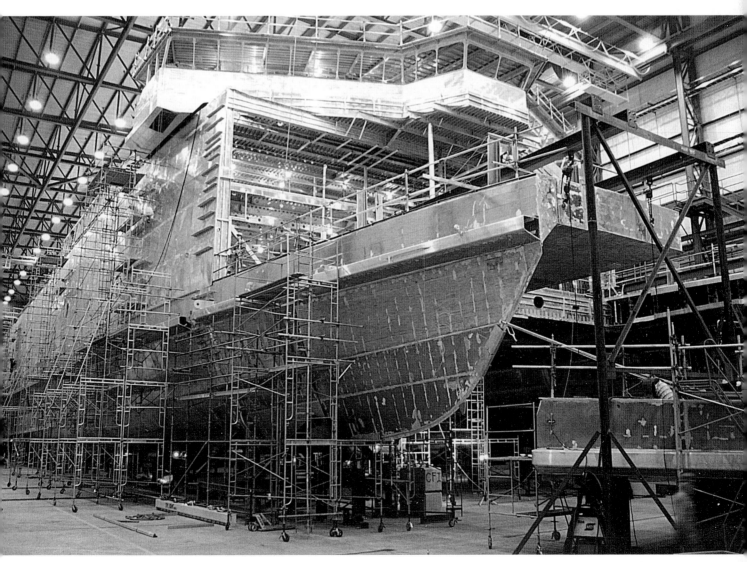

About the same time and not far to the east, three ships assembled on the city's waterfront became the focus of a controversy of provincial proportions. Known variously as the Fast Ferry Scandal and the FastCat Fiasco, the uproar began innocently enough with Premier Glen Clark's decision in 1994 to construct three new high-speed vessels to supplement the province's aging fleets of ferries. The FastCat program called for the construction of three aluminium-hulled catamaran vessels, each capable of making the Horseshoe Bay to Nanaimo crossing thirty minutes quicker. Clark also hoped to rejuvenate the province's ailing shipyards, believing that the successful production of state-of-the-art ferries in British Columbia would not only instil new skills among the province's shipbuilders, but also lead to orders for similar vessels from overseas.

By March 1996 the province had created a new firm, Catamaran Ferries International (CFI), to produce the vessels. Plants distributed throughout the province would produce its components, which would then be assembled in CFI's plant just east of Burrard Dry Dock. The enterprise seemed doomed from the outset. There were time delays, personnel changes, design problems and—once the ferries were commissioned—unanticipated operational issues. The greatest issue was the cost. By the time the last of the three ferries had been delivered in 2000, the project had cost close to $460 million—more than twice the $210 million originally budgeted.

While the FastCats were being built on the east side of the Burrard Dry Dock site, a smaller but more auspicious project was under way on the west. The city's old PGE railway station, no longer needed to house the North Vancouver Museum and Archives' collections, returned from Mahon Park to a site near its original location at the foot of Lonsdale Avenue. The idea of relocating the station had developed during discussions between city planners and museum director Robin Inglis, and was seen as an appropriate way to recognize the importance of heritage conservation in the revitalization of Lower Lonsdale. Substantial financial assistance

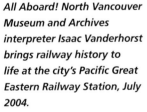

All Aboard! North Vancouver Museum and Archives interpreter Isaac Vanderhorst brings railway history to life at the city's Pacific Great Eastern Railway Station, July 2004.

North Shore News, *Kristin Bradford photo*

from the city's Kiwanis Club, BC Rail and the BC Heritage Trust made the project feasible. Once opened in September 1997, the old station became a focal point on the North Vancouver waterfront, presenting short-term exhibitions, providing information services and offering opportunities for waterfront interpretation.

Although the old station had been saved, a less auspicious fate awaited four other important heritage buildings in the Lower Lonsdale area. As 1996 drew to a close, the city expressed grave concerns about the state of repair of the old Syndicate Block, built in 1903 for the Western Corporation and the site of several of the city's earliest businesses. The structure was subsequently torn down, though parts of the original facade were incorporated in a reconstructed building. Other losses followed. On New Year's Eve 1997 fire raced through the Aberdeen Block, all but gutting the venerable structure and forcing the closure of Paine Hardware, its principal occupant for close to ninety years. Ten months later the Barraclough Block, whose domed turret had long been a landmark at the corner of Lonsdale and West Second, fell to the flames of another suspicious fire. Gross House, one of the few older single-family homes surviving in the area, was lost in yet another mysterious fire in October 2000.

Concerned by these repeated losses, the city took a pragmatic stand and encouraged the buildings' owners to restore and reconstruct rather than replace. In April 1999 plans were approved for the reconstruction of the Barraclough Block and the owner committed to incorporate surviving elements of the old building into the construction of the new. Although plans for the restoration of the Aberdeen Block were also approved, over seven years were to pass before new live-work units were built within and above the shell of the magnificent old building.

City of North Vancouver 1995 Council: Left to right: Councillor John Braithwaite, Councillor Stella Jo Dean, Councillor Barbara Perrault, Mayor Jack Loucks, Councillor Bob Fearnley, Councillor Barbara Sharp, Councillor Darrell Mussatto.
City of North Vancouver

Just as the face of the city was changing, so were the dynamics of the community. During its first eight decades males of British and mainland European extraction had dominated city council. Beginning in 1991 and continuing to 1999, council was more balanced, being composed of three male (one of whom—John Braithwaite—was black) and three female members, plus the mayor. Although none of the city's East Asian or Middle Eastern immigrants had been elected to council, several had let their names stand. Mohsen Shoja-Nia was the first, running for council in 1993.

Female ascendancy was also reflected in the community. After several false starts, North Vancouver's women reorganized once again. In 1995, the community's businesswomen established a new organization of their own: the Successful Women Always Network, generally known as SWAN. SWAN represented a new generation of women and its focus was on services for the business and professional women—no longer just teachers, secretaries and nurses—whom now formed a significant component of the North Vancouver workforce.

The 1990s were also significant for the North Shore's aboriginal population. Recent criticisms of the nation's Indian residential schools and the role that Oblate priests had played within them led the order's Canadian president, Father Douglas Crosby, to issue a public apology. In his statement, delivered on behalf of the order before twenty thousand people at a religious gathering in Alberta in 1991, Crosby expressed deep regret on behalf of the order for setting up and maintaining residential schools, for instances of physical and sexual abuse, and for dismissing "many of the riches of native religious tradition." Many band members considered the apology a hollow utterance. Speaking a decade and a half later, a Squamish student at Carson Graham Secondary School recalled how his grandmother had been abused at an Indian Residential School, being labelled a "savage" by the nuns: "She gets a lot of stress on her face and she can barely get to sleep when she talks about it."

As the 1990s came to an end, residents could not help but be conscious that one age had passed and that another had begun. Amid the furor over "Y2K"—the much-feared collapse of electronic technology at the turn of the millennium—the city paused to recognize two long-serving politicians, both of whom retired in 1999. The highly independent Stella Jo Dean had served on council on and off since 1969, often championing causes related to heritage and the arts. Jack Loucks' remarkable career had begun with his initial election to council in 1970 followed by an unprecedented twenty-three years as mayor. Loucks was honoured with a new plaza and park area on West First Street named "Jack Loucks Court." When opened in June 2001, the new development provided a pleasant link in a pedestrian route down the Lower Lonsdale slopes to the increasingly popular Quay—a fitting tribute to the man who had worked so hard on behalf of the area's revitalization.

INTO THE NEW MILLENNIUM 17

At the dawn of the new millennium much of what the city's founders had hoped for the community had finally been achieved. Indeed, if there was anything to lament it was the very growth that the founders had promoted in the first place. Many of the city's picturesque older homes and commercial buildings had fallen victim to the urge for greater density. Although two vehicular bridges provided a fixed link to the inlet's south shore, they were often congested and occasionally closed. The long-sought railway had arrived but it and its attendant industries prevented easy access to the waterfront that had attracted so many to settle in the city in the first place. Progress had finally come; the challenge lay in determining how to direct it.

In the early 2000s North Vancouver's population had grown to levels that would have made its founders proud. Since the date of its incorporation the city's population had grown tenfold, reaching an estimated 49,248 in 2006. Much of the city's recent growth was due to an influx of new Canadians. One in three residents had been born outside the country. By the time of the 2001 census North Vancouver was no longer a predominantly British

Young Iranian-Canadians dance on Lonsdale Avenue in celebration of Norooz, the Persian New Year, in March, 2006. Norooz is traditionally celebrated as the first day of spring and features symbolically-set tables (Haft Sîn), gift giving, fire jumping, house and business decorations, special foods and new clothes.

North Shore News *photo*

community. In 1911, 77.4 percent of the city's population had British roots. Eighty years later the rate was 46.5 percent. By 2001 immigration from continental Europe, East Asia and the Middle East had created a city, which though predominantly white was one in which visible minorities constituted 22.7 percent of the city's population. The overwhelming majority of immigrants were from the continent the city's founders had feared most. In 2001, about 45.3 percent of the city's immigrant population was Asian-born: 6 percent from China, 7.8 percent from the Philippines and 16.5 percent from Iran.

During the mid- to late 1990s, interracial strife had been commonplace in several North Shore neighbourhoods. By the early 2000s, however, increased familiarity had bred greater understanding. Students interviewed at Carson Graham Secondary School in 2006 had their own views of the situation. Arash Rahmanian, a student of Iranian descent, was optimistic: "There used to be quite a lot of tension, especially when more and more immigrants started to flow into North Vancouver . . . As the years have gone by . . . we've seen more acceptance." Jullian Kolstee saw not only greater tolerance, but also a blending of cultural influences:

> There's a large group . . . in the high schools today that are a somewhat mixed group. They take elements of culture from all the different minorities and it's become its own kind of culture within the community. I know lots of white kids

Faye Halls (Yeltsilewet),
director of the Esiha7an
Employment and Training
Centre in the former St.
Paul's Day School, June 2005.
North Shore News, Mike
Wakefield photo

*who know Persian words and Persian kids who snowboard and skateboard and
whatever else. I think everyone mixes and they share from each one of their
cultures here.*

A group of aboriginal students at Carson Graham saw the situation differently.
There may not have been interracial strife, but communication between various
cultures at the school was far from optimum: "They hang out with their own
race. They come up with some names too, like 'Rez Crew' and 'Persian Pride.' The
Chinese call themselves 'Flip flops' . . ." Gary Sum, whose parents were Chinese,
viewed interracial relations as a continuing challenge:

*I personally think we are doing something, but somehow I kind of get the feeling
we are not doing enough. In Carson it's great, you have all these First Nations
programs, but what happens is that the First Nations program is in this corner of
the school that the other kids never, ever go to—unless they're on their way to the
smoke pit . . . We need to reach out more.*

Like its Asian population, the community's First Nations population had also
grown substantially in the late twentieth century. In 1911, 262 people had lived
on the Mission Reserve compared to 339 in 2001. In 1911, only 54 city residents
claimed Native origins compared to 1,015 in 2001. The 1990s had been a watershed

Young Eagle: Sheldon Nahanee poised with his plume of feathers ready to perform the eagle dance at the 17th Squamish Pow Wow, July 2004. Events such as this reflected a renewed interest in aboriginal culture among Natives and non-Natives alike.

North Shore News, *Mike Wakefield photo*

in the history of Canadian First Nations. In 1991 after years of debate, the federal and provincial governments and the First Nations Summit agreed upon a process to negotiate the treaties that aboriginal people had long been denied. One of the Squamish Nation's hereditary chiefs, Joe Mathias, had served on the task force whose work had made the framework possible. In December 1993 the Squamish Nation submitted its statement of intent, the initial step in what promised to be a lengthy treaty negotiation process. As in other areas of the province the question of land claims proved to be complex; the territorial claims of the Musqueam and Tsleil-Waututh peoples overlapped those of the Squamish.

Entering the treaty negotiation process was but one of the positive steps the Squamish Nation had taken to improve the welfare of its members. By 2007 its council had initiated programs in areas as diverse as forest management, education, recreation, social services and economic development. Despite these successes, the early years of the new millennium also brought sorrow. In March 2000 Chief Joe Mathias suddenly died. Like his predecessors Chief Joe Capilano and Andy Paull, Chief Mathias had worked hard to advance the rights of the Squamish people. Although lauded by Natives and non-Natives alike, Chief Mathias had retained his humility, often describing himself simply as "that bow legged Indian from the other side of the tracks." Fourteen months after Mathias's death Chief Simon Baker, one of the Squamish Nation's favourite sons, passed away at the age of ninety. Baker, whose Squamish name Khot-la-cha meant "man with a kind heart," had lived a life full of years and honours but his loss was felt nonetheless.

During his lifetime Baker had not only witnessed phenomenal changes on his people's reserves but had also been instrumental in bringing much of it about. In the early 2000s the little houses on the Squamish reserves that Baker had known in his childhood had been all but forgotten. On the Mission Reserve newer, higher-quality houses stood not far from small, aging dwellings. The quality of housing on the reserves had generally improved but their population densities resulted in overcrowding. For the Squamish Nation, housing its 3,300 members—41 percent of whom lived off reserve—became an increasing challenge. Some Natives lived in crowded condominiums owned by the Squamish Nation but located within the city. In 2006 Native students who lived in and near "the condos" described the environment: "There's no playground, no lacrosse box. All we've got is a basketball court. It's all covered up in graffiti. A lot of dogs running all over the place. It smells a lot too. Dead rats and stuff." Many hoped that successful treaty negotiations would enable the First Nations to solve such issues, but when Squamish leadership proposed erecting billboards to finance the Nation's more immediate needs, the public outcry was predictable.

The city had housing issues of its own. Facilitating the development of affordable housing was a challenge that had varied over time. Market conditions, population growth rates, income levels and a number of other factors worked in concert to influence the situation. In the 1950s the city had worked with service clubs to provide affordable housing for seniors. From the 1960s to the 1980s programs of the federal and provincial governments had encouraged the development of social housing for specific populations. By the 1990s, however, both senior governments had all but withdrawn from the social housing field, leaving the city to deal with the issue virtually unassisted. The city's own Official Community Plan did little to mitigate the situation. Since its adoption in 1980 the OCP had encouraged high-rise residential development throughout Lower Lonsdale and up the Lonsdale corridor. As a result of this policy the city's population density had soared and by 2001 was over four times that of the neighbouring district. As the city soon discovered, urbanization came with its problems. By 2006 a buoyant market for self-owned

In the early 2000s both sides of Burrard Inlet witnessed a boom in condominium contruction, including these high-rise condominium towers on West First Street in the city's Lower Lonsdale area, January 2004.

North Vancouver Museum and Archives, 33-2

apartments encouraged property owners to evict their tenants, raze their buildings and erect high-rise condominiums.

With a high proportion of low-income families and a high percentage of rental households, the city was increasingly hard-pressed to facilitate the development of affordable housing. Despite the challenge, however, by 2007 the city had approved the creation of over one thousand units of non-market housing. Its own recent actions included the subsidization of project costs for the Quayview housing complex in Lower Lonsdale, the partnered purchase of an existing apartment building for conversion to non-market housing, and the purchase of a site for an adult shelter and transition housing. Such actions were timely; a 2005 study by the GVRD had documented growing homelessness throughout the region and a 168 percent increase in homelessness in the city and district in the previous three years.

Homelessness was by no means new to the city. In previous decades the city's homeless lived out of sight, taking shelter in the railway tunnel underneath Esplanade during inclement weather and living rough in ravines when the weather was warmer. By 2000 homelessness had become more visible. Over the years organizations had rallied to deal with the dilemma. From the mid-1990s the Harvest Project, one of the city's newer not-for-profit organizations, had dealt both with the causes and symptoms of homelessness. Speaking just before Christmas 2005, the Harvest Project's executive director Bob Rogers commented on a worsening situation: "The homeless part of our community is very visible. You see them sleeping outside; you see them as 'binners,' but the people who are at risk of becoming homeless are very hidden."

The city itself was also active in addressing the needs of its less fortunate residents. Council had a long history of involvement in dealing with social issues, having created the position of social planner in 1987, long before comparable jurisdictions even acknowledged a responsibility to deal with social issues. In 2001 the city facilitated the development of a temporary weather shelter on West Esplanade. Although the facility later closed, another temporary shelter was subsequently found. In April 2005 through strong support of the city and particularly Mayor Barbara Sharp, as well as assistance from others, the Lookout Emergency Aid Society was able to open a new shelter with year-round housing and counselling services.

Social issues notwithstanding, those who had founded the city in 1907 would have been pleased by its physical development. In 1907 the townsite had been a hodgepodge of wood-frame buildings, vacant lots, muddy trails, blackened stumps and second-growth forest. In the mid-2000s the city possessed an enviable mix of residential, commercial, industrial and institutional development in the midst of one of the most spectacular natural settings in the world. In 1907 considerable hopes had been held for extensive development along the North Vancouver waterfront. At the end of the twentieth century the city's sole remaining undeveloped site was the reclaimed land in its southwest corner. The area, popularly known as the Fullerton Fill, had long been anticipated as the site of a series of clean, light industrial and other business enterprises, but had lain as a virtual wasteland for over twenty years.

Shelter manager Richard Turton at the temporary North Shore Housing Centre at 705 West Second Avenue, March 2003. A permanent year-round shelter for the city's homeless was built on the same site in 2005 with the Lookout Emergency Aid Society serving as its operator.

North Shore News *Julie Iverson photo*

Part of the problem lay in an overabundance of industrial land elsewhere in the region. Much of it was cheaper than property of equal size in the Fullerton Fill. Furthermore, in North Vancouver there were rail yards to contend with. With freight trains shunting back and forth and nothing but level crossings to connect the area with the rest of the city, the Fullerton Fill held little appeal for potential investors. When an overpass was built in the 1990s, however, the area finally began to be developed. By September 2000 almost half of the acreage in what its owners now referred to as the Harbourside Business Park had been sold. For retired mayor Jack Loucks the achievement was bittersweet: "I campaigned for twenty years on the development of the Fullerton property and it just got developed about the time I retired!"

One of the earliest, and certainly the largest, developments in the area was the North Shore Auto Mall, a cluster of eighteen dealerships on a twenty-five-acre site that had once lain underwater. Several of the dealerships had moved from their previous locations in the district, lured by the development's pedestrian-friendly atmosphere. District mayor Don Bell put up a brave front, suggesting that the district's loss of business was a blessing in disguise. "I think that the concern that existed in the past was that there were perhaps too many auto dealerships along Marine Drive. I've heard descriptions that it was sort of the Kingsway of North Vancouver." The auto mall opened in the spring of 2000 and a new 6.5-acre park and walkway was developed in the years that followed. The M.B. King lumber mill was commemorated with an interpretive plaque and the naming of the waterfront walkway. In the ensuing years, a series of attractive light industrial and professional buildings moved into the area which, with sidewalks, plantings and expansive harbour views, became an increasingly popular destination for walkers, joggers and picnickers.

Residents enjoy a stroll along King's Mill Walk in the former Fell/Fullerton Fill area of the city, now the Harbourside Business Park, January 2003.

North Shore News, *Julie Iverson photo*

The Bodwell School opened on reclaimed land in the former Fullerton Fill in September 2003. The new school promoted cultural diversity, rather than ethnic exclusivity.

Courtesy of the Bodwell School, Paul Yuen photo

The Bodwell High School was one of the more intriguing organizations to move into "the fill." Its diverse student body was nothing if not reflective of the new North Vancouver. Founded in Vancouver in 1991, the non-denominational, co-educational day and boarding school moved to Harbourside Park in September 2003. Cultural diversity, rather than ethnic exclusivity, was at its very heart. Meanwhile on the public side of the system, Lonsdale School was suffering from falling enrolment. In May 2005 the school board voted to close the school and its last students left the building at the end of June.

Traditional schools and facilities only met traditional needs. When alternate recreational activities began to emerge among the North Shore's youth in the 1990s, the city was committed to address them. Skateboarders presented the biggest challenge as they skated along city streets, sidewalks, benches and retaining walls. Noting the success of skateboard parks elsewhere in the region, the city searched for a site of its own, initially looking at Waterfront Park but finally selecting a more central and publicly agreeable site adjacent to Centennial Theatre. The new facility, which opened in May 2004, was an instant success.

The city had long promoted recreational activity, having built its first recreation centre with the district in the mid-1960s. By the early 2000s population growth in the Lower Lonsdale area required the development of an additional facility. Working with the North Shore Recreation Commission, North Shore Neighbourhood House and other community partners, the city acquired space in a new condominium tower for a new community centre. Opened in 2004 as the John Braithwaite Community Centre—named in honour of the recently retired, long-serving city councillor—the new facility had much in common with the nearby neighbourhood house, facilitating community-based services as well as providing more traditional recreation programs.

Over the years, other community figures had also been honoured as council

*Zack Dolesky, of Canyon
Heights Elementary School,
shows his stuff at the City
Skate Park, opened in
May 2005 near Centennial
Theatre. The design of the
skate park was completed
with considerable input
from its intended users.*
North Shore News, *Cindy
Goodman photo*

chose names for facilities. Chief Dan George, the prominent actor, author and
First Nations ambassador had been recognized with the naming of a park. Chiefs
August Jack and Mathias Joe had been similarly honoured. Parks were named
to commemorate former mayor Jack Loutet, former alderman Sam Walker,
community volunteer Derek Inman and long-serving superintendent of public
works Jack Greenwood. Amateur historian Rodger Burnes, one of the city's most
avid supporters, was also remembered with a park. New streets near the waterfront
were named to recognize former mayors, aldermen and councillors: Noel Copping,

Ken Gostick, Jack Chadwick, George Hanes, Dugald Donaghy and Carrie Cates.

In the early 2000s, other community members whose contributions to the city were much more recent also received recognition. One of the first was Harry Jerome. After retiring from active competition, the acclaimed sprinter had gone on to teach and consult for Sports Canada. Jerome received the nation's highest accolade in 1971 when the Governor General awarded him the Order of Canada. Sadly, Jerome died from a brain seizure in 1982 at the age of forty-two. When Jerome's sister Valerie appeared with other family members at a council meeting in July 2001, council seized upon the suggestion that something significant in the city be named in the sprinter's honour. Various ideas came forward but in the end

Faces of the new North Vancouver: Cadets at a service of Remembrance in the city-owned North Vancouver Cemetery, September 2006.

North Shore News, *Victor Aberdeen photo*

2006 Council. Back Row (left to right): Councillors Craig Keating, Bob Fearnley, Bob Heywood, Sam Schechter. Front Row (left to right): Councillor Pam Bookham, Mayor Darrell Mussatto, Councillor Barbara Perrault.
City of North Vancouver

council chose to rename its premier facility, the Lonsdale Recreation Centre, as the Harry Jerome Recreation Centre while the centre and the other public facilities surrounding it became part of the Harry Jerome Complex. The rededication of the complex was a moving event with Charmaine Crooks, a five-time Olympian, 1984 Olympic silver medallist and member of the International Olympic Committee, delivering a memorable address.

Revered organizations and living residents were also honoured. The 103rd Squadron of the Royal Canadian Air Cadets had received the Freedom of the City in 1998; its naval counterpart the 105th Royal Canadian Sea Cadet Corps was similarly honoured in 2004. In the intervening years, four prominent politicians also received the designation: former mayor "Gentleman Jack" Loucks, former councillors Stella Jo Dean and John Braithwaite, and Ray Perrault, who had served the community as MLA, MP and finally senator. Becoming a freeman was a matter of considerable consequence; the designation was rarely given and required the unanimous consent of council.

Perhaps inspired by the work of past leaders, council endeavoured to create a legacy of its own. During past decades, successive councils had supported upgrades to the city's outdoor facilities in Mahon and Boulevard parks, working in partnership with the community's service clubs. As its centennial approached and its population multiplied, however, there was little undeveloped land left in North Vancouver for additional parkland. Eager to improve residents' quality of life, the city turned its attention to upgrading its existing assets. In 2002 the city unveiled an ambitious plan to complete the circle of parks originally envisioned by the city's founders. When completed, a "green necklace" would surround the city and mitigate much of the damage caused by the construction of the Upper Levels Highway in 1961. The project would include both passive and active areas, linking several city parks, public spaces and natural habitats while providing opportunities for pedestrians, people with mobility aids, inline skaters and cyclists alike. The

completion of the southern portion of the project, in 2005–06, provided residents with a sample of what was yet to come.

There was also funding for the arts. In 2000, recognizing that the Centennial Theatre was showing signs of wear, significant funding was provided for a major refit of several front-of-house areas in the thirty-four-year-old facility. That same year Sinfonia, the North Shore's own symphony orchestra, was founded with the popular Clyde Mitchell serving as its first musical director. In 2002 the city began to implement a new cultural plan while continuing to build upon its pre-existing public art initiatives. The visual arts community, however, remained underserved. Working with Wedgewood Developments, a firm building a condominium complex in Lower Lonsdale, the city negotiated for additional arts space to be provided as a community amenity. Despite a number of delays a new public gallery, the CityScape Community Arts Space—operated by the North Vancouver Community Arts Council—moved into its new facility in Lower Lonsdale in February 2001. Linda Feil, executive director of the arts council, recalled the gallery's creation:

> *The gallery came into being because the parties involved actually shared a common vision. Everyone involved—the Arts Council, the developer and the city—wanted to create a lively, welcoming and flexible place where people could come together to share and celebrate . . . Even before we opened, we decided that ideas for exhibitions and programs would come from the community, be themed, involve at least three artists, and include an interactive component to enable the community to participate.*

Library services—all but ignored by city councillors until the mid-1900s—were also enhanced. After extensive public consultation, plans for a new facility north of the 1973 library and city hall were approved by council. Rezoning of the site was sought in 2005 and site preparation began by the end of the following year.

But even as residents began to plan for the city's pending centennial celebrations, the amalgamation debate surfaced once again. Discussions began innocently enough at a North Vancouver Chamber of Commerce meeting early in 2001 when mayors Barbara Sharp and Don Bell were asked if the recent creation of a unified business licence application procedure signalled the beginnings of amalgamation. The two mayors cited their municipalities' traditional positions, and later summarized their respective views in the *North Shore News*. One year later, there seemed to be even less reason to amalgamate, as North Vancouver residents observed forced amalgamations in Ontario resulting in provincial downloading, tax increases, alienated residents and big government. The spectre of amalgamation might not have been laid to rest, but it had certainly been dealt a serious blow.

Issues with origins in the previous decade—such as the FastCat scandal and the Seven Seas/*No. 5 Ferry* controversy—continued to resurface. Battling the tide of scandal, Premier Glen Clark's successor Ujjal Dosanjh put the three fast ferries up for sale. But the damage to his party proved too great. In May 2001 the New Democratic Party government went down to a humiliating defeat. Sensing a need to rid itself of a political liability, Premier Gordon Campbell's new BC Liberal government auctioned the entire FastCat fleet in March 2003. When the auction was over, citizens were both shocked and appalled. The successful bidder, the Washington Marine Group, had acquired the ferries for just $19.4 million, $40.6 million less than the $60 million the firm had offered prior to the auction. Later, in a final twist, Washington announced that it was studying the feasibility of putting the FastCats back into service to compete against BC Ferries on a North Vancouver to Vancouver Island run.

Kathara Filipino Dancers perform at the North Vancouver Centennial Theatre, September 2002. North Shore News, *Julie Iverson photo*

Washington was no stranger to the North Vancouver waterfront. Largely owned by Montana transportation magnate Dennis Washington, the Washington Group of companies included several firms based or located in North Vancouver: Cates Towing, acquired in 1992 as a division of Washington's Seaspan International; Vancouver Shipyards, located in the district just west the Fullerton Fill; and Vancouver Drydock, whose floating dry dock had been built for Versatile Pacific in 1980–81.

Years after the FastCats had been auctioned, the ferries still sat moored near the foot of St. Andrew's Avenue, tangible reminders of a megaproject gone wrong. Until 2005, yet another disused, controversial vessel sat nearby. Three years after having been ordered to leave its moorings at the foot of Lonsdale Avenue, the Seven Seas restaurant—the former *No. 5 Ferry*—remained the subject of litigation. The city's marine surveyor had reported the vessel not seaworthy in January 1999, but many residents remained unconvinced. In a last-ditch effort to save the beleaguered vessel, the city invited proposals for a public-private partnership. Residents led by former newspaper publisher Peter Speck and retired city manager Gerry Brewer did their best to find both a use for the vessel and funding for its restoration. Brewer later recalled the sad but inevitable outcome of their efforts: "At the end of the day the city had it towed away in the middle of the night and had it broken up. When it was broken up one had to admit that the condition of the ferry was far worse than we had contemplated or than had been reported to us by our surveyor."

The city's waterfront industries had been a particular boon to its tax base, but in mid-2005 the city had a rude awakening. Western Stevedoring—lessee of Lynnterm, the city's easternmost bulk loading facility—appealed its property assessments for the years 2002 to 2004. Much to the city's chagrin, the province's Property Assessment Appeal Board ruled in Western's favour. The city protested, taking its case to the British Columbia Supreme Court. In March 2005 Justice Elizabeth Bennett ruled in favour of the company and the city faced the prospect of having to return hundreds of thousands of dollars in back taxes not only to Western Stevedoring but to other waterfront industries as well.

Joe Bustemente's legendary trumpet, used for navigational purposes during heavy fogs, became the inspiration for this whimsical sculpture in the city's Lower Lonsdale area.

Warren Sommer photo

In the mid-1900s one waterfront industry, the Wallace family's shipyards, had all but defined the city. In the early 2000s the site of the shipyards sat derelict as it awaited redevelopment. Pinnacle International, a large development company with offices in Vancouver, Toronto and San Diego, acquired the right to develop the property from receivers Price Waterhouse Coopers in November 2001. Following a comprehensive public consultation process, the former shipyard became the focus of a multi-million dollar redevelopment project. Unlike much that had happened on the waterfront in the preceding hundred years, the site would be transformed, but on the city's terms.

Marketed as "The Pier," the developer's concept called for a mix of commercial, residential and public uses on the site. By early 2005 a series of residential towers began to rise adjacent to the shipyard on the north side of Esplanade and two piers had been restored on the shipyard site itself. Dubbed the Burrard Dry Dock Pier and the St. Roch Dock, the two wharves helped revitalize the city's waterfront and created a destination for residents and tourists alike. A further rezoning of the shipyard site and the transfer to the city of several historic buildings for commercial and cultural use reconfirmed the status of the heritage precinct, extended public access to the waterfront and permitted the developer to build tall condominium towers elsewhere on the property.

Two decades after the loss or damage of several key historic buildings in Lower Lonsdale, residents were gratified to see the area recognized for what it was—the place where the city had been born. The area around the foot of Lonsdale Avenue was particularly significant, for it was there that Charles H. Cates, the Western Corporation and others had built the infant community's first docks. It was there that the Western Corporation had set up shop, building a number of commercial buildings to serve those who settled in the pre-war boom. The city had celebrated its incorporation at the first city hall at First and Lonsdale in 1907. Many important community events had happened in and around Pete Larson's nearby hotel. In the 1940s thousands had travelled through the area on a daily basis as they made their way to and from jobs in the shipyards.

On September 9, 2006, the National Historic Sites and Monuments Board met near the foot of Lonsdale Avenue and in a moving ceremony declared shipbuilding at Burrard Dry Dock as an "event of national historic importance." Unfortunately Jack Loucks, the fatherly mayor who had seen the potential of revitalizing the Lower Lonsdale area, had died just two days earlier. Loucks' legacy was no doubt in many minds as a succession of speakers rose to comment on the site. Robin Inglis, director of the North Vancouver Museum and Archives, remarked on how the shipyard and the community had risen to the challenge of providing ships for the Canadian and British fleets during the 1940s:

Local effort became a national story and Burrard Dry Dock and North Vancouver made a vital contribution to Canada's ultimately successful support for the winning of World War II. Winston Churchill is reputed to have said that the only thing that really frightened him at that time was whether the war of supply from North America could be won. It was a near run thing, and it was this shipyard and this community that had much to do with the outcome.

North Vancouver Museum director Robin Inglis was instrumental in preserving the stern and triple expansion steam engine of HMS Flamborough Head (subsequently known as HMCS Cape Breton) for display at the site of Burrard Dry Dock.
North Vancouver Museum and Archives photo

Riveting Presentation: North Vancouver Museum and Archives interpreter Sally Hamilton, alias "Shipyard Sal," brings the history of Burrard Dry Dock to life for visitors to Lower Lonsdale, July 2005.

North Shore News, *Mike Wakefield photo*

Six decades after the war, the city's ambitions for its own part of the site were considerable. Talks with the Vancouver Maritime Museum and other interested parties had resulted in a concept for a National Maritime Centre of the Pacific and Arctic. As envisioned, the new centre would incorporate interactive interpretive displays, multimedia presentations, research and training facilities, and historic artifacts as well as a marina. Maritime and arts-themed businesses located elsewhere on the site would complement the centre. The triple expansion engine and stern of the Victory Ship HMCS *Cape Breton*—built on the site as HMS *Flamborough Head* in 1944 and salvaged by the North Vancouver Museum and Archives in 2001—would likely find a home in the new development. On January 11, 2006, Mayor Darrell Mussatto formally announced the project as "an integral part of this community and Canada."

All in all, the Lower Lonsdale area was—after decades of neglect and delay—becoming exactly what its promoters had predicted twenty years before: a highly attractive place in which to live, work and play. There were residential towers, office blocks, cultural and entertainment amenities, and recreational facilities. Despite its highly urban character, the area possessed "green heat," an environmentally sustainable technology unique in the province. A centralized hot water heating system, owned by the city's Lonsdale Energy Corporation, provided its services to

over 46,000 square metres of commercial and residential development. Public art projects, such as a sculpture honouring Joe Bustemente and his famous trumpet, enlivened the Lower Lonsdale area. City planners dreamed of a continuous walkway that would form part of the Trans-Canada Trail, and take pedestrians and bicyclists from the eastern end of the old dry dock site to the western end of the Fullerton Fill. The Seabus terminal and the Lonsdale Quay market symbolized the changing nature of the city as diverse users conversed in a multitude of tongues, shopped, travelled to work or paused to enjoy the spectacle of a working waterfront.

Looking back on over sixty years of living in North Vancouver, old-timers such as Murray Dykeman reflected on how the social fabric of the city had changed:

The preserved stern of the Victory Ship Cape Breton *at the Burrard Dry Dock site, January 2007. The stern of the Burrard Dry Dock-built vessel was saved as an icon through an innovative "Save our Stern" campaign spearheaded by the North Vancouver Museum and Archives.*

North Vancouver Museum and Archives, Cecil Halsey photo

> *All you need to do is go down and stand in the Lonsdale Quay for an hour one day and you will realize that you don't know a single soul getting off the Seabus. For somebody like me who grew up here, when you knew nine out of ten people at the corner of Fifteenth and Lonsdale, to see a crowd of people, you realize that most of the people have only lived here five years. There's nothing wrong with that. They like it here. They came here because they like it, I'm sure. It still is a wonderful community, but my, it's different.*

Dick and Eva Hallaway, both born in the city in the mid-1920s, echoed Dykeman's views. When they were children, North Vancouver had been a small, sparsely settled town where chickens and cattle wandered the streets. Both had seen the city boom during and after the Second World War. Single-family houses had given way to apartments and condominiums. Vacant lots had disappeared.

Concrete towers supplanted wood-frame buildings, proclaiming the community's status as a regional town centre. The city had long since ceased to be an outpost of empire and was now remarkably cosmopolitan in tone. Despite the evolution, the Hallaways were adamant: "It's the best place in the world, but it sure has changed!" Regardless of all the growth, residents of both the city and the district retained a sense of living close to nature. As Murray Dykeman maintained, "I can be in the wilderness in ten minutes from my front door, and so can a hundred and eighty thousand other people. That's an unusual privilege . . . It's one of our greatest assets."

After a century of growth coupled with setbacks, and promise hampered by forces beyond its control, the ambitious city had finally been achieved. There was balance in its tax base with residents, merchants and industry each making appropriate contributions to the civic coffers. Residents' quality of life was high. Opportunities abounded. Within its five square miles residents had ready access to a fully modern hospital, ample emergency services, an expanding library, two recreation centres, specialized schools and facilities for the arts. There were parks throughout the city. The city's waterfront, once forbidden territory to those not there on business, had finally been made accessible. North Vancouver was a community in which its residents took pride and one that many would never choose to leave. The city across the inlet had ceased to be a rival and long-term residents took pleasure in saying, "Vancouver? Oh yes. Isn't that the place where the ferries used to go?"

Residents enjoy a walk on the Burrard Dry Dock Pier, opened to public use on April 23, 2005. With so much of its waterfront dedicated to bulk terminals and other industrial activity, residents embraced the pier with considerable enthusiasm.

City of North Vancouver, photo by Jon Pesochin, Green Tea Photography

ACKNOWLEDGEMENTS

···

Although one name may appear on the spine of this book, its publication owes much to the contributions of others: other writers, family, colleagues, and above all, the residents of North Vancouver. My greatest debt is to the latter. Some spoke with me on the telephone or communicated by email. Over two dozen attended a workshop to initiate the project. Others opened their homes to me, poured me tea and coffee, plied me with home baking, and endured endless questioning, much of it recorded on tape as a permanent record of our conversations. Age, ethnicity, and gender proved no barrier. People were proud of their city, aware of its challenges and achievements, and willing to share their perspectives.

The list is extensive and includes youth and seniors, Natives and immigrants, people in public life, former city staff, and residents at large: Doreen Armitage, Brad Baker, Emily Baker, John Braithwaite, Gerry Brewer, Levi Charles, John Cordocedo, Eric Crossin, Maureen Curtis, Travis Dapp, Kathleen Davidson, Anjie Dawson, Stella Jo Dean, Suzanne Dodson, Murray Dykeman, Linda Feil, Jim Galozo, Ron Gibbs, Ken Gostick, Dick Hallaway, Eva Hallaway, Margaret Herman, Bob Heywood, Lila Johnston, Matthew Johnston, Courtney Kessel, John King, Cole Klawikowski, Julian Kolstee, Mark Koop, Patricia Lambert, Beth Lawrence, Jim Lawrence, Jason Lee, Glynis Leyshon, Margaret Locke, the late Jack Loucks, Sue Macdonald, Gordon McConnell, Andrew Malbet, Mike Morgan, Dave Moulding, Robert Nahanee, Russell Bob Nahanee, Matthew Peters Nahanee, Roy Pallant, Eleanor Parkinson, Alana Paull, Simon Pickup, Arash Rahmanian, Ed Raymond, Eleanor Rienstra, Elizabeth Russell, Allan Sinclair, Desmond Smith, Gary Sum, Shirley Sutherland, George Thomas, Gertie Todd, Jim Warne and Jack Watts.

Commissioning a history of the city was the brainchild of Bruce Hawkshaw, former city clerk. Bruce anticipated the city's centennial well in advance and recommended the development of a book to the 1999 council. I am grateful to both Bruce and successive city councils for their support of this project, which I hope will be a lasting legacy of the city's centennial celebrations.

Other city staff have also been supportive of the project. Sandra Dowey, who succeeded Bruce as city clerk, has shown a remarkable ability to locate old bylaws and equally obscure documents in very short order. Paul Penner, Gary Penway, Cheryl Kathler, Larry Orr and Lisa McCarthy have provided valuable insights into a number of current community planning issues. Sandra and Gary have both served with Robin Inglis, director of the North Vancouver Museum and Archives, on a project steering committee, and their advice has been greatly valued.

Led by Robin, current and former staff of the museum and archives have often gone the extra mile to make the project a success. I am particularly grateful to retired archivists Francis Mansbridge, who introduced me to his facility's not inconsiderable collection, and June Thompson, whose encyclopedic knowledge of the archives' photograph collection has helped produce a highly attractive volume.

Current archivist Janet Turner and reference historian Daien Ide have tirelessly provided access to their records and responded cheerfully to my ongoing queries.

Although the museum and archives' collections are strong, locating photographs relating to the city's recent history proved a challenge. Terry Peters, managing editor of the *North Shore News*, has been particularly generous in making digital files of some of his paper's more recent images available for publication. Museum photographer and exhibit preparator Cecil Halsey also assisted by taking new photographs. Author Derek Hayes has encouraged me along the way and has provided digital copies of a number of difficult-to-photograph archival maps. City G.I.S. technician Perry Beck worked hard to generate additional maps.

During the course of my research I was able to locate descendants of Johann Wulffsohn, James Pemberton Fell and Edward Mahon, all major figures in the various land companies that in the 1890s and early 1900s owned most of what is today the City of North Vancouver. Jock Wulffson, Michael Fell and the late Bryan Mahon (together with his wife Marolyn) kindly delved through family photographs and papers and provided me with copies of several important items. Bob Heywood, a current city councillor and a distant relative of the Heywood-Lonsdale family, has been no less generous.

North Vancouver historian Dick Lazenby, whose knowledge of the community is prodigious, was most generous in sharing his research on a number of topics. Robin Inglis, Francis Mansbridge, John Stuart and my wife Bev, ever my most valuable critic, critiqued the manuscript in its entirety, while Len Corben, Eric Jamieson and Henry Ewert reviewed those portions relating to their particular areas of interest.

Naomi Pauls provided a valuable initial critique of the manuscript. Roger Handling created an excellent design for the book, Hugh Morrison provided expert indexing, while Silas White, Anna Comfort, Catherine Johnson and Marisa Alps at Harbour Publishing have carefully guided *The Ambitious City* to publication.

A final debt is owed to those who have written on North Vancouver before me, including Rodger Burnes, Kathleen Woodward-Reynolds, William Stott, James Morton, James Barr, Sally Carswell, Robin Williams, Henry Ewert, Francis Mansbridge, Verna Kirkness and Chief Simon Baker. Related studies by scholars such as Jean Barman, Cole Harris, Robert A.J. McDonald, Margaret Ormsby, Robin Fisher, Wilson Duff and Martin Robin have been no less valuable. Without their work my task would have been far more difficult, and the final product less successful.

Thank you to you all.

ENDNOTES

CHAPTER ONE

decrepit creature . . . Charles Hill-Tout, "Notes on the Cosmogony and History of the Squamish Indians of British Columbia," *Transactions, Royal Society of Canada*, 2, 3 (1897): Section 2, reprinted in R. Maud, ed. *The Squamish and the Lillooet*, vol. 2 of *The Salish People*, 19.

In a loud . . . Maud, 20.

In the beginning . . . Maud, 20.

The small pox most have had . . . quoted by Cole Harris, *The Resettlement of British Columbia: Essays on Colonialism and Geographical Change*, 13–14.

A dreadful skin . . . Maud, 22.

met by about . . . Capt. George Vancouver, *A Voyage of Discovery, 1791–1795*, June 13, 1792.

The shores of . . . Vancouver, June 14, 1792.

The shores are steep . . . John Kendrick, ed., *The Voyage of Sutil and Mexicana 1792: The last Spanish Exploration of the Northwest Coast of America*, 133–134.

All the lands . . . Robert E. Cail, *Man, Land and the Law: The Disposal of Crown Land in British Columbia, 1871–1913*, 9.

at prices lower . . . *British Columbian*, July 1, 1863.

On the west . . . F.W. Laing, *Colonial Farm Settlers on the Mainland of British Columbia, 1858–1871*, 23.

take away the post . . . Keith Thor Carlson, ed., *A Sto:lo-Coast Salish Historical Atlas*, 171.

The Indians have . . . Cail, 182.

seemed annoyed on . . . a great deal of trouble. Fr. Thomas A. Lascelles, *Mission on the Inlet: St. Paul's Indian Catholic Church, North Vancouver, BC, 1863–1984*, 10–11.

Everything possible is . . . Lascelles, 13.

that there be . . . Carlson, 171.

This is, without exception . . . *British Columbian*, August 25, 1866.

The beautiful sunny . . . wind and wave. *British Columbian*, May 27, 1868.

There is a library . . . James C. McCulley to his parents, September 5, 1875, BCARS, E/C/M13, McCulley Correspondence.

The crew here . . . Norman Hacking, *History of the Port of Vancouver*, n.p.

There is probably . . . quoted by Jean Barman, *The West Beyond the West: A History of British Columbia*, 92.

First they would . . . Matthews collection, file 03270, CVA.

My parents didn't . . . *North Shore Outlook*, May 5, 2000.

When we reached . . . "Moodyville's First Teacher was Young American Girl," undated newspaper clipping, Moodyville file, NVMA.

Out of the way . . . British Columbia, Superintendent of Education, *Annual Report*, 1872, 6.

CHAPTER TWO

Their great mill . . . Newton Henry Chittenden, *Travels in British Columbia*, 66.

Nearly every early . . . Major James S. Matthews, "Early Vancouver: Narratives of Pioneers of Vancouver, B.C.," vol. III, p. 284, typescript, CVA.

At the Moodyville Hotel . . . Matthews, "Early Vancouver," vol. 3, 284.

Around the mill . . . Matthews collection, file 04191, CVA.

The big shots . . . ILWU Pensioners Local 500, *Man Along the Shore!: The Story of the Vancouver Waterfront as told by Longshoremen Themselves*, 13.

Notices of deaths . . . *Moodyville Tickler*, July 20, 1878, CVA.

There was nowhere . . . Matthews collection, file 03268, CVA.

Invited to the . . . ceremony of it . . . Matthews collection, file 03270, CVA.

The people were moved . . . Wilson Duff, *The Indian History of British Columbia: Vol. 1, The Impact of the White Man*, 91.

[A watchman] would walk . . . Lascelles, 25.

I am happy . . . Canada, *Annual Report of the Department of Indian Affairs*, 1884, 104.

Seen from the bay . . . Lascelles, 18.

Instead of putting . . . George M. Grant, *Ocean to Ocean: Sir Sandford Fleming's Expedition Through Canada in 1872*, 319–320.

The Native Indians . . . ILWU Pensioners Local 500, 13.

The Chinese had . . . J. Rodger Burnes, "Moodyville as I Knew it," undated newspaper clipping, Moodyville file, NVMA.

Two years ago . . . *Vancouver Daily World*, November 18, 1895.

We had a teacher . . . Matthews collection, 03270, CVA.

I liked most . . . bother us, Matthews collection, file 03270, CVA.

[Louisa] had children . . . Matthews collection, file 03270, CVA.

The Mission Indians . . . Canada, *Annual Report of the Department of Indian Affairs, 1888*, 106.

the ghosts of a people . . . Aberdeen and Temair, Ishbel Gordon, Marchioness of, *Through Canada with a Kodak*, 202–203.

CHAPTER THREE

We were at Moodyville . . . Matthews collection, 03270, CVA.

this important section . . . North Vancouver. *Vancouver Daily World*, December 30, 1890.

determined to make . . . San Francisco. *Vancouver Daily World*, June 5, 1891.

entered into a new . . . *Times* of London, October 24, 1891.

To erect, construct . . . *British Columbia Gazette*, August 20, 1891, 642.

going to be . . . Conversation with Bryan Mahon, September 11, 2004.

In small blocks . . . *Vancouver Daily World*, December 20, 1890.

an extended pleasure . . . *Vancouver News-Advertiser*, January 20, 1892.

with an eye . . . Rudyard Kipling, "Something of Myself, " in John Beecroft, *Kipling: A Selection of his Stories and Poems*, 360.

The Squamish Mission . . . Canada, *Annual Report of the Department of Indian Affairs*, 1893, 120.

Only a few . . . Canada, *Annual Report of the Department of Indian Affairs, 1899*, 224.

a plentiful supply . . . Canada, *Annual Report of the Department of Indian Affairs, 1900*, 420.

All the pupils . . . Canada, *Annual Report of the Department of Indian Affairs 1902*, 401.

There is a lot . . . Simon Baker and Verna Kirkness, *Khot-La-Cha: The Autobiography of Chief Simon Baker*, 9–10.

This was a cheap . . . J. Rodger Burnes, "Saga of a Municipality in Its Formative Years: 1891–1907," typescript, NVMA.

not many . . . giants to us . . . Burnes, "Saga," 32.

CHAPTER FOUR

I got to know . . . J. Rodger Burnes, *Echoes of the Ferries*, 43.

Land covered but . . . Western Corporation, "Vancouver and North Vancouver, British Columbia," pamphlet, NVMA.

A separate ladies' . . . J. Rodger Burnes, *Echoes of the Ferries*, 44.

Why . . . because North Vancouver, *Express*, August 25, 1905.

some rather heated . . . in three years, *Vancouver Daily Province*, January 13, 1903.

the initial length of track . . . Ewert, 1.

Any possible loss . . . Henry Ewert, *The Perfect Little Streetcar System: North Vancouver 1906–1947*. North Vancouver: North Vancouver Museum and Archives, 2000, 2.

After the inspection . . . Burnes, *Saga*, 66.

a certain laxity . . . British Columbia, Superintendent of Education, *Annual Report*, 1904, quoted by Kathleen Woodward-Reynolds, "A History of the City and District of North Vancouver," unpublished M.A. thesis, University of British Columbia, 1943, 143. .

the most irresponsive . . . British Columbia, Superintendent of Education, *Annual Report*, 1905, quoted by Woodward-Reynolds, 143. .

in the hands of Mr. Hendry . . . *Express*, October 6, 1905.

CHAPTER FIVE

The large taxpayers . . . *Express*, December 14, 1905.

If the Dominion . . . *Express*, December 29, 1905.

Why should we . . . *Express*, November 24, 1905.

Burrard is a name...*Express*, November 24, 1905.

it did not take long . . . *Vancouver Daily Province*, August 30, 1906.

Those telephone people . . . J. Rodger Burnes. "Telephones Came Here in 1902," undated newspaper clipping, Services and Utilities – Telephones file, NVMA.

A dearth of good houses . . . *Express*, March 30, 1906.

the largest function . . . *Express*, April 6, 1906.

patriotic exercises . . . *Express*, April 6, 1906.

On the shores . . . *Express*, June 29, 1906.

the most prominent feature . . . Mahon, McFarland and Mahon, "North Vancouver, British Columbia: The Beginnings of a Great Port," pamphlet, NVMA.

what the Champs Elysées . . . Mahon, McFarland and Mahon, pamphlet, NVMA.

the first father . . . *Express*, June 7, 1907.

the official dry nurse . . . *Express*, July 5, 1907.

that would forever . . . *Express*, July 5, 1907.

whose character . . . *North Shore Press*, July 31, 1942.

on an almost direct line . . . Mahon, McFarland and Mahon, "North Vancouver, British Columbia: The Beginnings of a Great Port," pamphlet, NVMA.

As the railway company's charter . . . Mahon, McFarland and Mahon, "North Vancouver, British Columbia: The Beginnings of a Great Port," pamphlet, NVMA.

The thermometer rarely . . . *Westward Ho!*, August, 1908, 51.

CHAPTER SIX

The fact that Moodyville . . . *Express*, February 22, 1907.

Every year Sophie . . . Emily Carr, *Klee Wyck*, 23.

The Great White Chief . . . *Vancouver Daily Province*, March 26, 1910.

British Columbia is to be . . . Oriental labour here. *Express*, October 18, 1907.

The people of British Columbia . . . *Express*, October 18, 1907.

protesting against . . . *North Shore Press*, July 7, 1914.

The temper of the public . . . *North Shore Press*, July 24, 1907.

He was in his element . . . taste of sorrow. Charles W. Cates, "Lim Gong, Merchant and Friend," typescript, NVMA.

knots of ratepayers . . . board of aldermen. *Express*, June 3, 1910.

They protected the city . . . Gerry Brewer, interview, August 29, 2006.

A great transcontinental . . . *Vancouver Daily Province*, October 6, 1911.

construction will start . . . *Vancouver Daily Province*, November 11, 1910.

all the pioneering . . . Bentley C. Hilliam, "Oh, Why Didn't I Keep Those Vancouver Lots?," *Vancouver Sun*, February 8, 1964.

Now Lottie has . . . Hilliam, "Oh, Why Didn't I Keep Those Vancouver Lots?"

Real estate in North Vancouver . . . *Lonsdale Spectator*, November, 1910.

A repetition of the boom . . . in Vancouver. *Lonsdale Spectator*, November, 1910.

You washed all . . . Stella Jo Dean scrapbooks.

There will be . . . *Vancouver Daily World*, July 11, 1907.

The crowds were so large . . . quoted by Len Corben, "Having a Ball on Sunday," *North Shore Outlook*, May 12, 2000.

the most disorderly . . . quoted by Len Corben, "Having a Ball on Sunday."

Not merely a matter . . . *Express*, June 10, 1910.

With the club . . . *Lonsdale Spectator*, March, 1911.

The acme of high-class . . . *Express: Empire Day Prosperity Edition*, May 24, 1912.

as a token . . . "The Second Narrows Bridge: Spanning Burrard Inlet–Port of Vancouver, British Columbia," pamphlet, NVMA.

Bridge bylaws . . . "The Second Narrows Bridge: Spanning Burrard Inlet–Port of Vancouver, British Columbia."

CHAPTER SEVEN

the proper development . . . revenue purposes. William McKee, *Portholes and Pilings, City of Vancouver Archives, Occasional Paper No. 1*, 26.

The event is so . . . *Express*, July 4, 1913.

Several shareholders . . . George Morden to Edward Mahon, September 24, 1930, Mahon family papers.

British Columbia a very . . . Martin Robin, *The Rush for Spoils: The Company Province 1871–1933*, 168.

the big white elephant . . . Robin, 193.

We are not asking . . . *North Shore Press*, June 19, 1914.

Relief throughout the winter . . . *North Shore Press*, September 18, 1914.

To win glory . . . *North Shore Press*, August 25, 1914.

Your office work . . . J.P. Fell to Harry Bridgman, December 30, 1914, Fell family papers.

I have instructed . . . J.P. Fell to Henry Heywood-Lonsdale, January 23, 1915, Fell family papers.

This war is going . . . *North Shore Press*, July 7, 1916.

We're Canadian Engineers . . . *North Shore Press*, March 31, 1916.

not only the brains . . . "Canadian Engineers C.E.F., British Columbia, Headquarters, 6th Field Company, C.E., North Vancouver, BC," pamphlet, NVMA.

Selfish, unpatriotic . . . business [running]. *North Shore Press*, September 4, 1914.

an epoch in . . . *North Shore Press*, June 8, 1915.

a sunbeam . . . *North Shore Press*, June 2, 1916.

come to the conclusion . . . Francis Mansbridge, *Launching History: The Saga of Burrard Dry Dock*, 33.

I believe in . . . undated newspaper clipping from *North Shore Press*, c. 1913, Women–General file, NVMA.

Not conversant . . . *North Shore Press*, March 3, 1914.

unversed in the wily . . . *North Shore Press*, December 14, 1917.

hustled out Captain Falke . . . *North Shore Press*, November 15, 1918.

all the noise . . . chorus of shouting. *North Shore Press*, November 15, 1918.

in every patriotic . . . *North Shore Press*: Victory Number, July 18, 1919.

what should be . . . *North Shore Press*, January 16, 1920.

CHAPTER EIGHT

residents to show . . . *North Shore Press*, April 8, 1921.

one time the union . . . Hilda Mortimer, *You Call Me Chief: Impressions of the Life of Chief Dan George*, 115. Copyright 1981 by Hilda Mortimer. Reprinted by permission Doubleday Canada.

the Empress of Japan . . . ILWU, 52.

not less than . . . Mansbridge, 38.

demonstrate to the entire . . . are capable of. *North Shore Press*, September 2, 1921.

in future to build . . . *North Shore Press*, September 2, 1921.

the one thing . . . Marine Workers and Boilermakers Industrial Union Local No. 1. *A History of Shipbuilding in British Columbia: As told by Shipyard Workers 1927–1977*, 35.

I was in the yard . . . Marine Workers and Boilermakers Industrial Union Local No. 1, 35.

The damming of the Second Narrows . . . *North Shore Press*, May 14, 1920.

recommend the inclusion . . . *North Shore Press*, April 1, 1920.

Due to the fact . . . *North Shore Press*, April 22, 1921.

When you were boarding . . . Marine Workers and Boilermakers Industrial Union Local No. 1, 35.

take charge of . . . *North Shore Press*, June 9, 1922.

social and intellectual harmony . . . admitted to membership. Savage Club Fonds 4, NVMA.

The Chinese men seemed . . . Murdoch Grahame, typescript memoirs, Police file, NVMA.

to totally restrict . . . Undated newspaper clipping (c. 1921), George S. Hanes Fonds 48, Series 4, File 2, NVMA.

a one-way affair . . . J.S Terry, "The Story of the First Fifty Years of Lawn Bowling in North Vancouver," typescript, NVMA.

the pep and go . . . *North Shore Press*, July 13, 1923.

an unexpectedly large . . . *North Shore Press*, August 17, 1923.

mammoth photo spectacle . . . enraptured audience. *North Shore Press*, August 12, 1921.

They weren't allowed . . . Interview with Lila Johnston, Margaret Locke and Anjie Dawson, October 26, 2006.

His was a common . . . Robin Williams, *A Vancouver Boyhood: Recollections of Growing Up in Vancouver 1925–1945*, 83.

Mrs. Harry Bridgman . . . *North Shore Express*, June 3, 1921.

to become worthy citizens . . . undated newspaper clipping, Schools: Private – Girls file, NVMA.

the three nurses . . . Sally Carswell, *The Story of Lions Gate Hospital: The Realization of a Pioneer Settlement's Dream, 1908–1980*, 28.

best for its size . . . to the fore. Carswell, 63.

Within the next few years . . . *Vancouver Daily Province*, July 27, 1923.

the most important date . . . *North Shore Press*, September 14, 1923.

One old timer . . . funnier than that. *North Shore Press*, September 14, 1923.

the silken strand . . . overhead. *Vancouver Daily Province*, November 8, 1925.

The Cub Scout leader . . . Interview with Ken Gostick, May 21, 2002.

a standing reproach . . . *North Shore Press*, August 3, 1923.

Conditions are better . . . *North Shore Press*, January 7, 1921.

The span was hurled . . . *Vancouver Daily Province*, September 19, 1930.

CHAPTER NINE

They obviously had . . . Correspondence from Michael Fell, September 15, 2006.

I recall in those years . . . Clipping from *Citizen*, 1970, NVMA.

We had all the boulevard . . . Interview with Dick and Eva Hallaway, November 9, 2006.

It was illegal . . . Williams, 112.

Shaughnessy's manicured boulevards . . . Williams, 77.

There was no end . . . Williams, 77.

We did a lot . . . Interview with Lila Johnston, Margaret Locke and Anjie Dawson, October 26, 2006.

A woman primary . . . Williams, 139.

It wasn't easy . . . Jim Galozo, "It Wasn't Easy!," typescript, NVMA.

Jobs were scarce . . . Dora (Curry) Stacey, "My Days at Queen Mary School and Other Memories 1923 to 1930," *North Shore Historical Society, Newsletter*, December 1992.

the demoralizing . . . *The Homeroom*: www.mala.bc.ca

for the betterment . . . North and West Vancouver Council of Women Fonds 48, NVMA.

These seamen land . . . Undated newspaper clipping, *North Shore Press*, c. 1930, Missions to Seamen file, NVMA.

all powers and authority . . . *Minutes of the Honourable the Executive Council, approved by His Honour the Lieutenant Governor on the 24th day of January, A.D. 1933*.

given first call . . . *Proceedings of the Commissioner*, City of North Vancouver, January 24, 1933.

Arguments, theories . . . Williams, 151.

The company was proud . . . "Alf Donati's Notes," John King Papers.

Looking for a job . . . never hire you. "Side Stories of Bill's," John King Papers.

Jobs were hard to come by . . . Jim Galozo, "Working at Burrard Dry Dock in the Thirties," *North Shore Historical Society, Newsletter*, January, 1994.

It was a series . . . *North Shore Press*, August 26, 1938.

to find that . . . *North Shore Press*, August 26, 1938.

The discipline was certainly . . . Interview with Dick and Eva Hallaway, November 9, 2006.

Some of them . . . Interview with Dick and Eva Hallaway, November 9, 2006.

By the time boys . . . Williams, 188.

He made it his business . . . Williams, 186.

We don't quarrel . . . Williams, 197.

Families were large . . . Williams, 186.

My only hope . . . *North Shore Press*, August 12, 1938.

I don't think . . . ILWU, 99.

If the record . . . *North Shore Press*, July 28, 1939.

This city would benefit . . . *North Shore Press*, July 28, 1939.

We had nothing else . . . Baker and Kirkness, 90.

One of the amazing . . . ILWU, 99.

whatever took . . . Anne Silva, "Stroll Down Memory Lane," *The Centre Post* (Silver Harbour Centre), vol. 15, no. 6, June, 1987, 18.

It didn't take long . . . Anne Silva, "Stroll Down Memory Lane," *The Centre Post* (Silver Harbour Centre), vol. 15, no. 6, June, 1987, 18.

The Neighbourhood House . . . *North Shore Press*, November 17, 1939.

This was the only . . . Donald Luxton and Lila D'Acres, *Lions Gate*, 139.

When he comes . . . over the water. *Vancouver Daily Province*, May 30, 1939.

all too brief . . . commitment. *North Shore Press*, June 2, 1939.

CHAPTER TEN

pneumonia jackets . . . *North Shore Press*, September 29, 1939.

prepared to accept contracts . . . *North Shore Press*, September 29, 1939.

I remember that first day . . . Williams, 162–163.

If the truth were known . . . "The Story of a Community,"

At home we had . . . George Lewis, "Air Raid Patrol Days," typescript, NVMA.

We had a cadet . . . Interview with Dick and Eva Hallaway, November 9, 2006.

McDougall was very keen . . . Williams, 201.

By the summer . . . Williams, 165.

I remember the war . . . Interview with Murray Dykeman, July 6, 2006.

I don't think . . . Interview with Ken Gostick, May 21, 2002.

The other side . . . mostly bush, Interview with Ken Gostick, May 21, 2002.

McDougall had a . . . Williams, 195.

Building ships took . . . Williams, 167

When I was in the Yard . . . *Wallace Shipbuilder*, July, 1944, 11.

They flocked here . . . *Wallace Shipbuilder*, September, 1942, 5.

cheap buildings of . . . per month. *Proceedings of the Commissioner*, May 22, 1941.

be built in a . . . *Proceedings of the Commissioner*, August 14, 1941.

The architecture of . . . Jim Galozo, "Wartime Houses in North Vancouver," *North Shore Historical Society, Newsletter*, June, 1992.

What a shock . . . in 1941. Anne Silva, "Wartime Housing," typescript, April 13, 1994, NVMA.

very, very tiny . . . of this deal. *Vancouver Daily Province*, January 15, 1942.

The 500-block . . . Anne Silva, "Wartime Housing," typescript, April 13, 1994, NVMA.

The homes were . . . Jim Galozo, "Wartime Houses in North Vancouver," *North Shore Historical Society, Newsletter*, June, 1992.

There's a little . . . *Wallace Shipbuilder*, June, 1944, 2.

not an old-fashioned . . . *Wallace Shipbuilder*, July, 1945, 11.

Cutting spars . . . *Wallace Shipbuilder*, May, 1943, 5.

This community is . . . *Wallace Shipbuilder*, September, 1942, 5.

as soon as . . . *Vancouver Sun*, June 11, 1943.

If you'd been . . . Louise May and Robert McDonald, "In the Shipyard," in *Working Lives: Vancouver 1886 – 1986*, 63.

The main mechanic . . . Marine Workers and Boilermakers Industrial Union Local No. 1., 106.

For thousands of us . . . Marine Workers and Boilermakers Industrial Union Local No. 1., 107.

had the opposite . . . against his children. Williams, 194.

Limit trade licenses . . . of trade licenses. *Proceedings of the Commissioner*, November 4, 1941.

Take them back . . . in recent years. *Vancouver Daily Province*, January 15, 1942.

I don't remember . . . Williams, 193.

North Vancouver had . . . Williams, 193.

When conscription was . . . Jim Galozo, "It Wasn't Easy!," typescript, NVMA.

CHAPTER ELEVEN

If the City . . . *Proceedings of the Commissioner*, April 20, 1942.

I have it on . . . Capt. James Barr, *Ferry Across the Harbour*, 63.

The gambling fever . . . ILWU, 140.

During the war period . . . Correspondence from Ron Gibbs, August 3, 2001.

the present institution . . . turned away. *Proceedings of the Commissioner*, February 3 and March 22, 1943.

Each Saturday . . . Interview with Murray Dykeman, August 1, 2006.

We went down there . . . Interview with Murray Dykeman, August 1, 2006.

Bowling was the big thing . . . Interview with Murray Dykeman, July 6, 2006.

To me it was . . . Interview with Murray Dykeman, August 1, 2006.

The rehabilitation of returned men . . . *Proceedings of the Commissioner*, January 31, 1944.

Sam Sowden . . . Interview with Ken Gostick, May 21, 2002.

The three of us . . . Interview with Ron Gibbs, August 2, 2001.

Our Band didn't . . . Baker and Kirkness, 99.

On the whole . . . *North Shore Press*, May 11, 1945.

a wide-open chance . . . *North Shore Press*, May 11, 1945.

an old gal . . . in the middle. *North Shore Press*, November 9, 1945.

the most disgraceful . . . *North Shore Press*, November 9, 1945.

Cosily ensconced . . . Undated newspaper clipping from the *North Shore News*, Library file, NVMA.

until 15 or 20 . . . from it all. Alan Jessup, "North Van's Bonanza," *Vancouver Daily Province Magazine*, October 13, 1947.

Snorting bulldozers . . . Alan Jessup, "North Van's Bonanza," *Vancouver Daily Province Magazine*, October 13, 1947.

a medical-dental building . . . Christy McDevitt, "Stumps are Flying in North Vancouver," *Vancouver Sun Magazine*, October 16, 1948.

of quiet, simple people . . . McDevitt, "Stumps are Flying."

It was very close-knit . . . Interview with Ken Gostick, May 22, 2002.

I remember one . . . Interview with Murray Dykeman, August 1, 2006.

Until the Fifties . . . Interview with Dick and Eva Hallaway, November 9, 2006.

If you had a dollar . . . Interview with Murray Dykeman, August 1, 2006.

Their worldliness . . . blown apart. Interview with Gerry Brewer, August 29, 2006.

I do not understand . . . *Vancouver Daily Province*, December 13, 1966.

dazzling red . . . *North Shore Press*, September 27, 1946.

True enough . . . *North Shore Press*, September 27, 1946.

the sparkplug . . . *North Shore Press*, May 27, 1949.

In those days . . . Interview with Ron Gibbs, July 5, 2001.

The audience was . . . utterly amazed. Donovan Pool, "Players: The Early Days," *North Shore Historical Society, Newsletter*, April, 2000.

some promise and did manage . . . Pool, "Players."

In the past . . . McDevitt, "Stumps are Flying."

The recent spirit . . . to civic progress. McDevitt, "Stumps are Flying."

CHAPTER TWELVE

Kids from here . . . Peter Speck, "Memories," www.tomahawkrestaurant.com/news/memories.

There were all . . . Interview with John Braithwaite, October 3, 2006.

The stability that comes . . . Interview with Gerry Brewer, August 29, 2006.

In my young days . . . Interview with Murray Dykeman, August 1, 2006.

If you were smart . . . Interview with Murray Dykeman, August 1, 2006.

Discrimination is here . . . *Citizen*, September 11, 1970.

Let's look at . . . *Citizen*, September 11, 1970.

Everything was boarded up . . . Interview with Stella Jo Dean, September 18, 2006.

People always referred . . . Interview with John Braithwaite, October 3, 2006.

The creeks were . . . Interview with Gerry Brewer, August 29, 2006.

Coming from Toronto . . . Interview with John Braithwaite, October 3, 2006.

the best post office . . . *North Shore Press*, June 23, 1950.

now that the city . . . *North Shore Press*, June 23, 1950.

By the time . . . Interview with Murray Dykeman, July 6, 2006.

Sometimes I had . . . Interview with Murray Dykeman, July 6, 2006.

I look at the Squamish . . . Baker and Kirkness, 98.

The 'culture' of the 1950s . . . Speck.

Suddenly, everybody . . . Interview with Murray Dykeman, August 1, 2006.

They were quite cheap . . . would they? Interview with Murray Dykeman, August 1, 2006.

I'll say it arrived . . . Interview with Murray Dykeman, August 1, 2006.

When I first . . . Interview with Lila Johnston, Margaret Locke and Anjie Dawson, October 26, 2006.

I don't think . . . Interview with Murray Dykeman, August 1, 2006.

The unique thing . . . Interview with Ron Gibbs, July 5, 2001.

He ended up with . . . Interview with Murray Dykeman, July 6, 2006.

We started Little League . . . Interview with Ron Gibbs, July 5, 2001.

people generally were saddened . . . Barr, 69.

who had spent . . . Burnes, *Echoes of the Ferries*, 103.

well, that's it. *Barr. 69.*

just a kind of . . . what's going on. Interview with Dick and Eva Hallaway, November 9, 2006.

The library functioned . . . *Town Crier*, May, 1957.

Every eight weeks . . . Interview with Jack Loucks, May 16, 2002.

Both of my parents . . . Interview with Lila Johnston, Margaret Locke and Anjie Dawson, October 26, 2006.

CHAPTER THIRTEEN

It cut the city in half . . . Interview with Gerry Brewer, August 29, 2006.

Sometimes we'd slip up . . . Interview with Gerry Brewer, August 29, 2006.

The inlet itself . . . Interview with Gerry Brewer, August 29, 2006.

roared straight down . . . Interview with Gerry Brewer, August 29, 2006.

I used to be involved . . . Interview with Ron Gibbs, August 2, 2001.

It was my father . . . Jan-Christian Sorensen, "Walk's Dedication Remembers King's Mill," *North Shore News*, August 1, 2001.

He had a really . . . Sorenson, *North Shore News*, August 1, 2001.

would not only provide . . . North Vancouver Chamber of Commerce and West Vancouver Board of Trade, *Amalgamation Study of the City of North Vancouver, the District of North Vancouver and the District of West Vancouver.*

entertain further . . . City of North Vancouver, *Minutes of Council*, December 21, 1966.

There is no clear cut . . . *Citizen*, August 21, 1968.

Why a new city hall . . . *Citizen*, March 3, 1966.

don't want to do . . . *Citizen*, December 11, 1968.

Several matters deserve . . . *Citizen*, September 25, 1968.

there was only one tap . . . Interview with Lila Johnston, Margaret Locke and Anjie Dawson, October 26, 2006.

We lived in shacks . . . Baker and Kirkness, 98.

Just at that time . . . Baker and Kirkness, 100.

You have to pick . . . Baker and Kirkness, 100–101.

By god, things really started . . . Baker and Kirkness, 102.

Indian blood . . . Interview with John Cordocedo, November 14, 2006.

It has the same number . . . *Vancouver Sun*, December 7, 1988.

The RCMP are not . . . Roland Dean, untitled typescript, Stella Jo Dean scrapbooks.

Singing "God Save the Queen" . . . Interview with Murray Dykeman, August 1, 2006.

Sing, dance, shout . . . in the country. Stella Jo Dean scrapbooks.

First time I . . . *Citizen*, June 28, 1967.

Fifteen years ago . . . *Citizen*, August 14, 1968.

Discrimination against . . . Correspondence from Paul Winn, January 5, 2007.

And down at the bottom . . . Interview with John Cordocedo, November 14, 2006.

We are very concerned . . . *Vancouver Sun*, June 6, 1967.

concerned with the possibility . . . *Vancouver Daily Province*, May 6, 1969.

We are not going . . . *Vancouver Daily Province*, May 6, 1969.

We do not want . . . *Vancouver Sun*, June 17, 1969.

We intend to operate . . . *Vancouver Sun*, June 17, 1969.

become a model . . . *Vancouver Sun*, November 7, 1969.

I think the brochure . . . *Vancouver Sun*, November 7, 1969.

North Vancouver really . . . Interview with North Vancouver Youth Centennial Committee, September 26, 2006.

CHAPTER FOURTEEN

The stench of poverty . . . *Citizen*, October 14, 1970.

I wish the devil . . . tenants there. *Citizen*, October 14, 1970.

We had all those . . . Interview with Jack Loucks, May 16, 2002.

A couple of years . . . Interview with Bob Heywood, October 4, 2006.

They were tasked . . . Interview with Bob Heywood, October 4, 2006.

nobody else . . . Interview with Bob Heywood, October 4, 2006.

The senior NCOs . . . Interview with Bob Heywood, October 4, 2006.

Constables coached soccer . . . Roland Dean, untitled typescript, Stella Jo Dean scrapbooks.

There's a sort . . . *Citizen*, January 27, 1971.

At half past eleven . . . Mansbridge, 174.

We have had enough . . . *Citizen*, July 15, 1970.

Zoning bylaws should not . . . *Vancouver Daily Province*, July 21, 1970.

have the power to act . . . *Vancouver Sun*, November 25, 1970.

Members of staff . . . Interview with Ed Raymond, November 8, 2002.

Strikes go on . . . Interview with Gerry Brewer, September 7, 2006.

They had a full-sized . . . Interview with Dick and Eva Hallaway, November 9, 2006.

It was a sly move . . . Interview with Ed Raymond, November 8, 2002.

graphic evidence of the great strides . . . civic disgrace. *Citizen*, March 5, 1975.

to discuss the feasibility . . . City of North Vancouver, *Minutes of Council*, March 1, 1971.

to negotiate an agreement . . . City of North Vancouver, *Minutes of Council*, March 15, 1971.

We've been taken advantage of . . . *Citizen*, March 17, 1971.

The votes expressed . . . *Vancouver Sun*, November 19, 1972.

It is urgent . . . *Vancouver Daily Province*, February 3, 1973.

with a view to obtaining . . . City of North Vancouver, *Minutes of Council*, October 9, 1973.

And so the North Vancouver . . . *Citizen*, October 9, 1974.

Raising the $500,000 . . . *Citizen*, September 19, 1973.

There was pressure everywhere . . . *Vancouver Daily Province*, March 15, 1973.

The blast hurled . . . bread loaf. *Vancouver Daily Province*, March 15, 1973.

We think it started . . . Interview with Dick and Eva Hallaway, November 9, 2006.

They have failed miserably . . . *Citizen*, October 8, 1975.

This development is . . . *Citizen*, February 23, 1977.

This project was . . . *Citizen*, February 23, 1977.

We recognize it is an annoyance . . . *Vancouver Sun*, March 17, 1977.

That's all you're . . . *Vancouver Sun*, March 17, 1977.

In the seventies and eighties . . . Interview with Gerry Brewer, August 29, 2006.

He'd been asked . . . Interview with Gerry Brewer, September 7, 2006.

In those days the fire people . . . Interview with Stella Jo Dean, September 18, 2006.

We have inspected your City Hall . . . Honeyman and Curtis to Mayor and Council, February 13, 1930, Presentation House file I, NVMA.

This damned building. Interview with Gerry Brewer, August 29, 2006.

The PNE over here . . . Interview with Gertie Todd, October 3, 2006.

We want Pierre . . . and your country. *Citizen*, July 13, 1977.

CHAPTER FIFTEEN

I remember in one case . . . Interview with Gerry Brewer, September 7, 2006.

We had to move . . . Interview with Lila Johnston, Margaret Locke and Anjie Dawson, October 26, 2006.

Anyone who thinks . . . Doug Collins, "Get this Straight," *North Shore News*, November 6, 1987.

Indians Claim . . . Chris Lloyd, "Indians Claim Entire N. Shore," *North Shore News*, December 2, 1981.

We are not saying . . . Lloyd, *North Shore News*, December 2, 1981

You can imagine . . . Kim Pemberton, "Hose Reel Festival has Colourful History," *North Shore News*, May 8, 1987.

It was in decline . . . Interview with Gerry Brewer, August 29, 2006.

It was North Vancouver City's . . . *Citizen*, October 31, 1979.

a people place . . . sights and sounds. "Lonsdale Quay Progress," vol. 1, issue 3, February 1984, in *North Shore News*, February 19, 1984.

Lonsdale Quay could attract......"Lonsdale Quay Progress," vol. 1, issue 3, February 1984.

two hundred construction jobs . . . "Lonsdale Quay Progress," vol. 1, issue 3, February 1984.

Moral revolution . . . use of drugs, etc. . . . Douglas Knoll, "Standing to be Counted," *North Shore News*, October 19, 1980.

We had the ridiculous situation . . . Interview with Gerry Brewer, September 7, 2006.

It hit me all of a sudden . . . Timothy Renshaw, "Veterans Preserve Seamen's Heritage," *North Shore News*, December 27, 1985.

possibly the finest . . . *North Shore News*, October 18, 1981.

The interior was still there . . . Interview with Jack Watts, November 1, 2006.

The city got caught . . . Interview with Gerry Brewer, September 7, 2006.

While it looked alright . . . Interview with Gerry Brewer, September 7, 2006.

I think because of our work . . . Interview with Jack Watts, November 1, 2006.

happy as hell. Timothy Renshaw, "Overpass Gets Green Light," *North Shore News*, October 27, 1985.

CHAPTER SIXTEEN

Its roof sags . . . Evelyn Jacob, "Theatre Demise Slammed," *North Shore News*, November 8, 1992.

We're really not interested . . . Martin Millerchip, "City and District Amalgamation Unlikely," *North Shore News*, September 9, 1992.

Listen, the city . . . Anna Marie D'Angelo, "Councillors Debate NV Amalgamation," *North Shore News*, October 1, 1995.

Amalgamation will only . . . Bill Bell, "No Gain for City in Amalgamation," *North Shore News*, September 29, 1995.

We respectfully rejected proper ...Robert Galster, "NV Amalgamation Overture Rejected," *North Shore News*, October 22, 1995.

Boys lost at sea . . . Robert Galster, "Cenotaph to be improved in NV park," *North Shore News*, June 21, 1995.

square two . . . Timothy Renshaw, "Third Crossing Low Priority for Local Mayors," *North Shore News*, February 5, 1989.

This is really outrageous . . . *Vancouver Sun*, December 19, 1990.

In our opinion . . . *Vancouver Sun*, December 19, 1990.

The CNR weren't talking . . . Interview with Gerry Brewer, September 7, 2006.

When Stella Jo Dean . . . *Vancouver Sun*, August 27, 1998.

a heavy heart . . . Liam Lahey & Anna Marie D'Angelo, "Shape Up or Ship Out," *North Shore News*, February 8, 1999.

many of the riches . . . Doug Crosby, OMI, "An Apology to Native Peoples," 2.

She gets a lot . . . Interview with aboriginal program students at Carson Graham Secondary School, October 10, 2006.

CHAPTER SEVENTEEN

There used to be . . . Interview with North Vancouver Youth Centennial Committee, September 26, 2006.

There's a large group . . . Interview with North Vancouver Youth Centennial Committee, September 26, 2006.

They hang out . . . Interview with aboriginal program students at Carson Graham Secondary School, October 10, 2006.

I personally think . . . Interview with North Vancouver Youth Centennial Committee, September 26, 2006.

That bow-legged Indian . . . Wendy John, "Eulogy in Honour of Chief Joe Mathias," www.squamish.net.

There's no playground . . . Interview with aboriginal program students at Carson Graham Secondary School, October 10, 2006.

The homeless part . . . Jennifer Maloney, "Report Findings Underscore Problem," *North Shore Outlook*, December 8, 2005.

I campaigned for twenty years . . . Interview with Jack Loucks, May 16, 2002.

I think that the concern . . . Anna Marie D'Angelo, "Fullerton Site Selling Well," *North Shore News*, September 27, 2000.

The gallery came into being . . . Correspondence from Linda Feil, November 5, 2006.

At the end of the day . . . Interview with Gerry Brewer, August 29, 2006.

Local effort became . . . Robin Inglis, "Shipbuilding at Burrard Dry Dock: Speech Notes," September 9, 2006.

All you need to do . . . Interview with Murray Dykeman, August 1, 2006.

It's the best place . . . Interview with Dick and Eva Hallaway, November 9, 2006.

I can be in the wilderness . . . Interview with Murray Dykeman, August 1, 2006.

REFERENCES

Aberdeen and Temair, Ishbel Gordon, Marchioness of. *Through Canada with a Kodak*. Edinburgh: W.H. White, 1893.

Armitage, Doreen. *Burrard Inlet: A History*. Madeira Park: Harbour, 2001.

Baker, Chief Simon and Verna Kirkness, *Khot-La-Cha: The Autobiography of Chief Simon Baker*. Vancouver: Douglas & McIntyre, 1994.

Barman, Jean. *Stanley Park's Secret: The Forgotten Families of Whoi Whoi, Kanaka Ranch and Brockton Point*. Madeira Park: Harbour, 2005.

Barman, Jean. *The West Beyond the West: A History of British Columbia*. Toronto: University of Toronto Press, 1991.

Barr, Capt. James. *Ferry Across the Harbour*. Vancouver: Mitchell, 1969.

British Columbia, Superintendent of Education. *Annual Report on the public schools of the province of British Columbia*. Victoria: 1872–1910.

Burnes, J. Rodger. *Echoes of the Ferries: A History of the North Vancouver Ferry Service*. n.d.

Cail, Robert E. *Man, Land and the Law: The Disposal of Crown Land in British Columbia, 1871–1913*. Vancouver: UBC Press, 1974.

Canada, Annual Report of the Department of Indian Affairs. Ottawa: 1871–1960.

Carlson Keith Thor, ed. *A Sto:lo-Coast Salish Historical Atlas*. Vancouver: Douglas & McIntyre, 2001.

Carr, Emily. *Klee Wyck*. Toronto and Vancouver: Clark, Irwin & Co., 1971.

Carswell, Sally. *The Story of Lions Gate Hospital: The Realization of a Pioneer Settlement's Dream, 1908–1980*. West Vancouver: 1980.

Chittenden, Newton Henry. *Travels in British Columbia*. Vancouver: G. Soules, 1984.

Davis, Chuck. *Reflections: One Hundred Years: A Celebration of the District of North Vancouver's Centennial*. Vancouver: Opus, 1990.

Duff, Wilson. *The Indian History of British Columbia: Vol. 1, The Impact of the White Man, Anthropology in British Columbia Memoir No. 5*. Victoria: Provincial Museum of Natural History and Anthropology, 1964.

Ewert, Henry. *The Perfect Little Streetcar System: North Vancouver 1906–1947*. North Vancouver: North Vancouver Museum and Archives, 2000.

Grant, George M. *Ocean to Ocean: Sir Sandford Fleming's Expedition Through Canada in 1872*. Toronto: J. Campbell, 1873.

Hacking, Norman. *History of the Port of Vancouver*. Vancouver, 1977.

Harris, Cole. *Making Native Space: Colonialism, Resistance and Reserves in British Columbia*. Vancouver: UBC Press, 2002.

Harris, Cole. *The Resettlement of British Columbia: Essays on Colonialism and Geographical Change*. Vancouver: UBC Press, 1997.

ILWU Pensioners Local 500, *Man Along the Shore!: The Story of the Vancouver Waterfront as told by Longshoremen Themselves*. Vancouver, 1975.

Kahrer, Anna Gabrielle. "Logging and Landscape Change on the North Shore of Burrard Inlet, British Columbia, 1860s to 1930s." MA thesis, UBC, 1988.

Kendrick, John. ed. *The Voyage of Sutil and Mexicana 1792: The Last Spanish Exploration of the Northwest Coast of America*. Spokane: Arthur H. Clark, 1991.

Kipling, Rudyard. "Something of Myself," in John Beecroft, *Kipling: A Selection of his Stories and Poems*. Garden City, New York: Doubleday, 1956.

Knight, Rolf. *Indians at Work: An Informal History of Native Labour in British Columbia, 1848–1930*. Vancouver: New Star, 1996.

Koppel, Tom. *Kanaka: The Untold Story of Hawaiian Pioneers in British Columbia and the Pacific Northwest*. Vancouver and Toronto: Whitecap Books, 1995.

Laing, F.W. "Colonial Farm Settlers on the Mainland of British Columbia, 1858–1871." Typescript, Victoria: 1939.

Lascelles, Fr. Thomas A. *Mission on the Inlet: St. Paul's Indian Catholic Church, North Vancouver, BC, 1863–1984*.

Luxton Donald and Lila D'Acres, *Lions Gate*. Burnaby: Talonbooks, 1999.

McKee, William. *Portholes and Pilings: A Retrospective Look at the Development of Vancouver Harbour up to 1933, City of Vancouver Archives, Occasional Paper No. 1*. Vancouver: City of Vancouver Archives, 1978.

McNally, Vincent J. *In the Lord's Distant Vineyard: A History of the Oblates and the Catholic Community in British Columbia*. Edmonton: University of Alberta Press, 2000.

Mansbridge, Francis. *Launching History: The Saga of Burrard Dry Dock*. Madeira Park: Harbour, 2002.

Marine Workers and Boilermakers Industrial Union Local No. 1. *A History of Shipbuilding in British Columbia: As told by Shipyard Workers 1927–1977.* Vancouver: College Printers, 1977.

Matthews, Major James S. "Early Vancouver: Narratives of Pioneers of Vancouver, BC," vol. III, typescript. Vancouver: City of Vancouver Archives.

Maud, Ralph, ed. *The Squamish and the Lillooet*, vol. 2 of *The Salish People.* Vancouver: Talonbooks, 1978.

May, Louise and Robert McDonald, "In the Shipyard," in *Working Lives: Vancouver 1886–1986.* Vancouver: New Star, 1985.

Mortimer, Hilda. *You Call Me Chief: Impressions of the Life of Chief Dan George.* Toronto: Doubleday, 1981.

Morton, James. *The Enterprising Mr. Moody, the Bumptious Captain Stamp.* North Vancouver: J.J. Douglas, 1977.

Ormsby, Margaret. *British Columbia: A History.* Vancouver: Macmillan, 1958.

Perry, Adele. *On the Edge of Empire: Gender, Race and the Making of British Columbia 1849–1871.* Toronto: University of Toronto Press, 2001.

Reksten, Terry. *The Illustrated History of British Columbia.* Vancouver: Douglas & McIntyre, 2001.

Robin, Martin. *The Rush for Spoils: The Company Province 1871–1933.* Toronto: McClelland & Stewart, 1972.

Taylor, G.W. *Timber: History of the Forest Industry in BC.* Vancouver: J.J. Douglas, 1975.

Vancouver, Capt. George. *A Voyage of Discovery, 1791–1795.* London: John Stockdale, 1801.

Williams, Robin. *A Vancouver Boyhood: Recollections of Growing Up in Vancouver 1925–1945.* West Vancouver: Robinswood, 1997.

Woodward-Reynolds, Kathleen. "A History of the City and District of North Vancouver." MA thesis, UBC, 1943.

GOVERNMENT PUBLICATIONS
British Columbia Gazette.
British Columbia. *Superintendent of Education. Annual Reports.*
Canada. *Annual Report of the Department of Indian Affairs.*

NEWSPAPERS AND JOURNALS
British Columbian
British Columbia Saturday Sunset
The Centre Post (Silver Harbour Centre)
Citizen
Express
Lonsdale Spectator
Moodyville Tickler
North Shore Historical Society Newsletter
North Shore News
North Shore Outlook
North Shore Press
Times of London
Town Crier
Vancouver Daily Province
Vancouver Daily World
Vancouver News-Advertiser
Vancouver Sun
Wallace Shipbuilder
Westward Ho!

INTERVIEWS
Aboriginal program students, Carson Graham Secondary School. October 10, 2006.
Braithwaite, John. October 3, 2006.
Brewer, Gerry. August 29 and September 7, 2006.
City of North Vancouver Youth Centennial Committee. September 26, 2006.
Cordocedo, John. November 14, 2006.
Dean, Stella Jo. September 18, 2006.
Dykeman, Murray. July 6, July 12 and August 1, 2006.
Gibbs, Ron. July 5, July 19 and August 2, 2001.
Gostick, Ken. May 21, 2002.
Hallaway, Dick and Eva. November 9, 2006.
Heywood, Bob. October 4, 2006.
Loucks, Jack. May 16, 2006.
Mahon, Bryan. September 11, 2004.
Raymond, Ed. November 8, 2002.
Squamish Nation members Margaret Locke, Lila Johnston and Anjie Dawson. October 26, 2006.
Todd, Gertie. October 3, 2006.
Watts, Jack. November 1, 2006.

LIST OF MAPS

INDEX

Harbour Publishing Co. Ltd.
P.O. Box 219
Madeira Park, BC
V0N 2H0
www.harbourpublishing.com

Designed by Roger Handling, Terra Firma Digital Arts
Front endsheet, 1908 plan for Grand Boulevard, North Vancouver Museum and Archives, pamphlet 1908-2
Back endsheet, contemporary City of North Vancouver map by Roger Handling
Maps page 29, 65 and 82 courtesy Derek Hayes, *Historical Atlas of Vancouver and the Lower Fraser Valley*
Cover painting by Brian Croft, Acrylic on Canvas, "Lower Lonsdale–1919"
Cover, aerial photograph by Mike Wakefield, *North Shore News*
Back cover, launch of the *Princess Louise*, North Vancouver Museum and Archives, 27-2505
Printed in Canada

Harbour Publishing acknowledges financial support from the Government of Canada through the Book Publishing Industry Development Program and the Canada Council for the Arts, and from the Province of British Columbia through the British Columbia Arts Council and the Book Publisher's Tax Credit.

Library and Archives Canada Cataloguing in Publication

Sommer, Warren F. (Warren Frederick), 1951-
    The ambitious city : a history of the City of North Vancouver / Warren Sommer.
Includes bibliographical references and index.
ISBN 978-1-55017-411-3
    1. North Vancouver (B.C.)—History. I. Title.
FC3849.N67S66 2007   971.1'33   C2007-900091-6

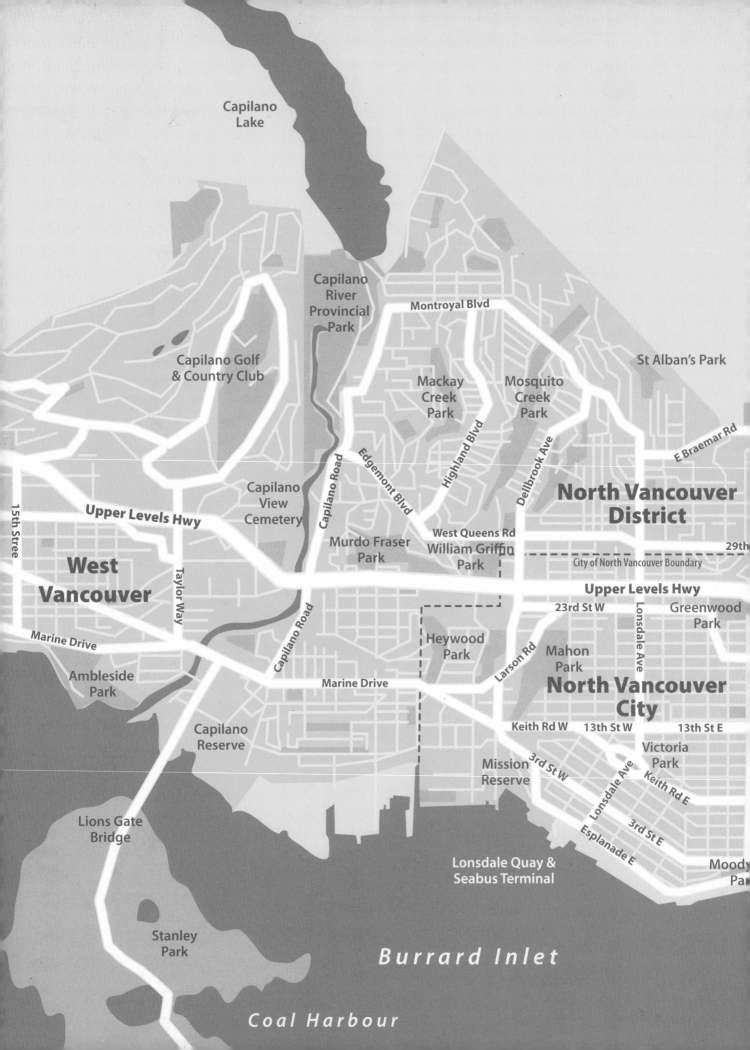